The Applied Theatre Reader

The Applied Theatre Reader is the first book to bring together new case studies of practice by leading practitioners and academics in the field and beyond, with classic source texts from writers such as Noam Chomsky, bell hooks, Mikhail Bakhtin, Augusto Boal and Chantal Mouffe.

This book divides the field into key themes, inviting critical interrogation of issues in applied theatre while also acknowledging the multi-disciplinary nature of its subject.

It crosses fields such as:

- Theatre in educational settings
- Prison theatre
- Community performance
- Theatre in conflict resolution and reconciliation
- Interventionist theatre
- Theatre for development.

This collection of critical thought and practice is essential to those studying or participating in the performing arts as a means for positive change.

Tim Prentki is Professor of Theatre for Development at the University of Winchester where he runs the MA in Theatre and Media for Development. He is co-author of *Popular Theatre in Political Culture* and is on the editorial board of *Research in Drama Education.*

Sheila Preston is a senior lecturer in Applied Theatre at the Central School of Speech and Drama, University of London. Her research interests are: theatre for development, the facilitator and critical pedagogies and theatre/performance for social change.

The
Applied Theatre
Reader

Edited by

**Tim Prentki and
Sheila Preston**

Routledge
Taylor & Francis Group

LONDON AND NEW YORK

First published 2009 by Routledge
2 Park Square, Milton Park, Abingdon, Oxon OX14 4RN

Simultaneously published in the USA and Canada
by Routledge
270 Madison Ave, New York NY 10016

Reprinted 2009

Routledge is an imprint of the Taylor & Francis Group, an informa business

Typeset in Joanna and Bell Gothic by
Florence Production Ltd, Stoodleigh, Devon
Printed and bound in Great Britain by
The Cromwell Press Group, Trowbridge, Wiltshire

British Library Cataloguing in Publication Data
A catalogue record for this book is available from the
British Library

Library of Congress Cataloging in Publication Data
The applied theatre reader/edited by Tim Prentki and Sheila
Preston.
     p. cm.
    Includes bibliographical references and index.
  1. Theater and society. 2. Community theater. I. Prentki,
  Tim. II. Preston, Sheila, 1968–.
PN2049.A66 2008
792.02′2 – dc22   2008005774

ISBN10: 0–415–42886–6 (hbk)
ISBN10: 0–415–42887–4 (pbk)

ISBN13: 978–0–415–42886–6 (hbk)
ISBN13: 978–0–415–42887–3 (pbk)

Contents

Notes on contributors

Josie Auger is a PhD candidate at the University of Alberta. Her research involved conducting a popular theatre and action research project in a First Nations community on STI/HIV prevention. As a sessional instructor, she teaches indigenous studies, history and drama.

Ananda Breed is Senior Lecturer at the University of East London. Her research explores justice and reconciliation in Rwanda, including *gacaca* courts, legendary theatre and grassroots associations. Ananda received her MA from NYU and PhD from the University of Manchester.

L. Dale Byam is Assistant Professor of Performance Studies in the Department of Africana Studies, Brooklyn College (CUNY). Publications: *Community in Motion: Theater for Development in Africa* (Greenwood 2000) and other articles. Works in progress: *The August Wilson Documentary* and *Vanishing Identities in Caribbean Performance Art*.

Penny Bundy is Associate Professor and Deputy Head of School, Education and Professional Studies, Griffith University, Australia. For the last four years her work has focused on using drama to assist adult survivors of institutional childhood abuse to live more fulfilling lives.

Jan Cohen-Cruz is Director of Imagining America: Artists and Scholars in Public Life, and a University Professor at Syracuse University. She wrote *Local Acts: Community-Based Performance in the United States*, edited *Radical Street Performance*, and, with Mady Schutzman, co-edited *Playing Boal: Theatre, Therapy, Activism* and *A Boal Companion: Dialogues on Art and Cultural Politics*.

Michael Etherton has taught in African and UK universities and published on African and Irish Drama. For the past twenty years he has been working in development and emergencies in Asia. He now lives in the Republic of Ireland.

Jonathan Fox is the founder of playback theatre, and the Director of the Centre for Playback Theatre in New York. He is author of *Acts of Service: Spontaneity, Commitment, Tradition in the Nonscripted Theatre*, 1994 and served as co-director of Recasting Reconciliation through the Arts & Culture, a program at Brandeis University.

Jane Heather teaches in Canada at the University of Alberta and at the Center for Indigenous Theatre. She has created community-engaged theatre projects with prison inmates, aboriginal youth, unions, teachers, seniors, women's groups and many social agencies and organizations.

Marina Henriques Coutinho is currently a PhD researcher at the University of Rio de Janeiro, investigating community theatre in Rio's slums. She received her MA in Theatre, Culture and Education. Since 1997 she has worked with children and young people as a drama teacher and social projects coordinator in Rio.

Anna Herrmann has worked in theatre and social change for 18 years, specialising in working with marginalised groups, both in the UK and abroad. Since 2002 she has been Head of Education at Clean Break. She is the co-author of *Making a Leap: Theatre of Empowerment – a practical handbook in creating issue-based theatre*.

Jenny Hughes is a Lecturer in Applied Theatre at the University of Manchester. Her research interests include theatre and conflict, theatre with offenders and young people 'at risk', research and evaluation in applied theatre, and theatre in the Middle East.

Adrian Jackson is Artistic Director of Cardboard Citizens, for whom he has directed over 20 productions – most recently *Timon of Athens* and *Pericles*, co-produced with the Royal Shakespeare Company. He has collaborated frequently with Augusto Boal, translated five of his books, and taught Theatre of the Oppressed (TO) widely abroad.

David Kerr has worked in both Malawi and Zambia in social activist theatre, has published academic works such as the prize-winning *African Popular Theatre* and has written plays and a poetry collection, *Tangled Tongues*. He is currently involved in the Media Studies Department at the University of Botswana.

Caoimhe McAvinchey is Convenor of the MA Applied Drama: Theatre in Educational, Community and Social Contexts at Goldsmiths College, London. Her research interests include performance practice with women in prison, the ethics and documentation of Applied Performance practice, and interdisciplinary collaboration.

Kathleen McCreery is a writer, director, facilitator, actor and counsellor. Kathleen's career has taken her from North America to Europe and Africa. She helped found Red Ladder and Broadside theatre companies. She is the author of many plays and co-author of *Theatre as a Weapon* (Routledge & Kegan Paul, 1986).

Paul Moclair is a Child Rights Theatre for Development consultant. He has worked with street children in Sierra Leone, with SCUK and UNICEF in Kenya and Sudan on HIV/AIDS and Child Rights programmes, and with social workers and trainee teachers in Palestine.

Helen Nicholson is Reader in Drama and Theatre at Royal Holloway, University of London. Her books include *Applied Drama: The Gift of Theatre* (Palgrave, 2005) and co-authorship of *Making a Performance: Devising Theatre and Contemporary Practices* (Routledge, 2007). She is co-editor of the journal *Research in Drama Education*.

Marcia Pompeo Nogueira is Associate Professor of the State University of Santa Catarina, Brazil. Her research interest is in community theatre and dialogical theatre for development. Her book *Theatre with Street Kids* was published in March 2008.

Tim Prentki is Professor of Theatre for Development at the University of Winchester where he runs the MA in Theatre and Media for Development. He is co-author of *Popular Theatre in Political Culture* and on the editorial board of *Research in Drama Education*.

Sheila Preston lectures in Applied Theatre at Central School of Speech and Drama, University of London. Her research interests are theatre for development, the facilitator and critical pedagogies, and theatre/performance for social change.

Simon Ruding is currently the Director of TiPP and was previously the Director of Geese Theatre Company. Over the last 19 years he has worked extensively in prisons, probation and with youth justice agencies throughout the British Isles.

Julie Salverson is a playwright, librettist and scholar. She is an Associate Professor at Queen's University, Canada. She is currently working on a clown opera about the atomic bomb and two books, one of which is titled *Witnessing a Tragic World: Theatre, Testimony and the Courage to be Happy*.

Jan Selman is Professor of Drama, University of Alberta, Canada. Previously, Artistic Director, Catalyst Theatre. Recent publications: *Popular Theatre in Political Culture*; articles in *Convergence* and *Journal of Adult Learning*. Recent popular theatre: *Transforming Dangerous Spaces*, investigating coalition within women's activist communities.

John Somers is an Honorary Fellow at Exeter University, Founder Editor of the journal *RIDE*, Founder Director of the *Exeter Research Conference* and Artistic Director of *Exstream Theatre Company*. He established the Exeter MA Applied Drama. He works extensively internationally.

Amanda Stuart Fisher is a Senior Lecturer in Applied Theatre at Central School of Speech and Drama. She has articles published in *TDR* and *Research in Drama Education*. Her research interests include theatre of testimony, verbatim and theatre's response to real events of trauma.

Liselle Terret is a Lecturer and Practitioner in Applied Theatre at Central School of Speech and Drama. Her research interests include participatory methodologies and aesthetics in applied theatre, particularly when working with children and young people; theatre and disability. She also performs feminist comedic neo-burlesque as Doris La Trine.

James Thompson is Professor of Applied and Social Theatre at the University of Manchester. He is director of *In Place of War* – a project developing performance practice in situations of armed conflict. He is author of *Applied Theatre: Bewilderment and Beyond* (Peter Lang, 2003) and *Digging Up Stories: Applied Theatre, Performance and War* (Manchester University Press, 2005).

Sarah Thornton founded Collective Encounters in 2004 as part of her research into Theatre for Social Change whilst Senior Lecturer at Liverpool Hope University. Following successful delivery of its first major project the company became a full-time commitment and Sarah is its Artistic Director.

Andy Watson trained in Paris with Lecoq, joining Geese Theatre Company in 1997, and becoming Artistic Director in 2003. His work involves devising and delivering theatre projects with offenders in both custodial and community settings. Andy is an Honorary Lecturer in Forensic Psychology at Birmingham University.

Lois Weaver is Professor of Contemporary Performance Practice at Queen Mary University of London and an independent performance artist, director and activist. Her interests include live art, solo performance, feminist and lesbian theatre, democracy and public engagement, and performance and human rights.

Joe Winston is Reader in Drama and Theatre Education at the University of Warwick and co-editor of *Research in Drama Education*. His publications include *Drama, Narrative and Moral Education* (Routledge Falmer, 1997) and *Drama and English at the Heart of the Curriculum* (David Fulton, 2004).

Acknowledgements

The editors would like, primarily, to thank the twenty-six authors – practitioners, artists and academics – who were commissioned to write chapters for *The Applied Theatre Reader* without whom this project would not exist. We are also indebted to the authors who gave personal permission for their work to be reprinted in this publication and especially to the generosity of Dorothy Heathcote, Renato Constantino, Jr and the Foundation for Nationalist Studies in the Philippines. Our gratitude also goes to Nick Moseley and to Edward Bond for contributing new thoughts and reflections that accompany the introduction to the Commentary on the War Plays in Chapter 10. With enormous gratitude to those communities and participants who are not named, but who have a presence in this book, and who are crucial in this work. Thanks go to Talia Rogers and Ben Piggott at Taylor & Francis, and to those at Florence Production. Finally, and not least, thank you to the BA and MA students of Central School of Speech and Drama, and the University of Winchester, for our lively discussions and whose needs inspired the project – you now have your Applied Theatre Reader.

Bakhtin, Mikhail, *Rabelais and His World*, 3215 word excerpt from pp. 197–277. © 1968. Massachusetts Institute of Technology, by permission of the MIT Press.

Boal, Augusto (trans. C. & M.-O. Leal McBride), *Theatre of the Oppressed*, pp. 120–42. © 1979, 2000. Reprinted by permission of Theatre Communications Group (TCG), New York.

Boal, Augusto (trans. C. & M.-O. Leal McBride), *Theatre of the Oppressed*, excerpt from pp. 120–42. ©1979, 2000. Reprinted by permission of Pluto Press.

Bond, Edward, *The War Plays*, 3608 word excerpt 'Commentary on the War Plays' from pp. 247–61. © 1985 (1991). Reprinted by permission of Methuen Drama, an imprint of A&C Black Publishers.

Bond, Edward, *Theatre Poems and Songs*, pp. 5, 59–60, 138. Eyre. © 1964. Reprinted by permission of Methuen.

Chomsky, Naom, *Profit over People*, excerpt from Chapter 1, 'Neoliberalism and Global Order', pp. 19–40. ©1999. Reprinted by permission of Seven Stories Press.

Constantino, Renato, *Synthetic Culture and Development*, excerpts from pp. 33–43. © 1985. Reprinted by permission of the Foundation for Nationalist Studies Inc.

Fo, Dario, *Mistero Buffo* (trans. Ed Emery), 2432 word excerpt from 'The Birth of the Jongleur', pp. 48–54. © 1988. Reprinted by permission of Methuen Drama, an imprint of A&C Black Publishers.

Freire, Paulo (trans. M. Ranos), *Pedagogy of the Oppressed*, pp. 160–4. © 1972. Reprinted by permission of Penguin Books, England.

Freire, Paulo (trans. M. Ranos), *Pedagogy of the Oppressed*, pp. 160–4. © 1972. Reprinted by permission of Continuum International Publishing Group, New York.

Giroux, Henry, *Border Crossings: Cultural Workers and the Politics of Education*, pp. 168–76. Reprinted by permission of Routledge, a division of Taylor & Francis Group.

Heathcote, Dorothy, *Drama as a Process for Change* © 2008. (originally 1997). By permission of Dorothy Heathcote.

Hoare, Quintin and Nowell Smith, Geoffrey (eds and trans), *Antonio Gramsci, Selections from the Prison Notebooks*, excerpt pp. 9–13 approx 980 words. © 1971 (2005). Reprinted by permission of Lawrence & Wishart.

hooks, bell, *Yearning*, 3315 word essay, 'Choosing the Margin as Space of Radical Openness', from pp. 145–53. Reprinted by permission of Between the Lines Press. © 1990.

Mda, Zakes, *When People Play People*. © 1993. Reprinted by permission of Zed Books.

Mouffe, Chantal, *On the Political*. © 2006 Routledge. Reprinted by permission of Taylor & Francis Books, UK.

Pretty, Jules N., Irene Guijt and John Thompson, *Participatory Learning and Action: A Trainers Guide*, excerpt 'A Typology of Participation', p. 61. © 1995. Reproduced with permission from International Institute for Environment and Development (IIED).

Rahnema, Majid, 'Participation', pp. 120–9. ©1999. In Wolfgang Sachs (ed.), *The Development Dictionary – A Guide to Knowledge as Power*. Reprinted by permission of Zed Books.

Wa Thiongo, Ngugi, *Decolonising the Mind*, pp. 34–61. Reprinted by permission of James Currey. © 1986.

Wilkinson, Sue and Kitzinger, Celia (eds), *Representing the Other*, 3085 word excerpt from pp. 10–19. © 1996. Reprinted by permission of Sage Press.

Willet, John, *Brecht on Theatre*, 1967 word excerpts from pp. 37, 186–201, 276–7. © 1964. Reprinted by permission of Methuen Drama, an imprint of A&C Black Publishers.

Prologue

Dario Fo (trans. Ed Emery)

.

Mistero Buffo (trans. Ed Emery) 'The Birth of the Jongleur', Methuen Drama (1988), excerpt from pp. 48–54.

KIND PEOPLE, GATHER ROUND AND LISTEN. The jongleur is here! I am the jongleur. I leap and pirouette, and make you laugh. I make fun of those in power, and I show you how puffed up and conceited are the bigshots who go around making wars in which *we* are the ones who get slaughtered. I reveal them for what they are. I pull out the plug, and . . . psss .˙. they deflate. Gather round, for now is the time and place that I begin to clown and teach you. I tumble, I sing and I joke! Look how my tongue whirls, almost like a knife. Remember that. But I have not always been . . . Well, I would like to tell you how it was that I came to be.

I was not born a jongleur; I didn't suddenly turn up as I am now, with a sudden gust from the skies and, hoopla, there I was: 'Good day . . . Hello.' No! I am the result of a miracle! A miracle which was carried out on me. Do you believe me? This is how it came about! I was born a peasant.

A peasant? Yes, a real countryman. I was happy, I was sad, I had no land. No! I worked as all of us work in these valleys, wherever I could. And one day I came by a mountain, a mountain all of rock. It was nobody's. I found that out. I asked people. 'No! Nobody wants this mountain!'

Well, I went up to its peak, and I scratched with my nails, and I saw that there was a little bit of earth there, and I saw that there was a little trickle of water coming down. So I began to scratch further. I went down to the river bank, and I wore my fingers to the bone bringing earth up onto this mountain. And my children and my wife were there. My wife is sweet, sweet and fair, with two round breasts, and a gentle way of walking that reminds you of a heifer as she moves. Oh, she is beautiful! I love her, and it gives me such pleasure to speak of her.

Anyway, I carried earth up in my own hands, and the grass grew so fast! Pfff . . . ! It grew of its own accord. You've no idea how beautiful it was! It was like gold dust! I would stick in my hoe, and pfff . . . a tree sprang forth. That earth was a miracle! A marvel! There were poplars, oaks and other trees everywhere. I sowed them when the moon was right; I knew what had to be done, and there, sweet, fine, handsome crops grew. There was chicory, thistles, beans, turnips, there was everything. For me, for us!

Oh, how happy I was! We used to dance, and then it would rain for days on end, and then the sun would blaze, and I would come, and go, and the moons were always right, and there was never too much wind, or too much mist. It was beautiful, beautiful! It was our land. This set of terraces was really beautiful. Every day I built another one. It was like the tower of Babel, beautiful, with all these terraces. It was paradise, paradise on earth! I swear it. And all the peasants used to pass by, saying:

> 'That's amazing, look what you've managed to bring forth out of this pile of rocks! How stupid that I never thought of that!'

And they were envious. One day the lord of the whole valley passed by. He took a look and said:

> 'Where did this tower spring up from? Whose is this land?'
> 'It's mine,' I said. 'I made it myself, with these hands. It was nobody's.'
> 'Nobody's? That "Nobody's" is a word that doesn't exist. It's mine!'
> 'No! It's not yours! I've even been to the lawyer, and he told me it was nobody's. I asked the priest, and he said it was nobody's. And I built it up, piece by piece.'
> 'It's mine, and you have to give it to me.'
> 'I cannot give it to you, sir. I cannot go and work for others.'
> 'I'll pay you for it; I'll give you money. Tell me how much you want.'
> 'No! No, I don't want money, because if you give me money, then I'll not be able to buy other land with the money that you give me, and I'll have to go and work for others again. No, I don't want to. I won't.'
> 'Give it to me.'
> 'No!'

Then he laughed, and went away. The next day the priest came, and he told me:

> 'The land belongs to the Lord of the Valley. Be sensible, give it up. Don't play the fool. Beware, because he is a powerful, evil lord. Give up this land. In the name of God, be sensible!'
> 'No!' I told him. 'I won't.'

And I made a rude gesture at him with my hand. Then the lawyer arrived too. He was sweating, by heaven, when he came up the mountain to find me.

'Be sensible. There are laws ... and you should know that you can't
... that, for you ...'
  'No! No!'

And I made a rude gesture at him too, and he went away, swearing.

But the lord didn't give up. No! He began by coming on hunting expeditions, and he sent all the hares chasing over my land. With his horses and his friends, he galloped to and fro across my land, breaking down my hedges. Then one day, he set fire to all my land. It was summer; a drought. He set fire to the whole of my mountain, and burned everything, even my animals and my house. But I wouldn't leave! I waited, and that night it began to rain. After the rain, I began to clear up, and put the fence posts back in position, and replace stones, and bring up fresh earth, and water everything. I was determined, by heaven, that I wouldn't move from there! And I did not move!

But one day he arrived, along with all his soldiers, and he was laughing. We were in the fields, my children, my wife and I. We were working. He arrived. He got down from his horse. He undid his breeches. He came over to my wife, grabbed her, threw her to the ground, ripped off her skirt and ... I tried to move, but the soldiers held me fast. And he leapt upon her, and took her as if she were a cow. And I and the children had to stand there, with our eyes bursting from our heads, watching ... I moved forward, with a leap. I managed to free myself. I took a hoe, and I shouted:

'You bastards!'
  'Stop,' my wife cried. 'Don't do it. That's all they want, that's exactly what they are waiting for. If you raise your stick, then they will kill you. Don't you understand? They want to kill you and take away your land. That's all they want. He is bound to defend himself. It's not worth taking your stand against him. You have no honour to defend. You're poor, you're a peasant, a country person, you cannot go thinking of honour and dignity. That is stuff for rich people, for lords and nobles! They are entitled to get angry if people rape their wives and daughters. But you're not! Let it be. The land is worth more than your honour, or mine. It's worth more than everything! I have become a cow, a cow for the love of you.'

And I began to weep, weeping and looking all around. The children were weeping too. And the soldiers, with the lord of the valley, suddenly went off, laughing, happy and satisfied. We wept, how we wept! We could not even look each other in the eye. And when we went into the village, they began throwing rocks and stones at us. They shouted:

'Oh you ox, you who don't have the strength to defend your honour, because you have no honour. You are an animal. The lord has mounted your wife, and you stood there, without saying a word, for a handful of earth. You wretch!'

And when my wife went around the village: 'Whore, cow!' they shouted after her. And then they ran off. They would not even let her go into church. Nobody would let her! And the children couldn't go out in the village without everyone picking on them. And nobody would even look us in the eye. My wife ran off! I never saw her again; I don't know where she ended up. And my children wouldn't look at me. They fell ill, and wouldn't even cry. They died. I was left alone, alone, with this land. I didn't know what to do. One evening, I took a piece of rope, and threw it over a rafter. I put the noose around my neck, and said to myself:

'Right. Now I am going to end it all, now!'

I was just about to do it, just about to hang myself, when I felt a hand on my shoulder. I turned around, and saw a fellow with big eyes and a pale face.

He says to me: 'Could you give me something to drink?'
'I ask you, in heaven's name, is this really the moment to come asking somebody for something to drink, when he's just about to hang himself?'

I look at him, and see that he too has the face of a poor wretch. Then I look further, and see that there are two more men, and they too have faces full of suffering.

'Alright, I'll give you something to drink. And *then* I'll hang myself.'

So I go to get them something to drink, and I take a good look at them:

'Instead of something to drink, you people look as if you could do with something to eat! It's been days and days since I last cooked anything to eat . . . But anyway, if you want, there is food.'

I took a pan and put it on the fire to heat up some broad beans. I gave them some, one bowl apiece, and how they ate! I, personally, wasn't very hungry. 'I'll wait till they've finished eating,' I thought, 'and then I'll hang myself.' Anyway, while they were eating, the one with the biggest eyes, who looked like a right poor devil, began to smile. He said:

'That's a terrible story, that you're going to hang yourself. I know why you want to do it, though. You have lost everything, your wife, your children, and all you are left with is your land. Yes, I know how it is! But if I were you, I wouldn't do it.'

And he carried on eating. How he ate! Then, in the end, he laid aside the utensils, and said:

'Do you know who I am?'
'No, but I've got an idea that you might be Jesus Christ.'
'Well done! You've guessed correctly. And this is St Peter, and that over there is St Mark.'

'Pleased to meet you! And what are you doing in these parts?'

'My friend, you've given me something to eat, and now I'm going to give you something to say.'

'Something to say? What is this "something"?'

'You poor fellow! It's right that you have held onto your land; it is right that you don't want bosses over you; it is right that you have had the strength not to give in; it's right . . . I like you. You're a good man, a strong man. But you're missing something which is also right, and which you should have: here and here. (*He points to his forehead and to his mouth.*) You shouldn't remain here stuck to your land. You should move around the country, and when people throw stones at you, you should tell them, and help them understand, and deflate that great bladder of a landlord. You should deflate him with the sharpness of your tongue, and drain him of all his poison and his stinking bile. You must crush these nobles, these priests, and all those who surround them: notaries, lawyers, etc. Not only for your own good, for your own land, but also for those like yourself who don't have land, who have nothing, and whose only right is the right to suffer, and who have no dignity to boast of. Teach them to survive with their brains, not just with their hands!'

'But don't you understand? I am not able. I have a tongue which refuses to budge. I stumble over every word. I have no education, and my brain is weak and useless. How am I supposed to do the things you suggest, and go about speaking to other people?'

'Don't worry. You will now see a miracle.'

He took my head in his hands, and drew me to him. Then he said:

'I am Jesus Christ. I have come to give you the power of speech. And this tongue of yours will lash, and will slash like a sword, deflating inflated balloons all over the land. You will speak out against bosses, and crush them, so that others can understand and learn, so that others can laugh at them and make fun of them, because it is only with laughter that the bosses will be destroyed. When you laugh at the rulers, the ruler goes from being a mountain, to being a little molehill, and then a nothingness. Here, I shall give you a kiss, and that will enable you to speak.'

He kissed me on the mouth. He kissed me for a long time. And suddenly I felt my tongue dart about inside my head, and my brain began to move, and my legs began to move with a mind of their own, and I went out in the streets of the village, and began to shout:

'Gather round, people! Gather round! Hear ye! The *jongleur* is here! I am going to play a satire for you. I am going to joust with the lord of the land, for he is a great balloon, and I am going to burst him with the sharpness of my tongue. I shall tell you everything, how things come and go, and how it is not God who steals! It is those who steal and go unpunished . . . it is those who make big books of laws . . . *They* are the ones . . . And we must speak out, speak out. Listen, people – these rulers must be broken, they must be crushed . . . !

PART 1

Chapter 1

Tim Prentki and Sheila Preston

APPLIED THEATRE
An introduction

Defining applied theatre

'APPLIED THEATRE' HAS EMERGED in recent years as a term describing a broad set of theatrical practices and creative processes that take participants and audiences beyond the scope of conventional, mainstream theatre into the realm of a theatre that is responsive to ordinary people and their stories, local settings and priorities. The work often, but not always, happens in informal spaces, in non-theatre venues in a variety of geographical and social settings: schools, day centres, the street, prisons, village halls, an estate or any other location that might be specific or relevant to the interests of a community. Applied theatre usually works in contexts where the work created and performed has a specific resonance with its participants and its audiences and often, to different degrees, involves them in it. Frequently those who engage in applied theatre are motivated by the belief that theatre experienced both as participant and as audience, might make some difference to the way in which people interact with each other and with the wider world. For both practitioners and participants there may often be an overt, political desire to use the process of theatre in the service of social and community change. For other practitioners and participants, the intention is less overt (but potentially no less political in its effect) and concerned with using theatre to draw attention to or reveal the hidden stories of a community.

Those practices existing (some rather reluctantly) under the umbrella of applied theatre might include: community theatre, community performance, theatre for social change, popular theatre, interventionist theatre, drama in education, theatre for integrated rural development, participatory performance practices, process drama/ theatre, prison theatre, theatre in health/education, theatre for development, theatre for conflict resolution/reconciliation, reminiscence theatre and so on. These categories evolved as responses to social conditions or as attempts to articulate the essence of the work created. As well as providing a way of 'grouping' common practice across many fields and cultural contexts, applied theatre over the last ten years has increasingly been used by practitioners to describe practice in community and educational settings.

As the applied theatre umbrella embraces a wide range of practice, it can be seen as an inclusive term. Just as we tend to understand 'community', so applied theatre, as a collective term, might allow possibilities for points of congruence and commonality to be found across different practices and contexts. On the other hand applied theatre, also like assumptions made of community, might equally be guilty of concealing 'difference' and inadvertently reveal conflicting ideologies and intentions behind its mask of sameness.

The assumption often lurking within the 'applied' in applied theatre is that theatre (assuming general agreement on what that is) is being attached to some other activity as a bandage might be applied to a wound. As **Helen Nicholson** discusses, the analogy might be with scientific bodies of knowledge that occur in two manifestations: pure and applied. In the example of mathematics there is the study and practice of it for its own sake, the pure form, and the use of it to solve a concrete problem, the applied version (Nicholson 2005: 5–8). However, no term in the field of cultural studies can be value free and the danger of using the term 'applied theatre' in this way is that it carries the implicit assumption that 'theatre' is a reified art form with a clearly defined aesthetic that can somehow be taken up and 'applied' in any context. In reality the division can never be so neat, for what is meant by theatre changes according to the manner and context of the application. The very form itself is responsive to the circumstances in which it is used. For instance, the material from which theatre is being made may draw exclusively on the factual (as in the case of verbatim theatre), or may be entirely fictional in form while still being based upon actual events. Yet in both cases the purpose of creating and staging this theatre may be to effect changes in the world outside the theatrical discourse. Conventionally, theatre requires the presence of an audience but in many examples of applied theatre there is no audience, only participants. In other applied theatre practice those involved commute between participation and spectating; while elsewhere the 'target' audience has no active role in shaping the performance.

Applied theatre practices may adopt the following theatrical transactions that involve participants in different participative relationships:

1   *Theatre 'for' a community*. An example could be a theatre company touring a piece of theatre or a workshop to young audiences in schools, or to local community groups.

2   *Theatre 'with' a community*. This could be workshop- or 'process'-based and involving participants in a devising or creative exploration that may or may not lead to presentation or performance to a wider audience.

3   *Theatre 'by' a community*. Here the community make and perform theatre themselves possibly to communicate to a specific audience and setting. This might involve a high level of facilitation by an applied theatre artist to enable decision making and performance by a community, or, become community

generated or 'comgen theatre' (see Mda, 1993) where the community/ participants direct and plan the entire event being directors, artists and performers with little or no outsider intervention.

Often, depending on the scope or intentions of the work, the course of a project might involve participants in a series of differing participative relationships and theatrical transactions according to the needs of the project.

Applied theatre defies any one definition and includes a multitude of intentions, aesthetic processes and transactions with its participants. In this Reader, academics and practitioners of applied theatre discuss and debate a wide range of case studies and offer examples of practice from all over the world which demonstrate the diversity, breadth and colour of the field. The emerging orthodoxies of Applied Theatre struggle to accommodate such a spectrum of practices and concepts.

Core conceptual themes have emerged which inform the theory and practice of applied theatre. In order to interrogate the broad field and its issues the editors have structured the Reader into sections according to the following themes: *poetics of representation, ethics of representation, intervention, participation, border crossings* and *transformation* with the acknowledgement that other related themes, such as *community, sustainability* and *facilitation*, are also themes across the book. We have resisted structuring the book conventionally by a subject-based categorisation around recognised areas within applied theatre such as TiE, prison theatre and TfD, etc. By doing this the editor's signal that the categories that have emerged are not necessarily separate areas of work with their own discrete methodologies but rather an interlocking set of practices based upon some common principles which can, to a degree, operate across the contexts in which these processes are applied; a process which is grounded in the principle of people-centred learning might be equally applicable in a school, a prison or a war zone.

The extracts from previously published work are intended to provide provocations to the reader that invite a wider consideration of the ideological discourses underpinning the concepts informing the section themes. In some instances the material that has been widely acknowledged as a seminal influence on the field might offer a predictable contribution, while others may invite readers to question the very existence of the applied theatre field as a discrete body of knowledge.

A brief history of applied theatre

While theatre has been used to intervene in social and political discourses since records of theatrical activity began, such as Euripedes' efforts to stir Athenian consciences in *The Trojan Women*, those practices which we recognise today as applied theatre have progressively gained currency throughout the second half of the twentieth century. Since the term 'applied theatre' alludes to a set of hybrid, interdisciplinary practices, it may be possible to trace its emergence to developments in those disciplines from which it draws most obviously.

The period after the Second World War witnessed an upsurge of interest in the social sciences, both at the macro level of national political organisation, reflected in the UK in the provisions of the Welfare State and the 1944 Education Act, and at the micro levels of personal fulfilment and community engagement. On an international level President Truman's Inaugural Address in 1949 and the establishment of the Bretton Woods organisations set in motion the subsequent decades of development where the USA and Europe laid down the blueprints for how the rest of the world should organise its economic, political and cultural life. These developments have found, sooner or later, a reflection in the various forms in which applied theatre has manifest itself although any suggestion of a direct causal relationship between a particular social science and an area of applied theatre would be a gross oversimplification. Drama therapy, for example, grew out of the expanding fields of psychology and psychiatry in the 1960s as a way of using drama processes to assist with the recovery of patients from mental illness. Today many practitioners of applied theatre are usually quick to assert that they are not therapists, either by training or inclination, and are concerned with social transformation rather than individual pathologies of rehabilitation. However, although purpose and outcome may be sharply differentiated, the kinds of processes through which the patients/ participants are put are frequently very similar. Lately the boundaries have been further blurred by the work of organisations such as Kids Company working therapeutically at the chalkface of urban deprivation in London in an attempt to tackle the roots of alienation and violence by young people which emanates, they feel, from a multitude of factors including poverty and lack of parenting.

Where applied theatre derives, albeit indirectly, from the discipline of sociology, the goal tends to be group (or social), rather than individual, transformation. Aspects of sociology are much exercised by notions of community and these are also prominent in that branch of applied theatre that calls itself 'community theatre' or 'community performance'. Practitioners are constantly on the lookout for suitable groups that constitute communities in order to work with a group of people who share certain common denominators, be these geographical, racial, experiential or circumstantial. Like sociologists, applied theatre practitioners tend to be sceptical of any tendencies towards a homogenised, essentialist concept of community and may prefer to use the theatre process itself as a form of community building, rather than starting from any preconceived idea that a given group of participants share any commonalities other than the fact of presenting themselves as participants for this process.

The idea of using theatre in the service of social change lies at the core of Bertolt Brecht's practice and theory. He took Marx's dictum articulated in the *Theses on Feuerbach*, 'the philosophers have only interpreted the world, the point is to change it', and applied it to the practice of theatre. In this sense Brecht might be viewed as the founding father of applied theatre and there is evidence that his project for the Major Pedagogy of the *Lehrstücke*, abolishing the distinction between actors and audience, would have accelerated developments in the field had not the Nazi election victory of 1933 abruptly curtailed these activities. Brecht's work only became accessible to the English-speaking world in the 1950s. Though it was as a playwright in the formal, conventional sense of the word that he became known in the West, his influence coincided with a period of social and theatrical experimentation related to the grass-roots activism of the 1960s.

One area where experimentation was rife was in education where ideas of child-centred learning and a problem-posing curriculum began to take hold. As Brecht was to Marx in the area of political philosophy, so Boal has become to Freire in the arena of education. Brazilian pedagogue, Paulo Freire, in his seminal work *Pedagogy of the Oppressed* and many subsequent volumes explored the possibilities of learning as a way of transforming the lives of students in a process that depends upon the establishment of a genuine dialogue between student and teacher in which both parties undertake the roles of both learner and teacher. Such a notion has much in common with ideas around the facilitation of applied theatre processes that have been developed in recent years. The theatre director **Augusto Boal** took many of Freire's educational theories and transposed them to the arena of theatre practice as acknowledged in the title of his first book, *Theatre of the Oppressed*. Due in large part to his publications and his tireless appetite for running international workshops, Boal has become a guru of applied theatre across the globe. However, the link between education and theatre was made in many parts of the world before his work was generally known. In Britain, from the 1960s, Theatre in Education developed a set of methodologies based on theories of active learning and subsequently exported these to North America, Australia and New Zealand where they have since flourished even as they withered in their native soil, afflicted by the blight of the Education Reform Act and the stifling of creativity in schools by successive Thatcherite and New Labour regimes. Even so, as this volume demonstrates, there is still much activity today in the field in both formal and informal educational contexts.

Besides community theatre and Theatre in Education, the other principal sub-set of applied theatre is Theatre for Development. This term emerged in the mid 1990s as the umbrella phrase to describe the various practices undertaken by non-government agencies (NGOs). As development expanded from its traditional spheres of operation in engineering, economics and agriculture into the 'softer' cultural arenas of governance, gender and, above all, health, so the role for theatre-based processes grew in line with concerns that sustainable change could only be accomplished by transforming attitudes and that theatre is a powerful means of engaging in transformation. The perceived failure of many of the clinical interventions to arrest the spread of HIV/AIDS has been a major reason for agencies looking more favourably upon Theatre for Development which started life as either a means of delivering messages to illiterate communities or as an event to mark the commencement or conclusion to a development project whose 'real' objectives lay elsewhere.

The politics of applied theatre

As the above history tends to suggest, the roots of applied theatre grew in the soil of progressive, radical people's movements in various places around the world. From this it might be tempting to assume that applied theatre is, per se, a left-wing or socialist methodology. This would be a false assumption: applied theatre is no more or less at the service of a particular ideology than any other kind of theatre. Its processes are as available to fascist regimes seeking to inculcate messages of obedience as they are to democratic regimes seeking to mobilise active citizens. As several of the following contributions indicate, it is often a very subtle and politically sophisticated business to facilitate without becoming a prey to the agendas of the sponsors; agendas that may contradict those of the participants. It is commonplace in the UK today for applied theatre projects to be undertaken directly or indirectly at the behest of the Government's social inclusion policies but a critique of those policies or an examination of the deeper causes of exclusion typically fall outside the scope of these projects. Philip Taylor articulates an ideal intention for many applied theatre projects:

> The theatre is *applied* because it is taken out from the conventional mainstream theatre house into various settings in communities where many members have no real experience in theatre form. The theatre becomes a medium for action, for reflection but, most important, for transformation – a theatre in which new modes of being can be encountered and new possibilities for humankind can be imagined.
>
> (Taylor 2003: xxx)

However, once a context for application imposes itself, the question of transformation, supposing such a thing can be measured or evaluated, raises all manner of circumstantial details concerning who is being transformed from what? Who is doing the transforming? Who judges when the transformation has been achieved? Questions about the transformative possibilities of applied theatre are contentious as they are key issues in the field and are explored at various points in the Reader. In short there is no mystery or magic to the processes of applied theatre that are subject to the same discourses of power that contain all the other cultural endeavours of humankind. As **David Kerr** has pointed out in relation to the growth in Theatre for Development in southern Africa, the control of the means of production goes a long way towards determining what is produced even when the producers would have it otherwise:

> My main concern is that in southern Africa at present, NGO-funded Theater for Development has become so dominant as a form of patronage for small-scale, resource-poor theatre troupes that it is difficult for artists to explore the full range of issues facing Africa, particularly those with roots in the past or those which cast light on global issues.
>
> (Adams and Goldbard 2002: 261)

Nevertheless the basis for this Reader lies in the belief that there is a field of related practices using aspects of the theatrical process that share sufficient common principles to enable them to operate under the umbrella term of applied theatre. Applied theatre therefore denotes the intention to employ theatre processes in the service of self-development, wellbeing and social change. However, as the forthcoming contributions will demonstrate, this intent is subject to differing interpretation and understanding by practitioners, and is influenced by context and the social, cultural or political landscapes which shape the artistic interventions that are created.

Bibliography

Adams, D. and Goldbard, A. (eds) (2002) *Community, Culture and Globalization,* New York: The Rockefeller Foundation.

Mda, Z. (1993) *When People Play People: Development Communication through Theatre,* London: Zed Books.

Nicholson, H. (2005) *Applied Drama,* Basingstoke: Palgrave Macmillan.

Taylor, P. (2003) *Applied Theatre: Creating Transformative Encounters in the Community,* Portsmouth, NH: Heinemann.

PART 2

Poetics of representation

Chapter 2

Tim Prentki

INTRODUCTION TO POETICS
OF REPRESENTATION

CONCEPTUALISING A POETICS OF applied theatre requires considera-tion of all those elements that contribute to the ways in which a theatrical communication is received and understood by its audience. The use of 'poetics' does not endorse a binary division between content and form that would privilege the 'content' as the maker of meaning and reduce the 'form' to the delivery of that meaning. Rather it is an acknowledgement that poetics, with all their contribution to the aesthetic development of form, play a crucial role in determining the content of a piece of theatre and further, what that content might mean in the collective and individual understanding of an audience. This is especially important in the context of applied theatre where there is a history of marginalising the aesthetic (taken to be the sole property or preoccupation of mainstream theatre) on the grounds that it is the 'applied' aspect of applied theatre that merits all critical attention and that the 'theatre' aspect is a given. In contrast there have been trends in applied theatre that counter this tendency, developing instead arts-led practices which privilege the form at the expense of community ownership of content. Thinking about the poetics of applied theatre necessitates critical analysis of the relationships *between* all aspects of the creative process: the theatre form, its application and its reception.

One of the key areas which differentiate the poetics of applied theatre from those of the mainstream is that of the target, or context-specific, audience. Typically with applied theatre practices there is a strong, intentional relationship between the manner in which the piece is created and the idea or picture of the audience for whom it is created. In relation, for example, to the desire to use the theatrical process to raise consciousness around a particular issue, applied theatre practitioners will often hope that their presentation will take their audiences beyond the point of awareness and into the arena of social action. So the choices around target audiences and the best means of stimulating them to action are likely to play a major role in any decisions about appropriate poetics to achieve an outcome beyond the theatre event. Unlike mainstream theatre, the distinction between participants – actors – and audience is not fixed. In many practices there may only be participants while in others there is the combination of both with the volatile or predetermined possibility of audience becoming actors, thereby relegating the protagonists to the role of spectators.

The content of applied theatre is commonly supplied by the participants directly in the form of their own stories or by the community who are often also the target audience through the research carried out in that community. However, the shaping of those stories and that research into dramatic forms that can communicate powerfully is often seen as the province of facilitators who use their experience to guide the participants through a bewildering array of poetic choices. These choices have themselves to be related to the cultural parameters of the participants so that the chosen forms can enter into a meaningful relation to their life experiences and understandings. A participatory poetics for rural African women is likely to involve very different choices from those appropriate for male inmates of a British prison, for example. Today, though, there is often a tension between local or indigenous forms of artistic and cultural expression and those deriving from the global dissemination of satellite technology. When asked to improvise a situation drawn from their daily lives, it is common for participants to ape the styles and manners of soap operas and crime series regardless of race, religion, gender, class or any other defining characteristic. Yet if earnest facilitators believe that part of their function is to support communities in resisting the global monoculture, it may be that they become guilty, themselves, of imposing a poetic that they deem appropriate or traditional upon the hapless participants. Within the questions arising around poetics, as with so many other aspects of applied theatre, contradictions abound.

Two figures who have exerted a profound influence upon the poetics of applied theatre during the second half of the twentieth century are Mikhail Bakhtin and Bertolt Brecht. Bakhtin, through his study of the French sixteenth-century novelist François Rabelais, reinvigorated the critical tradition of the popular as an alternative discourse existing independent of but in parallel with the official discourse of dominant culture, the so-called 'second world' of carnival and marketplace. Bakhtin's poetics of the popular have since been adapted and applied to many areas of cultural analysis, including the works of Shakespeare and the performances of Dario Fo. Of particular interest to the practice of applied theatre has been the focus upon the figure of the fool as an emblem of the popular tradition who is adept at spanning two worlds: the official and the popular; the scripted and the improvised; the fictional and the real; the stage and the auditorium; the spirit world and the material world, to name but a few. This trickster who juggles with simultaneous realities functions in many respects as the facilitator of the dramatic action, at once provoking the performers and interpreting for the audience: Puck, Feste and Lear's Fool from Shakespeare belong in this camp as do Schweik and Azdak from Brecht's plays.

Brecht's great contribution to the poetics of applied theatre was to develop a dramaturgy that answered his need for a theatre that could demonstrate the need for and inevitability of social change. Although historical circumstances, the Nazi election victory of 1933, forced Brecht to return to the writing of plays for formal theatrical production, the continuous search for theatrical means through which to highlight the contradictions of capitalist societies meant that he left a rich legacy for those who attempt to use theatre to stimulate social change. The development of his 'epic' theatre aesthetic with its emphasis upon narrative and the impact of social circumstances upon human actions underpins much of the story-based work of a wide variety of applied theatre practitioners. The *Verfremdungseffekt*, a key element of his epic theatre, is at its core a means by which to show up the contradictions that can undermine the official, dominant versions of history, politics and culture. *Verfremdungseffekte* are wedges driven into the heart of the assumptions by which our societies are organised in order that we can see whose interests are being served by the *status quo*. This counter-hegemonic practice is intended to work upon audiences as a form of intellectual empowerment that enables them to practise anti-oppressive social change outside the theatre. There is, however, no static, achieved formula for creating theatre for change but only a constant process of refining and reforming poetics in answer to changing social realities. At his death Brecht was still in the process of revising his epic theatre towards a more dialectical version that would enable epic and dramatic elements to operate within a framework of creative tension.

Chapter 3

Mikhail Bakhtin
(trans. H. Iswolsky)

RABELAIS AND HIS WORLD

Rabelais and His World, MIT Press (1968), excerpt from pp. 197–277.

[...]

HERE IS A DIMENSION in which thrashing and abuse are not a personal chastisement but are symbolic actions directed at something on a higher level, at the king. This is the popular-festive system of images, which is most clearly expressed in carnival (but, of course, not in carnival alone). In this dimension . . . the kitchen and the battle meet and cross each other in the image of the rent body. At the time of Rabelais these images were still alive and full of meaning in various forms of folk entertainments as well as in literature.

In such a system the king is the clown. He is elected by all the people and is mocked by all the people. He is abused and beaten when the time of his reign is over, just as the carnival dummy of winter or of the dying year is mocked, beaten, torn to pieces, burned, or drowned even in our time. They are "gay monsters." The clown was first disguised as a king, but once his reign had come to an end his costume was changed, "travestied," to turn him once more into a clown. The abuse and thrashing are equivalent to a change of costume, to a metamorphosis. Abuse reveals the other, true face of the abused, it tears off his disguise and mask. It is the king's uncrowning.

Abuse is death, it is former youth transformed into old age, the living body turned into a corpse. It is the "mirror of comedy" reflecting that which must die a historic death. But in this system death is followed by regeneration, by the new year, new youth, and a new spring. Therefore, abuse is followed by praise; they are two aspects of one world, each with its own body.

Abuse with uncrowning, as truth about old authority, about the dying world, is an organic part of Rabelais' system of images. It is combined with carnivalesque thrashings, with change of costume and travesty. Rabelais drew these images from the living popular-festive tradition of his time, but he was also well versed in the antique scholarly tradition of the Saturnalia, with its own rituals of travesties, uncrownings, and thrashings.

[. . .] the system of popular-festive images was developed and went on living over thousands of years. This long development had its own scoria, its own dead deposits in manners, beliefs, prejudices. But in its basic line this system grew and was enriched; it acquired a new meaning, absorbed the new hopes and thoughts of the people. It was transformed in the crucible of the people's new experience. The language of images developed new and more refined nuances.

Thanks to this process, popular-festive images became a powerful means of grasping reality; they served as a basis for an authentic and deep realism. Popular imagery did not reflect the naturalistic, fleeting, meaningless, and scattered aspect of reality but the very process of becoming, its meaning and direction. Hence the universality and sober optimism of this system.

[. . .] This old authority and truth pretend to be absolute, to have an extratemporal importance. Therefore, their representatives (the agelasts) are gloomily serious. They cannot and do not wish to laugh; they strut majestically, consider their foes the enemies of eternal truth, and threaten them with eternal punishment. They do not see themselves in the mirror of time, do not perceive their own origin, limitations and end; they do not recognize their own ridiculous faces or the comic nature of their pretensions to eternity and immutability. And thus these personages come to the end of their role still serious, although their spectators have been laughing for a long time. They continue to talk with the majestic tone of kings and heralds announcing eternal truths, unaware that time has turned their speeches into ridicule. Time has transformed old truth and authority into a Mardi Gras dummy, a comic monster that the laughing crowd rends to pieces in the marketplace.

[. . .] All the episodes we have discussed in this chapter, as well as the individual scenes of battles, fights, beatings, the uncrowning of people and objects (for instance, the bells) are presented by Rabelais in the popular-festive carnival spirit. Therefore, all the episodes are ambivalent: destruction and uncrowning are related to birth and renewal. The death of the old is linked with regeneration; all the images are connected with the contradictory oneness of the dying and the reborn world. Not only the episodes discussed but the entire novel is filled with that carnivalesque atmosphere. More than that, a number of important scenes are directly related to feasting and festivity.

We give here a broadened meaning to the word "carnivalesque." As a special phenomenon, carnival has survived up to our time. Other manifestations of popular-festive life, related to it in style and character (as well as origin), have died out long ago or have degenerated so far as to become undistinguishable. Carnival is a well-known festivity that has been often described throughout many centuries. Even during its later development in the eighteenth and nineteenth centuries it still preserved certain fundamental traits in a quite clear, though reduced, form. Carnival discloses these traits as the best preserved fragments of an immense, infinitely rich world. This permits us to use precisely the epithet "carnivalesque" in that broad sense of the word. We interpret it not only as carnival per se in its limited form but also as the varied popular-festive life of the Middle Ages and the Renaissance; all the peculiarities of this life have been preserved in carnival, while the other forms have deteriorated and vanished.

But even in its narrow sense carnival is far from being a simple phenomenon with only one meaning. This word combined in a single concept a number of local feasts of different origin and scheduled at different dates but bearing the common traits of popular merriment. This process of unification in a single concept corresponded to the development of life itself; the forms of folk merriment that were dying or degenerating transmitted some of their traits to the carnival celebrations: rituals, paraphernalia, images, masques. These celebrations became a reservoir into which obsolete genres were emptied.

Obviously, this consolidation took place in its own way, not only in various countries and at various seasons but even in different cities. The clearest, classic carnival forms were preserved in Italy, especially in Rome. The next most typical carnivals were those of Paris. Next came Nuremberg and Cologne, which adopted a more or less classic form at a somewhat later period. In Russia this process did not develop at all; the various aspects of folk merriment of a national or local character (shrove days, Christmas, fairs) remained unchanged. They offered none of the traits typical of Western European amusements. Peter the Great, as we know, tried to bring to Russia the later European style of the "feast of fools" (for example, the election of the all-clowns' pope) and the pranks of the April fool, but these customs did not take root and did not mix with local traditions.

Even in the cities where the process of development acquired a more or less classic character (as in Rome, Paris, Nuremberg, and Cologne), local festivities formed the basis of carnival. Its ritual was enriched by these local traits, which otherwise were doomed to vanish.

Many of these popular-festive forms that had lent some of their essential elements to carnival continued to lead contemporaneously their own pallid existence. This was, for instance, the case of the French charivari; its main traits had been transferred to carnival, but it still retained a feeble resemblance to bridal mockery (if the marriage for some reason or other was not considered normal). It is still presented in our days, as a cat-concert under the windows of newlyweds. Furthermore, all the elements of folk merriment which constituted the second, unofficial part of holy days and legal feasts continued to exist independently; however, they had many traits in common with the carnival rituals: the election of kings and queens for a day on the feast of the Epiphany ("the feast of beans") and on St. Valentine's day. These common elements are determined by the fact that they are all related to time, which is the true hero of every feast, uncrowning the old and crowning the new.[1] These popular unofficial forms of merriment continued, of course, to surround the feasts of the Church. Every fair, usually scheduled for the dedication of a church or a first mass, preserved carnivalesque traits. Finally, the carnivalesque character appeared on private family occasions, christenings and memorial services, as well as on agricultural feasts, the harvest of grapes (*vendage*) and the slaughter of cattle, as described by Rabelais. We also saw the carnivalesque character of the *nopces à mitaines*, a typical bridal ritual. The common denominator of the carnivalesque genres is the essential link of these feasts with "gay time." Whenever the free popular aspect of the feast is preserved, the relation with time is maintained, and this means the persistence of its carnivalesque flavor.

But when carnival developed in the narrow sense of the word and became the center of all popular forms of amusement, it diminished all the other feasts and deprived them of almost every free and utopian folk element. The other feasts faded away; their popular character was reduced, especially because of their connection with ecclesiastic or political rituals. Carnival became the symbol and incarnation of the true folk festival, completely independent of Church and State but tolerated by them. This was true of the Roman carnival described by Goethe in his famous sketch in 1788; and true also of the 1895 carnival in that city, pictured by Dietrich for his *Pulcinella* (and dedicated to his Roman friends and to the similar 1897 celebration). In Dietrich's time this festival was the only surviving vivid and colorful testimony of true popular life as it existed in bygone centuries.

In the time of Rabelais folk merriment had not as yet been concentrated in carnival season, in any of the towns of France. Shrove Tuesday (*Mardi Gras*) was but one of many occasions for folk merriment, although an important one. A considerable role in the festive life of the marketplace was played, as we have said, by the fairs held three or four times a year in several towns. The amusements offered at the fairs usually bore a carnivalesque character.

[. . .] A [. . .] sense of unity was brought to the people by all the forms and images of medieval popular-festive life. But the unity did not have such a simple geometric character. It was more complex and differentiated; most important of all, it had an historic nature. The body of the people on carnival square is first of all aware of its unity in time; it is conscious of its uninterrupted continuity within time, of its relative historic immortality. Therefore the people do not perceive a static image of their unity (*eine Gestalt*) but instead the uninterrupted continuity of their becoming and growth, of the unfinished metamorphosis of death and renewal. For all these images have a dual body; everywhere the genital element is emphasized: pregnancy, giving birth, the procreative force (Pulcinella's double hump, the protruding belly). . . . Carnival with all its images, indecencies, and curses affirms the people's immortal, indestructible character. In the world of carnival the awareness of the people's immortality is combined with the realization that established authority and truth are relative.

Popular-festive forms look into the future. They present the victory of this future, of the golden age, over the past. This is the victory of all the people's material abundance, freedom, equality, brotherhood. The victory of the future is ensured by the people's immortality. The birth of the new, of the greater and the better, is as indispensable and as inevitable as the death of the old. The one is transferred to the other, the better turns the worse into ridicule and kills it. In the whole of the world and of the people there is no room for fear. For fear can only enter a part that has been separated from the whole, the dying link torn from the link that is born. The whole of the people and of the world is triumphantly gay and fearless. This whole speaks in all carnival images; it reigns in the very atmosphere of this feast, making everyone participate in this awareness.

[. . .] The influence of carnival, in the broadest sense of the word, was great during all periods of literary development. However, this influence was in most cases hidden, indirect, and difficult to detect. During the Renaissance it was not only exceptionally strong but direct and clearly expressed, even in its exterior forms. The Renaissance is, so to speak, a direct "carnivalization" of human consciousness, philosophy, and literature.

The official culture of the Middle Ages was evolved over many centuries. It had its heroic, creative period and was all-embracing and all-penetrating. This culture enveloped and enmeshed the entire world and every segment, even the smallest, of human consciousness. It was supported by an organization unique of its kind, the Catholic Church. In the time of the Renaissance the feudal structure was nearing its end, but its ideological domination of the human mind was still extremely powerful.

Where could the Renaissance find support in the struggle against the official culture of the Middle Ages, a struggle which was as intense as it was victorious? The ancient literary sources could not per se offer a sufficient basis, because antiquity was also still seen by many through the prism of medieval ideology. In order to discover humanist antiquity, it was necessary at first to be free from the thousand-year-old domination of medieval categories. It was necessary to gain new ground, to emerge from ideological routine.

Such support could be offered only by the culture of folk humor which had developed throughout thousands of years. The progressive leaders of the Renaissance participated directly in this culture and first of all in its popular-festive, carnivalesque aspect. Carnival (and we repeat that we use this word in its broadest sense) did liberate human consciousness and permit a new outlook, but at the same time it implied no nihilism; it had a positive character because it disclosed the abundant material principle, change and becoming, the irresistible triumph of the new immortal people. This was indeed a powerful support for storming the stronghold of the Gothic age; it prepared the way for a new, free and sober seriousness.

In one of his articles, Dobrolyubov expressed a thought that deserves our notice: "It is necessary to work out in our soul a firm belief in the need and possibility of a complete exit from the present order of this life, so as to find the strength to express it in poetic forms."[2] At the base of Renaissance progressive literature there existed such a "firm belief." It was only thanks to this conviction that a radical change and renewal of all that exists became "necessary and possible," that the initiators of the Renaissance movement could see the world as they did. But this conviction also inspired the culture of folk humor; it was no abstract thought but a living experience that determined this culture's forms and images. Official medieval culture tried to inculcate the exactly opposite belief in a static unchanging world order and in the eternal nature of all existence. This teaching, as we have said, was still powerful. It could not be overcome by individual thinking or scholarly perusal of antique sources (not seen in the light of "carnival consciousness"). Popular culture alone could offer this support.

This is the reason why in all the great writings of the Renaissance we clearly sense the carnival atmosphere, the free winds blowing from the marketplace. We find this element in the very structure of Renaissance writings and in the peculiar logic of their images, although nowhere more clearly than in Rabelais.

The analysis we have applied to Rabelais would also help us to discover the essential carnival element in the organization of Shakespeare's drama. This does not merely concern the secondary, clownish motives of his plays. The logic of crownings and uncrownings, in direct or in indirect form, organizes the serious elements also. And first of all this "belief in the possibility of a complete exit from the present order of this life" determines Shakespeare's fearless, sober (yet not cynical) realism and absence of dogmatism. This pathos of radical changes and renewals is the essence of Shakespeare's world consciousness. It made him see the great epoch-making changes taking place around him and yet recognize their limitations.

Shakespeare's drama has many outward carnivalesque aspects: images of the material bodily lower stratum, of ambivalent obscenities, and of popular banquet scenes.

The carnivalesque basic element in Cervantes' *Don Quixote* and in his novellas is quite obvious: his novel is directly organized as a grotesque play with all its attributes. The depth and consequent nature of his realism are also typical of this pathos of change and renewal.

Renaissance literature still needs special study in the light of correctly understood popular-festive forms.

Rabelais' novel is the most festive work in world literature. It expresses the very essence of the people's gay spirit. This is why this novel stands out so sharply against the background of the humdrum solemn literature of the following periods, especially of the nineteenth century. This is why it is impossible to understand him if we adopt the nonfestive posture that prevailed during those later years.

However, even within bourgeois culture the festive element did not die. It was merely narrowed down. The feast is a primary, indestructible ingredient of human civilization; it may become sterile and even degenerate, but it cannot vanish. The private, "chamber" feast of the bourgeois period still preserves a distorted aspect of the ancient spirit; on feast days the doors of the home are open to guests, as they were originally open to "all the world." On such days there is greater abundance in everything: food, dress, decorations. Festive greetings and good wishes are exchanged, although their ambivalence has faded. There are toasts, games, masquerades, laughter, pranks, and dances. The feast has no utilitarian connotation (as has daily rest and relaxation after working hours). On the contrary, the feast means liberation from all that is utilitarian, practical. It is a temporary transfer to the utopian world. The feast cannot be reduced to any specific content (for instance to the historical event commemorated on that day); it transgresses all limited objectives. Neither can it be separated from bodily life, from the earth, nature, and the cosmos. The sun shines in the festive sky, and there is such a thing as "feast-day" weather. All these elements have been preserved in the bourgeois truncated forms of these celebrations.

Characteristically enough, modern Western philosophy of anthropology has sought to discover the festive awareness of man and this special aspect of the world, in order to overcome the pessimistic conception of existentialism. However, philosophical anthropology with its phenomenological method, alien to the historic, social element, cannot solve this problem. Moreover, this philosophy is guided by the narrow spirit of the bourgeois period.

Notes

1   Actually, every feast day crowns and uncrowns, and has therefore its own king and queen. See this theme in the *Decameron*, where a king and queen are elected for every day of the festive discourses.

2   Dobrolyubov: "Poems of Ivan Nikitin." Collected works in nine volumes, Goslitisdat Leningrad, 1963. Vol. 6, p. 167.

Chapter 4

John Willett

BRECHT ON THEATRE

Brecht on Theatre, Methuen Drama (1964), excerpts from pp. 37, 186–201, 276–7.

Notes to the opera *Aufstieg und Fall der Stadt Mahagonny*

[. . .]

THE MODERN THEATRE is the epic theatre. The following table shows certain changes of emphasis as between the dramatic and the epic theatre:

DRAMATIC THEATRE	EPIC THEATRE
plot	narrative
implicates the spectator in a stage situation	turns the spectator into an observer, but
wears down his capacity for action	arouses his capacity for action
provides him with sensations	forces him to take decisions
experience	picture of the world
the spectator is involved in something	he is made to face something
suggestion	argument
instinctive feelings are preserved	brought to the point of recognition
the spectator is in the thick of it, shares the experience	the spectator stands outside, studies
the human being is taken for granted	the human being is the object of the inquiry
he is unalterable	he is alterable and able to alter

eyes on the finish	eyes on the course
one scene makes another	each scene for itself
growth	montage
linear development	in curves
evolutionary determinism	jumps
man as a fixed point	man as a process
thought determines being	social being determines thought
feeling	reason

Extracts from *A Short Organum for the Theatre*

23

The bare wish, if nothing else, to evolve an art fit for the times must drive our theatre of the scientific age straight out into the suburbs, where it can stand as it were wide open, at the disposal of those who live hard and produce much, so that they can be fruitfully entertained there with their great problems. [. . .] A theatre which makes productivity its main source of entertainment has also to take it for its theme, and with greater keenness than ever now that man is everywhere hampered by men from self-production: i.e. from maintaining himself, entertaining and being entertained. The theatre has to become geared into reality if it is to be in a position to turn out effective representations of reality, and to be allowed to do so.

35

We need a type of theatre which not only releases the feelings, insights and impulses possible within the particular historical field of human relations in which the action takes place, but employs and encourages those thoughts and feelings which help transform the field itself.

36

The field has to be defined in historically relative terms. In other words we must drop our habit of taking the different social structures of past periods, then stripping them of everything that makes them different; so that they all look more or less like our own, which then acquires from this process a certain air of having been there all along, in other words of permanence pure and simple. Instead we must leave them their distinguishing marks and keep their impermanence always before our eyes, so that our own period can be seen to be impermanent too. [. . .]

37

If we ensure that our characters on the stage are moved by social impulses and that these differ according to the period, then we make it harder for our spectator to identify himself with them. He cannot simply feel: that's how I would act, but at most can say: if I had lived under those circumstances. And if we play works dealing with our own time as though they were historical, then perhaps the circumstances under which he himself acts will strike him as equally odd; and this is where the critical attitude begins.

42

The kind of acting which was tried out at the Schiffbauerdamn Theater in Berlin between the First and Second World Wars, with the object of producing such images, is based on the 'alienation effect' (A-effect). A representation that alienates is one which allows us to recognize its subject, but at the same time makes it seem unfamiliar. The classical and medieval theatre alienated its characters by making them wear human or animal masks; the Asiatic theatre even today uses musical and pantomimic A-effects. Such devices were certainly a barrier to empathy, and yet this technique owed more, not less, to hypnotic suggestion than do those by which empathy is achieved. The social aims of these old devices were entirely different from our own.

43

The old A-effects quite remove the object represented from the spectator's grasp, turning it into something that cannot be altered; the new are not odd in themselves, though the unscientific eye stamps anything strange as odd. The new alienations are only designed to free socially-conditioned phenomena from that stamp of familiarity which protects them against our grasp today.

44

For it seems impossible to alter what has long not been altered. We are always coming on things that are too obvious for us to bother to understand them. What men experience among themselves they think of as 'the' human experience. A child, living in a world of old men, learns how things work there. He knows the run of things before he can walk. If anyone is bold enough to want something further, he only wants to have it as an exception. Even if he realizes that the arrangements made for him by 'Providence' are only what has been provided by society he is bound to see society, that vast collection of beings like himself, as a whole that is greater than the sum of its parts and therefore not in any way to be influenced. Moreover, he would be used to things that could not be influenced; and who mistrusts what he is used to? To transform himself from general passive acceptance to a corresponding state of suspicious inquiry he would need to develop that detached eye with which the great Galileo observed a swinging chandelier. He was amazed by this pendulum motion, as if he had not expected it and could not understand its occurring, and this enabled him to come on the rules by which it was governed. Here is the outlook, disconcerting but fruitful, which the theatre must provoke with its representations of human social life. It must amaze its public, and this can be achieved by a technique of alienating the familiar.

45

This technique allows the theatre to make use in its representations of the new social scientific method known as dialectical materialism. In order to unearth society's laws of motion this method treats social situations as processes, and traces out all their inconsistencies. It regards nothing as existing except in so far as it changes, in other words is in disharmony with itself. This also goes for those human feelings, opinions and attitudes through which at any time the form of men's life together finds its expression.

47

In order to produce A-effects the actor has to discard whatever means he has learnt of getting the audience to identify itself with the characters which he plays. Aiming not to put his audience into a trance, he must not go into a trance himself. [. . .]

48

At no moment must he go so far as to be wholly transformed into the character played. The verdict: 'he didn't act Lear, he was Lear' would be an annihilating blow to him. He has just to show the character, or rather he has to do more than just get into it; this does not mean that if he is playing passionate parts he must himself remain cold. It is only that his feelings must not at bottom be those of the character, so that the audience's may not at bottom be those of the character either. The audience must have complete freedom here.

61

The realm of attitudes adopted by the characters towards one another is what we call the realm of gest. Physical attitude, tone of voice and facial expression are all determined by a social gest: the characters are cursing, flattering, instructing one another, and so on. The attitudes which people adopt towards one another include even those attitudes which would appear to be quite private, such as the utterances of physical pain in an illness, or of religious faith. These expressions of a gest are usually highly complicated and contradictory, so that they cannot be rendered by any single word and the actor must take care that in giving his image the necessary emphasis he does not lose anything, but emphasizes the entire complex.

65

Everything hangs on the 'story'; it is the heart of the theatrical performance. For it is what happens *between* people that provides them with all the material that they can discuss, criticize, alter. Even if the particular person represented by the actor has ultimately to fit into more than just the one episode, it is mainly because the episode will be all the more striking if it reaches fulfilment in a particular person. The 'story' is the theatre's great operation, the complete fitting together of all the gestic incidents, embracing the communications and impulses that must now go to make up the audience's entertainment.

67

As we cannot invite the audience to fling itself into the story as if it were a river and let itself be carried vaguely hither and thither, the individual episodes have to be knotted together in such a way that the knots are easily noticed. The episodes must not succeed one another indistinguishably but must give us a chance to interpose our judgment. [. . .] The parts of the story have to be carefully set off one against another by giving each its own structure as a play within the play. To this end it is best to agree to use titles [. . .]. The titles must include the social point, saying at the same time something about the kind of portrayal wanted, i.e. should copy the tone of a chronicle or a ballad or a newspaper or a morality.[. . .]

Appendices to the Short Organum

4

a   If we now discard the concept of EPIC THEATRE we are not discarding that progress towards conscious experience which it still makes possible. It is just that the concept is too slight and too vague for the kind of theatre intended; it needs exacter definition and must achieve more. Besides, it was too inflexibly opposed to the concept of the dramatic, often just taking it naïvely for granted, roughly in the sense that 'of course' it always embraces incidents that take place directly with all or most of the hall-marks of immediacy. In the same slightly hazardous way we always take it for granted that whatever its novelty it is still theatre, and does not turn into a scientific demonstration.

b   Nor is the concept THEATRE OF THE SCIENTIFIC AGE quite broad enough. The Short Organum may give an adequate explanation of what is meant by a scientific age, but the bare expression, in the form in which it is normally used, is too discredited.

45

The theatre of the scientific age is in a position to make dialectics into a source of enjoyment. The unexpectedness of logically progressive or zigzag development, the instability of every circumstance, the joke of contradiction and so forth: all these are ways of enjoying the liveliness of men, things and processes, and they heighten both our capacity for life and our pleasure in it.

Every art contributes to the greatest art of all, the art of living.

46

The bourgeois theatre's performances always aim at smoothing over contradictions, at creating false harmony, at idealization. Conditions are reported as if they could not be otherwise; characters as individuals, incapable by definition of being divided, cast in one block, manifesting themselves in the most various situations, likewise for that matter existing without any situation at all. If there is any development it is always steady, never by jerks; the developments always take place within a definite framework which cannot be broken through.

None of this is like reality, so a realistic theatre must give it up.

Note

This table does not show absolute antitheses but mere shifts of accent. In a communication of fact, for instance, we may choose whether to stress the element of emotional suggestion or that of plain rational argument.

Chapter 5

Julie Salverson

CLOWN, OPERA, THE ATOMIC BOMB AND THE CLASSROOM

O**NE MORNING I RECEIVED AN EMAIL** asking me to contribute a short blurb to a grant application. I'm the librettist on this project and I needed to send a snappy sound bite that could capture a four-year journey distilled into ninety minutes of performance. Trying to attract the funder's interest, I wrote: 'A radioactive child, a village of widows in northern Canada, a haunted pilot and an infamous and ignored physicist hurtle down the Highway of the Atom in a clown opera about the atomic bomb'. The email disappeared into the ether, and I wondered again at the numerous ways I am challenged with the task of passing on this remarkable event. This chapter looks at an experiment with the fundamentals of clown – as taught by Jacques Lecoq and Phillipe Gaulier – and a new model for working theatrically with testimony in both professional and community situations. The project has brought together opera singers and clowns; archival, critical-theory and artist-based research; drama students; and a major opera company with a twenty-five-year history of community involvement.

The event

Several years ago Peter van Wyck, a writer and scholar at Concordia University in Montreal, telephoned me with an extraordinary invitation. Would I accompany him on a trip to explore the geography, archive and stories along 'The Highway of the Atom?' This adventure would eventually lead us to the top of Canada in minus forty-degree winter, to a nuclear-waste disposal site one mile below the New Mexico Desert, and to the Trinity Site where the world's first atomic bomb was detonated. 'Highway of the Atom' was the name given the Canadian trade route over which uranium ore was transported from northern Canada. The uranium was carried on men's backs and river barges over a two-thousand-mile water and portage route.

It was then loaded onto trains and sent south to be refined in Port Hope (a port town just outside Toronto with access to Great Lakes shipping) and ultimately used by the American government to build atomic bombs. Many of the Dene First Nation of the community around Deline, Great Bear Lake (the Sahtúgot'ine), were employed to transport this uranium. Over the years a number have died of cancer (Peter Blow's 1999 documentary about Deline is called 'Village of Widows'). In the late 1990s, the Dene discovered that 'their' uranium had been used in the bombs dropped on Hiroshima and Nagasaki, and they undertook a most extraordinary expedition. A small group from the community flew to Japan to apologize to the survivors, the *hibakusha*. This conveyance of apology, this act of witness and responsibility in the face of events over which the Dene had no control, startled and challenged us. Peter and I saw ourselves as bewildered strangers stumbling down the highway of the atom in search of an ethics of memory. We asked what it means to be implicated and to take ownership in the face of a catastrophic event. An excerpt from our project description states how we viewed our task:

> This research program investigates, translates and performs an encounter between the researcher and a Canadian trade route, between the cultural theorist and the artist, between the witness and the translator, between the archival and the memorial, and between the placed and the displaced. It is by no means always evident who belongs to which role. The enormity of what may be reductively called 'the story' makes inadequate any conventional claims to authorship, ownership, clear constituency. And yet there are stakes, implications, responsibilities.

The challenge

My part of the project is a deliberate investigation into clown and the absurd as an alternate vocabulary to what have become common methods for artists working in community with people's stories: popular-education-based scene development, theatre of the oppressed, storytelling, playback theatre. For years as a community-based playwright I have grappled with the problem of how to tell stories of violence with integrity and a faithfulness to the living and the dead that allows the inevitability of my shaping the telling aesthetically, politically and personally. I have been concerned with the relationship between aesthetics and politics, with the importance of artistry and imagination in plays that reference 'true stories', and with expanding the aesthetic vocabulary of theatre that testifies. Above all, I've grown disturbed by what I call an aesthetic of injury, a tendency in socially motivated theatre to focus on pain at the expense of agency and to reduce stories to a cast of victims, heroes and helpless witnesses. One problem for the witness/artist is the danger of fixing trauma in presumed configurations of how loss looks and sounds. Preconceptions about pain and how to recognize it restrict our ability to receive the strength and resilience in a survivor, and the possible vulnerability in ourselves as we listen to accounts of violence.

Philosopher Emmanuel Levinas puts it well, I think, when he suggests that the problem with tragedy is that it isn't tragic enough. Beyond the hopeless, self-enclosing indulgence of a tragic response to existence, there is an alternative in the relationship with others. For the person or the community willing to hear accounts of violence from survivors, this means that those who listen and those who speak are both fully subjects, reducible neither to their pain nor to a sentimental closure where everything can be overcome, healed, reconciled. It is impossible to face the story of the atomic bomb and its consequences with comprehension.[1] Clown offered a way to name this impossibility. It also provided us with an opportunity for the kind of story our research made necessary: a story of both immense magnitude and ordinary humanity, where the relationship between suffering and survival, tragedy and love, the visible and the invisible might be explored. Beckett talked about the quest to 'fail better'. How can we fail and still witness this story?

Creating a working team

I wrote a letter to Tapestry New Opera Works in Toronto. The company invited me to join their summer librettist/composers' laboratory where I met composer Juliet Palmer. It turned out her father was a fighter pilot and she'd grown up in New Zealand, which declared itself a nuclear-free zone in 1985. I'd grown up next door to Port Hope and a neighbouring nuclear station. We teamed up. Our collaboration crosses a number of borders: geographic, historic, cultural, archival, social, pedagogic and aesthetic. In 2003 Juliet and I wrote a fifteen-minute opera commissioned for the opening of Tapestry's studio theatre. My libretto came from two notebooks filled with scribbles from my accumulated readings (atomic history, testimonies from workers, scientists and communities attached to nuclear testing) and the trips Peter and I had taken to the North West Territories and New Mexico. 'Over the Japanese Sea' is about a young businessman meeting an old office cleaner who turns out to have been the pilot of the plane that dropped the bomb. The young man is losing his lover, and asks the older man for advice when he overhears the cleaner reminiscing about a lost love. This love turns out to be his experience of flight over the Japanese sea. This piece was staged partly in the Tapestry offices with the audience on their feet among the singers (in promenade style familiar to community play projects but new to opera) and partly in the studio with the audience seated. The response of the audiences encouraged us. Instead of sitting back immobilized by the idea of the bomb, people chatted together and with us about their connections to the atomic story: a cousin who was an engineer, an uncle who was a miner, a neighbour who worked in a physics lab. All of us wanted to produce this engagement from people, this energy, and the reaction confirmed our desire to make the opera about the effects of the atomic age on ordinary people, not a creation of iconic figures, heroic or tragic.

The class[2]

Next I invited my undergraduate acting class at Queen's University to explore what would happen when the element of clown was introduced into the research material. I hired three senior students to work with me as a team.[3] Our first session, held just before the winter break, was an introduction to the topic. We began by asking: 'What comes to mind when you think of the atomic bomb?' The class created images, devised text, told stories, played with word association. Three hours later this valiant crew dragged themselves from the studio, somber, serious, nervously committed to the next six weeks of exploration. They returned after the week's break with their first assignment: to bring back, word for word, someone's answer to the question 'What do you think of when you hear the words atomic bomb?' from a peer, a parent or a grandparent. The students then selected from a group of research topics (The Manhattan Project, the atom, physicists Lise Meitner and Robert Oppenheimer, the Deline community) and were asked to return the following week with a performance piece that combined what they judged the most important elements from the personal texts with one key element from the researched material. A week later they performed the results. The exercise had selected what mattered to the students, but the form of the pieces was unintentionally melodramatic, 'weighted with worthiness', the team and I said to each other. The scenes were exhausting to watch, draining energy from actors and audience both.

Several days later the research team and I met and agreed that the work presented had been exactly what we didn't want: earnest, ponderous and self-conscious in a manner that highlighted the inexperience of the students. They stood apart from a topic they were in awe of, and it showed. We decided that from then on every theatrical idea, no matter how devastating the content, had to be shown through a clown exercise. The next day, just before class, I was presented with my first challenge. Eliza, a conscientious student who had missed the last session, came up to me in the hall, out of breath and anxious. She had been researching the effects of nuclear testing on the environment and was eager to present her findings to the group. I told her she would have to tell us about what mattered through one of the exercises. No, she insisted, what she had read about was too important, she had to make sure everyone 'got it', as she put it. I managed to get her to agree to try the exercises and see what would happen, and I promised her that if she didn't feel she had sufficiently made her point, she could then talk to the class.

The following class was conducted by two visiting clown artists, Charlotte Gowdy and Lisa Marie DiLiberto, with coaching from our team. Juliet also sat in. Clown and text was one thing, but what about clown and text and music and singing? Eliza had to wait while several groups worked. In one scene three 'pilots' knelt (with sweaters on backwards that tied their hands behind them and padding that amplified their bodies to bouffon grotesque shapes) and used their elbows as hands to fold a paper airplane and send it off to drop the bomb over Japan. In another a military commander danced for his life to convince the audience that he could keep the public reassured while burying more troops. Eliza kept sending me worried glances and checking her pages of notes, which no doubt she wanted to read aloud. Finally it was her turn. She joined a small group who waited outside the door for instructions. 'Your job', we told them, 'is to stand at the front of the room with your backs to the audience, turn when given the signal, and run into the audience, startling them.' While the small group waited outside the door, we gave the audience (the rest of the class) pieces of newspaper they were told to crumple up into balls. 'When the group at the front turns and runs toward you, on a signal from me, throw the balls at the students.'[4] The group entered, turned to the class, ran forward and were met by a slew of paper hurled at them from their delighted classmates. 'Freeze', Lisa yelled. They did, holding grotesque misshapen positions. Then, one by one, Lisa and Charlotte played the patron, or mean teacher, with each student, drawing from them extreme voices and physicality, asking questions about their names, what they had for breakfast, and most importantly, what impossible exploit they were proud of that they had come to show us. The exercise caught the students off guard. Though they are usually so determined to impress with their acting skills or the physical attractiveness they believed (as young actors and young people) so important, this awkward game allowed them to play, to reveal their true vulnerability and their pleasure. Each showed the 'patron' something, perhaps a song, a dance, a way to brush one's teeth. In the interaction between actor and patron, a childlike character emerged, with a strong and recognizable trait. For some, it was a bratty child, for others an innocent and awestruck one. If the students stayed too much in their heads, became too uncomfortable to let the game unfold, both the game and the student were frustrated. But most of the time actors and audience were fascinated and alert.

When it was Eliza's turn, she morphed into a kind of old woman. She chanted a spell. As the character became stronger, the old woman more clearly took shape. I realized with a chill that she reminded me of the wise old woman in fairy tales, who often lives in the woods. Just at that moment, Charlotte introduced the next element of the exercise. She asked Eliza: 'What do you have to tell us?' This was the moment where we would hear about her research, her story of atomic science and the environment. Eliza gathered herself up to a great height, casting her glance over the entire class, and whispered forcefully, 'It's not gone! It's still here!' Everyone was silent, stunned, the image of atomic particles and radiation hovering among us. Eliza was the last student in her group. We took a breath, and Charlotte said 'Ok, done. Good. Thanks.' Eliza didn't move. 'Do you want to say anything more?' I asked her. She looked at the class, noticed the response to what she'd done. No, that was all. She'd made her point.

Why clown

The experience of boiling things down to their essence proved central to the rest of the class. It also influenced the scenes that emerged from the exercises and the subsequent work on the opera. Eliza, in this unexpected role as wise woman – comic one moment and deadly serious the next – found a solid place where she could honestly tell us what was most urgent to her. This juxtaposition gives the inexperienced actor – as it would, I believe, a community participant – a framework that brings together several key factors. We see Eliza herself behind the mask of the actor. What is revealed is her desire and conviction to tell the story held up against her awkwardness and inexperience. As audience members caught in this contradiction, we recognize our own failings and we appreciate her bravery and love her for trying. Perhaps we might be willing to try too. This ability to fail and still try, not with resignation but with pleasure, is important to the context for witnessing testimony. To listen well has become an increasingly terrible burden. We are immersed in history and questions about how to pass on stories fairly, fully, and with integrity. Inevitably, this is an unforgiving task, the clown's ultimate impossible exploit. Instead of being paralyzed by or denying the impossibility of the endeavour, the clown insists she will try. She screws up, and we laugh. She tries again. It is the laughter of recognition, relief, astonishment and of horror.

In much community practice we ask actors to deliver with confidence and urgency. Clown offers a theatrical convention that can unpin our expectations about what it means to hear tragic stories and thus, perhaps, allow us to listen differently. Too often our methods offer Eliza a narrow range of choices. She either pretends to stand unambiguously confident in her story or she apologizes that she is overwhelmed and inadequate beside its enormity. Clown presents Eliza to an audience and allows us to see her as imperfect, caring deeply, having a right to care, and having something to say. Beside her passion, which is evident in other theatrical forms of testimony, the ridiculous clown body, the dress-up clothes and the red nose, these signal to us that Eliza is not really important. Her silliness, her grotesqueness, these are her humility, even her apology if you like. She admits that she has no right to be taken seriously in the face of this enormous event, and yet she is determined to be heard. This juxtaposition, paradoxically, lets us love her and take her seriously. Our laughter reminds us that we, also, are ridiculous and have no right. The silence that follows appalls us, shocks us, forces us to perhaps think 'What have I laughed at? What huge story is this pathetic but brave woman asking me to listen to? I am as ordinary and inadequate, yet I am also as willing. I too could address this event!' This is not a theatrical approach that makes light of tragedy. It is, perhaps, an approach that is tragic enough.

After that agonizing first class, we had six weeks with energized, vibrant, laughing, curious and hard-working students who seemed delighted to arrive and reluctant to leave. These students were engaged and, dare I say it, happy, while wanting to learn all they could about the bomb and its historic, personal, environmental and social fallout. Six months later in Toronto we held a three-day workshop with professional opera singers, clowns and bits of text and improvised music. Again there was a sense of awe at the topic, mutual wonderment at the power of each of these art forms, and deep pleasure and astonishment at the spark generated by bringing it all together. The following March we presented two scenes from the opera to an audience at Queen's University that included my students. Again the atmosphere of excitement, curiosity and energy prevailed. As my former class watched director Steven Hill act the patron with Charlotte Gowdy now playing the distraught wife about to give birth to a radioactive baby, they saw that it was not unique to them as students to be unpinned, on edge and terribly human when risking a performance with clown. Listening to the audience around them, they realized it was not only them who could laugh and cry at what clown Karen Hines calls 'this terribly beautiful world'. The philosopher Adorno asked the question: 'What would happiness be that is not measured by the immeasurable grief at what is?' But what, I wonder – turning his comment slightly – is grief that is not measured by the astonishment of living, the awakening from death that continues to surprise?

As I finish writing this chapter, I hear that North Korea has exploded a nuclear weapon. This news, announced on a warm thanksgiving weekend in Canada amidst the richness of friends, food and family, and the brilliant reds and oranges of dying autumn leaves, makes the notion of a courageous happiness dreadfully relevant. It seems so frivolous to be happy. Brecht asked how we can make poems about trees in the face of horror. But Robert Desnos, a poet writing from the Holocaust, asks an even more penetrating question:

You who are living, what have you done with these treasures?
Do you regret the time of my struggle?
Have you raised your crops for a common harvest?
Have you made my town a richer place?

Carolyn Forche quotes this poem in her book *Against Forgetting: Twentieth-Century Poetry of Witness* and responds by asking: 'if we have not, if we do not, what, in the end, have we become? And if we do not, what, in the end, shall we be?' (Forche 1993: 47).

Lecoq and Gaulier teach that clown refuses consolation, including the consolation of forgetting.[5] In their approach to teaching and performance there are a number of key elements: a world from which there is no escape; an audience, implicated and present; clowns on stage, constantly seeking to love and be loved, and above all offering their naked selves; and the tyrant clown or patron, stronger than the rest, in charge. The tyrant runs the show and the game is to play anyway, to live anyway. 'Amusez-vous, merde!' ('For God's sake, joy!') says Gaulier to his students. Have pleasure, complicite and contact; act from your spirit not from your will; and, always give more of yourself.[6] I am not suggesting a kind of traditional comedy where everything works out in the end. A story told through the comedic 'does not depend on a happy ending but on a different sense of the real . . . when laughter "breaks us up," it asserts our freedom . . . The comic hero recognizes the risk involved but takes his chances, learning to live beyond the tragic polarities where new possibilities emerge . . .' (McLelland 1970: 83). The clown is not a hero but she is heroic in her courage, in being available to the possible, no matter how absurd and unlikely. Pleasure, joy and fun in this context are not spectacle or escape, but rather the deadly game of living with loss, living despite failure, living even despite the humiliation of trying endlessly. 'Always stay in the shit' says Steven Hill, 'that is where the humanity and the possibilities lie.'[7] It is this idea of 'amusez-vous, merde' – live and love in the shit – which I believe can bring new energy to theatre that grapples with risky stories: a tenacious, nonsentimental insistence on life within loss that is honest, ready to risk failure, and absolutely courageous.

Bibliography

Forche, C. (ed.) (1993) *Against Forgetting: Twentieth-Century Poetry of Witness*, New York and London: W.W. Norton & Company.

McLelland, J.C. (1970) 'Beyond Tragedy – the Comic Vision', in J.C. McLelland, *The Clown and the Crocodile*, Toronto: John Knox Press.

Martin, J. (2002) 'The Theatre Which Does Not Exist: Neutrality to Interculturalism', in F. Chamberlain and R. Yarrow (eds), *Jacques Lecoq and the British Theatre*, London and New York: Routledge, pp. 55–70.

Salverson, J. (2006) 'Witnessing Subjects: A Fool's Help', in J. Cohen-Cruz and M. Schutzman (eds), *A Boal Companion: Dialogues on Theatre and Cultural Politics*, New York and London: Routledge, pp. 146–57.

Notes

1   Much of my learning has come from Steven Hill, artistic director of Leaky Heaven Circus in Vancouver. Steven has worked for many years in multiple community and

professional situations, and his approach to clown is informed by Lecoq and Gaulier. The term 'risky stories' is used by Roger I. Simon and Wendy Simon in their essay: Teaching Risky Stories: Remembering Mass Destruction Through Children's Literature. *English Quarterly*. Vol.28 no.1(Fall 1995): 27–31.

2   My discussion of clown in this context is necessarily abbreviated. The work referenced (Lecoq and Gaulier) is highly skilled, takes years to teach, and has distinctions I am not addressing. Red nose and Bouffon are the two approaches we are using, more often red nose despite my example with bouffon. Clown is the final stage of two years of study in both the Lecoq and Gaulier schools, and not many master it. I am convinced, however, from what I have seen in Steven Hill's work and my experiences in Toronto, that this approach to clown has tremendous potential with untrained people of all ages.

3   Students Aaron Stern, Michael Lenic and Karen Kugelmass studied some clown with my colleague Michelle Newman and had participated in a workshop with Karen Hines. They planned each class with me and coached the class through the process.

4   An exercise we had learned from Karen Hines.

5   Parts of this paragraph come from my essay 'Witnessing subjects: a fool's help' (2006).

6   From notes I took during a few weeks in Gaulier's clown class in Paris, February/March 2006.

7   From notes I took during Shelter workshop, September 2004, Toronto.

Chapter 6

Adrian Jackson

PROVOKING INTERVENTION

HAVING SPENT MUCH OF THE past 20 years working with the Theatre of the Oppressed and especially Forum Theatre as a tool for social and individual change, both with my own company, Cardboard Citizens, and in training and development situations all around the world, a major preoccupation of mine has been finding the methodology to make the game of Forum work in an unforced way – to create the conditions whereby the participation of Boal's *spectactor* is natural, easy and productive. Much of this of course resides in the skill of the joker and his or her ability to solicit participation from an initially recalcitrant or too well-behaved audience. But the real forces creating the possibility of intervention are the seduction and provocation provided by the model, the piece of theatre whose outcome is to be rewritten in action by the audience. At best Forum Theatre retains the subversive intentions of its origins, as a counterweight to the standard power relations obtaining in the theatre context, and by extension, in the society which supports that theatre.

Sometime in the late eighties or early nineties, I went, on two occasions, to see versions of a show by the avant-garde Belgian director, Jan Fabre, entitled *The Power of Theatrical Madness*. By no stretch of the imagination would this kind of work fall within the ambit of the at-that-time-unused designation *applied theatre* – indeed it might even be described as being at the opposite end of that spectrum, as *unapplied theatre*, being work that appeared to be made solely for an art-crowd audience, with no declared goal of social change, art for art's sake (whatever that means). However, on both occasions, the work succeeded in provoking quite extreme reactions, and indeed interventions, from members of the audience. Whether this was the desired response or not, to this day, I have no idea, but, apart from being a very beautiful, concentrated, strange and difficult meditation on the nature of theatre, paradoxically there were also things to be learnt from it which overlap into the subject areas discussed in this book, and how an audience may be coaxed or challenged into moving beyond the role of passive spectator into active critic or subversive participant.

The Power of Theatrical Madness was very much *auteur* theatre, a grand design with much stylisation, occasional literary or other references, choreographed grace and ugliness, performers, both male and female clad, as I remember it, in smart suits and open-necked shirts. It contained wonderful moments and enduring images, most particularly one which clearly referenced the tale of the 'Emperor's New Clothes', with a naked crowned figure parading round the stage; it also had the repetitive tics and over-long sequences which characterised the rather self-regarding theatrical avant-garde of that time. Maybe the whole thing was a pun on the Emperor's new clothes, the Emperor being Fabre and his troupe, awaiting the brave little boy who would point out their preposterous self-important aesthetic nakedness. Or maybe not. I liked the experience enough to watch it twice, though I also thought it contained moments of unutterable tedium. On both occasions, however, a version of the brave little boy appeared, to puncture the pretension with enjoyable irreverence and break the rules of theatrical convention.

The first time, in the small auditorium of the Institute of Contemporary Arts in London, there came a point in the show when a tray of live frogs was brought on stage, and they hopped off in various directions. After a few minutes, a number of performers whipped off their white shirts and each appeared to trap one of these hapless reptiles under their shirts on the floor. Then, with much gusto, they appeared to stamp vigorously on the shirts, crushing their ranine victims underneath, as seemingly evidenced by large red stains that appeared on the shirts.

At about this point, a female voice came from the back of the auditorium, prefaced by a very British, 'Excuse me', asking 'Are you really killing those frogs?' The company ignored the question and went on with their show. So she asked again, louder. Again, no response. She left the auditorium, and we could hear her loudly persisting outside the theatre space, repeating her question to the staff and remonstrating generally about cruelty to animals. The show continued and came, eventually to its conclusion. Later, in conversation with other theatre-goers, I established from a more zoologically minded punter that had they really been 'killing those frogs', the stain that appeared on their shirts would have been blue, not red, frogs being cold-blooded animals (please do not ask me for a more detailed chemical or biological explanation – suffice it to say that apparently this detail of colour would have proved the actors' innocence without the need for more detailed forensics). It seemed certain to me that the company's intention was to provoke, though whether they experienced these animal-loving interventions in other countries to which they toured seemed less certain. They did nothing with the intervention, however, seemingly simply ignoring it – but perhaps knowing that this was the reaction most likely to increase the level of protest.

A year or so later, I saw the same company performing a version of the same show at the Albert Hall – a venue which combines a very stuffy and well-behaved British Empire feel with a circular configuration which forces members of an audience to be conscious of their fellows. This time the piece, though again undeniably brilliant and striking in parts, had considerable *longueurs*, which seemed like a statement, a taunt, a deliberate taxing of the audience's patience; of course, it may be that the audience was simply not considered as a factor in the construction of the piece – that this was the vision of a creator, taking the artist's prerogative to do as he liked, to make the piece he wanted, at the length he wanted. Or maybe it was a bit of both.

Anyway, after an agonisingly slow sequence, in which little happened over a long repetitive period, a member of the audience from the stage right side – the performance effectively being played on a thrust stage surrounded on three sides – shouted out: 'Get on with it!' At which another member of the audience from the other side shouted sternly: 'Shush (PAUSE) . . . I'm doing the crossword'. After a further short pause, a third member of the audience joined in the dialogue from elsewhere with: 'Give us a clue'. Again, at no point did the company acknowledge or react to these interventions, which released a healthy critical dialogue and irreverent levity in their audience.

I tell this story because this was my first serious experience of theatre audiences breaking the rules and thereby creating a more interesting spectacle. This was before I myself started experimenting with the Theatre of the Oppressed, specifically Forum Theatre, in which intervention is a *sine qua non*, an anti-rule even, though of course not an obligation (except in the worst of forced Forum Theatre events). A considerable preoccupation of mine since then has been how to provoke and seduce meaningful intervention from audiences – and how sometimes one sees Forum Theatre in which intervention is solicited (or even begged) for all the wrong reasons and by all the wrong methods.

Why does an audience member intervene, and what is a meaningful intervention? At first, my Bible was the story Augusto tells of the powerfully built woman – her dimensions used to increase with his every telling of the story, to the point where these days she is girthed like a sumo wrestler – who intervened in a session of the precursor of Forum Theatre, Simultaneous Dramaturgy, because she was so angry, both with the oppressor in the story and with the pathetic attempts of the actors to use the strategy she was suggesting, that she simply could not stay passively in her seat any longer. The drivers here for intervention were frustration and anger, and a sense that she had to do it otherwise no one else would.

Augusto attributes to this moment, the Ur-Intervention if you like, the birth of Forum Theatre as we know it. Solidarity, fellow feeling, coupled with a sense of, in the immortal words of the bleakly brave protagonist in Alan Bleasdale's seminal eighties TV drama, The Boys from the Blackstuff – 'I can do that'. She was neither bored by artistic pretension nor outraged by animal abuse, but she was angry both with a character whose type she knew and the ineffectual responses of those faced with this oppressor on the stage.

Unlike the barrackers and questioner in the Fabre performances, this woman waited till Boal (belatedly) gave her permission to intervene – but then her intervention, actually taking the stage and taking control of the action (to administer a sound beating to the erring oppressor-husband), was obviously on a different scale. It takes a lot of courage to enter someone else's stage without a script.

Much Forum intervention does work on those lines, implicating the audience in the action of the piece by stimulating the essential, but often dormant, human urge to put right injustice. The comparative safety of the theatrical environment works with the driver of *anger* to overcome the restrictors of *fear* and *convention*. Spect-actors forget their fear for a few precious moments – and the hope is that by forgetting their fear in the theatrical conceit, they may then be encouraged to forget their fear of upsetting convention in their real lives. The power of theatrical solidarity, if you like. The audience provides the backup, if the intervention is not totally misguided, and proves to the intervening spect-actor that they are not alone, and that it is possible to take arms against a sea of troubles.

The theatre must provoke, if the target is truly to move people beyond the normative conventions which keep the spectator passive, the citizen obedient. Of course if you simply provoke, you run the risk of meaningless outrage – the question is what you do with that provocation and the resulting release of energy. You also have to seduce, by the power of the narrative and the quality of the theatrical experience. Seduction and provocation in equal measure. The experience has to be seductive enough to warrant participation. And to make the experience truly seductive, the art must be good enough. Good enough for the circumstances you find yourselves in, with the resources you have at hand.

Jan Fabre's piece, seductive and provocative enough to elicit transgressive audience response, no doubt supplied material for many post-show drinks and dinner-party conversations, but there, I imagine, it ended. I doubt that many personal or social acts of real-life revolution resulted from it. The best *applications* of Forum Theatre link the event of performance to follow-up, working with organisations and bodies which can harness the initial transgression and embed it in programmes to enable concerted long-term change and development.

For many years now, Cardboard Citizens has used Forum Theatre in hostels and day centres, first of all just as an event in itself, and more latterly in its Engagement Programme in which after the initial performance and Forum session, the ex-homeless actors, trained as short-term mentors, hook up with members of the homeless audiences to offer suggestions of how or where they might best follow up the ideas or changes initiated or implied during the Forum. Many participants will start attending the various weekly workshops offered by the company, in a range of performance-related disciplines – and the workshop group, composed of people in similar situations, becomes a launch-pad for embedding the change. Or a meeting might be arranged for the day or week after the performance, and an actor might even accompany individuals on a trip to one of the numerous schemes and charities the company has links with, to capture the urge displayed in the moment of intervention and allow the person to solidify their desire for change into action in real life. Or, to paraphrase Augusto, *to extrapolate from rehearsal in the theatre to performance in real life.*

What is the seduction? At bottom, always, a good piece of theatre – the better the theatre, the easier the seduction. The seduction in a Cardboard Citizens show is also, in part at least, the nature of the seducers – the performers are mostly ex-homeless people – for the audience, these are people like us, telling stories like ours. The seduction will often be by the use of a lighter form to clothe a more difficult issue; for instance, treating the subject of abuse and homelessness under the guise of a pantomime version of Dick Whittington – Dick and his Dog, the world's first *panto-forum* (there is a longer story to be told here one day, of the adaptation of this noble British theatre form, with its subversion and apparent interactivity, into a genuine tool for political debate . . .). People came on stage to play with the Dame (*ooh er missus* . . .), and found themselves engaged in deeper questions.

The provocation can be as simple as the visible mistreatment of a homeless person – in ways familiar to the audience. The small device of a beggar harangued or spat upon by a passing commuter has often worked an easy trick of provoking the first five or six interventions, bringing the audience onto the stage simply to remonstrate or reason with the ignorant character who stops long enough to say 'you people make me sick – why don't you get a bloody job like the rest of us . . .' Once this first transgression has been performed, others will follow with more ease, seeing that this original sin has not resulted in cataclysmic consequences for its perpetrators – indeed discovering that it can be fun.

The best Forum Theatre acts with this combination of seduction and provocation to release the innate dissatisfaction in its audience members so that, without coercion, they feel an overwhelming urge to make their thoughts and feelings known by taking action; in the form of *intervention*. The worst manifestations of Forum Theatre simply replace one set of rigid theatrical and social conventions with another, even to the extent that the audience feels compelled to participate as a sort of penance, and sometimes even to save a vicarious embarrassment for the performers as to whether the game is working or not. At its least subversive, civic duty can take the place of the art and pleasure of theatre; at best, theatricality combines with content to produce the perfect conditions for an audience to take an active part, to the point of genuinely taking the power.

To end with a similar story of transgression from the world of the Theatre of the Oppressed, in 1992 I attended a festival of Forum Theatre in Paris at which companies and organisations around the world showed pieces they had made. Amongst them was a so-called Forum Theatre play from one of the newly independent Eastern bloc countries. In this disastrously (and possibly unpleasantly) misconceived production, the scenario featured a number of shipwreck survivors washed up on a desert island. The survivors were, we were told by an interpreter, representative of various ethnic groups: there was an Arab, a Jew, an African prince from the Ivory Coast (*sic*, as translated to us), a Red Indian (*sic*, as before), a French lady, and I forget the rest. Since the play was made for an international audience, with little or no knowledge of the originating language, it was to be performed out of verbal language; each performer was to speak in 'characteristic' sounds, though we were not told who was who. One's suspicions were aroused when one character made 'ooga-wooga' sounds, while another, dressed in a long black coat, made nasty rasping throaty noises.

I had the misfortune to be sitting in the front row. The audience of over 200 was in festival mode, and (overly) respectful of each international contribution. The first event in the narrative was the awakening of the rasping black-coated character, whilst all the rest of the survivors lay exhausted on the shore. This character made as if to steal a wallet from the pocket of another, till the latter awoke in the nick of time. Later all the survivors were making offerings of coats and such-like for the building of a fire, and some were striking sticks together to try to make sparks to light it. While this was going on, the rasper was calmly standing elsewhere, not offering his coat, and lighting a cigar with his lighter. By now the general tenor of the production was clear.

The 'model' ended fairly rapidly, and we were told that now ALL THE PARTS were to be replaced by members of the audience (rather than the protagonist as is the working norm in Forum). As it happened the rasping actor approached my neighbour to take his place – no question here of voluntarism, we were to do as we were told in this woeful misunderstanding of the methodology and function of Forum. I took the opportunity to ask him, in various languages, whether he by any chance represented the Jew. On receipt of an affirmative answer I started to leave, horrified to find that some members of this polite audience were playing along and happily taking people's places, as if they had left their brains at the door. On my way out, I passed Boal slumped in his seat and said to him: 'Augusto, this is racist shit of the worst order'. He replied disconsolately: 'I know, you should say something'. So I did, and was rapidly joined by others. I became the protesting audience member, provoked in this case by the utter ineptitude and offensiveness of the production to speak out, against polite convention.

Various discussions and protests followed, Boal gave his damning verdict on this woeful adaptation of his form ('C'est bon pour Club Mediteranée, mais cela n'a rien à faire au Theatre de L'Opprimé') and eventually the whole group made images of their reactions to the piece. Finally the presenting company, horrified by the responses they had provoked but still, I fear, sadly not in full comprehension of why their piece had been so ill-received, made their own mea culpa image.

Here, for a dangerous moment in which the audience was starting to play along, it might have appeared as if one set of theatrical conventions had been replaced by another, equally unthinking one. The rule to be quiet and passive had been replaced by the rule to be active and participate, but was being followed with the same level of docile unthinkingness that Forum Theatre had been created to counter. Thankfully, normal subversive service was resumed in time, and hopefully some lessons were learnt. There was no seduction here, merely provocation, but still that provocation caused a revaluation of the theatrical event, along with a sobering awareness that however revolutionary any form, even in the Theatre of the Oppressed, its power can still be commandeered by the enemy and consciously or unconsciously applied with a completely different end in mind.

Forum Theatre should always retain at least a frisson of the 'original sin' of transgression – in the image of the spect-actor as unknown quantity, marching from floor to stage to execute an action, who knows what – and should always provoke dialogue and debate, expected or unexpected. If one model of thoughtless obedience has simply replaced another, the game is not worth the candle. However popular and widely used the form, it must never lose its subversive edge, even when its audiences come to be as well-versed in its conventions as the other theatre's punters are. And it should always be ready for the still small voice of protest. . . .

Chapter 7

Andy Watson

'LIFT YOUR MASK'
Geese Theatre Company in performance

SINCE 1987 GEESE THEATRE COMPANY (UK) has been developing theatre projects with offenders and people at risk of offending. The company works from the principle that theatre and drama are highly effective vehicles for exploring behaviour and contemplating the possibility of change. Whilst acknowledging that there exists a wide range of factors which influence people's decision making, the company focuses on individuals' responsibilities for their offending, and invites those individuals to challenge the attitudes and beliefs which underpin their offending behaviour. Geese's work asks questions and stimulates debate; it prompts participants to stand outside themselves and to evaluate who they are. Although the company's work follows an agenda, that of reducing re-offending, we do not deliver projects that teach participants not to re-offend, or which provide a moral or lesson to be learned. We present theatre and deliver groupwork which encourages offenders to consider the roles they play, have played or could play in the future, and invites them to consider whether or not they are content with those roles. Any changes that participants make are their own – our work provides the catalyst or framework but any changes are instigated and owned by the participants themselves.

The majority of our projects incorporate performance, whether it is an hour-long five-person full-mask piece, or a two-minute solo scene spontaneously created by a practitioner and integrated into a wider groupwork programme. This chapter will focus on the company's use of performance, as opposed to concentrating on our more participatory groupwork projects, of which there has been much discussion.[1]

A detailed analysis of Geese's performance work must consider some of the important factors which influence our decision making about those performances.

Firstly, the audience: as with all applied theatre we are creating theatre with a specific audience in mind. Our audience consists of offenders; however, offenders are not a homogenous group. In a prison there is only one definite assumption we can make about the composition of our audience: they have all been convicted of a crime (unless we are working with people on remand). Beyond that there may be little we know about who we are working with or what their motivations are for attending the project. A performance of Lifting the Weight[2] could attract eighty inmates, drawn from all sections of the prison, with a variety of reasons for attending. We cannot assume that they are attending because they are interested in theatre, in the project or in the process of change. Although we ask that participants are volunteers, 'volunteering' in prison is often a little different from more traditional notions of volunteering. When asked about their motivations for attending, some people will inform us that they were 'told to come'. Others might see it as an opportunity to meet associates whom they seldom see; some attend because it gets them out of other activities; others might see it as an opportunity to get out of their cell for a couple of hours. This degree of uncertainty about the make-up and motivations of our audience demands that we employ specific strategies in order to ensure the theatre is immediately engaging to a potentially disparate and disengaged group.

In contrast, some Geese performances operate in much more tightly defined parameters than Lifting the Weight. Stay[3] and So Far[4] were both designed to be delivered as part of probation service groupwork programmes with men who have been convicted of violence against a partner or sexual offending against children respectively. As with a prison audience, the eight to ten men who watch Stay are not a homogenous group, but in addition to the knowledge we have about their offending (they have been convicted of violence against a partner or ex-partner) we also know that their attendance is as part of a court order. They have not volunteered: they must attend or risk being returned to court for breaching an order, with the additional risk of a more severe sentence being handed down. Consequently, audiences for Stay and So Far are often very resistant, and this resistance demands that we make very clear choices about the nature of our performance.

Another primary consideration for us in the creation of our work is an understanding of the function of the piece, and how it relates to other work which we (or others) might be delivering with the same group. Our performances are seldom delivered in isolation, but often as part of a wider project, delivered either by ourselves, or, as in the case of Stay, by the probation services who have commissioned us. Therefore it is vital to understand what it is we are trying to achieve with our theatre.

Gutted[5] provides a useful example of how we create theatre within clearly defined parameters according to the project's function. The project is designed to explore masculinity and to look at the ways in which a man's underlying schema, his attitudes, thinking and feelings, impact on the way in which he interacts with the world and those around him. The performance which prefaces the project therefore had to reflect and enhance that groupwork process. In devising the performance we wanted to: provide an easily accessible narrative which the audience could recognise; show a man's struggle with the choices he has made and the impact of those choices on his friends and family; illustrate, using highly visual metaphors, some of the man's internal processes.

In addition, we are choosing to use theatre because we believe that the performance itself has a power to motivate, to shift people's thinking, to create affect and to act as a catalyst for the change process. As one inmate in HMP Elmley recently commented after watching a performance of *Gutted*, 'it gave me for probably the first time an objective look at the effects of my lifestyle on my family.' This power can then be harnessed when we enter the more participatory aspects of the work – if an audience member has recognised an aspect of himself in the performance, and also experienced a moment of dissonance or ambivalence in that recognition, we can move forward in the groupwork process exploring what might need to happen if that participant wants to begin to make changes.

In discussing the early development of Geese Theatre in America in 1980, Bergman and Hewish (Liebmann 1996: 97) describe a significant moment which helped to clarify the company's remit and scope. The first Geese performance took place in Stateville Correctional Centre in Chicago, a 'didactic historical/political treatise entitled "Gimme a Dollar" '. As Bergman and Hewish reflect, 'It did not take long for us to realise that our theatre was amusing to the inmates but wholly irrelevant. We knew that if we were to continue working in prison, we had to find theatre that was relevant.' It was this understanding that led the company to decide that 'the work must: create and mirror the inmate's special world, accurately' and this is one of the principles which still holds true for the performances created by Geese Theatre (UK) today.

All the company's performances are designed to accurately mirror the audience's world: our characters, their stories and the situations in which they are placed are immediately recognisable by the audience. In the example already cited, *Gutted* is designed to be delivered to an audience of fathers who have had several short prison sentences. The performance itself follows the story of Craig, a young male recidivist who is also a father. The audience immediately recognise Craig; they are familiar with the situations he finds himself in, the debates he has with himself, the emotions he feels, and the strategies he employs. The performance is clearly designed to encourage each man in the audience to 'catch sight of himself' (Liebmann 1996: 102).

This close mirroring has several distinct advantages when working with an offender audience. If offenders attend a theatre project for a number of different reasons, not all necessarily about wanting to engage with the performance itself, showing that the performance is relevant to their lives can help to unify those offenders into an audience. If they are witnessing characters who, although not them, bear a striking resemblance to them, in situations which they recognise, they are more likely to 'see the point' and be willing to engage with what is presented. In *The Plague Game*,[6] the audience watch an inmate struggle to communicate with his family on a prison visit. This is a scene which the vast majority of the audience will recognise for themselves – they have been there. In this moment of recognition they become 'hooked' into the performance – they want to know how the fictional inmate is going to deal with the situation, what impact any decisions will have on his partner and, most importantly, how he might be feeling during the visit. The offender in the audience is able to make direct connections between his own experience of being in a prison visit and the fictional version he is witnessing being played out before him.

The significance of this close mirroring goes beyond the initial moment of recognition; it is more than a rapport-building device to get an audience 'onside'. By presenting characters in recognisable situations we are able to invite the audience to reflect upon some of their own decision making, to explore some of their motivations and to consider potential alternative strategies. In *Lifting the Weight*, a character who has been released from prison and who has made a commitment not to offend again could be in a scene in which old associates are putting pressure on him to return to his old lifestyle. In theatrically presenting a scene which many of the audience will recognise we are positioning them as active observers in something very close to their own lives. Our character can articulate how it feels to be placed under pressure, can demonstrate potential ways out of the problem, and can illustrate some of the difficulties posed by the encounter. In this articulation of exactly what is going on for the character at that moment we are inviting the audience to consider what goes on for them in similar moments; by externalising the character's internal process we are inviting the audience to consider their own internal processes, their own decision making.

Of course, a professional theatre company consisting of trained actors/ practitioners who do not necessarily have experience of offending themselves, creating performances for offenders and *about* offenders' lives can be seen as problematic. Geese takes this issue very seriously and the company takes great pride in reflecting the offenders' world accurately. All Geese practitioners have a dual role – they are performers but they are also groupwork practitioners, working in a variety of participatory contexts with offenders. It is through these groupwork processes that we learn about the offender's world; through listening to offenders' stories and asking questions about their experiences we are able to accurately reflect that world back to them in our performance work. As two former Geese practitioners, Farrall and Mountford, stress:

> My map of the world is not the same as yours, because my experiences are different. The Company moves on therefore, by continually asking those we work with to share with us the landscape they inhabit so that we, through theatre and drama, can assist them in living their lives in a different world.
>
> (Thompson 1998: 125)

Adrian Jackson, in his introduction to the UK edition of Boal's *Games for Actors and Non Actors*, discusses why the traditionally 'reserved' British might intervene in a Forum Theatre piece. He states that 'if the model is right, if it is true to life, and is sufficiently effective at making the audience angry about the treatment of the protagonist, then up on stage they will come' (Boal 1996: xxii). Something similar is true for Geese's performance work in prisons: if the model is right, if it is true to life, and the audience invest in the characters and the world they inhabit because they recognise it, they will engage with what is being presented. The key is getting the model right and true to life – an audience of eighty inmates in a prison do not hold back when providing feedback about what you are presenting – if they do not recognise the characters and the world which you are holding up as a supposed mirror for them, they are entitled to challenge your interpretation of their world. An offender who witnessed a performance of *Hooked on Empty*[7] clearly summarises some of the attitudes we might be presented with when working in a prison, but also goes on to demonstrate the power that the theatre can hold if delivered sensitively and accurately:

Before I went in to watch your play, I said to myself, 'Yeah, yeah, here we go again, people that don't know what they're talking about.' How wrong I was. In every aspect you got it down to a 'T' . . . I think it hurt me to see what I had been through and what I had been putting up with . . . The play most definitely put a lot of things in perspective for me. Before I stepped into the room yesterday, I had an 'I don't give a fuck' attitude towards drugs . . . But I swear, if I've got anything to do with it, my life is not going to go on like my past.

(Baim, Brookes and Mountford 2002: 198)

By observing a world which is recognisable and believable, this offender is galvanised into wanting to make changes in his life. The theatre serves as a catalyst, propelling that offender into wanting to make changes but only because he believes that the fictional theatre world created resembles the world in which he is living.

Another of the defining features of Geese's performance work, namely, inter-activity and responsivity, helps to clarify Geese's position with regards to a professional's representation of an offender's world. The earliest of Geese perform-ances, *Lifting the Weight* and *Plague Game* and some of the more recent creations such as *Inside/Outside*,[8] have audience interaction at their core. Audience members are positioned not as passive observers of a narrative which unfolds before their eyes but as active participants who are integral to both the development of the characters and the direction of the narrative. As Baim, Brookes and Mountford explain:

The drama takes place between the characters on stage, but even more crucially, between the characters and the audience. A character will often need help or advice when facing a desperate situation. He or she turns to speak with the audience: 'What can I do next?' Now the character and the audience are directly linked; the character serves as the conduit for the audience's ideas, fears, frustrations and, often, their disbelief that there is a way out of the cycle of offending.

(Baim, Brookes and Mountford 2002: 182)

The performances act as a forum in which the audience can debate, often very passionately, the situations presented. The audience may be provoked into discussing the best course of action in a given situation, or to analyse what certain individuals (not just the protagonist) might be thinking or how they might be feeling. They may be asked to suggest advice or to consider some of the obstacles which might stand in the way. The structure of the theatre performance creates a dialogue between the on-stage action and the audience. This dialogue allows the audience of offenders to engage directly with versions of themselves, to suggest alternative ways of behaving and to view the consequences. The audience is encouraged to take ownership of the action, of the narrative, and in doing so they are invited to consider the role of the fictional offender not as a passive victim of circumstance, but as an active participant in the narrative who makes clear decisions about how that narrative will unfold. In effect, audience members are encouraged to reflect upon their own role of offender and consider how some of their decisions have influenced the narrative of their own lives.

The audience are carefully positioned to respond; they are often subtly placed in the role of 'expert'. In *Stay*, the male abuser character periodically turns to the audience of male abusers and seductively attempts to explain away his violence against his partner using the distortions, minimisations and justifications that the men in the group will have used. After a sustained period of physical and verbal abuse directed towards his partner, he will invite the group members to collude with his distortions: 'I don't do it with anyone else so it must be something about her that makes me . . .' The group, many of whom will have used similar distortions, experience cognitive dissonance: a tension arises from holding two conflicting thoughts at the same time. On the one hand they may want to agree with the character's distortions, as they are distortions they themselves have used to justify their behaviour; on the other hand, they have just witnessed a set of behaviours which clearly show the fictional perpetrator being in control and making clear choices about his use of violence. This dissonance is often uncomfortable. The men will challenge the distortion and confront the man with the reality of what he has done, what they have just witnessed. In so doing, their interaction becomes not only a challenge of the fictional character but of themselves. In the groupwork process the men might be asked how it felt to witness the abuse taking place. The majority of them find it uncomfortable and it makes them angry. If one probes a little further to examine that discomfort, they are angry not with the character, but with the bits of the character they recognise in themselves. This dissonance, created by the performance, is one of the key components in promoting the possibility of change.

Integral to the structure of all our performance work has been the development of highly accessible visual metaphors. The search for appropriate metaphors has been at the heart of the company's work from the outset, driven by a belief that visual images which reflect some part of the audience's experience can be strong 'hooks' in the process of change. For Geese, metaphor provides a tool, a language which can be interpreted, analysed and explored in follow-up groupwork processes. The whole set for *Gutted* serves as a metaphor – a large wall within which the central protagonist locks away uncomfortable or difficult feelings; the character of the 'Fool' from *Lifting the Weight* and *Plague Game*, a larger than life master of ceremonies who continually throws problems at the protagonist and who physically embodies the things in life which are beyond our control; the 'Consmith' from *Gutted*, who symbolises, amongst other things, the part of the offender that does not want to change, that wants to maintain an offending lifestyle; the child's drawing of a female figure which is periodically ripped up in *Stay* which might represent the gradual destruction of the female partner; and the oversized blanket which is carried into every scene by Ellie, the central character in *Journey Woman*,[9] and which represents her maladaptive coping strategies, and which she uses to hide away from the possibility of making changes in her life. These metaphors have several commonalities: they are highly visual; they are open to interpretation; they are theatrically powerful and therefore memorable; and they provide a common language to talk about personal experiences.

In the groupwork process which is delivered in conjunction with our performances, the power of these metaphors comes alive. The images and metaphors resonate with the audience – they provide meaning for some of the experiences which they have not fully been able to articulate. In a discussion after a performance of *Gutted* the men may be asked to consider the character of the 'Consmith' and each will place a different interpretation on the role. Many men describe the 'Consmith' as the destructive, negative voice that we all carry with us; others see him as a negative father figure, an anti-role model. The majority of the men make very strong personal connections with the character – for many the 'Consmith' is an external, visual representation of an internal process. By concretising this internal process we are able to invite the men to challenge the Consmith, to unpick what holds him in place and gives him power, and to rehearse the counter-arguments which might work against him. The metaphor provides a vehicle and a language for that exploration.

One of Geese's most recognisable metaphors is that of the mask and the concept of mask lifting. In performances such as *Lifting the Weight, Plague Game, Gutted* and *Inside/Outside* actors wear character half-masks. These half-masks represent the 'front' that people show to the outside world. With the mask down the character is demonstrating their external, presenting behaviour. However, audiences are encouraged to ask the characters to 'lift their masks' throughout the performance. When requested to do so, an actor will literally lift the mask from their face and the character will reveal something to the audience, and to the other characters, that they have kept hidden, thoughts and feelings which are not publicly shared. The mask is not necessarily about lying; when we lift the mask we are inviting the character to verbalise their 'inner voice', often revealing attitudes and beliefs which might motivate the behaviours we are witnessing, or allowing the character to reveal vulnerabilities, insecurities and fears which might otherwise remain hidden. Audience members, especially inmates, quickly comprehend the metaphor. They acknowledge that survival in a prison environment often involves the use of masks or fronts but also that the masks which are used to justify offending can be very destructive.

Of course, the company acknowledges that everyone wears masks throughout their life, and probably different masks for different situations, and also that some masks might actually be useful and constructive. It is the destructive masks which we concentrate on when working with offender groups; the masks that they accept cause damage to themselves and others; the masks which support and justify their offending; the masks which hold them in role as offender. The mask and the concept of mask lifting allows the audience direct access to a character's internal world and becomes a powerful groupwork tool for challenging distortions and exploring the underlying thoughts, feelings and behaviours which contribute to a presenting behaviour.

Geese utilises other masks in its repertoire of performances and groupwork projects. Half masks such as the Fragment Masks which represent key behaviours or coping strategies[10]; helmet masks such as Death Bird[11] which represents the impulse to offend; and Buzz, Suck, Wheedler and Crash, four masks used as representations of different elements of addiction in *Hooked on Empty*. Again, these are highly visual, powerful theatrical images which make concrete attitudes, behaviours or feelings which otherwise might be hard to explore. By inviting participants to recognise the masks they use we are also inviting them to become aware of how they might be perceived by others, aware of the internal processes which feed into their more destructive behaviours, and aware of the situations which might provoke their appearance. It is through this awareness and recognition that the men and women we work with are able to consider the efficacy of their choices, and can start to generate alternative strategies and rehearse new skills and roles.

Bibliography

Baim, C., Brookes, S. and Mountford, A. (eds) (2002) *The Geese Theatre Handbook*, Winchester: Waterside Press.

Boal, A. (1996) *Games for Actors and Non-Actors*, London: Routledge.

Liebmann, M. (ed.) (1996) *Art Approaches to Conflict*, London: Jessica Kingsley Publishers.

Thompson, J. (ed.) (1998) *Prison Theatre Perspectives and Practices*, London: Jessica Kingsley Publishers.

Notes

1   For further reading on Geese Theatre Company see the Bibliography at the end of this chapter.

2   A structured improvisation exploring the difficulties faced by prisoners post-release. *Lifting the Weight* was originally created by John Bergman for Geese Theatre (USA).

3   A semi-improvised play about domestic abuse. Co-created by Geese Theatre (UK) with John Bergman, Geese Theatre (USA).

4   An exploration of the experiences of men who commit a range of sexual offences, primarily created for sex offender treatment settings. Co-devised by Geese Theatre (UK) under the direction of James Neale-Kennerly.

5   Co-devised by Geese Theatre (UK) under the direction of Tony McBride.

6   An improvisational play about prisoners and their families. Originally created and directed by John Bergman for Geese Theatre (USA).

7   A play about drug and alcohol addiction. Co-devised by Geese Theatre (UK) under the direction of John Bergman, Geese Theatre (USA).

8   A play exploring the hopes, fears and anxieties for lifer prisoners contemplating release and their families. Co-devised by Geese Theatre Company (UK) under the direction of Andy Watson.

9   A full-mask performance for women offenders. Co-devised by Geese Theatre Company and directed by Andy Watson.

10   For more information on Geese Theatre Company's Fragment Masks, see Baim, Brookes and Mountford (2002: 184 and 185).

11   For more information on Death Bird see Thompson (1998: p 114).

Chapter 8

Lois Weaver

DOING TIME

A personal and practical account of making performance work in prisons

The minute you walked in the joint,
I could see you were a [girl] of distinction,
A real big spender,
Good looking, so refined.
Say, wouldn't you like to know
What's going on in my mind?
> Lyrics from *Hey Big Spender* by
> Cy Coleman and Dorothy Fields

THESE WERE THE LYRICS CHOSEN BY a notorious pickpocket who loved the film *Sweet Charity* and had always wanted to be Shirley MacLaine. She first came to the workshop, not to participate, but to challenge anything or anyone who might come in from the outside to challenge her. Finally, after a few days of watching and taunting, she stepped into the circle and said, 'Lady, we don't do drama here, we do time . . . and I've decided to *sp-e-end a little time* with you.'

The minute I walked in the joint, I could tell this was going to be an experience distinct from any other. Approaching the gate was like approaching the border control of a foreign and forbidden country. I knew that on the other side of this arbitrary line everything would be different: the language, the customs, the currency. And I knew it was not a difference of nations but of jurisdiction. I stood there with my passport in hand and my innocence somehow in question knowing that while many of its citizens were hoping, if not struggling, to get out, there was a real possibility that I would not be allowed in. Any challenge of authority, even the slightest unconscious gesture or uninvited joke, could send me home with all my bags, cameras and anticipation in tow. Even after I gained entrance to this strange land, I felt as if I was always approaching the gate. Every door had a key, every action had a protocol. Each individual had her own language, each encounter required an exchange of currency and each hour of a workshop, no matter how carefully planned, could be turned inside out if not turned away. It was true. We weren't doing drama we were doing time. Everything was based on what we had right there, in that moment, in that room. Nothing was guaranteed, only the possibility of time.

From 2002 to 2003, Peggy Shaw and I designed and ran workshops in four women's prisons in Brazil and the UK as part of a People's Palace Project entitled STAGING HUMAN RIGHTS. Prior to this project, People's Palace Projects worked primarily in partnership with Augusto Boal and the Center for the Theatre of the Oppressed, implementing Forum Theatre techniques and analysing their effectiveness in addressing issues of human rights. STAGING HUMAN RIGHTS was a project set up to research alternative methodologies. Peggy and I based the workshops on our own process of making performance with the hope that these methods could be used not only as a means of personal and social transformation but might also be effective in getting women in prison to talk about human rights. Like Boal-based methodologies, our performance work is rooted in individual experience, based on community concerns and invested in the power of the imagination to bring about change. However it doesn't 'do drama' in the conventional sense. It doesn't set up scenarios or interrogate actions. It works with portraiture, both real and fantasy; with forms of personal communication, like lies and letters and is rooted in the details of daily life, like laundry and teacups. Rather than using a narrative approach to making scenes and solving problems, our performance making relies on the imagistic and associative strategies of contemporary performance.

Doing time in the UK

Approaching the gate of the UK prison was as mundane as it was terrifying. We waited outside gates as high and grey as a typical English morning. We stood next to a truck delivering thin-sliced white bread and just ahead of a few family members awaiting a release. Like most, this prison sits between towns and outside the reach of public transportation as if daring anyone to make the journey. Our passports were checked and our cameras inspected with the warning that under no circum-stances were we to point the cameras in the direction of any doors or locks. Keys could be cut from the information gathered from the picture of a keyhole. I wondered how one image of entry could inspire such complicated narratives of compromise and escape. I then realised it was exactly that respect for the power of the image that had brought us here.

The locking and unlocking of in-between gates punctuated our walk down the municipal green halls. We were attentive and tense, trying to understand the language of this architecture. There was a room full of odd school desks with seats attached to both sides. 'For visiting' the guard told us, 'Red seat for the prisoner, blue seat for the visitor and no touching.' Crossing the courtyard, we asked why the rubbish containers were locked down with such a heavy chain. 'They'll make a ladder out of anything' the guard said.

The workshop space was equipped with computers, interview rooms and tea supplies, a conducive workspace except for the radio coming from the workshop next door where women had opted for a job filling bags with plastic forks and spoons. Fifteen women chose to work with us but we were told that those numbers could change. A lock down could cancel the morning, mid-morning meds could eliminate the concentration and a disagreement at lunch could alter the course of the next day and a half. Once women are incarcerated, any sense of rhythm is lost. Families are broken, children are scattered and identities threatened. It is different for men. There is usually at least one woman, wife, mother or girlfriend, on the outside looking after things, keeping the beat. I decided to work with the lack of rhythm and apply the principles of our process: shift on impulse, make association from disruption; transform quickly with the moods and the meds. We would spend time trying to 'make ladders out of anything' we could keep our hands on.

Beginning any workshop is difficult. So we acknowledged that feeling of standing at the edge of a great unknown by playing a game of ANY QUESTIONS.

> We'll go around the circle and everyone can ask the workshop leaders one question. It can be personal, professional, mundane or profound. Express your curiosity or concerns and we will answer on impulse with responses based on truth, untruths or in-between.

In the process of making personal performance, lying is always an option and creating truth is the goal. In this workshop, accessing the personal and the mundane was essential. We played FILL IN THE BLANKS.

> On a blank sheet of paper, write these sentences as I read them out then fill in the blanks with the first thing that comes into your mind. Last night before I _____; It wasn't the first time I _____; You should have seen me when _____ etc.

This exercise was not looking for specific information, like time or crime, but for associations. We relied on rhythm and pace to keep images flowing and the longer the list of questions, the freer the responses. At the end, I asked them to select a sentence and tell its back-story, reminding them that a story can be a word, a phrase, a paragraph, a fantasy or a lie. After a short session of story telling, we introduced STAR QUALITY.

> Think of someone or something you've always wanted to be or do. Name it. Think about the one quality that best describes that person or thing (sexy, confident, skilful). Now perform an everyday action (walking in the door, taking money out of a pocket) using that quality. Perform it again, this time saying the line 'I am_____' (fill in the blank with your word). The whole group will repeat your line and your action after you. Think of your performance as a public assertion of possibility and the mirrored response as a chorus of affirmation.

The group repetition not only provided a mirror, it gave the women courage. It seemed easier to throw themselves into it when they knew it would be thrown right back, quickly and without judgement. Real mirrors are scarce. Everything in the prison seems focused on what is not there, what is absent and past. We tried to shift the focus to the present and future. We continued to look for mirrors in their words, gestures and desires. We decided to TAKE A PICTURE.

> Strike a pose from your star quality performance. Take a digital or Polaroid picture of that pose. If it is digital, download the photos onto a computer or connect to a TV monitor and

*call the images up on screen one at a time. When your picture comes up, imagine that it
is a picture of someone else. Give her a gender, name, place of birth, favourite pastime.
Introduce us. Tell us his or her story – true, false or in-between.*

Seeing the image on a screen gave the women a sense of importance and
authority and telling the story enabled them to reveal things about themselves
without the risk of disclosure. They understood this blending of the real and the
fantasy and understood from their own experience the value and necessity of a
'creative truth'. We wanted to reinforce this sense of play and fantasy. Referencing
established applied theatre terminology of the 'tool box', we developed DRESS UP
BOX.

*Think of the person on the screen as your super star or fantasy persona. Using the wardrobe
of costumes provided, DRESS UP like this persona. Introduce yourself to the group.*

FANTASY MANIFESTOS

*While in costume, think about how the persona performs in their daily life – an act of
bravery, song, dance, soap opera scene, a private ritual, speech to parliament, skilful
manoeuvre. Decide on a series of gestures from this that you can repeat. Stay in costume
but return to your real self and finish the sentence, I BELIEVE _____. Develop this
into a three-sentence monologue. Now introduce yourself as your fantasy persona and perform
the gestures with the monologue. Create video portraits of these manifestos.*

FANTASY PERFORMANCES

*Answer this question: What kind of performance would I do if money, time, gender, race,
circumstance or ability was not an issue? Make notes about this fantasy on a piece of paper.
Add notes on all the material created in the exercises so far. Help each other imagine how
to create a 3–5 minute presentation using any and all of this material. The only requirement
is to include one thing you believe in or believe to be true. It can be glaringly obvious or
hidden like a message in a bottle. Perform for each other.*

Our notorious pickpocket sang *Hey Big Spender*, pausing occasionally to talk about
the importance of giving young people individual support in order to ensure our
collective future. A middle-aged Afro-Caribbean woman took on the role of Prime
Minister and initiated a debate on how and why incarcerating women is a waste of
public money. A first-time offender invented the character, Betty No Boobs, and
announced her intentions to start a national campaign to help raise money for breast
augmentation surgery. A host of others from rap artists to teletubbies performed
fantasies and talked about personal health, family welfare and governmental failures.
We did not intend to present a formal or public showing of these fantasy performances
but the women decided they wanted to MAKE AN EVENT.

*Choose a format for public performance – TV show, music video, sports event, beauty pageant,
church service. Look for ways to incorporate the fantasy performances into this larger
context. Do not alter the fantasies but construct the event around the existing performances.
Outline the structure of the event and look to see where the performances intersect.*

We ended our time together by creating a breakfast talk show. The magazine format accommodated celebrity driven characters as well as those who wanted to deal with specific and urgent issues. It provided cameo spots for those who wanted to share their problems with the show's 'agony aunt', read the prison news or report on the weather in their section that morning. They dressed up and performed their fantasies and manifestos in front of each other, the prison staff and an imagined TV audience. Betty No Boobs appeared on the show in order to make her appeal. At the end of her rehearsed performance she unexpectedly turned to the audience and said 'Actually I have decided, after doing this work with all of you, that I do not need to have breast implants or anything that extreme done to my body. I can be accepted and beautiful just the way I am.'

Doing time in Brazil

Getting through the gate of the prison in Rio seemed hindered only by the fact that it was Friday afternoon. We exchanged our passports for a red plastic ID that looked like it had passed a thousand Fridays. We pushed through a rusty turnstile and a disinterested bag search into the courtyard of the prison. Our only obstacle was a dog and a litter of nine pups lying on the threshold, fast asleep in spite of the flies buzzing around their eyes. The courtyard served two prisons, one for women, one for men, and consisted of a patch of grass and the remains of a blue tiled fountain the colour of the Brazilian sky. When I looked up I saw a favela climbing like a lush wild vine up the hill just beyond. It had been planted there by families who wanted to be close. Walking into the women's building, I realised I wasn't able to distinguish between inmates and staff. Women walked by covered in paint, followed by a man who introduced himself as the Head of Education. He apologised for not being able to invite us into his office. 'The women decided to redecorate it,' he said. A woman in a sexy red suit invited us into her office for tiny cups of coffee. She was the director of the prison. As she led us upstairs to meet the workshop participants, a truck backed up to the main door and three very strong women pulled heavy pots from the back of the truck and lugged them up the two flights of stairs. 'These are the prison men,' she told us, 'you'll find things quite normal here.'

There were 12–18 women in each 20- by 20-foot cell. They performed daily rituals and watched us watch them as we passed. Inside the cells were rows of concrete cubicles, bunks built in honeycomb shapes that gave the illusion of private space. They were miniature houses squeezed into one room like favelas squeezed onto a hillside. Life here was not hidden. It was on display. Whole families arrived on visiting day with food and news from home. They sat outside, in the halls, in their cells. The rhythm was not broken. It was reinforced.

We worked in the only communal room in the building. Immovable concrete tables and benches occupied two-thirds of the room. There were two toilets and a dripping sink on one side of the 10 by 10 floor space where 22 women came to stand in a circle. There was no door and a hallway surrounded by cells encircled the room. Sounds bounced off the concrete walls. Twice during each session sounds of women coming and going from daily sunbathing would remind our participants of what they had sacrificed to work with us. Guards chatted in the doorway. Doctors arrived unexpectedly to set up a clinic. Suited evangelists overtook the room for prayer and laying on of hands. I wondered how we would ever work here but the women seemed to have a great capacity for chaos. They listened. They waited for translation.

Working in both English and Portuguese was easier than expected. We found a rhythm of talking, then waiting. I explained that we would be using performance to talk about human rights. This touched off a lengthy display of excitement and approval. Unlike the women in the UK, they had an energy and a collective vocabulary for the subject of human rights. However, they had difficulty understanding exactly what we were going to DO? A play? A movie? A soap opera? I told them we were going to spend time together making something. I struggled to make this clear. Suggesting that we all know what it means to make something: a dress, a cake, a mistake, a friend, a mess, I introduced this exercise.

MAKING SOMETHING

Take one piece of paper and a pen. Write two true facts about yourself and one lie. Add to this list, a place you have always wanted to go and a person you have always wanted to be. Think of the information on the paper as raw material or a list of ingredients. Think of an object that you could make from the paper that relates to something on the page. Tear, crumple or fold the paper into the object. Show the object and tell its story using any combination of information from the raw material.

They made boats, hats, typewriters, hearts and eyeglasses, and talked of travel. This provoked questions about the United States and England. What was it like – the food, government, prisons, education system, crime? Why were we here? Was it philanthropy or were we doing it for the money? What life could we offer them once they were out? They talked about desires. Some wanted to be on TV. Another had a friend who couldn't read or write. 'Can she come to the workshop if I sit next to her and help?' she asked. A young Thai woman who spoke neither English nor Portuguese made it clear that she was hungry for the food of her own country. An English woman who was arrested mid holiday would be here for at least two years before possibly being transferred to an English prison. She had no sweater for the Brazilian winter nights. I picked up on this and asked them to PACK A BAG.

Draw your favourite or fantasy suitcase. 'Pack' it with items such as: favourite food, precious object, favourite music, fantasy outfit, map of home or a place you have always wanted to go, a piece of dirty laundry you can't leave behind, a letter never sent. Display the drawings and give a guided tour of your belongings.

Performing this was a delight and a personal politic coloured each detail of their stories and fuelled their desire to tell. They moved quickly through the STAR QUALITY, DRESS UP and FANTASY PERFORMANCE exercises. I had purchased a pair of turquoise shoes from a woman on the street outside the prison. She had crocheted the top and attached it to recycled wooden soles. When I introduced these and marvelled at the creativity, one of the women casually remarked, 'We make to live.' Fantasy and creative necessity were common currency. It was the language of Carnival and of daily life. Capitalizing on this bounty, I moved the focus to forms of communication. I asked them to WRITE A LETTER.

Write a letter from your prison self to your STAR QUALITY persona. Imagine the letter will be found and read in public (newspaper, TV). Reveal a secret, appeal for help, tell a pack of lies. DRESS UP and read the letter as your persona. Make a video of the reading.

There were impassioned letters to judges calling for an end to corruption, appeals to celebrities and to God for better circumstances, to lovers for love and to children for remembrance. The messages prompted stories about secret signs and codes that develop between the women and that communicate across the courtyards. We immediately started DOING THE LAUNDRY.

Draw a life-size version of the piece of dirty laundry in your suitcase. Fill the clothing with messages both written and drawn that will be flown like flags when the laundry is hung out. Make a performance, exhibition and or video portrait of yourself talking about your piece of laundry.

Laundry is one of the most hopeful things in the prison yard. It is a constant rhythm, a dependable display of individuality, a message sent when things can be seen but not heard. For us, it became a canvas, a costume and a political banner and hanging laundry in public became our method of declaring our human rights. When it came time to MAKE AN EVENT, we decided on an exhibition. We made life-sized paper laundry. The women stood holding the drawings like ill-fitting clothes and described in detail their dreams and discontents. They sang, danced and performed these manifestos to a room full of mothers, boyfriends, children, prison staff and officials. This was not a mock TV variety show made and performed in isolation but a public installation for visiting day. They hung out their laundry for all to see and we documented it, then took it down, folded it and agreed to take it with us and hang it out wherever we go.

Getting out

No laws were changed, no sentences lifted. The Universal Declaration of Human Rights was neither invoked nor challenged. We have no statistics, no measurements for levels of imagination or degrees of transformation but some incarcerated women in Brazil and the UK declared their right to spend some time in imagined and improved circumstances, to dress up, to sing, to dance and to air their views and hang their laundry in public.

PART 3

Ethics of representation

Chapter 9

Sheila Preston

INTRODUCTION TO ETHICS
OF REPRESENTATION

THE CONCEPT OF REPRESENTATION, defined here as a powerful system of communication whereby meaning is culturally constructed and received, is of deep relevance for cultural practices of film, theatre, visual arts and social research; and for cultural workers involved in the making, shaping and creating of representations in these spheres. Analysing the politics of representation requires consideration of how and why identities are depicted, and naming the influence of dominant ideologies against social and political landscapes. The need to consider ethics and representation as interrelated discourses is a key imperative for applied theatre practice and informed by the rich debate happening betwixt and between the academic fields of anthropology, film (and documentary), feminism, disability studies, social research and lesbian and gay studies.[1]

The reality that representations depict the real lives of individuals or groups who may be vulnerable and/or marginalised from the dominant hegemony is an ethical as well as political concern. As cultural workers,[2] whether we are researchers writing about individuals, theatre makers constructing narratives and stories, or facilitators enabling people to write or perform their own stories, we have a responsibility towards ensuring that the representations that are made are produced through a climate of sensitivity, dialogue, respect and willingness for reciprocity. Ethical practice however cannot be separated from awareness that representations, however sensitively and carefully handled, will carry their own political significance and resonance in the broader socio-political sphere and will be constantly vulnerable to appropriation and redefinition. A good example can be found in considering representations of disability. There are many narratives of disability that the media employ, but often disability is represented through the idea of individuals either failing or triumphing over adversity and achieving 'against all odds' (Morris 1997). One might identify on a personal level with the nature of struggle, but on a wider, political level, the proliferation of this narrative in mainstream communications (such as movies) succeeds in reinforcing ideologies of normalcy and individualism while failing to consider the role of society in disabling people.

Giroux, writing on the liberatory possibilities of a counter pedagogy that can redefine dominant representations, suggests that we need to provide:

> opportunities to read texts as social and historical constructions, to engage texts in terms of their presences and absences, and to read texts oppositionally. This means teaching [students] to resist certain readings while simultaneously learning how to write their own narratives.
>
> (Giroux, Chapter 36, this volume)

Giroux highlights a need to facilitate dialogue with communities on the representations that are created. Developing a 'knowingness' of the narratives and mythologies that perpetuate media representations (such as the disability example described) might be an important step in developing critical awareness by all (including ourselves) of how these narratives might influence the texts created in an applied theatre intervention, and allow for the possibilities of the creation of counter-representations.

The broad terrain of applied theatre encompasses a range of aesthetic models and values of practice. The poetic choices made (whether intended at the outset, or produced throughout the creative process) will define the applied theatre paradigm and ultimately whether it tends to speak 'for', 'about' or 'with' communities and the issues concerning them. Each of these paradigms may be influenced (intentionally or unintentionally) by differing ethical–political priorities, as well as aesthetic sensibilities which may, or may not be exclusive of each other.

Tension between the artist and issues of voice and authority can be informed by the similar journeys of documentary and anthropology. Ruby (2000), writing on documentary film anthropology, outlines key influences that illustrate 'fundamentally different conceptions of the relationship between the filmmaker and those who are filmed' (2000: 197).[3] First, there was that pioneered by documentary film director Dziga Vertov where the camera represents the world as seen through the eyes of the filmmaker: 'I, a machine, show you the world as only I can see it' (Vertov quoted in Ruby ibid.). Here the 'art' of film is paramount as it is the creative medium for the expressing of the filmmaker's 'sensibility' (ibid.). In contrast, there is the approach pioneered by Robert Flaherty and his experiences filming Inuit communities in which he attempted to 'replicate the view of the world held by the people he filmed' (ibid.). To do this, Flaherty showed a genuine attempt at reciprocity 'by seeking the subjects' response to his vision' (ibid.); this example reveals early attempts to share the ownership and authorship of the medium. Finally Ruby outlines a third approach; that of the cooperatively produced and subject-generated films that 'offer the possibility of perceiving the world from the viewpoint of the people who lead lives that are different from those traditionally in control of the means for imaging the world' (Ruby 2000: 196). Here the means of production are literally handed over to the subjects where film and video becomes a tool for them to speak of their social and political realities. The technological revolution of the past ten years, combined with the literacy of a media-obsessed society, has enabled an abundance of films created by individuals and communities from the margins creating, what bell hooks would call, spaces of 'radical possibility' (Chapter 12, this volume).

These examples from documentary film reveal how the development of the aesthetic has been brought about by challenges to the politics and ethics of representation and illuminates similar tensions that are operating in applied theatre between artist-led practices where the artists (playwright, director, professional actors/dancer, etc.) as 'professionals' employ their artistic vision to develop a poetic that represents the stories of the community which either speaks to that community or to a different audience; theatre forms such as verbatim theatre and theatre of testimony that may attempt a reciprocity and a shared-authorship with their subjects; and community-led, collaborative approaches that believe firmly in handing over the means of production to the subjects.

The role of the professional artist, their vision, and aesthetic competency in the field is important as Winston, speaking of the ethical importance of artistry, and Stuart-Fisher, articulating the need for the expression of trauma which can feel 'incommunicable', (Chapters 14 and 16 respectively, this volume) both testify. In such senses the political power of theatre as a form of advocacy finds its potency in ways that may be therapeutic and political depending on context.

However, any representation created to speak 'for' a community is vulnerable to misrepresentation or simplification. Similarly, in the field of ethnography the intention may well be to represent a culture as well as possible through the eyes of the community being studied. However, as Clifford and Marcus suggest, the previous assumption that there is some *given* determining that *others* are 'unable to speak for themselves' and that the ethnographer has some 'automatic authority' to speak for them (1986: 10) has been challenged. bell hooks, deeply critical of the colonizing impact of attempts to 'liberate' and speak 'for' oppressed communities, writes vividly and uncomfortably, illuminating the power relationship between author and subject: 'No need to hear your voice. Only tell me about your pain. I want to know your story. And then I will tell it back to you in a new way. Tell it back to you in such a way that it has become mine, my own. Re-writing you, I write myself anew. I am still author, authority' (bell hooks, Chapter 12, this volume).

The ethos of community-generated theatre circumvents the inescapable problem of representing or speaking for marginalised communities in the same way as the following (feminist) position articulates: 'Instead of speaking for others, we maintain a respectful silence and work to create the social and political conditions which might enable Others to speak (and be heard) on their own terms' (Wilkinson and Kitzinger, Chapter 13, this volume). Here, the refusal to represent 'other' redefines the priority; effort is made, instead, towards self-advocacy enabling others to represent themselves. It is the personal and political importance of being able to speak critically from a position of marginality that creates radical possibilities (bell hooks, Chapter 12, this volume). In applied theatre and social research this may feel the 'preferred' standpoint although, as discussed, without critical awareness of its ideological and political impact, self representation might be equally vulnerable to appropriation when it appears in the public sphere.

Here, the ethical-political complexity of constructing representations creates a dissonance in applied theatre; the dilemma between safeguarding and protecting people's right to speak *or* not speak in private or public with the urgent need to challenge society and its marginalising hegemonies. To compound this dilemma is to consider that the ideological interests involved in representation act both personally and socio-politically. In each respect, representations of the disenfranchised can so easily become a problematic commodity (see Thompson, Chapter 17, this volume).

Exploring the politics of representation is therefore complex and highlights the need to interrogate the choices that are made in applied theatre texts for, with and by communities in particular social and political contexts. We might ask ourselves the following critical questions:

1   How appropriate is our preferred aesthetic for engaging with the politics of speaking *with, for* or *about* communities?
2   How do we deal with moral and/or political tensions at the heart of the stories and texts that are created?
3   How can we work sensitively, and create a genuine climate of dialogue and reciprocity?
4   How are issues of voice, authority and ownership reconciled in the process of constructing narratives and representations that result?
5   How will representations that have been created impact in diverse, unpredictable and political contexts?

Bibliography

Clifford, J. and Marcuse, E. (1986) *Writing Culture: The Poetics and Politics of Ethnography*, London: University of California Press.

Giroux, H. (1995) *Border Crossings – Cultural Workers and the Politics of Education*, New York: Routledge.

Morris, J. (1997) 'A Feminist Perspective' in A. Pointon and C. Davis (eds), *Framed – interrogating Disability in the Media*, London: Routledge, pp. 21–31.

Ruby, J. (2000) 'Speaking For, Speaking About, Speaking With, or Speaking Alongside', in J. Ruby, *Picturing Culture: Explorations of Film and Anthropology,* London: University of Chicago Press, pp. 195–219.

Wilkinson, S. and Kitzinger, C. (1997) *Representing the Other.* London: Sage Publications.

Notes

1   For further reading on representation and its related discourses see the references in this Bibliography, in this volume and: Hall, S. (1997) *Representation: cultural representations and signifying practices*, Sage. Barthes, R. (1993) *Mythologies*, Vintage. Beauvoir, S. (1997) *The Second Sex*, Vintage. Said, E. (1995) *Orientalism – western conceptions of the orient*, Penguin. bell hooks (1995) *Art on my Mind – visual politics*, The New Press.
2   Giroux's concept of cultural worker is conceptualised in its broadest sense to mean artists, writers and media producers, but also intended to encompass other professions involved in cultural work such as those working in law, medicine, education, theology,

etc. in order to 'rewrite the concept and practice of cultural work by inserting the primacy of the political and the pedagogical' (Giroux 1992: 5).

3   For this section I am indebted to the discussion put forward in Ruby's chapter *Speaking for, speaking about, speaking with, or speaking alongside* (in Ruby 2000), and recognise that this is merely a simple introduction to a complex field of study.

Chapter 10

Edward Bond

COMMENTARY ON THE WAR PLAYS

The War Plays, 'Commentary on the War Plays', Methuen Drama (1985, 1991), excerpt from pp. 247–61.

Introduction

Edward Bond's *The War Plays* are not documentaries on the politics of war, but stories about ordinary, everyday lives in a future world of almost constant conflict. Above all, they give insights into the extremes of human behaviour when the need to be human conflicts with the demands of living in ordered but unjust society. In the commentary which accompanies the plays, Bond outlines aspects of his philosophy of humanness and culture, including the pivotal notion of *radical innocence*. He says this is the natural disposition all children bring into the world and which marks them as human. Their innocence is not 'goodness', but the need to seek to act in a good way so as to be 'at home' in the world. For example, in drama, Lear's childlike generosity, rage and existential despair may all be understood as radically innocent. The problem is that the child learns to survive in corrupt society by turning its need for justice into the lust for revenge. Bond calls this the great ur-text of all drama, from the Greeks to the present day, and sees it as struggling to assert itself again in the enfeebled theatre of our own time. In the extremes of drama the characters – and the audience – are confronted with the return of their own imperative but forgotten radical innocence. Bond says this sudden reassertion is the enactment of humanness itself, and is the original function of Tragedy and Comedy. Bond calls it the *Palermo Paradox* because it was first articulated in an exercise he devised with drama students at Palermo University.

In the field of Applied Theatre these concepts may shed potent light not only on the behaviour of the dispossessed and the deeply wrought victims of war and famine, but also on the complacency and violence of the powerful and affluent. It is a radical new way of categorising human motives and interpreting actions and character that has implications for playwriting, acting and directing. Bond says it restores meaning to the stage and rescues it from the superficiality of mere 'theatre'. He believes the *Palermo Paradox* is the foundation of modern drama.

Palermo improvisation

I DEVISED A SCHEME FOR improvisation by students at Palermo University. A soldier returns home with orders to choose a baby from his street and kill it. Two babies live in his street: his mother's and a neighbour's. His mother welcomes him and shows him her baby. He goes to the neighbour and she shows him her baby. He kills it and goes home. What would this show? Airmen killed children in Vietnam and were demobbed and went home to their children; soldiers train with nuclear weapons and go home on leave to their children; technicians make nuclear weapons and at the end of each shift go home to their children; and civilians give their children a home and their soldiers threaten other children with nuclear death. When the soldier in the improvisation returned to his mother and her baby we would see one of the contradictions in which we live. But as I planned the improvisation I realised how it would end. I noted the end in my notebook.

Next day the students improvised. I asked them to act honestly what the soldier would do. The soldier came home and was welcomed by his mother. She showed him her baby. He went next door. His neighbour welcomed him and gave him her baby to hold. The action became very slow. The soldier seemed to be staring into a watch as if he tried to tell the time from its workings. He gave the baby back to the neighbour. Then he went home and killed his mother's baby. In my notebook I had written that is what he would do. He and the other students were surprised that he had done it. They were surprised when the next student to play the soldier also murdered the 'wrong' baby. All the students played the soldier and none of them could bring himself to kill the 'right' baby. It was a paradox.

Was the paradox true only on stage? In a Nazi prisoner-of-war camp in Russia in 1942 prisoners were paraded every night for roll call. After all of them had responded to their number a few were killed in front of the others. They were not killed because they had committed what we would recognize as an offence, but to frighten the others into obedience. The commandant and his guards were not sadists – killing made life easier for everyone, it was an aid to discipline.

Some of the guards were Russian. Every few days new prisoners were brought in. One day it happened that one new prisoner was the brother of one of the guards. Two Russians: a Nazi and a communist. Being a good administrator the commandant abhorred all waste and made the best use of every murder. That night after roll call he told the prisoners they would see a demonstration of Nazi discipline. The communist brother was brought forward and the commandant ordered the Nazi brother to shoot him. He pointed his pistol at his brother's head. The commandant shouted 'Fire!'. The guard lowered his pistol. He asked the commandant to let someone else shoot his brother.

The commandant probably relished the moment and approved of the request. Didn't it show the great resistance Nazis overcame to do their duty? Again he ordered the guard to fire. This time the guard did not even raise his pistol. The commandant would not have relished that. It was military insubordination in front of his prisoners. It is said to be easier to kill someone at a distance than when you are face to face with them. But the Nazi guard had often placed his gun as close to his victim's head as we place pen to paper or knife to bread. In those days Nazis killed as other people pick their teeth – to remove a nuisance. The commandant told the guard that his refusal would not save his brother. He – the commandant – would shoot the prisoner and then the guard. He ordered the guard to shoot. He would not. A paradox! The commandant shot the guard and his brother. Surely this is one of the world's great stories?

I do not know what was in the commandant's mind as he walked from the square and the bodies – as the commandant had been upset, there would have been seven or eight at the end – were dragged to the ovens. For years he had been taught that Slavs were vermin and wasn't this one more proof? But I am sure – and this is as true of the commandant as it is of the guard – that no one willingly gives up the name of human. It takes a great deal of culture to make us human, it takes even more culture to make us beasts.

Does the paradox occur only in crises, or is it present in much or even all of what we do – creating an ambiguous struggle which determines who we are? If, as I think, that is so, then we are constantly struggling to express our humanity in ways which society, because it is still inhuman, first discourages, then forbids and then corrupts – and finally rewards, calling the corruption 'duty'. This would explain much of human suffering. It would mean that we can only be human in conflict with society – yet society demands the right to define what is 'good'. Good – after love – is the most ambiguous of words.

But the problem is even stranger. Human nature is not 'natural' but is created by society. I do not mean that society imposes a social form on an instinctual, animal nature. Except when it regulates purely physiological functions – such as stabilizing the body's temperature – the human brain works holistically. The higher, learnt cortical synapses are involved in the lower brain's functioning. It is because of this that we can be human. Whenever we act we must do so for human reasons and from human motives. Our unconscious is not more animal than our conscious, it is often even more human. The unconscious sees through us and our social corruption and sends us messages of our humanity, ingeniously and persistently trying to reconcile the divisive tensions in our lives. Our unconscious makes us sane; it is only in an insane society that our unconscious colludes in insanity.

[...]

Radical innocence

In the Palermo improvisation the soldier killed his brother or sister. In the camp the soldier refused to kill his brother. Both decisions came from the same paradox. The paradox is never absent from our mind. It is the crux on which humanness is poised, an expression of the radical innocence which makes us human. We are born radically innocent, and neither animal nor human; we create our humanness as our minds begin to think our instincts. As we grow our radical innocence becomes embroiled in the social contradictions which turn our cities into armed camps in peace and ruins in war.

Dostoevsky and Blake understood that evil is a form of innocence; and even the church accepted that this is so when it taught that the devil is a fallen angel. Radical innocence is the state in which infants discover and interpret the world. The discoveries and interpretations structure the mind's early learning. The mind cannot lose this structure any more than the unlesioned brain can return to a state without language. Radical innocence is the psyche's conviction of its right to live, and of its conviction that it is not responsible for the suffering it finds in the world or that such things can be. To believe that it was would be to believe that it had no right to exist. The mind that believed that could not functionally integrate itself or even intellectually discriminate – it would lose its symbolic ability and be dead. There is no other way we can lose our innocence, even when it turns into our curse. It is the innocence of evil that makes it so terrible.

Children think of the future as adults think of the past. For children the future is the place from which come determined events – events they often rage against. The child cannot escape from the future or its parents'– all authority's – secret knowledge of the future. It does not know the law yet is judged by it. It sees its offences as if they were forced on it, just as we are forced to accept the events of history. We accuse children of committing the crimes of the dead – back to the earliest generations. When they are accused of doing wrong they feel as we would if we were accused of burning Joan of Arc or causing the Black Death. That is why children cannot abandon their sense of innocence – or their knowledge of it. Because we bring consciousness, reason and morality into the world, we must see it as unjust and absurd. It is our primal shock.

In its innocence the child judges its judges as guilty – it is a judgement not only against people but against the fact of the world. If a child is to be persuaded that it is responsible for its own wrongs it must be persuaded of the rightness of social teaching. Before radical innocence can submit to authority the child must adopt its judges' judgements. But it cannot simply replace radical innocence with radical guilt; that would mean it had no right to be born, and a mind that attacked itself so radically would destroy itself. So innocence protects itself by becoming corrupt. It accepts that authority's right to be is like the right of pain and evil to be – greater than its own right to be. And as the child passes from being the subject of parental control to being the political subject of the state, radical innocence adopts the political injustice of class society. Education prepares it to be corrupted in this way. We inculcate morality as part of the child's social learning; but the morality is a social teaching based on society's structure, with its practical necessities but also its unjust social distortions. In this way we are corrupted by being made good, consenting, dutiful, law-abiding citizens. The individual gives to his corruption all the force of his innocence. The great social injustices, the class divisions, economic exploitation, wars of conquest and greed, the charade of law-and-order, the prisons and punishments – all these barbarities are sanctioned in the name of the highest good and carried out in the conviction of innocence. We ruin the world by our honest efforts to make it better.

[. . .]

The paradox creates social tensions which society uses to strengthen its distorted social relations. Society, which creates us, deforms us. That is why often, to be good citizens, it requires us to live lives of violence and colossal indifference. This is achieved, and innocence turned to righteousness and reaction, by the creation of guilt. The mind panics and flees to the protection of its accusers. Guilt enables society to manipulate people without coercing them with open force. Indeed guilt is society's way of making people agents of its force. The innocence in guilt makes social power, for the guilty, effective and distorting; and by turning the guilty into agents of social force, innocence is the cause of social violence. Righteousness is guilt wearing a uniform. Society cannot deal justly with its problems because it is founded on misinterpreting them.

[. . .]

Radical innocence is not a natural state, an aspect of human nature existing outside history and society. The need for moral discrimination precedes any particular moral code. A child's 'why' questions cannot be answered by scientific cause-and-effect answers. Like a judge, the child seeks motives, and it judges the world. As it subjectively develops a living relationship with its home, society and state it cannot resolve all the tensions in the relationship. The unresolved tensions may be corrupted if the unjust state subordinates them to its needs. The will has only to accept that its radical right to be is represented and expressed by the state. The proposition is plausible. Even unjust states pass good laws and perform good deeds – society's mere practical existence depends on it. Even corrupt radical innocence must act from good motives. If the morally corrupt were not motivated by innocence they could not commit their crimes and brutalities. That is why human conflicts are so intransigent and destructive. Himmler said 'We gas the Jews out of love'. That is terrible, but it is true. It is the most important remark of the twentieth century – it is its sermon on the mount. If we do not understand it we are left with cynicism, apathy, or the illusions of religion – and what is theology but frozen despair? If it could have been possible for any Nazi leader to tell his killers that they were corrupt and that what they did was wrong, then it would have been ontologically impossible for the Third Reich to have come into the world. Instead, the corrupt go to great lengths to do good. Even lonely psychopaths – who have no flashy uniforms or nuclear bombs to encourage their self-esteem – justify their crimes by claiming to be moral agents ('a higher power possessed me') or innocent ('a lower power possessed me') and prove it to their satisfaction – and their judges' bewilderment – by acts of innocent kindness.

When radical innocence is not corrupt it is a force of reason. History is the slow removal of social injustices and distortions and the slow creation of democracy, not only formally but in freedom of the mind. Uncorrupted radical innocence learns from society just as corrupted radical innocence does. Corruption, not innocence, nurtures the child in grown people; if anything of the child survives in adult innocence it is a very old child. Nor do we retain radical innocence by being in the right social class at the right historical time – as if, for example, the industrial revolution made a place in the working-class into a holy niche. If democratization is to continue, the working-class – the lower class of consumers – must have not merely formal democratic rights, freedom from physical coercion and freedom to choose possessions and goods – it must gain freedom of mind, which is freedom of self and freedom to choose the future.

[. . .]

Paradoxical actions alone cannot change society but they are part of the forces of change. They show people making history rational and the community moral. Even when the actions are as 'meaningless' as the guard's refusal to murder his brother, they show the irrepressible insubordination that forces reaction to become what it is. Radical innocence must retain its autonomy and self-justification in order to persuade itself of the rightness of the social teaching it adopts; if it did not, the teaching would have no force. Ironically, tyrants govern by consent: a thing is not good because God does it but God does it because it is good – and that, for the faithful, is as true of the leader as it is of God. The leader knows best. This ensnares even people of good will. It is not only why the gaoler handed Socrates the hemlock, it is why Socrates took it: the form of the state was good. It is why the Nazis murdered and why we make bombs. Our humanity is not given by the state's answers, but by our questions.

We are sent to the theatre

In the early world of jungles and deserts, and in the classical world of fifth-century Athens, the whole community went to the drama. If slaves, convicts, the mad and women were sometimes excluded that is because they were not fully members of society. Society sent people to the drama just as it sent them to the fields, the hunt and the well. It seems that now we are not sent to the theatre but choose to go. This is an illusion. We are still sent there by society. It must send us to the theatre even when it can only send representatives. It needs theatre as much as it needs its other institutions – its prisons, universities, parliaments and so on. But just as democratic society wrongly assumes that everyone in it, and not merely the ruling class, has power, so it wrongly assumes that when society sends representatives to the theatre it is sending the community there. Unjust society not only manipulates force by disguising violence as law and order, it also manipulates the rest of culture. Just as it usually sends the wrong people to prison and parliament, so it usually sends the wrong people to theatre. The others it sends to the petrified drama of most film and television – and their frenetic activity is a sign of their moribund state: giving electric shock treatment to a skeleton does not bring it to life.

When theatre is commercially exploited it corrupts society because the product it exploits – it is the only one it has – is the human image. To exploit that causes more apathy and pain, and in the end more destruction, than chaining and exploiting human bodies. It is the same with modern religion. Religion is a form of drama, an off-shoot of the human psyche – but it cannot develop because it cannot forget its gods when its machines no longer need them. When a society which creates a religion is technologically superceded, what was progressive becomes regressive. The modern church's excited agitation is really the empty obverse of its weariness.

It trivializes morality and by this brutalizes its believers, and so becomes the servant of commercial secularism and waste. The church is now a force for social profanity.

Society needs drama (even in debased commercial forms) because in it it seeks the human image. It must do this even when theatre degrades the human image. Great national institutions – national theatres, national galleries and so on – promote culture but also control and repress it. They make the whole of society a ghetto. Theatre is comparatively free of technology. A few people in a room can make a play. This is a strength because often it frees it from political control, in both its police and commercial forms. But it is also a weakness. Our times are too fast and chaotic for the stages in attics and cellars, on their own, to be able to study and recreate the human image. We also need to show how the whole of modern technology belongs to our creative psyche. But there is a conflict between financial resources and creative forces. In unjust society creative forces can no longer come from the state, because it no longer represents a progressive class that flourishes on human reason: it represents only an exploiting class and its ability to exploit. Now the creative forces of art come from the street. There is no more folk art, it has become the kitsch of commercialism. But street art is creative. We should not romanticize the street – as much garbage and cruelty are found there as in the cultural institutions. But street skills and disciplines are as astringent and liberating as those of academies. And more important, it is in the street – though we may wish it did not have to be so – that radical innocence is most potent. Authority in unjust society must lie, the street may lie but need not. Academies and national theatres cannot develop the skills of art because they no longer need art. The street needs art.

We think art has its source in truth, but its source is in lies. A child asks what, why, how – the questions of the great philosophers. It asks these questions because its brain is over-capacious and holistic. A child asks the profoundest philosophical questions, but it asks them about its room because that is its world. And as it grows it seeks a reason even for the stars. In that they have meaning, the questions – how, what and why – are truthful, but the answers are confusions and lies. The child gives the first answers itself. They are imagistic – the images 'see' its feelings. This early language expresses more than it describes, but it is intellectual and discriminates and analyses; even the first images are symbolic because they point to the nothingness that surrounds them. Lear tells his child 'nothing will come of nothing', but everything comes of nothing. This is the infant's first encounter with truth, and from it comes the dependence on art. Later it will be taught answers – but these will be lies or full of error. Primitive societies mix error and truth in order to exist; they dig wells but worship the rain God. Authority uses phenomena still beyond its understanding to coerce and stimulate society – it surrounds it in mystery. The sacred is a way of keeping the world in thrall. The priests' function is to be so possessed by illusions that they become real – that is, people act on them – and when this is not possible, to lie. Dostoevsky's inquisitors lie to everyone except God, whom they offend with the truth.

A society that uses a hydraulics technology may still demand belief in the rain God and found its institutions on his existence. The society that does this is constantly torn apart. To preserve the 'great social truth' – what society believes in order to maintain its structure – the 'truths of society' – the knowledge it needs to exist in the world – are constantly denied. So the 'great social truth' is a lie.

Chapter 11

Chantal Mouffe

ON THE POLITICAL

On the Political, Routledge (2006), pp. 29–34.

Agonistic confrontation

MANY LIBERAL THEORISTS REFUSE to acknowledge the antagonistic dimension of politics and the role of affects in the construction of political identities because they believe that it would endanger the realization of consensus, which they see as the aim of democracy. What they do not realize is that, far from jeopardizing democracy, agonistic confrontation is the *very* condition of its existence. Modern democracy's specificity lies in the recognition and legitimation of conflict and the refusal to suppress it by imposing an authoritarian order. Breaking with the symbolic representation of society as an organic body — characteristic of the holist mode of organization — a pluralist liberal democratic society does not deny the existence of conflicts but provides the institutions allowing them to be expressed in an adversarial form. It is for this reason that we should be very wary of the current tendency to celebrate a politics of consensus, claiming that it has replaced the supposedly old-fashioned adversarial politics of right and left. A well functioning democracy calls for a clash of legitimate democratic political positions. This is what the confrontation between left and right needs to be about. Such a confrontation should provide collective forms of identification strong enough to mobilize political passions. If this adversarial configuration is missing, passions cannot be given a democratic outlet and the agonistic dynamics of pluralism are hindered. The danger arises that the democratic confrontation will therefore be replaced by a confrontation between essentialist forms of identification or non-negotiable moral values. When political frontiers become blurred, disaffection with political parties sets in and one witnesses the growth of other types of collective identities, around nationalist, religious or ethnic forms of identification. Antagonisms can take many forms and it is illusory to believe that they could ever be eradicated. This is why it is important to allow them an agonistic form of expression through the pluralist democratic system.

Liberal theorists are unable to acknowledge not only the primary reality of strife in social life and the impossibility of finding rational, impartial solutions to political issues but also the integrative role that conflict plays in modern democracy. A democratic society requires a debate about possible alternatives and it must provide political forms of collective identification around clearly differentiated democratic positions. Consensus is no doubt necessary, but it must be accompanied by dissent. Consensus is needed on the institutions constitutive of democracy and on the 'ethico-political' values informing the political association – liberty and equality for all – but there will always be disagreement concerning their meaning and the way they should be implemented. In a pluralist democracy such disagreements are not only legitimate but also necessary. They provide the stuff of democratic politics.

Besides the shortcomings of the liberal approach, the main obstacle to the implementation of an agonistic politics comes from the fact that, since the collapse of the Soviet model, we are witnessing the unchallenged hegemony of neo-liberalism with its claim that there is no alternative to the existing order. This claim has been accepted by social democratic parties which, under the pretence of 'modernizing', have been steadily moving to the right, redefining themselves as 'centre-left'. Far from profiting from the crisis of its old communist antagonist, social democracy has been dragged into its collapse. In this way a great opportunity has been lost for democratic politics. The events of 1989 should have provided the time for a redefinition of the left, now liberated of the weight previously represented by· the communist system. There was a real chance for a deepening of the democratic project because traditional political frontiers, having been shattered, could have been redrawn in a more progressive way. Unfortunately this chance has been missed. Instead we heard triumphalist claims about the disappearance of antagonism and the advent of a politics without frontiers, without a 'they'; a win–win politics in which solutions could be found favouring everybody in society.

While it was no doubt important for the left to come to terms with the importance of pluralism and liberal democratic political institutions, this should not have meant abandoning all attempts to transform the present hegemonic order and accepting the view that 'really existing liberal democratic societies' represent the end of history. If there is a lesson to be drawn from the failure of communism it is that the democratic struggle should not be envisaged in terms of friend/enemy and that liberal democracy is not the enemy to be destroyed. If we take 'liberty and equality for all' as the 'ethico-political' principles of liberal democracy (what Montesquieu defined as 'the passions that move a regime'), it is clear that the problem with our societies is not their proclaimed ideals but the fact that those ideals are not put into practice. So the task for the left is not to reject them, with the argument that they are a sham, a cover for capitalist domination, but to fight for their effective implementation. And this of course cannot be done without challenging the current neo-liberal mode of capitalist regulation.

This is why such a struggle, if it should not be envisaged in terms of friend/enemy, cannot be simply envisaged as a mere competition of interests or on the 'dialogic' mode. Now, this is precisely how most left-wing parties visualize demo-cratic politics nowadays. To revitalize democracy, it is urgent to get out of this impasse. My claim is that, thanks to the idea of the 'adversary', the agonistic approach that I am proposing could contribute to a revitalization and deepening of democracy. It also offers the possibility of envisaging the left's perspective in an hegemonic way. Adversaries inscribe their confrontation within the democratic framework, but this framework is not seen as something immutable: it is susceptible of being redefined through hegemonic struggle. An agonistic conception of democracy acknowledges the contingent character of the hegemonic politico-economic articulations which determine the specific configuration of a society at a given moment. They are precarious and pragmatic constructions which can be disarticulated and transformed as a result of the agonistic struggle among the adversaries.

Slavoj Žižek is therefore mistaken to assert that the agonistic approach is unable to challenge the status quo and ends up accepting liberal democracy in its present stage. What an agonistic approach certainly disavows is the possibility of an act of radical refoundation that would institute a new social order from scratch. But a number of very important socioeconomic and political transformations, with radical implications, are possible within the context of liberal democratic institutions. What we understand by 'liberal democracy' is constituted by sedimented forms of power relations resulting from an ensemble of contingent hegemonic interventions. The fact that their contingent character is not recognized today is due to the absence of counter-hegemonic projects. But we should not fall again into the trap of believing that their transformation requires a total rejection of the liberal-democratic framework. There are many ways in which the democratic 'language-game' – to borrow a term from Wittgenstein – can be played, and the agonistic struggle should bring about new meanings and fields of application for the idea of democracy to be radicalized. This is, in my view, the effective way to challenge power relations, not on the mode of an abstract negation but in a properly hegemonic way, through a process of disarticulation of existing practices and creation of new discourses and institutions. Contrary to the various liberal models, the agonistic approach that I am advocating acknowledges that society is always politically instituted and never forgets that the terrain in which hegemonic interventions take place is always the outcome of previous hegemonic practices and is never a neutral one. This is why it denies the possibility of a non-adversarial democratic politics and criticizes those who, by ignoring the dimension of 'the political', reduce politics to a set of supposedly technical moves and neutral procedures.

bell hooks

CHOOSING THE MARGIN AS A SPACE OF RADICAL OPENNESS

Yearning, "Choosing the Margin as Space of Radical Openness", Between the Lines Press (1990), essay from pp. 145–53.

A S A RADICAL STANDPOINT, perspective, position, "the politics of location" necessarily calls those of us who would participate in the formation of counter-hegemonic cultural practice to identify the spaces where we begin the process of re-vision.

[. . .]

I have been working to change the way I speak and write, to incorporate in the manner of telling a sense of place, of not just who I am in the present but where I am coming from, the multiple voices within me. I have confronted silence, inarticulateness. When I say, then, that these words emerge from suffering, I refer to that personal struggle to name that location from which I come to voice – that space of my theorizing.

Often when the radical voice speaks about domination we are speaking to those who dominate. Their presence changes the nature and direction of our words. Language is also a place of struggle. I was just a girl coming slowly into womanhood when I read Adrienne Rich's words, "This is the oppressor's language, yet I need it to talk to you." This language that enabled me to attend graduate school, to write a dissertation, to speak at job interviews, carries the scent of oppression. Language is also a place of struggle. The Australian aborigines say "that smell of the white man is killing us." I remember the smells of my childhood, hot water corn bread, turnip greens, fried pies. I remember the way we talked to one another, our words thickly accented black Southern speech. Language is also a place of struggle. We are wedded in language, have our being in words. Language is also a place of struggle. Dare I speak to oppressed and oppressor in the same voice? Dare I speak to you in a language that will move beyond the boundaries of domination – a language that will not bind you, fence you in, or hold you? Language is also a place of struggle. The oppressed struggle in language to recover ourselves, to reconcile, to reunite, to renew. Our words are not without meaning, they are an action, a resistance. Language is also a place of struggle.

It is no easy task to find ways to include our multiple voices within the various texts we create – in film, poetry, feminist theory. Those are sounds and images that mainstream consumers find difficult to understand. Sounds and scenes which cannot be appropriated are often that sign everyone questions, wants to erase, to "wipe out." I feel it even now, writing this piece when I gave it talking and reading, talking spontaneously, using familiar academic speech now and then, "talking the talk" – using black vernacular speech, the intimate sounds and gestures I normally save for family and loved ones. Private speech in public discourse, intimate intervention, making another text, a space that enables me to recover all that I am in language, I find so many gaps, absences in this written text. To cite them at least is to let the reader know something has been missed, or remains there hinted at by words – there in the deep structure.

Throughout *Freedom Charter*, a work which traces aspects of the movement against racial apartheid in South Africa, this statement is constantly repeated: *our struggle is also a struggle of memory against forgetting*. In much new, exciting cultural practice, cultural texts – in film, black literature, critical theory – there is an effort to remember that is expressive of the need to create spaces where one is able to redeem and reclaim the past, legacies of pain, suffering, and triumph in ways that transform present reality. Fragments of memory are not simply represented as flat documentary but constructed to give a "new take" on the old, constructed to move us into a different mode of articulation. [. . .]

I have needed to remember, as part of a self-critical process where one pauses to reconsider choices and location, tracing my journey from small town Southern black life, from folk traditions, and church experience to cities, to the university, to neighborhoods that are not racially segregated, to places where I see for the first time independent cinema, where I read critical theory, where I write theory. Along that trajectory, I vividly recall efforts to silence my coming to voice. In my public presentation I was able to tell stories, to share memories. Here again I only hint at them. The opening essay in my book, *Talking Back*, describes my effort to emerge as critical thinker, artist, and writer in a context of repressions. I talk about punishment, about mama and daddy aggressively silencing me, about the censorship of black communities. I had no choice. I had to struggle and resist to emerge from that context and then front other locations with mind intact, with an open heart. I had to leave that space I called home to move beyond boundaries, yet I needed also to return there. We sing a song in the black church tradition that says, "I'm going up the rough side of the mountain on my way home." Indeed the very meaning of "home" changes with experience of decolonization, of radicalization. At times, home is nowhere. At times, one knows only extreme estrangement and alienation. Then home is no longer just one place. It is locations. Home is that place which enables and promotes varied and ever-changing perspectives, a place where one discovers new ways of seeing reality, frontiers of difference. One confronts and accepts dispersal and fragmentation as part of the construction of a new world order that reveals more fully where we are, who we can become, an order that does not demand forgetting. "Our struggle is also a struggle of memory against forgetting."

This experience of space and location is not the same for black folks who have always been privileged, or for black folks who desire only to move from underclass status to points of privilege; not the same for those of us from poor backgrounds who have had to continually engage in actual political struggle both within and outside black communities to assert an aesthetic and critical presence. Black folks coming from poor, underclass communities, who enter universities or privileged cultural settings unwilling to surrender every vestige of who we were before we were there, all "sign" of our class and cultural "difference," who are unwilling to play the role of "exotic Other" must create spaces within that culture of domination if we are to survive whole, our souls intact. Our very presence is a disruption. We are often as much an "Other," a threat to black people from privileged class backgrounds who do not understand or share our perspectives, as we are to uninformed white folks. Everywhere we go there is pressure to silence our voices, to co-opt and undermine them. Mostly, of course, we are not there. We never "arrive" or "can't stay." Back in those spaces where we come from, we kill ourselves in despair, drowning in nihilism, caught in poverty, in addiction, in every postmodern mode of dying that can't be named. Yet when we few retain in that "other" space, we are often, too isolated, too alone. We die there, too. Those of us who live, who "make it," passionately holding on to aspects of that "down-home" life we do not intend to lose while simultaneously seeking new knowledge and experience, invent spaces of radical openness. Without such spaces we would not survive

Our living depends on our ability to conceptualize alternatives, often improvised. Theorizing about this experience aesthetically critically is an agenda for radical cultural practice.

For me this space of radical openness is a margin – a profound edge. Locating oneself there is difficult yet necessary. It is not a "safe" place. One is always at risk. One needs a community of resistance.

In the preface to *Feminist Theory: From Margin to Center*, I expressed these thoughts on marginality:

> To be in the margin is to be part of the whole but outside the main body. As black Americans living in a small Kentucky town, the railroad tracks were a daily reminder of our marginality. Across those tracks were paved streets, stores we could not enter, restaurants we could not eat in, and people we could not look directly in the face. Across those tracks was a world we could work in as maids, as janitors, as prostitutes, as long as it was in a service capacity. We could enter that world but we could not live there. We had always to return to the margin, to cross the tracks to shacks and abandoned houses on the edge of town.
>
> There were laws to ensure our return. Not to return was to risk being punished. Living as we did – on the edge – we developed a particular way of seeing reality. We looked both from the outside in and from the inside out. We focused our attention on the center as well as on the margin. We understood both. This mode of seeing reminded us of the existence of a whole universe, a main body made up of both

margin and center. Our survival depended on an ongoing public awareness of the separation between margin and center and an ongoing private acknowledgement that we were a necessary, vital part of that whole.

This sense of wholeness, impressed upon our consciousness by the structure of our daily lives, provided us with an oppositional world-view – a mode of seeing unknown to most of our oppressors, that sustained us, aided us in our struggle to transcend poverty and despair, strengthened our sense of self and our solidarity.

Though incomplete, these statements identify marginality as much more than a site of deprivation; in fact I was saying just the opposite, that it is also the site of radical possibility, a space of resistance. It was this marginality that I was naming as a central location for the production of a counter-hegemonic discourse that is not just found in words but in habits of being and the way one lives. As such, I was not speaking of a marginality one wishes to lose – to give up or surrender as part of moving into the center – but rather of a site one stays in, clings to even, because it nourishes one's capacity to resist. It offers to one the possibility of radical perspective from which to see and create, to imagine alternatives, new worlds.

This is not a mythic notion of marginality. It comes from lived experience. Yet I want to talk about what it means to struggle to maintain that marginality even as one works, produces, lives, if you will, at the center. I no longer live in that segregated world across the tracks. Central to life in that world was the ongoing awareness of the necessity of opposition. When Bob Marley sings, "We refuse to be what you want us to be, we are what we are, and that's the way it's going to be," that space of refusal, where one can say no to the colonizer, no to the downpressor, is located in the margins. And one can only say no, speak the voice of resistance, because there exists a counter-language. While it may resemble the colonizer's tongue, it has undergone a transformation, it has been irrevocably changed. When I left that concrete space in the margins, I kept alive in my heart ways of knowing reality which affirm continually not only the primacy of resistance but the necessity of a resistance that is sustained by remembrance of the past, which includes recollections of broken tongues giving us ways to speak that decolonize our minds, our very beings. Once mama said to me as I was about to go again to the predominantly white university, "You can take what the white people have to offer, but you do not have to love them." Now understanding her cultural codes, I know that she was not saying to me not to love people of other races. She was speaking about colonization and the reality of what it means to be taught in a culture of domination by those who dominate. She was insisting on my power to be able to separate useful knowledge that I might get from the dominating group from participation in ways of knowing that would lead to estrangement, alienation and, worse, assimilation and co-optation. She was saying that it is not necessary to give yourself over to them to learn. Not having been in those institutions, she knew that I might be faced again and again with situations where I would be "tried," made to feel as though a central requirement of my being accepted would mean participation in this system of exchange to ensure my success, my "making it." She was reminding me of the necessity of opposition and simultaneously encouraging me not to lose that radical perspective shaped and formed by marginality.

Understanding marginality as position and place of resistance is crucial for oppressed, exploited, colonized people. If we only view the margin as sign marking the despair, a deep nihilism penetrates in a destructive way the *very* ground of our being. It is there in that space of collective despair that one's creativity, one's imagination is at risk, there that one's mind is fully colonized, there that the freedom one longs for is lost. Truly the mind that resists colonization struggles for freedom of expression. The struggle may not even begin with the colonizer; it may begin within one's segregated, colonized community and family. So I want to note that I am not trying to romantically re-inscribe the notion of that space of marginality where the oppressed live apart from their oppressors as "pure." I want to say that these margins have been both sites of repression and sites of resistance. And since we are well able to name the nature of that repression we know better the margin as site of deprivation. We are more silent when it comes to speaking of the margin as site of resistance. We are more often silenced when it comes to speaking of the margin as site of resistance.

Silenced. During my graduate years I heard myself speaking often in the voice of resistance. I cannot say that my speech was welcomed. I cannot say that my speech was heard in such a way that it altered relations between colonizer and colonized. Yet what I have noticed is that those scholars, most especially those who name themselves as radical critical thinkers, feminist thinkers, now fully participate in the construction of a discourse about the "Other." I was made "Other" there in that space with them. In that space in the margins, that lived-in segregated world of my past and present. They did not meet me there in that space. They met me at the center. They greeted me as colonizers. I am waiting to learn from them the path of their resistance, of how it came to be that they were able to surrender the power to act as colonizers. I am waiting for them to bear witness, to give testimony. They say that the discourse on marginality, on difference has moved beyond a discussion of "us and them." They do not speak of how this movement has taken place. This is a response from the radical space of my marginality. It is a space of resistance. It is a space I choose.

I am waiting for them to stop talking about the "Other" to stop even describing how important it is to be able speak about difference. It is not just important what we speak about, but how and why we speak. Often this speech about the "Other" is also a mask, an oppressive talk hiding gaps, absences that space where our words would be if we were speaking, if there were silence, if we were there. This "we" is that "us" in the margins, that "we" who inhabit marginal space that is not a site of domination but a place of resistance. Enter that space. Often this speech about the "Other" annihilates, erases: "No need to hear your voice when I can talk about you better that you can speak about yourself. No need to hear your voice. Only tell me about your pain. I want to know your story. And then I will tell it back to you in a new way. Tell it back to you in such a way that it has become mine, my own. Re-writing you, I write myself anew. I am still author, authority. I am still the colonizer, the speaking subject, and you are now at the center of my talk" Stop. We greet you as liberators. This "we" is that "us" in the margins, that "we" who inhabit marginal space that is not a site of domination but a place of resistance. Enter that space. This is an intervention. I am writing to you. I am speaking from a place in the margins where I am different, where I see things differently. I am talking about what I see.

Speaking from margins. Speaking in resistance. I open a book. There are words on the back cover, *Never in the Shadows Again*. A book which suggests the possibility of speaking as liberators. Only who is speaking and who is silent. Only who stands in the shadows – the shadow in a doorway, the space where images of black women are represented voiceless, the space where our words are invoked to serve and support, the space of *our* absence. Only small echoes of protest. We are re-written. We are "Other." We are the margin. Who is speaking and to whom, Where do we locate ourselves and comrades?

Silenced. We fear those who speak about us, who do not speak to us and with us. We know what it is like to be silenced. We know that the forces that silence us, because they never want us to speak, differ from the forces that say speak, tell me your story. Only do not speak in a voice of resistance. Only speak from that space in the margin that is a sign of deprivation, a wound, an unfulfilled longing. Only speak your pain.

This is an intervention. A message from that space in the margin that is a site of creativity and power, that inclusive space where we recover ourselves, where we move in solidarity to erase the category colonized/colonizer. Marginality as site of resistance. Enter that space. Let us meet there. Enter that space. We greet you as liberators.

Spaces can be real and imagined. Spaces can tell stories and unfold histories. Spaces can be interrupted, appropriated, and transformed through artistic and literary practice.

As Pratibha Parma notes, "The appropriation and use of space are political acts."

To speak about that location from which work emerges, I choose familiar politicized language, old codes, words, like "struggle, marginality, resistance." I choose these words knowing that they are no longer popular or "cool" – hold onto them and the political legacies they evoke and affirm, even as I work to change what they say, to give them renewed and different meaning.

I am located in the margin. I make a definite distinction between that marginality which is imposed by oppressive structures and that marginality one chooses as site of resistance – as location of radical openness and possibility. This site of resistance is continually formed in that segregated culture of opposition that is our critical response to domination. We come to this space through suffering and pain, through struggle. We know struggle to be that which pleasures, delights, and fulfils desire. We are transformed, individually, collectively, as we make radical creative space which affirms and sustains our subjectivity, which gives us a new location from which to articulate our sense of the world.

Chapter 13

Sue Wilkinson and Celia Kitzinger

REPRESENTING THE OTHER

Representing the Other, Sage Press (1996).

Negotiating the problems of Othering

THIS CHAPTER EXPLORES various ways in which feminists have attempted to negotiate the problems of Othering: by speaking only for ourselves; by speaking of Otherness only to celebrate it; by attempting to destabilize Otherness; and by interrupting Othering.

Speaking only for ourselves

Contemplating the problems consequent upon representing Others, some feminists suggest that the solution is to refuse to be drawn into representing Others at all. Speaking only for *ourselves*, we leave Others to represent *themselves*. Instead of speaking for Others, we maintain a respectful silence, and work to create the social and political conditions which might enable Others to speak (and to be heard) on their own terms.

The idea that we should speak only for ourselves, and eschew speaking for Others, derives in part from a sense that the Others have been too much spoken for and about already. It comes from the belief that it might be more appropriate to silence the cacophony of dominant voices busily regulating, explaining, justifying, exonerating or celebrating Others in favour of simply pointing to the silence of those Others and thereby helping to create a space for them to speak for themselves. However well intentioned our speech on behalf of an Other, it acts to reinforce precisely that Otherness which speaking may be intended to undermine. The Other is silenced *because* she is Other, and the speech of the dominant group on her behalf reinscribes her Otherness simply through the fact of its being spoken, and irrespective of its content:

> A conversation of 'us' with 'us' about 'them' is a conversation in which 'them' is silenced. 'Them' always stands on the other side of the hill, naked and speechless, barely present in its absence. Subject of discussion, 'them' is only admitted among an 'us', the discussing subjects, when accompanied or introduced by an 'us', member, hence the dependency of 'them'.
>
> (Trinh, 1989: 65)

[. . .]

This position of speaking only for oneself is in direct contradistinction to the conventional practice of the social sciences, within which speaking 'for' or 'about' Others has been the norm. Indeed, the methodological and epistemological assumptions expressed in traditional psychology give the clear impression that the scientific psychologist's 'subject' bears more than a passing resemblance to Edward Said's (1978) 'oriental', who must be represented and spoken for by the 'expert'. The traditional 'objectivity' of the social sciences (especially psychology), in pursuit of which a rigid detachment is maintained between researcher and 'subject', has been replaced, in much contemporary feminist research, by an ethic of involvement. Pointing out that men's representations of their Other (women) have been self-interested and inadequate 'science', much feminist research (especially in psychology) eschews any attempt at objective distance, emphasizing instead the shared experience of researcher and researched. 'We' research 'ourselves'. The contemporary feminist researcher is likely to construct herself as sharing personal experience and/or identity with the people she is researching and to use this as warrant for her 'findings'; she is speaking, 'for herself' and for her 'community'. The titles and subtitles of much feminist writing reflect this preoccupation with 'speaking for ourselves' (e.g. Seifer, 1976; White, 1990).

One problem for feminists who take this position lies in defining who, exactly, 'we' are and what constitutes 'our community'. In much of this work, 'we' are, of course, 'women'. [. . .] The claim that 'there's nobody out there but us women' results in 'a homogenizing of "women's experience" and an obliteration of the full range of oppressions to which we are subject, the diversity of communities from which we draw our strengths' (Kitzinger and Wilkinson, 1993: 8–12). But attempts to define 'us' with more precision inevitably become reductionist: can we (the authors) speak on behalf of all women, or only all white women, all white middle-class women, all white middle-class childless lesbian women, all white middle-class childless lesbian British women? . . . and so on. [. . .]

A second problem with 'speaking only for ourselves' lies in the peculiar composition of the group 'academic feminists', such that to do this would result (indeed, has resulted) in a massive over-representation of the views of white, middle-class, western women. Speaking only from, about, and in relation to our own (untheorized) positions of relative privilege has, in fact, been part of the *problem of* feminism, contributing to its false universalizing and imperializing tendencies to the extent that it is hard to reconceptualize 'speaking only for oneself' as part of the *solution*.

Thirdly, there is the problem of the continued silencing and exclusion of Others in feminist theory and practice. Although it is clear that *speaking on behalf of Others* serves to reinscribe their silence and their Otherness, it is equally the case that feminist insistence on 'speaking only for ourselves' can serve the same function. If 'we' are prevented from representing Others, those Others are equally barred from theorizing 'us' and so excluded from the process of developing feminist theory and method which *interrupts* dominant assumptions. For example, in relation to the hegemony of heterosexuality, speaking only for oneself, while authorizing lesbians to speak *qua* lesbians *on lesbianism*, serves equally to disauthorize lesbian theories of heterosexuality. Lesbian theories of heterosexuality can be challenged as not being based in (current) identity or experience (only heterosexuals can speak of hetero-sexuality); and, conversely, heterosexual feminists are relieved of the burden of theorizing lesbianism (see Kitzinger, 1994, for an extended discussion of these problems). [. . .]

In sum, whatever the intentions, the *effects* of speaking only for ourselves are often the silencing of Others, the erasure of their experience, and the reinscription of power relations.

Celebrating Otherness

Others by definition are oppressed and marginalized by the dominant culture: consequently, their cultures and traditions are typically represented as inferior or pathological. A common representational strategy of some feminists is to seek to refute this dominant representation by documenting and celebrating the survival skills, the inherent strengths, and the positive cultures and traditions of Others. The celebration of woman's Otherness is familiar from the work of some of the French-speaking feminists (e.g. Cixous, 1983/92; Irigaray, 1981), and has been described as characterizing the writings of psychologists committed to revealing women's 'different voice' (Gilligan, 1982) or different 'ways of knowing' (Belenky *et al.*, 1986). [. . .] This is an important corrective to the traditional focus on the weakness and suffering of the Other.

However, one of the problems endemic to 'studying down' (Olson and Shopes, 1991: 198) is 'the temptation to exaggerate the exotic, the heroic, or the tragic aspects of the lives of people with little power'. The danger lies in romanticizing Others and in using our representation of them to delineate 'our' vision of the Good Life. Some early ethnographers saw in 'primitive' cultures the nobility of the 'savage', the healing rituals and harmonies of the 'natural' life, and the pure essence of the precolonial (Van Maanen, 1995). In 'reclaiming' the lives of Others for feminism, we run the risk of representing in their lives what we would like to see in our own. Heterosexual women, for example, when not expressing overtly anti-lesbian views, often represent lesbian lives in extraordinarily romanticized terms: lesbians are supposed to enjoy the 'luxury' of 'doing away with men' (Yuval-Davis, 1993: 52), and it is to lesbians 'that heterosexual feminists look in the hope of finding a model of equality which can eventually be applied to our relationships with men' (Croghan,

1993: 244). Similarly, white western women, when not expressing overtly racist views, often idealize and romanticize the lives and traditions of black women, and/or women from other cultures. [. . .]

Part of the feminist 'celebration' or 'romanticization' of Other women's lives often involves the claim that Other women are always aware of, and actively acting to resist, their oppression (cf. Salazar, 1991). In part, this is a reaction against the notion of 'false consciousness', whereby 'we' saw the truth and Other women were emeshed in patriarchal ideologies from which it was 'our' duty to rescue them. Instead Other women are now often assumed to possess their own (often implicit) critique of gender (and other power) relations. [. . .]

[. . .]

There is no possibility of completely evading the grasp of power: power is deeply implicated in constructing the discourse of the Other. As Linda Alcoff (1994: 200) points out, 'the speech of the oppressed is not necessarily either liberatory or reflective of their true interests.' In choosing to represent Others as always resisting, undermining or subverting the dominant order, feminists, in our anxiety to avoid apparent criticism of Others, fall into the opposite trap of romanticizing them. In sum, celebrating Others, as much as derogating them, may project onto those Others our own political agenda, appropriating them to our own 'cause'.

Destabilizing Otherness

As strategies for dealing with the problems of Othering, 'speaking only for ourselves' and 'celebrating Otherness' share some epistemological assumptions both about the nature of Otherness, and about the meaning of 'representation'. Feminists writing from a range of perspectives, but particularly those influenced by postmodernism, have challenged these assumptions and have attempted to destabilize the entire problem.

First, in both the strategies already discussed, the Other is conceptualized as a member of an oppressed group in relation to which the person doing, or refusing to do, representational work is a dominant group member. We have, however, already alluded to the fact that there are many dimensions of power and powerlessness along which Otherness can be constructed, and it is clear that these multiple intersecting discourses of Otherness can position researcher and researched in shifting ways. [. . .]

[. . .]

No theoretical discussion of 'representing the Other' can fail to take up the question of the category itself. We cannot write about the Other as if some totalizable intelligible object simply 'exists' out there, waiting to be represented. Others are constructed − by those who do the Othering, by those who reflect upon that Othering, and by the Others' own representations of themselves.

[. . .] Most feminist research in psychology continues to be governed by the norms of representational realism. Feminist social psychologists (like many feminists across the social sciences) attempt in their work to present their female research participants 'as they really are' (as opposed to the way men have presented them) and 'in their own voices' (as opposed to the authoritative voice of the researcher–interpreter). Sceptical of the possibility of any such presentation of women's experience in direct, 'pure' or authentic form, Spivak (among others) recommends that feminists should proliferate no more accounts of the sort entitled '—Speak', where the Other is simply a name that provides the alibi for erasing the investigator's intervention into the construction and representation of the narrative (Spivak, 1986: 229). Representation is never merely descriptive: it serves also a constitutive and regulatory function which is obscured in (but not absent from) accounts relying upon the conventions of representational realism.

Interrupting Otherness

The problem, then, is how to go on conversing about theorizing and attempting to challenge structural power, whilst recognizing the multiple intersecting forms of power and powerlessness; how to think about our own and/or others' Otherness without fixing it as an essential attribute; how to speak without our words serving to disempower Others; and when to remain silent. For feminist psychologists engaged in empirical research, these problems raise potentially intractable questions. Whom shall we include in our samples? In what ways will they be the same as, and in what ways different from, us? How will we represent their views? As feminist researchers, we are 'chronically and uncomfortably engaged in ethical decisions about how deeply to work with/for/despite those cast as Others' (Fine, 1994: 75).

Wrestling with problems of Othering, feminists and other critical social scientists have suggested ways out of the apparent impasse. Linda Alcoff (1994: 301–2), for example, who writes powerfully and passionately on issues of Othering, recommends four 'interrogatory practices' to evaluate instances of 'speaking for Others': firstly, she suggests that we should analyse, and perhaps resist, the impulse to speak at all; secondly, she asks us to engage in a critical interrogation of the relevance of our autobiographies (e.g. as white, heterosexual etc.) on what we say – and not simply as a disclaimer against ignorance or errors; thirdly, she suggests that we maintain an openness to criticism; and fourthly, she asks us to analyse the actual *effects* of speaking on the discursive and material context. These concerns are increasingly incorporated (in a variety of forms) into contemporary feminist social science practice – with the aim of interrupting the process of Othering. Feminist psychologist Michelle Fine, to whose sophisticated and sensitively argued writing we owe an important debt in thinking about these issues here, suggests that we can interrupt Othering by 'working the hyphen' in the Self-Other equation:

> Self and Other are knottily entangled. This relationship, lived between researchers and informants, is typically obscured in social science texts, protecting privilege, securing distance, and laminating the contradictions. Despite denials, qualitative researchers are always implicated at the hyphen. When we opt, as has been the tradition, simply to write about those who have been Othered, we deny the hyphen . . . When we opt, instead, to engage in social struggles with those who have been exploited and subjugated, we work the hyphen, revealing far more about ourselves,

and far more about the structures of Othering . . . By working the hyphen, I mean to suggest that researchers probe how we are in relation with the contexts we study and with our informants, understanding that we are multiple in all those relations.

(1994: 72)

In practice, 'working the hyphen' seems to include the following approaches (here our taxonomy overlaps with, and extends, Fine's 1994, classification): (a) checking out with Others the validity of one's representations of them; (b) listening to Other's accounts of 'us' as a way of exposing the operation of Othering; (c) listening to members of the powerful group to hear the ways in which they construct Others: and (d) finally (perhaps more in hope than with any sense of current possibility) developing opportunities for dialogue between 'us' and Others. We now (briefly) discuss each of these in turn.

First, an approach not unfamiliar to feminist social psychologists is to give representations back to the represented for comment, feedback, and evaluation; the idea is that the researcher should negotiate representations with those represented and, in some versions of this, they are described not as 'subjects' or even 'research participants' but as 'co-researchers'. [. . .]

Secondly, many feminists emphasize listening to Others – creating conditions under which it is possible to hear the voices of Others 'talking back': to 'us', over 'us', regardless of 'us', to each other, or to other Others. As we have seen, Others' representations of themselves, and certainly their representations of 'us', are routinely de-authorized and dismissed as neither credible nor coherent. Some researchers have stressed the possibilities inherent in the 'inversion' of Othering, whereby Others are given legitimacy as informants on Othering (rather than heard – if at all – merely as subjects' descriptions of their own subjugated position). [. . .] Writing about the domination enacted by elite white women in the USA on the women of colour who work for them as domestics, sociologist Judith Rollins (1985) delivers her analysis from the vantage point of the women employed as domestics: 'reversing who would typically be relied upon to tell the "real" story and who would be portrayed as Other, Rollins allows readers to hear how much subjugated women know about them-Selves and about Others' (Fine, 1994: 77). [. . .] To look instead at the Others looking at 'us' is to relativize and problematize 'our' own perspective: it can be uncomfortable, unsettling or painful, but it is an essential beginning if the process of Othering is to be interrupted.

Thirdly, the study of dominant group members can yield information about the ways in which Self is constructed through and against the construction of Other. Just as accounts written by early ethnographers reveal more about their authors' own social and cultural preoccupations than they do about the 'primitive' tribes which were the object of their study, so more generally the words of people with power speaking or writing about Others can reveal the process involved in Othering. For example, researchers have usually read the traditional psychological and psychiatric literatures on lesbianism in order to find out about lesbians, so colluding in the process of Othering. An alternative approach, embodied in the first two chapters of Celia Kitzinger's (1987) book, The Social Construction of Lesbianism, is to ask instead: 'What can we learn from the literature about the construction of social scientific accounts?' and 'What can we learn from the literature about attempts to manage and control homosexuality?' In other words, what is said by psychologists and psychiatrists about lesbians is understood as revealing information about their preoccupations as members of a (predominantly heterosexual) academic elite, charged with the special responsibility of constructing authorized accounts of Others. In a parallel study, Harlan Hahn (1983, cited in Fine, 1994) has reviewed the work of non-disabled researchers on disability:

> only to conclude that by reading their work we learn more about these researchers' terror of disability than we do about the persons with disabilities about whom they presumably have written. Hahn theorizes that nondisabled researchers carry existential and aesthetic anxieties about bodily dis-integrity that they project onto the bodies of persons with disabilities. Their narratives are laced with anxieties as if they were simply in the bodies of 'them' rather than (un)settled within the (un)consciousness of the researchers.
>
> (Fine, 1994: 78)

As Michelle Fine (1994) points out, listening to the voices of privilege to understand how Othering works involves processes which differ depending on the social location of the listener. To listen, as a lesbian, to the voices of researchers on lesbianism is different from listening, as a non-disabled woman, to the voices of researchers on disability: our own contradictory 'partialities and pluralities' (Fine, 1994: 79) have to be part of the interrogation.

Finally, there are repeated suggestions that 'dialogue' with Others can be more illuminating than the monologue of the single researcher presenting 'data' about Others (Fowler, 1994): our work should be not so much about the Other as about the interplay between the researcher and the Other. In the introduction to *Writing Culture*, Clifford (1986) argues that ethnographers should attempt to create a text within a context of collaborative story-making which celebrates dialogue over monologue, polyphony over monophonic authority. [. . .]

[. . .]

Bibliography

Alcoff, L. (1994) 'The Problem of Speaking for Others' in S. Ostrov Weisser and J. Fleishner (eds), *Feminist Nightmares — Women at Odds: Feminism and the Problem of Sisterhood*, New York: New York University Press.

Belenky, M., Clinchy, B., Goldberger, N., and Tarule, J. (1986) *Women's Ways of Knowing*, New York: Basic Books.

Cixous, H. (1983/92) 'The Laugh of the Medusa' in E. Abel and E.K. Abel (eds), *The Signs Reader: Women, Gender and Scholarship*, Chicago: University of Chicago Press.

Clifford, J. (1986) 'Introduction' in J. Clifford and G.E. Marcus (eds), *Writing Culture*, Berkeley: University of California Press, pp. 1–26.

Croghan, R. (1993) 'Sleeping with the Enemy: Mothers in Heterosexual Relationships', in S. Wilkinson and C. Kitzinger (eds), *Heterosexuality: A Feminism and Psychology Reader*, London: Sage, pp. 495–7.

Fine, M. (1994) 'Working the Hyphens: Reinventing the Self and Other in Qualitative Research' in N.K. Denzin and Y. Lincoln (eds), *The Handbook of Qualitative Research*, London: Sage, pp. 70–82.

Fowler, C.S. (1994) 'Beginning to Understand: Twenty Eight Years of Fieldwork in the Great Basin of Western North America', in D.D. Fowler and D.L. Hardesty (eds), *Others Knowing Others: Perspectives on Ethnographic Careers*, Washington, DC: Smithsonian Institution Press.

Gilligan, C. (1982) *In a Different Voice*, Cambridge, MA: Harvard University Press.

Irigaray, L. (1981) 'This Sex which is Not One' in E. Mark and I. de Courtivron (eds), *New French Feminisms* London: Harvester, pp. 99–106.

Kitzinger, C. (1987) *The Social Construction of Lesbianism*, London: Sage.

Kitzinger, C. and Wilkinson, S. (1993) 'Theorizing Heterosexuality' in S. Wilkinson and C. Kitzinger (eds), *Heterosexuality: A Feminism and Psychology Reader*, London: Sage, pp. 1–32.

Kitzinger, C. and Wilkinson, S. (1994) 'Virgins and Queers: Rehabilitating Heterosexuality', *Gender and Society* 8 (3): 444–63.

Olson, K. and Shopes, L. (1991) 'Crossing Boundaries, Building Bridges: Doing Oral History among Working-class Women and Men', in S. Berger Gluck and D. Patai (eds), *Women's Words: The Feminist Practice of Oral History* London: Routledge.

Rollins, J. (1985) *Between Women: Domestics and their Employers* Philadelphia, PA: Temple University Press.

Said, E. (1978) *Orientalism*, New York: Pantheon.

Salazar, C. (1991) 'A Third World Women's Text: Between the Politics of Criticism and Cultural Politics', in S. Berger Gluck and D. Patai (eds), *Women's Words: The Feminist Practice of Oral History*, London: Routledge.

Seifer, M. (1976) *Nobody Speaks for Me! Self Portraits of American Working Class Women*, New York: Simon & Schuster.

Spivak, G. (1986) *In Other Worlds: Essays in Cultural Politics*, London: Methuen.

Trinh, T.M.A. (1989) *Woman, Native, Other: Writing Postcoloniality and Feminism*, Bloomington, IN: Indiana University Press.

Van Maanen, J. (1995) 'An End to Innocence: The Ethnography of Ethnography', in J. Van Maanen (ed.), *Representation in Ethnography* London: Sage.

White, E.C. (1990) *The Black Women's Health Book: Speaking for Ourselves*, Seattle, WA: Seal Press.

Yuval-Davis, N. (1993) 'The (Dis)Comfort of Being "Hetero"' in S. Wilkinson and C. Kitzinger (eds), *Heterosexuality: A Feminism and Psychology Reader*, London: Sage, pp. 52–4.

Chapter 14

Joe Winston

'FIT FOR A CHILD?'
Artistry and didacticism in a theatre in health education programme for young children

A FEW YEARS AGO I ATTENDED a musical Theatre in Education (TiE) performance for two classes of five-year-old children. It told the story of a donkey that was brutalised and suffered constant misfortune before eventually sacrificing its life in order to save a young girl from drowning. The play was mawkish in the extreme, uncritically following a sub Hans Christian Anderson plot propounding sainthood through suffering, and within ten minutes of its start the children were already restless. The inappropriateness of the play's content was matched by the poor quality of its artistry, limited as it was to expensive costumes and the vocal gusto of the two young performers who sang a range of songs, each as if they were auditioning for a part in *Phantom of the Opera*. Before the hour was through the children were openly bored, paying practically no attention to the death throes of the donkey, whose dying song, being a gentle ballad, was only partially audible above their restless chatter. I ceased to worry about the inappropriateness of the play's didactic agenda as the theatrical experience had evidently made no impact whatsoever on its young audience. The glossy notes for teachers that accompanied the performance included extensive referencing to National Literacy objectives and suggested written follow-up work. I didn't leave with the impression that teachers were rushing back to their classrooms eager to have their children write about the character of the donkey or list the trades of his various tormentors.

It has long been understood by practitioners of Theatre in Education that the negotiation of the tensions at the heart of their practice is key to its success. We might define these tensions as: entertainment versus education or artistry versus didacticism. Is there also a tension for performers between the aesthetics and the ethics of TiE for young children; between the pleasurable effects of a play's artistry and the ethics of presenting a programme that honestly and with integrity addresses the concerns of the stakeholders (schools, funding agencies), providing children with a programme that is neither pleasurable at the expense of its educational agenda nor vice versa? This chapter will argue that it is, in fact, only when they attend fully to issues of artistry and the aesthetic that devisers of TiE are being truly ethical in their approach; that only through such attention can their work engage their audiences and begin to address whatever didactic objectives they might be claiming to have. The argument will take the form of an analysis of a programme for Year 1 children (five- and six-year-olds) that toured Birmingham schools in 2004 and for which I was the external evaluator. It was devised and performed by *Language Alive*, part of the Playhouse, a well established TiE company with a strong reputation for participatory work that skilfully addresses learning outcomes whilst always placing issues of artistry at the forefront of its concerns.

The programme

Fit for a King was a participatory programme for first-year primary school children developed to explore the topic of healthy eating. An ethical principle that underpins all of the work of *Language Alive* is to limit the audience to thirty children at any one time in order to ensure maximum participation for every child.

The play was performed by just two actor-teachers, one in the role of Yannis, a boisterous, playful and above all excessive young prince, the other in the role of his long-suffering servant, Cookie, whose many duties included organising Yannis' meals for him. The programme began with Cookie enrolling the children as his advisers, with the task of helping him design a healthy banquet for the Prince's coronation ceremony. This was a challenge, as the children soon found out when they met Yannis, for he had no sense of healthy food and was only interested in eating cakes, sweets, chips, crisps and tomato ketchup. Through two shadow puppet shows, the children learned how the prince had made himself violently sick at a recent banquet and also witnessed a replay of the previous year's dragon chasing competition, in which Yannis had been so unfit that the dragon had caught up with him and scorched his bottom.

The animated discussions between the children and the Prince, and the children and Cookie, which constituted the didactic elements of the play, focussed on what foods constituted a balanced diet and why, and led to each child designing a healthy, balanced meal which they drew with coloured pens on individual paper plates. These didactic activities were skilfully interspersed with comic exchanges between Cookie and the prince and various physical clowning activities – Cookie chasing the prince, the prince chasing Cookie, the prince juggling rather than eating his fruit, Cookie dressing as a fitness instructor and pompously leading the prince and the children through a series of physical exercises. The show culminated in the Prince actually winning this year's dragon chasing competition and realising that this was due to his having become fit through exercise and a healthy diet. The children showed him the meals they had prepared for his banquet, which pleased him, and a large, red crown arrived in time for Cookie to proudly announce his coronation.

Out comes the learning . . .

Learning outcomes can be a thorny issue for theatre in education companies as they are currently subject to a technicist ideology which defines them in terms of the visible and the immediately evident. To use Eisner's terminology, the instrumental objectives are privileged above the expressive, or those that are less prescriptive, less expansive, less obvious (Eisner, 1985). In the case of a programme devoted to promoting healthy eating, the company did, in fact, feel compelled to try to find evidence as to whether the play actually did lead children to make healthier choices at their school dinners. Three teachers in separate schools agreed to monitor a selection of children's choices at mealtimes for the three days before and after the performance. Leaving aside the shaky evidence such a small sample would inevitably provide, the results were far from clear. Two schools saw no change in children's choices and in the school where they were noted, for every child who changed their option from chips to mashed potato, another child was seen to do the opposite!

On the whole, the company had a wiser approach to its learning outcomes, defining them in terms of helping children articulate what they already knew about diet and healthy living and encouraging them to make informed choices; both of which were evidenced within the context of the play itself. As such the company recognized itself as in partnership with the schools they visited, in one obvious and one not so obvious sense. The obvious sense was to see their play as complementing what schools were already doing vis-à-vis teaching and promoting healthy eating. At the time of the tour, the children in all the schools were being taught the facts; the play therefore provided a fictional and entertaining context within which these facts could be applied. The less obvious sense of partnership is just as important but more risky. When theatre enters schools, it has a real power to transgress the normal institutional codes and practices, a carnivalesque potential to uncrown the adult and invert the power structures. Its more comic and playful elements are key to this, as I have proposed in two previous analyses of practice.[1] Paradoxically, I propose, it is in this potential, at the heart of a play's artistry, that its true ethical agenda as education lies. In addressing this artistry, we tap into the power of theatre as education and it is to an analysis of how this can be done that I devote the rest of this chapter.

In comes the artistry

> The actors are so skilled! I mean they hold the children like that, I mean that's the greatest thing. If they didn't have the control of the children then they wouldn't learn anything anyway. But they have got them spellbound!
>
> (Extract from interview with teacher)

The material presence of the actors was what held the attention of the children and the skill of their performances was central to this. It was they who orchestrated the fun – and fun, laughter and above all *playfulness* were what drew in the children and held them within the theatrical experience. The verbal repartee between Cookie and Yannis was important but more so, perhaps, was the physicality and clowning.

Two moments the children particularly loved were when Cookie and Yannis chased one another around a partition and when Yannis juggled four pieces of fruit very skilfully. One audience of children I saw were relatively quiet but they roared with laughter at the chase; the first group of children I interviewed as part of my evaluation mentioned that the prince could juggle before they mentioned anything else.

Less exuberant but equally physical was the constant exchange of glances and gestures between the actors. Yannis' register of gestures was limited by his naivety, and signalled petulance, excitement and anticipation, whereas Cookie's range was more varied and signalled to the children a clear 'moral' response to Yannis: growing discontent and frustration, for example, as he listed the excesses he had planned for his proposed feast; or a mixture of admiration and frustration as Yannis juggled the fruit instead of eating it. There was also smug self-satisfaction as he later entered as a fitness inspector; and surprise, gratitude and admiration toward the end of the play as he thanked the children for the wondrous way in which they had changed Yannis for the better. The tension between the characters was first and foremost *performative*, one of physical energy – the loud, boisterous, hyperactive Yannis versus the quiet, restrained calm (though increasingly frustrated) Cookie. This gave the play both its balance and its dynamic and matched the *referential* tension, i.e. the moral tension at the heart of the play's subject matter, centred as it was around the struggle to get the Prince to eat more healthily.[2]

Here, too, however, to understand the play's efficacy we need to analyse it in theatrical terms, seeing it as a classic confrontation between two standard, comic types; Yannis and Cookie – youth versus age; excess versus restraint; naughtiness versus common sense; disorder versus order; master versus servant. The key to the comedy was in this latter, carnivalesque inversion of real life adult/child relationships. Yannis (the child) was master, Cookie (the adult) was servant. Yannis' characteristics therefore appealed to children as a release from the normal power structures of family and school. He was clearly a child – in fact, in many ways, his behaviour positioned him as younger than the children themselves, like a baby brother, permanently attached to a cuddly toy and displaying the excessive appetite of a toddler. He also knew a lot less than they did about the world and its hazards, as symbolised in the dragon chasing contest, as much as in his attitude to food. The educational trick, however, lay in making Cookie also endearing to the children. He was the adult at his wit's end who couldn't control an unruly child. Kind-hearted and polite to the children, he had the Prince's best interest at heart. Children know about such adults and they know about naughty children who frustrate and annoy them.

In this way the play set up a moral tension that pulled the children in opposing directions. It worked because children implicitly understood its human context as one congruent with their own lives and, crucially, they liked both of the characters for their differing but positive human qualities. This affective bonding to each character was at the heart of the play's potential dilemmas; the children agreed with Cookie's agenda but they enjoyed Yannis' subversion of it. As with most comedy, this was resolved at the climax (the feast) where moral order was finally restored; when Yannis eventually learned how to eat well and stay healthy. But the real enjoyment, and the real learning, lay in the tensions along the journey rather than in the moral stability of the final resolution.

Enlisting children as experts is a well-tried convention in participatory drama. Where TiE or Drama in Education (DiE) programmes sometimes falter, however, is in seeing this primarily as an imaginative or, more precisely, a *mental* activity, which results in the *physicality* of the roles often remaining under-explored. For younger children, physicality is very significant in helping them internalise their involvement and maintain concentration. The ritual of bowing on the entrance of the Prince, the drawing of the menus, the engagement in physical exercise were all crucial in providing children with a rhythm of physical as well as mental involvement. Such physicality works best in a theatre programme when it is aesthetically integrated into the plot and not seen as a desirable interlude, like a bout of 'brain gym', so popular in contemporary primary classrooms.

Vocal involvement is a form of physicality when the voice is harnessed for its dynamic qualities rather than simply as a carrier of literal meaning – in other words, when its use has a playful rather than a didactic feel to it. Yannis' excesses were meant to stir children into admonishing him, sanctioning them to use their superior knowledge to correct him or even tell him off a little. When he interrupted and subverted Cookie's sensible agenda, the children were highly amused and had a great time shouting 'NO!' at him. Such verbal exchanges are more motivating and energising for children than the question–answer routines that typified some of Cookie's dialogue with them, reminiscent as it was of classroom discourse with its questions about whether certain foods were healthy or not. Although this did have a purpose within the plot – and hence made sense to the children – it was inevitably less fun. Similarly, the ritual presentation of the menus at the end of the play, although laudably equable and participatory, was nonetheless rather low on energy, both physical and psychic, as each child was called upon to explain their meal and receive due praise for their efforts. I wondered if some further layers of comic tension here might suitably have energised these vocal sessions – tensions arising from a shortage of time (will we be ready before the crown arrives?); from one group trying to keep something secret (a healthy cake?) so that the Prince wouldn't see it; or from the real possibility that the Prince might not become King after all as his residual silliness kept breaking through.

The didactic aspects of the programme, as located within its physical activity and symbolic objects as well as its utterances, worked better the more they were integrated into its artistic logic. The children's drawings served both to reinforce their own knowledge *and* as the menus for the Prince's feast. Cookie's words of praise and the Prince's words of thanks were those of teachers *and* of actors *and* of characters in the drama. When the Prince said to the children 'I need to get used to telling people what to do' he was contracting their behaviour both as pupils *and* as his fictional subjects. The deeper all aspects of a programme can be embedded into its aesthetic – in other words, the more complex its layers of symbolic meaning – the better, I suggest, will be both the artistry and the learning.

To explore this a little more deeply let us take one example of a symbolic object whose potential I felt remained under-explored in the play; that of the crown. The crown made its appearance at the end of the show and was a potent symbol of the Prince's passage from irresponsibility to responsibility. It had a direct parallel with Bettelheim's proposition that the journey of central characters in fairy tales to King/Queen symbolises the child's eventual and inevitable journey into adulthood, whilst signalling that this journey carries with it moral responsibilities (Bettelheim, 1976). Yet very little was made of the crown. It was never on display but this absence was not built into the plot. What if the children were waiting for it to arrive? (What if it didn't?) Could some of them have been called upon to unpack it secretly and check that it was indeed the red one and not the awful, dark green one that the Prince would refuse to wear? Little was made of the coronation ceremony, which could have incorporated children as heralds, as cheering populace, the rehearsal for which might have permeated the show as another of Cookie's endless stream of duties. Instead, the climax of the play saw the triumph of didacticism over theatricality as the children brought out their individual meals in a tedious and predictable procession.

Research has shown that the visuals of theatre, particularly when there is something of the surprising, unusual or unexpected about them, are what children remember most (Deldime and Pigeon, 1989). Hence those children who, when I interviewed them, immediately remarked upon the Prince's juggling, telling me exactly what fruits he had juggled and in what order. The following short extract is also revealing:

> Girl 'He had a little King's hat on first and then got a big crown'
> Boy 'And it's got lights on it'
> Me 'Oh did it? That's nice'
> Boy 'He had two lights that didn't light'

I did not solicit this information; the children volunteered it as it was fixed so strongly in their memories. The boy had obviously been particularly struck by the lights on the crown and by the fact that two weren't working. His observation left me nonplussed as the lights flashed quickly on and off, so it was difficult to notice whether they were all working or not. At the next performance I looked closely and he was right. Although this observation might seem peripheral to the play's concerns, I conclude the analysis with it as it reminds us of what commands children's attention in theatre, of what they acutely observe and remember, whatever our didactic agenda. When it comes to theatre, artistry is what we must harness as the most effective and hence the most ethical quality of our pedagogy.

Bibliography

Bettelheim, B. (1976) The Uses of Enchantment: The Meaning and Importance of Fairy Tales, London: Penguin.
Deldime, R. and Pigeon, J. (1989) La Mémoire du Jeune Spectateur, Brussels: de Boeck Wesmael.
Eisner, E. (1985) The Art of Educational Evaluation, London: Falmer Press.

Notes

1   See Winston, J. (1998) Drama, Narrative and Moral Education, London, Falmer (Chapter 9) and (2005) 'Between the aesthetic and the ethical: analysing the tension at the heart of Theatre in Education', Journal of Moral Education, vol.34, no.3.

2   See Jackson A. (2001) 'Researching Audiences for Educational Theatre', in Playing Betwixt and Between: the IDEA Dialogues, 2000, IDEA Publications.

Chapter 15

David Kerr

'YOU JUST MADE THE BLUEPRINT TO SUIT YOURSELVES'
A theatre-based health research project in Lungwena, Malawi

SINCE IT FIRST SPRANG INTO popularity in the late 1970s, social theatre
in Africa has met numerous challenges, mostly arising from neo-colonial, top-
down attitudes and practices, either bequeathed directly from the colonial period
or indirectly from a neo-colonial political economy of donor funding.

Drama designed by missionary teachers or colonial information officers as
propaganda for developmental innovation in such fields as agriculture, health and
literacy created strategies predicated on an ideology investing colonial communicators
with unlimited wisdom. Such plays constructed African audiences in the role of
backward children, who needed constant paternal guidance (Kamlongera 1989).

This premise was most notable in the theatre motif that has often been referred
to as the 'Mr. Wise and Mr. Foolish' formula. In colonial health plays, for example,
a wise colonial doctor struggled to convince a foolish, superstitious African (usually
influenced by an evil 'witch-doctor'). The formula has remained surprisingly common
in post-colonial plays created by African theatre companies and is particularly popular
in plays about HIV and AIDS. Mr. Wise, the colonial health expert, has evolved into
a Western-trained doctor or health worker while Mr. Foolish is still a superstitious
recalcitrant, often influenced by an identikit evil or mercenary 'witch-doctor' (Rohmer
1999).

NGOs have tried to offset neo-colonial, simplistic characterization by introducing
participatory research and performance techniques in order to link social theatre
more closely with African traditions of communication. The recruitment of local
theatre practitioners allows professional communicators to create appropriate stories
using African proverbs, songs and dances to ensure local acceptance. But such
attempts to pack new messages into old cultural forms may sometimes be closer to
appropriation than respect for 'traditions'.

The difference between the lessons of Theatre for Development and those of indigenous performance is that the latter used multi-layered performance techniques and motifs rather than blatant didacticism. For example, trickster tale narrative drama had an overt message (such as condemning laziness), but also a counter-ethic in which the audience empathized with the socially outrageous antics of the spider or hare anti-hero. Work songs condemned members of the community, such as wives drawing attention to their husbands' defects in grain-pounding songs, but did so with a density of metaphor and allusion that saved the faces of the satire's victims (Timpunza-Mvula 1985). Dilemma folktales presented three or more alternative endings to a story and then allowed audiences to debate and choose the most appropriate outcome. By contrast, the didacticism of much Theatre for Development is painfully tendentious and one-dimensional with stereotyped characterization and banal motivation.

Simplistic message formation is linked to the sectoral interests of specific NGOs. The briefs that NGOs give to African theatre groups for creating plays are usually restricted to the issue that the NGO has as its 'portfolio'. In real life the causes of illiteracy or HIV infection are not restricted to the obvious. Each superficial cause is linked to a much larger chain that embraces politics, kinship systems, economics, class, ethnicity, global communications and local/global ideologies. Owing to their strict financial and cultural auditing systems, NGOs rarely have time or resources to push their research analysis into this more complex, historically contextualized and ideologically sensitive field. As a result, the action plans that emerge from typical Theatre for Development evaluation sessions are doomed to tinker with solutions that only superficially address problems identified during the research process.

As a result audience participation techniques rarely lead to free and open discussion. Extreme poverty gives power to local elites (chiefs, elders, traders, religious or political leaders) so discussions are almost always monopolized by dominant sections of the audience who manipulate the discussion in ways they feel the visiting theatre team and their NGO backers want to hear. Thus the liberatory language of Freire and Boal found in project proposals rarely finds fruition in social theatre practice (Kidd and Kumar 1981).

A theatre-based health research project in Lungwena

The following case study explores an NGO-funded theatre project I was involved with in Malawi, 2003–4.

The process I describe is a long-term health project, funded by the Norwegian Centre for Cooperation in Higher Education (NUFU), in Lungwena, a deprived area about 50 kilometers North of Mangochi on the unfashionable East bank of Lake Malawi, close to the Mozambique border. Lungwena, a small trading center two kilometers from the Lake itself, is chosen because it has a clinic providing primary health care in the area, including accommodation for visiting health workers. The project is a long-term attempt to improve the health of the area by calling upon the skills of academic researchers and communicators in all five of the constituent colleges of the University of Malawi.

Unlike many health projects, the NUFU coordinators of the Lungwena project realize that poor health is not primarily a medical but a social problem. For that reason, although Dr. Maleta of the Medical College in Blantyre coordinates the project, the research and implementation aspect also involves: the Polytechnic (in Blantyre) on issues of sanitation and water supply; Chancellor College, Zomba KAP[1]; Bunda College of Agriculture near Lilongwe on nutrition; and Kamuzu College of Nursing, Lilongwe, on primary health care. I participate in the contribution by Chancellor College.

The project attracts me because of its multi-sectoral approach and because the NUFU project coordinators are determined to keep a low profile, thus allowing Dr. Maleta and his directorate to design research and intervention processes themselves in ways that encourage appropriate communication methods. Thus the directorate enthusiastically accepts my proposal to use theatre both as a form of qualitative research into KAP and as a tool for implementing the intervention strategy.

My brief from the directorate for the first stage of the process is to help build a local drama group that can create a play to tour around key villages in the area and ascertain KAP problems contributing to low levels of health. In this task, my colleagues from some of the other colleges make useful suggestions for issues to research. Dr. Maleta also puts me in touch with an existing drama group in Lungwena (Tukumbusyane Travelling Theatre).

One of my first tasks is to look at issues of language and culture. I can understand the national language, chiChewa, and speak it quite well, but Lungwena is in a chiYao speaking area. The Yao have a unique culture which has been influenced by nineteenthth-century contacts with the Swahili. Most of them are Muslim, although their religious beliefs are synthesized with indigenous African customs. Everyone in Lungwena can understand chiChewa, but are more comfortable with chiYao; for that reason I recruit a Masters student at Chancellor College, Syned Muthathiwa. Although not having many drama skills he is a fluent chiYao speaker and familiar with Yao culture.

Our first tasks are to contact Tukumbusyane Travelling Theatre, undertake research in the chosen villages and create a play with them that can explore some of the issues about KAP in the area. This process is accomplished over a two-week period. Dr. Maleta and other members of the NUFU project organizing committee are able to give us much information, particularly about quantitative research that has already been undertaken, and about the grass roots primary health care network in the area. The latter consists of community nurses at the Lungwena clinic, along with village committees under the supervision of a prominent traditional leader, chief Fowa.

One of the greatest resources is Tukumbusyane Travelling Theatre, an amateur troupe of seven; four men and three women. Unlike many similar groups in Southern Africa, these are not teenagers recently dropped out of school and looking for money or glory. They are all mature married men and women, ranging from 25 to 52 years old, living in several different villages in the area. Apart from the group leader, Stanford Chisale, who has a junior certificate and a salaried job with the Ministry of Agriculture, the others have little if any formal education, and occupations mainly relate to the fishing industry, either as fishermen or fish/vegetable vendors.

Drama is not a traditional art form among the Yao but the members of Tukumbusyane have all had exposure to indigenous performance skills of narration, singing, dancing, mime and drumming, and have highly developed ensemble skills of improvisation. They have also received some social theatre training in an earlier workshop held by my University colleague, Joe Chimwenje.

Tukumbusyane's repertoire comprises a combination of commercial satires about love, marriage, work and status, and didactic plays commissioned by the Lungwena primary health team. Our workshop and rehearsal area is a sandy space under a tree outside the clinic's hostel where Syned and I are staying. The tree shade is necessary in temperatures which creep towards 40 degrees every day. After some introductory warm-up and trust games I ask the group to show us one of their commercial plays.

The play, called *Za Ukwati* ('Concerning Marriage'), is a comedy about adultery and marital finances in a style based on a folk story motif of two tricksters (in this case husband, Yuda, and wife, Maggie) trying to outwit each other. The humour is dependent upon caricature, comic timing and plot ironies. After the mini-performance the group explains how some of the characters – Yuda, the husband, with his macho stubbornness; Che Richard, the traditional healer; Maggie, the cunning adulteress; and Che Ndogo, the wise, modernizing authority figure – are stock characters who appear in many of the plays. When we travel around the villages it is clear that the actors are minor celebrities known by their stage names.

Over four days we tour eight chosen villages to prepare for performances, seek approval of the headmen, research issues and pick up local information to incorporate into the play. We also devise the play we are to use to elicit responses from the audiences on KAP issues. For the play-devising, Syned and I explain the major issues on which NUFU wants to acquire information, namely: reasons for early marriage of young girls; polygyny[2], and reluctance to attend the clinic or to use birth control; the impact of initiation ceremonies for both boys and girls; the influence of traditional attitudes to food consumption; and reluctance to build pit latrines or to preserve food resources during harvest time. We leave the theatre group to discuss the issues on their own. Within two hours the group orally builds a scenario, allocates roles, and without any rehearsal performs a play on these issues.

The performance is in chiChewa for my benefit, but on the understanding that most of it will be translated into chiYao for the village performances. I'm rather alarmed at the short time they have taken to create the play, fearing that the analysis may be superficial. There are some obvious problems of stagecraft, but it is very difficult to evaluate the content, because the whole play is designed around opening up the dialogue to the audience, which does not yet exist.

The plot of *Lingongochichi?* ('What are the Reasons?') is very simple. A married couple, Yuda and Make Bibi, are quarreling about not having enough food to celebrate the Jando, male initiation, rites for their son. The quarrel raises many targeted issues particularly those concerning early marriage, polygyny, family planning and food conservation. Most of the rest of the play involves unsuccessful attempts to reconcile the couple, both by relatives (especially Che Mangame, Make Bibi's maternal uncle) and by the community's authority figure (Che Ndogo). The escalating argument explodes in Yuda's threat to abandon Make Bibi. The outcome is left to the audience to debate. Several elements of the play are based on existing traditions. Make Bibi's complaints about Yuda's irresponsibility are similar to those found in grain-pounding songs and in the rhetoric of traditional court marriage disputes. The clash between Yuda and Che Ndogo is similar to the Mr. Wise and Mr. Foolish that I referred to earlier, and the final appeal to the audience for settlement of the issues is similar to the dilemma tale formula.

Syned and I work on making some improvements to the play: I concern myself with stagecraft issues of sightlines, entries, exits and mime technique; Syned with language in the translation into ChiYao. In fact, the finished version uses code-switching between chiYao and chiChewa, as well as some phrases of English and kiSwahili for comic or role status reasons. We also discuss ways of ensuring that in performance, the Mr. Wise and Mr. Foolish contrast is not too didactic and that the whole debate is one designed to elicit substantial audience feedback rather than pre-packaged responses.

One of the most important issues we have to decide is to find out whether we are allowed to use drums in the performances. The reason for the doubt is that the performances fall within the last few days of Ramadan in an area that is about 90 percent Muslim. Some headmen feel that there is no problem, but one imam we consult pronounces against using drums and we opt for the conservative option. This means that we have to work on songs and drum-free dances for major transitions.

On 23 and 24 November we perform in four of the eight villages, one performance at about noon, the other in the late afternoon. We have a NUFU vehicle; a 4x4 twin cab, ideal for touring around the sandy, rocky tracks linking the villages. Warm-up songs, dances and sketches, either by the group or by performers of the villages we are visiting, precede each performance of *Lingongochichi?*.

The first performance in Ntumbula village under a large Baobab tree is not a success. There is a group of representatives from the clinic, who assume VIP seats. Women and children sit in a semi-circle on the sand while the subaltern men stand on the verandah of a house far from the performing area. After warm-ups a member of the primary health care committee, Mai Mbela, uses a loudhailer to introduce the visitors. During the play she sometimes interrupts the action to elucidate a health moral she feels has not been sufficiently emphasized. This encourages the actors to simplify motivation and create a tendentious rather than open play. Worse still, only the women in the audience respond to the participation techniques, expressing their approval for 'modern' approaches to reproductive health issues. The men stand aloof, laughing at the jokes, but refusing to intervene in any dialogue with a play that seems unfairly weighted towards a woman's point of view on such issues as polygyny, birth control and early marriage of girls.

During a quickly taken late lunch we discuss the performance. The group explains that the attitude of men in Ntumbula is typical of local reaction to health messages. I explain that the whole function of the NUFU-funded project is not, at this stage, to teach the communities, but to allow the Medical school research team to learn what the problems and issues are in the community concerning health issues. I manage to persuade Mai Mbela not to use the loudhailer for future performances or to try to influence the message of the play, and also urge the acting team not to tilt the balance of the argument too much in Make Bibi's favour, but to allow men in the audience to support Yuda's arguments. This is very different from the techniques they have previously used, which have been in a tradition of top-down message packaging.

These changes elicit a much more successful performance in Chironga village, where the gendered-debate structure of the play becomes very clear. As in Ntumbula, the women fervently support Make Bibi's points of view when she appeals for their support, but the men also get involved in the debate, good-naturedly cheering their own gender's viewpoint. At times the play stops for debates between men and women, but the main analysis comes at the end of the play. I am astonished at the frankness of the discussion, with women asking their husbands searching questions about polygyny, sex practices, HIV infection and early marriage of children.

This pattern continues over several days, performances, a mini-evaluation and further work on the developing play to deepen the analysis, linking it to more fundamental social issues about political and economic change.

The performances of the newly re-workshopped version of *Lingongochichi?* resume on 28 November with visits to Mwanjati and Mponde and to Milombwe and Taliya the next day. The attempt to deepen the analysis works particularly well in Mponde and Taliya. Mponde is a large village close to Lungwena, and the audience is the biggest in our whole tour. As usual, the early exchanges are very gendered, but the dynamic is rather different from other villages because two of the actors, James and Yuda, are prominent Mponde residents, with James one of the elders who advise the headman. As the play ends, the audience creeps closer to the actors. Yuda steps in and out of role, projecting stereotyped male chauvinist attitudes while in role, and supporting some of the women's points of view when he is out of role. The effect of this is to shift the balance of the argument away from gender towards social rights. More complex questions begin to be discussed. Is it good for girls of 13 to be married instead of finishing their education? Is it good for fishermen to spend their profits from fish sales in wooing a new wife, rather than supporting their existing families? How do the money economy and the new multi-party democracy introduced since 1994 affect families? There is a highly charged atmosphere as people realize that the issues laughed at in the play affect the community in the deepest ways. The debate is fierce but conducted in a constructive and hopeful manner.

The performance at Taliya in hilly country towards the Mozambique border provokes even more challenging community self-analysis. Some members of the project directorate have made the long journey to witness how theatre can be used as a research tool. Considering the scattered nature of the village, the audience is quite large, partly because one of the actors, Patuma Marten, is from Taliya.

In Taliya the actors use more chiChewa than chiYao, so that the visitors can understand; many in the audience also do the same during discussions. As usual, *Lingongochichi?* sets up a major debate between the men and the women. I sit with the members of the directorate. One of them, appalled at views expressed by Yuda and many men in the audience, says she would like to intervene to correct their attitudes. I am opposed to this on the grounds that it would take the debate back to the artificial imposition of political correctness, which prevented active participation of the men in Ntumbula. Dr. Maleta agrees with me and the play process continues.

The after-play discussion focuses much on 'miyambo' (traditional customs). As with other villages the men support miyambo such as polygyny, early marriage of girls and excluding pregnant women from eating certain foods. The women are almost equally united in their view that these miyambo are outdated. At the hottest point of the debate one young man gives a passionate defense of miyambo saying, 'they are a blueprint given to us by our forefathers'. Several other men pick up this metaphor of the blueprint and apply it to issues raised in the play.

Eventually, an old man, who is one of the village elders and much respected in the community, stands up to speak:

> You young men have just made up this blueprint to suit yourselves. This marrying of young girls is not what our forefathers did. When I was a

young man I married a girl of 18 not 13. At that time a father had to keep his girls until they were 17 or 18 before they could be married. You young men want to run away from your responsibilities. You don't want to spend money on educating and bringing up your girls. You just want to make money, selling fish and marrying other wives. You just want money. That is not a blueprint from our forefathers.

At each statement the women in the audience dance and ululate in agreement. Some of the younger men look shamefaced, and the debate moves to a much deeper level, examining the relationship between traditions (real and invented), gender, class and the cash economy.

Unfortunately, a sudden rainstorm breaks up the debate and everyone scatters to their homes. The members of the directorate meet briefly at the clinic and are fulsome in appreciation of theatre's ability to open up many levels of discussion and solicit cultural information. They realize that drama may not only help support the research process, but also delivery of behavior-change strategies at the implementation stage.

On the following day we have an evaluation session with Tukumbusyane Travelling Theatre and Chief Fuwa. One unanimous criticism is that the schedule of two performances a day including travel between villages has been too demanding. Most of the reaction, however, is very positive. Chief Fuwa and the actors are all convinced that audience participation has been spectacularly better than for previous performances and agree that this has been because of the play not assuming a judgmental stance.

The following morning is taken up with housekeeping issues, and at lunchtime Syned and myself return to Zomba. Since November 2003 the NUFU project has continued in Lungwena beyond the pilot stage. Unfortunately, I have not been involved in the expansion of the theatre segment of the project. For personal reasons I decided to leave Malawi. During the months before my departure, I wrote up my report on the theatre research findings, participated in evaluation sessions, and also helped in the recruitment of two young women from the Chancellor College English Department, Agnes Chimbiri and Mervis Kamanga, to continue the research and communication work.

Analysis of the theatre pilot research project in Lungwena

In many respects the Lungwena Project shared some of the problems I have outlined in the earlier part of this chapter. My own role as a British facilitator, despite my knowledge of chiChewa and aspects of Yao culture, made me something of an outsider. NUFU's role as the agency organizing the Project also met some of the problems of all NGOs undertaking such work. In particular, the tendency of the primary health care team and even Tukumbusyane Travelling Theatre to impose modernizing health messages on the rural communities was a typical consequence of NGO intervention. The sudden influx of researchers in the new Pajero 4x4 was recognized as a powerful economic and ideological force that elicited reactions ranging from mild hostility, through good-humoured interest to cooperation.

Although Tukumbusyane were involved in the evaluation, they were cut off from the directorate's planning process in Blantyre.

On the other hand, the NUFU organizers avoided many of the pitfalls that other NGOs have fallen into. By putting almost all the project design, management and implementation in the hands of hard-working and intelligent Malawian academics and medical professionals they minimized negative effects produced by 'parachuting' in external experts. The Malawian directorate showed great flexibility and innovation by encouraging theatre as a research and communication vehicle. Despite the Pajero, the research visitors did not live in ostentatious luxury when they were in Lungwena. The clinic's spartan rest-house, infested with scorpions and with only three hours of generator-supplied electricity, was visibly part of the community, so that the theatre team's devising work there provided word-of-mouth publicity for the later visits.

The popularity of Tukumbusyane Travelling Theatre, and the intimate local knowledge derived from their subaltern status within various villages, provided easy entry into the community. The use of village performers as part of warm-ups created an unthreatening context for the more instrumental *Lingongochichi?*. The group's adaptability in dropping the Mr. Wise and Mr. Foolish formula and moving in and out of role during after-performance discussions let them push the play's themes beyond superficial, medical problems to deep-rooted causes of class, ethnicity, gender, economics and global power dynamics.

In the current socio-economic context it is difficult for social theatre groups to survive without NGO support. However, with local involvement in extensive research, a determination to create plays examining multi-sectoral issues, and the recruitment of subaltern, linguistically and culturally skilled local actors, some obvious pitfalls of neo-colonial message packaging can be avoided. In its place a genuine rather than token participation can allow communities to achieve a sense of ownership and free speech through debates generated by the social theatre process.

Bibliography

Kamlongera, C. (1989) *Theatre for Development*, Bonn: Zed Press.
Kidd, R. and Kumar, K. (1981) 'Co-opting Freire: A Critical Analysis of Pseudo-Freirean Adult Education', *Economic and Political Weekly* 16 (1–2): 27–36.
Rohmer, M. (1999) *Theatre and Performance in Zimbabwe*, Bayreuth: Bayreuth African Studies.
Timpunza-Mvula, E. (1985) 'Chewa Pounding Songs', *Cross Rhythms* 2: 68–79.

Notes

1   KAP is a common piece of developmental jargon meaning Knowledge, Attitudes and Practices, the field of enquiry normally addressed by qualitative research.
2   Polygyny is the form of polygamy in which a man has several wives.

Chapter 16

Amanda Stuart Fisher

BEARING WITNESS
The position of theatre makers
in the telling of trauma

'All sorrows can be borne if you put them into a story or tell a story about them'.

(Isak Dinesen in Arendt 1998: 175)

WHEN ARENDT DRAWS OUR attention to this quotation by Dinesen she is referring to the way that the human subject uses 'word and deed' to '[insert] himself into the human world' (Arendt 1998: 176). 'This insertion', which as Arendt states 'is not forced upon us by necessity' (Arendt 1998: 177), is a distinctly *human* impulse. It is self-initiated by a drive to provide an account of oneself and to formulate and communicate something that is ours and ours alone – a distinctive 'self' which can be shared, communicated and enunciated through words and through the process of telling our story. As Arendt points out, the drive to speech and action signifies the 'beginning' of the human subject. Through word and deed we are able to respond to the 'primordial' (Arendt 1998: 178) question 'Who are You?' (ibid.).

For the survivors of *trauma*, however, the human desire to provide an account of oneself can become a profoundly troubling process. The traumatic eludes comprehension and communicability. It shatters our self-perception and disables our capacity to process, understand and express what has been encountered. In *Beyond the Pleasure Principle* [1920], Sigmund Freud identifies the traumatic as an event that 'breaks through the protective shield' (Freud 1985: 301) of the self or 'the ego'. Trauma, then, is that which lies *beyond* experience and which cannot be absorbed into the cognitive framework of experience and our own personal narratives. In Felman and Laub's book *Testimony*, Dori Laub says: 'The trauma is thus an event that has no beginning, no ending, no before, no during and no after. This absence of categories that define it lends it a quality of "otherness"' (Felman and Laub 1992:

69). The traumatic therefore *exceeds* the human capacity for language and self-articulation. This raises critical questions for Applied Theatre practitioners as well as playwrights who seek to create theatre texts that are derived from 'real' personal accounts of trauma. The traumatic should not be confused with the experience of hardship or suffering – however severe. On the contrary: there is no 'story' of trauma and the absence of the restitutive narrative categories of beginning, middle and end means that theatre must engage with that which is by definition incomplete and incomprehensible.

Furthermore, personal trauma is often precipitated by geopolitical or historical trauma. In these instances, and as is exemplified in the writings about the *Shoah*, the suffering of the victim becomes inexpressible precisely because of the enormity of the event. Elevated to a quasi-transcendental status, such global traumas signify something irreducible to and incommensurable with lived experience. Indeed what exceeds the bounds of all representability – that which it is impossible *to know* – inevitably brings representation itself into question. This painful and lacunary aspect of bearing witness is something survivors of such historical catastrophes know all too well. For instance, Primo Levi, reflecting on his own attempts to come to terms with his experience of the Camps through an act of testimony, writes: 'There is another lacuna in every testimony: witnesses are by definition survivors . . . No one has told the destiny of the common prisoner, since it was not materially possible for him to survive' (Levi in Agamben 1999: 33).

When personal and epochal trauma is interwoven in this way, the very possibility of bearing witness and providing an account of what has occurred becomes extremely problematic. As the Italian philosopher Giorgio Agamben indicates, the testimony of the survivor is always incomplete for it is impossible 'to bear witness from the inside of death' (Agamben 1999: 35). Furthermore, as we shall see below in the interview with Yael Farber, when historical or political trauma occurs, often communicable language is itself eradicated, destroying the subject's framework of comprehension and self-expression. Here we witness not only the shattering of subjectivity but the fragmentation of all historicity in the face of an event that is essentially dehumanising.

There is not enough space in this chapter to further develop an in-depth analysis of the impact of trauma on our understanding of subjectivity and experience, instead let us consider the essence of the problem: whilst the traumatic results in the *collapse* of experience, the human subject who lives through it can speak. The bodies and voices of the survivors bear witness to that which is incomprehensible and 'unimaginable' (Lewental in Agamben 1999: 12). The survivors of trauma are indeed often seized by a *compulsion* to speak – to testify to 'the rest' – to those who were not there: 'The need to tell our story to "the rest", to make "the rest" participate in it, had taken on for us . . . the character of an immediate and violent impulse, to the point of competing with our other elementary needs' (Levi 1979: 15).

So what is this 'testimony' that speaks *on behalf* of those who are forever silenced and *of* something that lies beyond the bounds of everyday experiential intercourse? As Giorgio Agamben explains, the testimony of the witness draws our attention to the 'aporia of historical knowledge' (Agamben 1999: 12). Testimony is not a faithful account of the factual or historical *truth* of an event; on the contrary it is not comprised of facts and comprehensible events. It is instead a fragmented collection of emotional, physical and bodily associations, and remembrances. These physical and concrete traces of the past are reawakened and shaped by the imperative to speak despite the incommunicability of what must come to expression. In this way, the performance of testimony can be seen to *intervene* in the historical process, rather than simply 'reflect' it in a representational form. It bears witness to that which lies beyond knowable and comprehendible facts and draws us into what Agamben describes as the 'non-coincidence between facts and truth, between verification and comprehension' (Agamben 1999: 12). In this way testimony disrupts and destabilises our conception of a unified and explanatory historical process. Furthermore, in the performance of testimony we, as listeners, are drawn into the testimonial process. Laub expresses this concisely when he says that 'testimonies are not monologues' (Felman and Laub 1992: 70). In fact the witness speaks through a necessity *to be heard*. For Laub the testimonial process contributes to what he calls 'undoing the entrapment' (ibid.) of the traumatic. Writing from a psychoanalytic perspective, Laub draws a connection between speaking of the past and the potential 'release' for the 'victim' from the firm grip of the traumatic event.

To summarise, there are three central challenges that confront practitioners who engage with accounts of personal and political trauma: How do we negotiate the telling of trauma whilst recognising its incommunicability? What is the appropriate language with which to speak of trauma? And what are the ethical implications of being a listener and performer of testimony?

The two playwrights interviewed for this chapter, Sonja Linden and Yael Farber, have each created theatre texts that have derived from the testimony of individuals who have been subject to extreme personal, political or historical trauma. Sonja Linden is a playwright and founding member of *Ice and Fire Theatre*.[1] In 1997 she set up the *Write to Life* project at the *Medical Foundation for the Care of Victims of Torture*, London. It was the experience of working with these clients that inspired her two latest plays *I Have Before Me a Remarkable Document from a Young Lady from Rwanda . . .* (2003) and *Crocodile Seeking Refuge* (2005). Yael Farber is a South African playwright and director. She describes her creative process as a *collaboration* with the people whose life experiences the plays explore – in each play the subjects of the stories are also the performers. Her three testimonial plays *Woman in Waiting*, *AmaJuba (Like Doves we Rise)* and *He Left Quietly* have toured nationally and internationally. Whilst the work of Sonja Linden and Yael Farber is very different, the interviews explore, in very different ways, the use of language and the ethical responsibility that underpins this kind of work.

Crocodile Seeking Refuge (2005)

Destin: I come here to the UK to escape persecution and they put me in prison! I made the same mistake as the crocodile that tries to escape from the rain. You know that story? . . . The first time he feels the rain on his back, he doesn't like it, so he jumps into the river. Stupid eh? . . . Rain, river, same thing. He jumps into the river to escape water only to find more water! (Linden 2005: 24–25)

ASF: In the introduction to 'I Have Before Me . . .' you say that the process of testimonial writing can become an 'act of healing.' Could you say something more about this?

SL: There were two very dramatic examples of that. One was a young Rwandan woman, that I've written about in the introduction of *I Have Before Me . . .* But the other example was an Iranian woman who inspired the character of Parvaneh in *Crocodile Seeking Refuge*. She had been trying, for a long time, to write about her experiences as a political prisoner. Her psychotherapist referred her to me saying she was desperate to write but was blocked. Parvaneh then came to see me. She had a huge story to tell. Her English was quite good so I suggested she write in the present tense. That became a really powerful tool because it made it very dramatic. And the other interesting thing was writing in a foreign language had a distancing effect.

We gradually built up discrete units of her experience through question and answer in the sessions. In the end she wrote an entire book that subsequently she translated back into Farsi and which she had published.

After about a year of working with me she reported that the headaches and the nightmares that she'd had since her prison experience fifteen years before had actually stopped and she really felt it was to do with the writing of the book.

ASF: Can you tell us a little about the creative process of *Crocodile Seeking Refuge*?

SL: There were several very distinct stages. The first stage was, of course, working with individual clients of the Foundation, hearing their stories and encouraging them to write them. Because some of their writing was very impressive my initial impulse was to make the play verbatim, so it started out as being a sort of documentary style.

ASF: You were using their own writing at this stage?

SL: Yes, originally their writing was the main source. On the first day we worked with five actors and we gave them some background material. And then we had an amazing full day where they actually met their counterparts at the Medical Foundation.

ASF: And what was that like?

SL: It was a wonderful day, a lot of bonding and sharing . . . initially a bit scary for the actors! At a later stage the actors went to visit the 'real life' character in their own homes, did an interview and came back and improvised around that. We set ourselves a target of a work-in-progress – this was then performed at the Royal Court Theatre Upstairs and at the Actor's Centre. It wasn't totally successful but it was a very good first start which could have been developed further but actually I'd sort of shifted direction after that because I found it quite confining and limiting in many ways.

A: Why was that?

SL: I suppose at one level I thought 'well I'm actually a playwright' and I want to be able to use my creativity, be more inventive. But it was a really difficult decision. My loyalty to these people made me, for a long time, not want to break away from their own writing. Once I'd made the decision, though, I found it very liberating.

ASF: And the people whose stories inspired the piece, what were their feelings about the play? Did they come and see it?

SL: They did. They gave us fantastic feedback for both stages of the project – I have to say. At the work in progress, we invited them up on stage at the end and that was possibly the most moving part of the evening. When they came to the Lyric, I was very nervous. It felt like a huge responsibility.

Linden suggests that the *strangeness* or 'otherness' of English enabled Parvaneh, one of the people she worked with at the Medical Foundation, to feel psychologically safe enough to access her past experiences – something that had been difficult when using her native Farsi. In the interview that follows with South African playwright Yael Farber, we see how an alternative approach was adopted, yet which still circulates around the problem of language. Farber's testimonial theatre work is threaded through with the poetry, song and vernacular text of the black South African people. In this way the language of the play discloses a diversity of histories that had hitherto been silenced by the domination of the colonial language of Afrikaans. Thus the spoken word enables us to access that which lies *beyond* representation. By this, I mean that language can disclose its own material history. Throughout Farber's plays the characters switch from one language to another, from English and Afrikaans, to their own indigenous vernacular. Farber uses these shifts in language to highlight the stark contrast between the personal, domestic and familial domain of the individual and the oppressive social (and educative) context, where black indigenous people were forced to speak the language of their colonisers. In this way our attention is drawn to what Farber later describes in her interview, as the 'psychic violence' of apartheid.

Woman in Waiting (2002)

Thembi:
>When I walk through this museum in me, I finally understand the power of facing the past.
>(*She walks to the childhood Christmas shoes and picks them up.*)
>Its over half a century since that heavy gale first blew me into this world.
>This little girl . . .
>(*She holds the small shoes to her heart.*)
>Who was too shy to even raise her hand in class – would find herself here tonight . . . Akhulume! [speaking!]Telling my story!
>(*She places the shoes before her on the floor.*)
>And we must speak . . . or it will eat us inside.
>We must speak . . .
>Or our hearts will burst.
>
>(Farber 2008: 84)

ASF: Can you begin by telling us about why you wrote these three plays?

YF: As a South African artist, I wanted to be a part of revealing how individual lives were violated by Apartheid – as well as documenting these stories in a way that history text books fail to convey.

ASF: And how would you describe this kind of work?

YF: I've called the trilogy *Theatre as Witness: Three testimonial plays from South Africa*. I think 'testimonial' is a good word.

ASF: In your work the characters often talk about the importance of the *listener* – and the need for a story to be *listened* to. Could you say something more about this?

YF: What first sparked my fascination with the dynamic between listener and speaker was the *Truth and Reconciliation Commission*, and the dramatic dynamic that inevitably unfolded between testifier, persecutor and witness. The essential component of testimonial theatre lies in its capacity for healing through speaking, hearing and being heard.

ASF: One of the interesting aspects of your work is your use of direct address. This somehow seems to *implicate* the audience. It's as if an ethical demand is placed upon them in terms of recognising their responsibility . . .

YF: Precisely . . . This is different from the protest theatre of the eighties, which implicated through direct and dynamic accusation. I recall watching *Woza Albert*,[2] at The Market Theatre when I was a teenager. The anger was powerful and compelling for the time . . . necessary to mobilise. But testimonial theatre – by confiding in its audience – creates intimacy and accountability with the audience.

ASF: Can you tell me a little bit about your creative process?

YF: Piles of notes from weeks of intensive interviews and memory recall exercises offer unstructured material from which I then develop a trajectory, script dialogue and shape the narrative to make the story cohesive, true and moving. When gathering raw material, the subject cannot be looking at how to create a compelling narrative. They should not be in a conscious act of creation. That is my job. The survivor needs to be facilitated in offering random, chaotic raw truth – from which I then craft a scripted text. I will then work with the cast to retain natural speech patterns, vocabulary and vernacular language so that the authenticity of the individual's use of language is honoured. We collaboratively layer the work in this way.

ASF: When I was reading your plays I thought of a quote that I'd read in J.M. Coetzee's novel *Disgrace*, where he says that the story of South Africa should not be reduced to the English Language. How important is the inclusion of different languages in your work?

YF: Incredibly important. There's an intrinsic connection between the psyche of the country and the languages that people speak. The denigrating of indigenous language through colonialism is a psychic violence. It was central to the work that authentic language was present in the scripts. When the actor then breaks from vernacular, turns to the audience and speaks in English, the audience no longer takes this for granted, but is aware that this storyteller is reaching out in a language imposed upon them . . . which is a profoundly generous act.

Linden's and Farber's work throws open crucial ethical questions for Applied Theatre practitioners and theatre makers, such as: how does the playwright negotiate the 'truth' of the story and the dramatic demands of playwriting? What kind of reciprocal relationship exists between the individual (whose story is being told) and the creative process?

To tell one's story to another is, as Farber indicates, a profoundly generous act and furthermore to be entrusted with this story places great responsibility on the theatre maker and subsequently the audience member. As Shoshana Felman points out, testimony is a 'radically unique, noninterchangeable and solitary burden' (Felman and Laub 1992: 3). It belongs only to the witness, it is a story that is theirs and theirs alone. To enter into the confidence of this testimony draws the listener into an *ethical* relationship with the other. 'Ethical', because: to become a listener or an audience member of testimony, is to encounter what Emmanuel Levinas describes as the 'infinite responsibility to the other person' (Critchley 2002: 6). In other words, for Levinas, whose own philosophical outlook was formed through the traumatic events of the *Shoah*, our responsibility for another person can never be constituted on the basis of our desire to comprehend the totality of the other. Such a desire always effectively entails a reduction of the other to the bounds of self knowledge, effacing the other's radical exteriority.

To create a playtext that performs or mediates the testimony of the other, is to bear responsibility for that testimony and for the other. As we have seen, testimony is unique, it is the witness's story and as such responds to Arendt's primordial question, 'who are you?' (Arendt 1998: 178). The act of giving testimony is in effect an ethical demand: listen to me, hear my story, let me tell you what I have encountered. As custodian and listener to this testimony, the playwright (and subsequently the audience) is called upon to open themselves to the testimony of the other. This 'call' has less to do with empathy, understanding and comprehension; rather, it has the character of an ethical demand, which in being listened to, is also acknowledged. In other words, the correlate of bearing witness (the act of testimony) is the requirement that we – the listener - should open ourselves up to the unknowable and radical difference, the 'alterity', as Levinas puts it, of the other.

In the performance of testimony the language of the other performs that which exceeds experience and is unknowable. To hear this testimony is, to some degree, to enter into the traumatic in a way that is immediate and unsettling. For testimony, as we have seen, is not an ordered, coherent series of events, it is incomplete, fragmentary; revealing an encounter that lies beyond explanation and comprehension. For that reason, the performance of testimony should perhaps always remain unsettling and never reassuring. This is because it brings us before our own vulnerability in the face of the incommunicable and allows us to glimpse the limits of our understanding of the world and our place within it. In order to respond to the demands of testimony we must open ourselves up to this unsettling encounter with the other. In this way we allow ourselves to be disturbed by the world that the testifier opens up before us – an encounter which perhaps resonates with what Levinas describes as 'the restlessness of the same disturbed by the other' (Levinas 1998: 25).

Bibliography

Agamben, G. (1999) *Remnants of Auschwitz: The Witness and the Archive*, New York: Zone Books.
Arendt, H. (1998) *The Human Condition*, Chicago: University of Chicago Press.
Critchley, S. and Bernasconi, R. (eds) (2002) *The Cambridge Companion to Levinas*, Cambridge: Cambridge University Press.
Farber, Y. (2008) *Theatre as Witness: Three Testimonial Plays from South Africa*, London: Oberon Books.
Felman, S. and Laub, D. (1992) *Testimony: Crises of Witnessing in Literature, Psychoanalysis and History*, New York: Routledge.
Freud, S. (1985) *On Metapsychology: The Theory of Psychoanalysis*, Buckinghamshire: Pelican Books.
Levi, P. (1979) *If This is A Man: The Truce*, London: Abacus Books.

Levinas, E. (1998) *Otherwise than Being or Beyond Essence* (trans. A Lingis), Pittsburgh, PA: Duquesne University Press.

Linden, S. (2004) *I Have Before Me A Remarkable Document Given to Me by a Young Woman from Rwanda*, London: Aurora Metro Press.

Linden, S. (2005) *Crocodile Seeking Refuge*, London: Aurora Metro Press.

Notes

1   See *Ice and Fire*'s website for more information (www.iceandfire.co.uk).
2   *Woza Albert* by Percy Mtwa, Mbongeni Ngema and Barney Simon was first performed at the Market Theatre, Johannesburg, in 1981.

Chapter 17

James Thompson

THE ENDS OF APPLIED THEATRE
Incidents of cutting and chopping

Q: Did any incident occur while you were with these others?
A: An incident occurred of cutting and chopping.
> (Jaganathan Uttamanathan to court dealing with
> Bindunuwewa massacre)

The rehabilitation program went well. The government even used it as a showpiece.
> (Sri Lankan Observer 27 October, 2000)

THIS CHAPTER REPORTS ON AN applied theatre project in a child soldiers' rehabilitation centre in the village of Bindunuwewa, Sri Lanka, that was followed some three months later by a massacre – *an incident of cutting and chopping*. The nature of the applied theatre programme is explained in my book *Applied Theatre* (Thompson 2003) but to give context to this discussion it is worth noting that the programme was supported by UNICEF and the Sri Lankan government's National Youth Services Council. It took place in two parts. In July 2000 I ran a training course in applied theatre techniques for the staff of the rehabilitation centre (teachers and trainers) and then immediately afterwards I ran workshops for nearly one week with the young men and boys in the centre. This was jointly planned and run with Sri Lankan colleagues from an applied theatre network called Big Circle. The focus was on a range of theatre games and improvisation exercises leading to a performance for people living and working in the camp. While some of the young men did talk about their personal experiences in the conflict and in a range of armed groups, this was not the concern or the theme of the theatre work.

The argument presented in this chapter starts from the end of my book on applied theatre where, on briefly mentioning this massacre, I asked whether '[t]his is the place where it ends?' (Thompson 2003: 197). This chapter takes on this question in an attempt to reveal the complex web in which this initiative was caught. It seeks to unravel the project to examine whether it should in fact mark an end of applied theatre.

An international incident

Sri Lanka has experienced a civil conflict lasting over twenty years in which one of the main protagonists, the Liberation Tigers of Tamil Eelam (LTTE), has been frequently accused by international bodies of actively recruiting child soldiers. UNICEF has been at the forefront of these accusations although in recent years it has been working closely with the LTTE to support programmes through which recruits under the age of 18 are released back to their families. In June 2004, however, the cooperation appeared to have broken down when UNICEF once again called on the LTTE to halt child recruitment from Tamil areas. A press statement from 26 June 2004 announced:

> After promising signs in April that the LTTE was taking seriously its pledge to release the children in its ranks, recruitment has been accelerated in recent weeks, including of children under the age of 18.
>
> (UNICEF 2004)

While reports differ as to the exact number of children under the age of 18 who currently serve with the LTTE, it is clear that international attention to the existence of these young people has been one area in which the Tigers have gained notoriety. As Frances Harrison, the former BBC reporter to Sri Lanka notes, 'allegations of child recruitment have dogged the Tamil Tiger rebels for years . . . so much so that they have become a powerful propaganda tool used against them by the Sri Lankan military and other opponents' (Harrison 2003).

This emphasis on propaganda is significant for this first area of discussion. The 'Tamil struggle' is waged very directly in the international arena with Tamil diasporic organisations, particularly in Europe and Canada, driving fundraising campaigns for the Tamil people based on a sense of the injustices committed by the Sri Lankan state. On the other side the international community has listened to the case made by Sri Lankan government officials for the LTTE to be proscribed as a terrorist organisation – partly because of its continuing use of children in active service. Although already a banned terrorist organisation in the UK and the USA, the LTTE joined a European-wide list on 30 May 2006. Part of the credit for the action taken by the international community has been given to the former Foreign Secretary Lakshman Kadirgamar, who came to international attention for his campaign to starve the LTTE of funds. The existence of child soldiers remained a powerful *propaganda tool* in his work on this matter.

It is possible to argue therefore that the child-soldier centre in Bindunuwewa had a function beyond the immediate boundaries of the camp. It was necessary as a concrete example of the existence of child soldiers and a double-edged proof of the abusive nature of the Tigers and the humanity of the Sri Lankan government. Kadirgamar spoke of the '[a]bominable crimes . . . being committed against young

Tamil children' by the LTTE and the camp thus gave him a living example of them (Kadirgamar 2000). The camp – *and perhaps all that went on in it* – performed a particular task and must therefore be understood within a geopolitical enterprise undertaken principally by the foreign secretary to cut off international support for the LTTE. What happened inside the centre was important insomuch that it maintained or at least did not disturb the smooth running of that wider performance.

The international pressure on the LTTE's child-soldier recruitment was directed by the Sri Lankan government and supported by the 'non-political' UNICEF. While I have no problem condemning child-soldier recruitment, the Sri Lankan government can have no monopoly on virtue in the civil war. The Bindunuwewa centre however provided a site from which the good will of the government could be proved in international arenas and the existence of foreign consultants (me) in liaison with international agencies (UNICEF) running programmes in this centre, further strengthened the impression that the government was part of the international mainstream pursuing decent projects under both a Human Rights and a Trauma Relief banner.

The anthropologist Alex Argenti-Pillen in her work on the effect of International NGOs on local discourses of violence in Sri Lanka has examined how in a complex, conflict-ridden political arena many projects seem to avoid or ignore context in their justifications of their activities. Her attention is focused principally on what she names as the 'trauma industry' that has come to dominate the programmes of agencies such as UNICEF. I would argue that the practice emanating from that approach, which allows theatre, for example, to be framed as 'helping people heal through the telling of stories or expressing their pain', also becomes divorced from this wider environment. Agenti-Pillen explains how 'elites in Colombo have thereby acquired a paradigm by means of which they can discuss violence without having to mention its context' (Argenti-Pillen 2003: 186). This I believe is what had happened with the applied theatre project in Bindunuwewa. In allowing the discourse of 'healing' or 'trauma' and at times 'human rights' to frame and explain the activities, less attention was paid to the local/international political machinations that permit projects to exist and gain legitimacy. Whether the 'trauma discourse' or the 'human rights paradigm' are the most appropriate or not for applied theatre is of course relevant, but here my point is that in conflict situations these discourses operate (and are manipulated) at a macro level within historically and culturally particular parameters. They are operationalised; they are made to perform in order to ensure the maintenance of certain forms of power and control or within the competitions of power that exist in many crisis situations. Since applied theatre operates primarily in sites that are bound by historically structured conflicts; whether that be prison, classroom, hospital, camp or war zone; attention to what I am here calling the *political* becomes vital. It is not good enough to understand the discourses that operate within a particular location: we must understand who is using them, for what ends and in what circumstances.

A showpiece

When the Officer in Charge of the camp, Captain Abeyratna, came down to the camp edge to help disperse a crowd that had gathered outside the camp the night before the massacre, he is reported to have said to the police, 'this is an international question; get rid of those people' (Abeyratna 2000). Although it is impossible to understand the exact reason for him combining the mention of an international context with the demand to the police to move on a mob, the coupling of the two does suggest that he was aware of the wider significance of his work. The local disquiet interrupted the international appearance that perhaps it was his job to maintain. In the end the disturbance was not quietened and by the morning many more people were clamouring at the camp's boundary. By early morning they had stormed into the grounds and within less than one hour 24 young men were left dead from cut, burn and crucially gun shot wounds. Although the crowd were largely identified as 'villagers', there were 60 police present who have been viewed as complicit to some degree in most reports on the massacre (Keenan 2005a, 2005b).

What I want to discuss here is the *show* of the camp. All contexts in which applied theatre projects take place show themselves in some way and the organisation and reception of that show is important for understanding the problems faced by particular projects. The Sri Lankan Observer described Bindunuwewa as a 'showpiece' and the Captain's awareness of its significance indicates that one vital audience for that show was international. Its priorities were outside the boundaries of the village and the activities inside the camp were perhaps only important in the degree to which they did little to disturb that projected image. Marginally contributing to it would be fine, even being invisible would be all right but the smooth relaying of a broader mission was to be untroubled. The theatre project thus was either to conform to the image of rehabilitating surrendered child soldiers or remain a trouble-free *private* activity; one that did not interfere with the wider performance.

However, Kadirgamar's use of the camp was within a contested international terrain that competed to interpret the rationale for the incarceration of these Tamil youth. There were many other readings based on a range of historical and cultural positions that offered radically different visions of the camp's purpose. These were both international but crucially also local. It is these more local interpretations that I believe were forgotten by the policy makers and could be partly responsible for the massacre. The Captain's pleading for the crowd to be dispersed illustrates a literal moment when different versions of the camp's purpose collided. The Captain wanted the emerging angry response from the local community to disappear — not to compete and thus complicate the international version that he was entrusted to maintain.

In a return visit to Bindunuwewa village in 2006, a number of local people were interviewed[1] about the massacre five years previously. There were many different memories but a dominant theme was the fear that the Tigers were now in the hills above them plotting their revenge on the community below. There was a clear sense of a deep fear at the power and reach of the Tigers. It is not the job of this chapter to deal in detail with the differing versions of the causes of the massacre, but it is frequently noted that a disturbance within the camp on the previous night led a number of local people to fear that the 'Tigers' in the camp were about to come flooding out of the centre and kill them. The fear of the Tigers, a product of years of civil conflict during which the LTTE have been accused of a number of massacres and have been subsequently demonised in the majority Sinhala community's press, meant that for many an attack on the centre was viewed as defensive. Clearly there was manipulation of that sense of vulnerability and there was massive negligence (if not co-operation) from the police, but hundreds of previously non-homicidal individuals did approach the camp that morning. To take up work tools and engage in *chopping and cutting* means that deeply held structures of belief were somehow threatened by the existence of the camp or news of the disturbance. The anthropologist Bruce Kapferer has analysed 'the interface between nationalist mythologizations drawn from textual sources and popular action' (1988: xi) in relation to Sri Lankan violence, and although the exact mechanisms for this connection are outside the scope of this chapter, clearly a set of meanings and processes were generated by the camp, and particular incidents within it, that provoked a certain terrible response. These readings of the camp created an 'interface' with the local community that was both outside the control of the supranational picture and 'showpiece' that others were trying to sustain.

The camp had a number of different uses before being transferred to a centre for the training of surrendered child soldiers in the late 1990s. The local, predominantly Sinhala, village had varied responses to the arrival of the Tamil youth in their area. In most reports there are discussions of the good relations between camp and village with tales of young Tamil internees working in the village or helping out locals with a variety of tasks. However, within these reports there is also an undercurrent of disquiet with indications of a fear of possible relations between the young men and local young women and also the availability of services (particularly water) to the camp that were not made available to the village. The showpiece thus appears to have *shown* the local community a number of competing visions of the relations between Tamil people and Sinhala. Linked to the international display was a humanist discourse that insisted that Sinhala and Tamil people had no problem with each other and many people in the area would urge this interpretation. However, competing was the view that the government was more preoccupied with helping Tamil 'terrorists' than supporting the impoverished Sinhala villagers. This discourse also directed its criticism to the national government that was seen to be more concerned to maintain its international image than fighting the Tigers vigorously. In a sense the political position that argued that the national politicians were too soft on the Tigers and were too concerned about international opinion found an easy symbol in the existence of the camp. A fairly insecure institution located above a village became a shortcut symbol for the discrimination *against the Sinhala* that was at odds with the international message hoped for in the showpiece.

Once again the theatre project is caught up in these different positions. While the staff at the camp were at pains to emphasise the degree to which the young men were welcomed into the village, the post-massacre analyses indicate that this was the product of a hoped for local *show* of the camp and perhaps less than accurate vision of how it played out in different communities of interest in the region. The belief that the Tamils were treated favourably (the access to water), that there was more care to their Human Rights than local Sinhalese (the fact they received rehabilitation, when returning Sri Lankan army recruits got little support) was a mobilising rhetoric which the knowledge of UNICEF's programmes (including the theatre project) could have sustained. An applied theatre project *behind closed doors* therefore cannot claim that it was only an event within the parameters of the camp. It may have been benign; it did nothing that made the massacre more likely; but at worst it could have contributed (however slightly) to the emerging hostility to the young men in the centre. Benign might be fine but I would argue, undoubtedly with the benefit of hindsight, that this is not good enough for the aspirations of applied theatre practice.

Therefore, although asking 'which show are we part of?' is a vital part of the critical examination of applied theatre practice, it is not sufficient. When considering applied theatre projects in complex situations we might be able to discern the different operating, competing or complementing positions that condition the context but we cannot subtract ourselves from one in a hope that we can be singularly attached to another. If, for the sake of argument, we had asserted that we were there specifically to draw attention to the Human Rights abuses of the Tamil Tigers, the work could still have been claimed by other competing discourses. Within the region it could have proved a Sinhala nationalist position that their rights were marginalised and in the international arena it could have confirmed that the government was dutifully obeying human rights norms. We were however problematically silent about what we were doing because there were few opportunities for speaking about the work. I now feel that articulating a clear position would have not necessarily prevented the co-option of this practice into some dubious and ultimately murderous positions. Many of the rationales for the practice, for example drawing on trauma relief or human rights logics, could be co-opted to support the decisions that left a large group of young people vulnerable on this hillside in the first place.

In his seminal chapter on the massacre, Alan Keenan notes that 'almost as soon as the attack was over, a number of competing narratives and explanations began to vie for supremacy in the public sphere, feeding off the lack of clear information available from trustworthy sources' (Keenan 2005a: 21, 2005b). I have emphasised here that this process was also happening in the period leading up to the massacre with a range of actors (from government ministers to the local Buddhist high priest) contributing. The argument here is that applied theatre projects frequently take place in sites that produce and are produced by narratives competing in the public sphere. Perhaps in deliberately seeking to work with refugees, prisoners, troubled teens, the disabled or the elderly we are seeking out those places in which that competition is most acute and highly contested. If we accept this *applied theatre tendency*, my point is that the relationship between the *vying in the public sphere* and the actual work of applied theatre is not sufficiently explicit.

Applied theatre as strategy or tactic?

The necessity for a more carefully planned and deliberate development of the interrelation between the public and private aspects of applied theatre is not only a call for the private practice to have a correlating act of 'public' explanation or advocacy. The relationship between the private and public is not the dichotomy that this implies. In contested situations applied theatre needs to consider the complex interrelation of the private and public and understand the shifts between tactical and strategic performance practice. According to De Certeau *tactics* are the actions that take place within situations and cannot operate over and above the moment. So they are 'ways of operating' – everyday practices such as 'clever tricks, knowing how to get away with things' (De Certeau 1984: xix). *Strategies* on the other hand are acts where 'a subject of will and power ... can be isolated from an "environment"' (ibid.). Strategic acts are thus those that seek to intervene in a situation 'with an exterior distinct from it' (ibid.). Many applied theatre projects, when working with marginalised or oppressed communities, hope they can generate strategic action with that community when in fact, because of the structured position they occupy, they can only operate at the level of tactics. Applied theatre projects might instil in participants rich and complex means of coping and subtly resisting the worst of a context, but rarely are they able to equip people to transcend it. In not noticing how many communities are held in cultural, spatial and temporal settings from which a strategic vision of change is very difficult, applied theatre may be making those communities more vulnerable. The celebratory theatre workshop, the problem-solving role play, and the forum theatre session in most applied theatre circumstances are therefore *tactical* performance practices that might provide immediate means of living through and dealing with the present but cannot claim that they structurally alter a situation. As De Certeau claims, what a tactic wins 'it does not keep' (ibid.).

My argument here is that, because applied theatre operates in situations that are governed by both tactical and strategic actions, operating solely at the level of the tactical and private means that our private acts can be subsumed into the public strategies of others. Jaganathan Uttamanathan as an arrested and accused villager from Bindunuwewa could only use the tactic of minimisation in his response to the questions about the incident during the court case. Calling it 'cutting and chopping' was a tactic within the structure of a judicial process. However, Kadirgamar through his position of Foreign Secretary of Sri Lanka could operate strategically by trying to transform international law that put pressure on the LTTE. Our private activity became a small part of his strategy because it had no clear public or *strategic* site of operation itself. One of the causes of the massacre within these terms could be that the young men and boys in demanding that they be given more assurances about their release[2] started to realise the limits of the tactics open to them. They were in a position from which, to echo De Certeau's words, they could not win. Whether we like it or not however, as guests of a UN agency, my Sri Lankan colleagues and I had some access to a more public world in which, with the benefit of hindsight, we should have engaged.

I make no claim to know the shape of these 'public/strategic' projects. If my criticism of the theatre project in Bindunuwewa is that it operated solely in the realm of the tactical and that it thus gave up the realm of the strategic, it follows that perhaps a connected, simultaneous strategic *more public* performance response is needed. While I am not urging a return to grandstanding 'political' theatre, I am arguing for new alliances that might interweave the strategic and the tactical: for some way of linking more explicitly the care and resilience hoped for in those private projects with the assertively strident possibilities of public performance. Bindunuwewa was caught into a web of powerful strategic performances that 'vied for supremacy' after the massacre and sought to use the 'showpiece' prior to it. These manipulations, provocations and half-truths needed to be acknowledged, revealed and questioned. This is a task in which some forms of public performance might be able to engage. This is not to reject the act of creating the participatory, tactical project with the young men, but perhaps in the absence of careful research into the wider performances and an explicit engagement with them, our project could be one that left them vulnerable.

Throughout this chapter I have used the word 'performances' to describe in particular Kadirgamar's use of his camp showpiece and also referred to the camp itself performing for certain constituent groups. My argument is that because this institution and the policies that permitted its construction performed in different ways for certain audiences, public performance practice might be a way to reveal how those discursive and institutional performances operated. This echoes the former University of Belgrade theatre professor Dragan Klaic who urged that 'artists focus not on the unfolding tragedy itself but on the ways it is being presented, reported, perceived and metaphorized by other dominant discourses' (Klaic 2002: 160). While it might be a tall order to claim that this is the job of those applied theatre practitioners whose art lies in working creatively with groups and communities, without that wider focus, I believe, applied theatre is liable to be an easy target for the strategic manipulations of others.

Perhaps the alliance to make – or the barrier to break – is between the applied theatre practitioners and those performance artists who specialise in public spectaculars, site-specific interventions and transgressive critical acts. And a conversation between what urgently need to be allied fields of practice will help applied theatre people remember the potential of intervening publicly (or more strategically) and perhaps allow performance practitioners to experience the power of intervening privately (or more tactically). Bindunuwewa and the subsequent tragedy was thus, for me, the end of a narrow vision of applied theatre, and a demand for a form of enmeshed public/private/tactical/strategic performance practice . . . whatever it may be called.

Bibliography

Abeyratna, Y.K. (2000) Transcript of an interview with Captain Abeyratna, the officer in charge of the Bindunuwewa camp, taken on 6 November 2000 at Police CID HQ, Bandarawela (grey literature).

Argenti-Pillen, A. (2003) *Masking Terror: How Women Contain Violence in Southern Sri Lanka*, Philadelphia, PA: University of Pennsylvania Press.

De Certeau, M. (1984) *The Practice of Everyday Life*, London: University of California Press.

Harrison, F. (2003) 'Analysis: Sri Lanka's Child Soldiers', available at http://news.bbc.co.uk/1/hi/world/south_asia/2713035.stm (accessed 4 October 2006).

Kadirgamar, L. (2000) 'Address to Winnipeg Conference', available at www.satp.org/satporgtp/countries/shrilanka/document/papers/lakshmans_address_in_winnipeg_canada.htm (accessed 1 September 2006).

Kapferer, B. (1988) *Legends of People/Myths of State: Violence, Intolerance and Political Culture in Sri Lanka and Australia*, Washington, DC and London: Smithsonian Institution Press.

Keenan, A. (2005a) 'Making Sense of Bindunawewa – from Massacre to Acquittal', *Law & Society Trust* 15 (212): 19–42.

Keenan, A. (2005b) 'No Peace, No War: Have International Donors Failed Sri Lanka's Most Vulnerable?' *Boston Review*, available at www.bostonreview.net/BR30.3/keenan.html (accessed 16 July, 2008).

Klaic, D. (2002) 'The Crisis of Theatre? The Theatre of Crisis!', in M. Delgado and C. Svich (eds), *Theatre in Crisis: Performance Manifestos for a New Century*, Manchester: Manchester University Press, pp. 19–42.

Thompson, J. (2003) *Applied Theatre: Bewilderment and Beyond*, Bern: Peter Lang.

UNICEF (2004) 'Children Being Caught Up in Recruitment Drive in North East', available at www.unicef.org/media/media_21990.html (accessed 4 October, 2006).

For more information on the Bindunuwewa massacre please see:

The Law and Society Trust Review (2000) *The Bindunuwewa Massacre: Interim Report of the Human Rights Commission* 11 (158).

Presidential Commission of Inquiry (2000) *Report of the Presidential Commission of Inquiry into Incidents that Took Place at Bindunuwewa Rehabilitation Centre, Bandarawela,* 25 October.

University Teachers for Human Rights (Jaffna) (2005) *Sri Lanka, Special Report No. 19: The Curse of Impunity Part I – Bindunuwewa, the Thin End of the Wedge of Impunity.*

Notes

1   I was accompanied by colleagues involved in a new performance project that is being developed in response to the massacre.
2   This apparently is the source of the disturbance the night before the massacre.

PART 4

Participation

Chapter 18

Sheila Preston

INTRODUCTION TO
PARTICIPATION

FOR SOME TIME NOW THE rhetoric of participation has had currency across a broad spectrum of social and public agencies including education, development and health, and applied theatre practice in these areas. It is widely understood, now seen as 'common sense', that encouraging participation and involvement by people in their own developmental change, whether these be changes in knowledge, attitude, behaviour and health practices seems a pragmatic and effective pedagogic strategy whilst, seemingly, being an ethical one. Drama can be enjoyable, involving and dynamic. It demands its participants to be active and collectively creative and for this reason can be a useful medium for luring people, even those unused to drama, into participation. For this reason the participative features of theatre, performance and creativity in general are increasingly called upon to foster involvement by people in different settings and to meet various developmental, educational and change agendas.

Nonetheless, the authors in this section reveal that an aim of participation, even if liberatory in intention and highly desirable, is far from trouble-free in practice; to achieve genuine participation is in itself complex and difficult amidst the myriad of agendas, power relations and competing ideological interests rife in most projects and settings.

Gramsci's seminal writing on hegemony offers a lens through which to analyse, critically, common sense notions of participation. Gramsci describes hegemony as: 'The "spontaneous" consent given by the great masses of the population to the general direction imposed on social life by the dominant fundamental group' (Chapter 20, this volume). In this way, harnessing the consent of a group through the communal spontaneity of 'participation' might carry a 'useful' hegemonic function in society. The seductive 'feeling' of participating and 'joining in' with others is less a neutral or benign act but, rather, manipulation into compliance with a social order.

Compliance, variable as its cultural context, can potentially serve a variety of interests, such as a project needing to meet a quota of participants for funding purposes or a government wanting more popularity. Key to hegemony is the seemingly willing participation of a community in carrying out or complying with the wishes of the dominant ideology even if it seems not to be in their interests. We see this in the extreme in the orchestration of genocides where communities have participated in killing their neighbours.

The meaning of participation and its 'usefulness' (for what? or for whom?) depends on one's ideological and political standpoint. Participation therefore can serve to reproduce the hegemony or run counter to it.

For Freire and other radical and grassroots activists, enabling collective partici- pation is an intrinsic part of the transformative, counter hegemonic intentions of a project (we say 'intentions' as the outcome or 'reality' may not end up transformative or counter hegemonic at all). The facilitator or artist creates a relationship with participants which Freire describes as co-intentional:

> Teachers and students (leadership and people), co-intent on reality, are both Subjects, not only in the task of unveiling that reality, and thereby coming to know it critically, but in the task of re-creating that knowledge. As they attain this knowledge of reality through common reflection and action, they discover themselves as its permanent re-creators. In this way, the presence of the oppressed in the struggle for their liberation will be what it should be: not pseudo participation, but committed involvement.
>
> (1996: 51)

Although facilitating co-intentional participation might be concerned with enabling the participants' genuine ownership of the work and their critical engage- ment with reality, and supporting their potential transformative action, this may conflict with the starting point of those participating in the first place. These participants, like the facilitator/artist, are themselves embroiled in culture and its influences and so may support value systems that serve to maintain the hegemony rather than transform it. The facilitator/artist needs then to decide if their 'participatory project' extends to supporting the participants wishes in maintaining existing power structures even if they are unequal or problematic in other ways.

As well as being aware of our own ideological 'limits' as practitioners of applied theatre, it is worth exploring how the participatory possibilities of applied theatre practice may be limited by the 'model' it proposes for itself. The following 'typology of participation', arising out of the field of participatory development and the emerging practice of Participatory Learning and Action (PLA) which has been acutely aware of the possibilities and limitations of participation, illustrates a range of possible participative relationships in any project or part of a project:

1   *Passive participation.* People participate by being told what is going to happen or what has already happened.

2   *Participation in information gathering.* People participate by answering questions posed by extractive researchers using questionnaire surveys or similar approaches. People do not have the opportunity to influence proceedings.

3   *Participation by consultation.* External people listen to the views of local people. External professionals define both problems and solutions, and may modify these in the light of people's responses.

4   *Participation for material incentives.* People participate by providing resources, for example labour, in return for food, cash or other material incentives. People have no stake in prolonging activities when the incentives end.

5   *Functional participation.* People participate by forming groups to meet pre-determined objectives related to the project. Such involvement tends to occur after major decisions have been made. These institutions tend to be dependent on external initiators and facilitators, but may become self-reliant.

6   *Interactive participation.* People participate in joint analysis, which leads to action plans and the formation of new local institutions or the strengthening of existing ones. Groups take over local decisions, and so people have a stake in maintaining structures or practices.

7   *Self-mobilisation.* People participate by taking initiatives independent of external institutions to change systems. They develop contacts with external organisations for resources and technical advice they need, but retain control over how resources are used.

(Pretty *et al*. 1995: 61)

It is not too difficult to see how such a typology might be employed to critically interrogate applied theatre forms and the scope of projects in the field, their relationship to their participants, and theatre models that exist 'for', 'by', 'with' or 'about' their communities. Such a critical analysis needs to happen with an understanding of context. The well-used strategy of forum theatre, intended as a poetics of the oppressed (see Boal, Chapter 19, this volume), could as effectively serve to enable 'functional participation' via a message-based theatre with perfunctory, predetermined participation and little opportunity for community analysis. In its more radical application a forum theatre performance might enable community analysis (the content of which having been arrived at through a participatory process) and thus leave open the potential for a community group to become 'self mobilising.' Whether an applied theatre practice allows for the more radical possibilities of participation within a project depends on the ideological intentions of the project (and the interests being served in it), the scope of the work and the openness of the creative strategies offered. Lastly but no less important: if genuine participation exists through co-intentionality, the relationship nurtured by the facilitator or artist is crucial and therefore their sensitivity and skill in working 'with' participants and enabling democratic ownership of creative mediums is key.

Bibliography

Freire, P. (1996) *Pedagogy of the Oppressed*, Harmondsworth: Penguin.

Pretty, J.N., Guijit, I., Thompson, J. and Scoones, I. (1995) *Participatory Learning and Action: A Trainer's Guide*, London: IIED.

Chapter 19

Augusto Boal
(trans. C. and M.-O. Leal McBride)

THEATRE OF THE OPPRESSED

Theatre of the Oppressed (trans. C. and M.-O. Leal McBride), Pluto Press and TCG (1979, 2000), excerpt from pp. 120–42.

Experiments with the People's Theater in Peru

THESE EXPERIMENTS WERE carried out in August of 1973, in the cities of Lima and Chiclayo, with the invaluable collaboration of Alicia Saço, within the program of the Integral Literacy Operation (*Operación Alfabetización Integral* [ALFIN]), directed by Alfonso Lizar-zaburu and with the participation, in the various sectors, of Estela Linares, Luis Garrido Lecca, Ramón Vilcha, and Jesús Ruiz Durand. The method used by ALFIN in the literacy program was, of course, derived from Paulo Freire.

[. . .]

The training of the educators, chosen from the same regions where literacy was to be taught, was developed in four stages according to the special characteristics of each social group:

1   *barrios* (neighborhoods) or new villages, corresponding to our slums (*cantegril, favela*, . . .);
2   rural areas;
3   mining areas;
4   areas where Spanish is not the first language, which embrace 40 percent of the population. Of this 40 percent, half is made up of bilingual citizens who learned Spanish after acquiring fluency in their own indigenous language. The other half speaks no Spanish.

[. . .] What I propose to do here is to relate my personal experience as a participant in the theatrical sector and to outline the various experiments we made in considering the theatre as language, capable of being utilized by any person with or without artistic talent. We tried to show how the theatre can be placed at the service of the oppressed, so that they can express themselves and so that, by using this new language, they can also discover new concepts.

In order to understand this *poetics of the oppressed* one must keep in mind its main objective: to change the people – 'spectators,' passive beings in the theatrical phenomenon – into subjects, into actors, transformers of the dramatic action. [. . .] Aristotle proposes a poetics in which the spectator delegates power to the dramatic character so that the latter may act and think for him. Brecht proposes a poetics in which the spectator delegates power to the character who thus acts in his place but the spectator reserves the right to think for himself, often in opposition to the character. In the first place, a 'catharsis' occurs; in the second, an awakening of critical consciousness. But the *poetics of the oppressed* focuses on the action itself: the spectator delegates no power to the character (or actor) either to act or think in his place; on the contrary, he himself assumes the protagonist role, changes the dramatic action, tries out solutions, discusses plans for change – in short, trains himself for real action. In this case, perhaps the theatre is not revolutionary in itself, but this is surely a rehearsal for revolution. The liberated spectator, as a whole person launches into action. No matter that the action is fictional; what matters is that it is action.

I believe that all the truly revolutionary theatrical groups should transfer to the people the means of production in the theatre so that the people themselves may utilize them. The theatre is a weapon, and it is the people who should wield it.

But how is this transference to be achieved? As an example I cite what was done by Estele Linares, who was in charge of the photography section of the ALFIN plan.

What would be the old way to utilize photography in a literacy project? Without a doubt, it would be to photograph things, streets, people, landscapes, stores, etc., then show the pictures and discuss them. But who would take these pictures? The instructors, group leaders, or coordinators. On the other hand, if we are going to give the people the means of production, it is necessary to hand over to them, in this case, the camera. This is what was done in ALFIN. The educators would give a camera to the members of the study group, would teach them how to use it and propose to them the following:

> We are going to ask you some questions. For this purpose we will speak
> in Spanish. And you must answer us. But you cannot speak in Spanish:
> you must speak in 'photography'. We ask you things in Spanish, which
> is a language. You answer us in photography, which is also a language.

The questions asked were very simple, and the answers – this is, the photos – were discussed later by the group. For example when people were asked, where do you live, they responded with the following types of photo-answers:

A picture showing the interior of a shack. In Lima it rarely rains and for this reason the shacks are made of straw mats, instead of with more permanent walls and roofs.

In general they only have one room that serves as kitchen, living room, and bedroom; the families live in great promiscuity and very often young children watch their parents engage in sexual intercourse, which commonly leads to sexual acts between brothers and sisters as young as ten or eleven years old, simply as an imitation of their parents. A photo showing the interior of the shack fully answers the question, where do you live? Every element of the photo has a special meaning, which must be discussed by the group; the objects focussed on, the angle from which the picture is taken, the presence or absence of people in it, etc.

[. . .]

One day a man, in answer to the same question, took a picture of a child's face. Of course everyone thought that the man had made a mistake and repeated the question to him:

'You didn't understand; what we want is that you show us where you live. Take a picture and show us where you live. Any picture; the street, the house, the town, the river . . .'

'Here is my answer. Here is where I live.'

'But it's a child . . .'

'Look at his face: there is blood on it. This child, as all the others who live here, have their lives threatened by the rats that infest the whole bank of the river Rímac. They are protected by dogs that attack the rats and scare them away. But there was a mange epidemic and the city dog-catcher came around here catching lots of dogs and taking them away. This child had a dog who protected him. During the day his parents used to go to work and he was left with his dog. But now he doesn't have it any more. A few days ago, when you asked me where I lived, the rats had come while the child was sleeping and had eaten part of his nose. This is why there's so much blood on his face. Look at the picture; it is my answer. I live in a place where things like this still happen.'

I could write a novel about the children of the *barrios* along the river Rímac; but only photography, and no other language, could express the pain of that child's eyes, of those tears mixed with blood. And, as if the irony and outrage were not enough, the photograph was in Kodachrome, 'Made in U.S.A.'

The use of photography may help also to discover valid symbols for a whole community or social group. It happens many times that well intentioned theatrical groups are unable to communicate with a mass audience because they use symbols that are meaningless for that audience. A royal crown may symbolize power, but a symbol only functions as such if its meaning is shared. For some a royal crown may produce a strong impact and yet be meaningless for others.

What is exploitation? The traditional figure of Uncle Sam is, for many social groups throughout the world, the ultimate symbol of exploitation. It expresses to perfection the rapacity of 'Yankee' imperialism.

In Lima the people were also asked, what is exploitation? Many photographs showed the grocer; others the landlord; still others, some government office. On the other hand, a child answered with the picture of a nail on a wall. For him that was the perfect symbol of exploitation. Few adults understood it, but all the other children were in complete agreement that the picture expressed their feelings in relation to exploitation. The discussion explained why. The simplest work boys engage in at the age of five or six is shining shoes. Obviously, in the *barrios* where they live there are no shoes to shine and, for this reason, they must go to downtown Lima in order to find work. Their shine-boxes and other tools of the trade are of course an absolute necessity, and yet these boys cannot be carrying their equipment back and forth every day between work and home. So they must rent a nail on the wall of some place of business, whose owner charges them two or three *soles* per night and per nail. Looking at a nail, those children are reminded of oppression and their hatred of it; the sight of a crown, Uncle Sam, or Nixon, however, probably means nothing to them.

It is easy enough to give a camera to someone who has never taken a picture before, tell him how to focus it and which button to press. With this alone the means of photographic production are in the hands of that person. But what is to be done in the case of the theatre?

The means for producing a photograph are embodied in the camera, which is relatively easy to handle, but the means of producing theatre are made up of man himself, obviously more difficult to manage.

[. . .]

Third stage: the theater as language

This stage is divided into three parts, each one representing a different degree of direct participation of the spectator in the performance. The spectator is encouraged to intervene in the action, abandoning his condition of object and assuming fully the role of subject. The two preceding stages are preparatory, centering around the work of the participants with their own bodies. Now this stage focuses on the theme to be discussed and furthers the transition from passivity to action.

First degree: *Simultaneous dramaturgy*: This is the first invitation made to the spectator to intervene without necessitating his physical presence on the 'stage.'

Here it is a question of performing a short scene, of ten to twenty minutes, proposed by a local resident, one who lives in the *barrio*. The actors may improvise with the aid of a script prepared beforehand, as they may also compose the scene directly. In any case, the performance gains in theatricality if the person who proposed the theme is present in the audience. Having begun the scene, the actors develop it to the point at which the main problem reaches a crisis and needs a solution. Then the actors stop the performance and ask the audience to offer solutions. They improvise immediately all the suggested solutions, and the audience has the right to intervene, to correct the actions or words of the actors, who are obligated to comply strictly with these instructions from the audience. Thus, while the audience 'writes' the work the actors perform it simultaneously. The spectator's thoughts are discussed theatrically on stage with the help of the actors. All the solutions, suggestions, and opinions are revealed in theatrical form. The discussion itself need not simply take the form of words, but rather should be effected through all the other elements of theatrical expression as well.

[. . .]

This form of theater creates great excitement among the participants and starts to demolish the wall that separates actors from spectators. Some 'write' and others act almost simultaneously. The spectators feel that they can intervene in the action. The action ceases to be presented in a deterministic manner, as something inevitable, as Fate. Man is Man's fate. Thus Man-the-spectator is the creator of Man-the-character. Everything is subject to criticism, to rectification. All can be changed, and at a moment's notice: the actors must always be ready to accept, without protest, any proposed action; they must simply act it out, to give a live view of its consequences and drawback. Any spectator, by virtue of being a spectator, has the right to try his version – without censorship. The actor does not change his main function: he goes on being the interpreter. What changes is the object of his interpretation. If formerly he interpreted the solitary author locked in his study, to whom divine inspiration dictated a finished text, here on the contrary, he must interpret the mass audience, assembled in their local committees, societies of 'friends of the *barrio*,' groups of neighbors, schools, unions, peasant leagues, or whatever; he must give expression to the collective thought of men and women. The actor ceases to interpret the individual and starts to interpret the group, which is much more difficult and at the same time much more creative.

Second degree: *Image theater*: Here the spectator has to participate more directly. He is asked to express his views on a certain theme of common interest that the participants wish to discuss. The theme can be far-reaching, abstract – as, for example, imperialism – or it can be a local problem such as the lack of water, a common occurrence in almost all the *barrios*. The participant is asked to express his opinion, but without speaking, using only the bodies of the other participants and 'sculpting' with them a group of statues, in such a way that his opinions and feelings become evident. The participant is to use the bodies of the others as if he were a sculptor and the others were made of clay: he must determine the position of each body down to the most minute details of their facial expressions. He is not allowed to speak under any circumstances. The most that is permitted to him is to show with his own facial expressions what he wants the statue-spectator to do. After organizing this group of statues he is allowed to enter into a discussion with the other participants in order to determine if all agree with his 'sculpted' opinion. Modifications can be rehearsed: the spectator has the right to modify the statues in their totality or in some detail. When finally an image is arrived at that is the most acceptable to all, then the spectator-sculptor is asked to show the way he would like the given theme to be; that is, in the first grouping the *actual image* is shown, in the second the *ideal image*. Finally he is asked to show a *transitional image*, to show how it would be possible to pass from one reality to the other. In other words, how to carry out the change, the transformation, the revolution, or whatever term one wishes to use. Thus, starting with a grouping of 'statues' accepted by all as representative of a real situation, each one is asked to propose ways of changing it.

[. . .] A young woman, a literacy agent who lived in the village of Otuzco, was asked to explain, through a grouping of live images, what her home town was like.

In Otuzco, before the present Revolutionary Government, there was a peasant rebellion; the landlords (that no longer exist in Peru) imprisoned the leader of the rebellion, took him to the main square, and, in front of everyone, castrated him. The young woman from Otuzco composed the image of the castration, placing one of the participants on the ground while another pretended to be castrating him and still another held him from behind. Then at one side she placed a woman praying, on her knees, and at the other side a group of five men and women, also on their knees, with hands tied behind their backs. Behind the man being castrated, the young woman placed another participant in a position obviously suggestive of power and violence and, behind him, two armed men pointing their guns at the prisoner.

This was the image that person had of her village. A terrible, pessimistic, defeatist image, but also a true reflection of something that had actually taken place. Then the young woman was asked to show what she would want her village to be like. She modified completely the 'statues' of the group and regrouped them as people who worked in peace and loved each other – in short, a happy and contented, ideal Otuzco. Then came the third, and most important part, of this form of theater: how can one, starting with the actual image, arrive at the ideal image? How to bring about the change, the transformation, the revolution?

Here it was a question of giving an opinion, but without words. Each participant had the right to act as a 'sculptor' and to show how the grouping, or organization, could be modified through a reorganization of forces for the purpose of arriving at an ideal image. Each one expressed his opinion through imagery. Lively discussions arose, but without words. When one would exclaim, 'It's not possible like this; I think that . . .,' he was immediately interrupted: 'Don't say what you think; come and show it to us.' The participant would go and demonstrate physically, visually, his thought, and the discussion would continue. In this particular case the following variations were observed:

1)   When a young woman from the interior was asked to form the image of change, she would never change the image of the kneeling woman, signifying clearly that she did not see in that woman a potential force for revolutionary change. Naturally the young women identified themselves with that feminine figure and, since they could not perceive themselves as possible protagonists of the revolution, they left unmodified the image of the kneeling woman. On the other hand, when the same thing was asked of a girl from Lima, she, being more 'liberated,' would start off by changing precisely that image with which she identified herself. This experiment was repeated many times and always produced the same results, without variation. Undoubtedly the different patterns of action represent not chance occurrence but the sincere, visual expression of the ideology and psychology of the participants. The young women from Lima always modified the image: some would make the woman clasp the figure of the castrated man, others would prompt the woman to fight against the castrator, etc. Those from the interior did little more than allow the woman to lift her hands in prayer.

2)   All the participants who believed in the Revolutionary Government would start by modifying the armed figures in the background: they changed the two men who were aiming their guns at the victim so that they would then aim at the powerful figure in the center or at the castrators themselves. On the other hand, when a participant did not have the same faith in his government, he would alter all figures except the armed ones.

3)   The people who believed in magical solutions or in a 'change of conscience' on the part of the exploiting classes would start by modifying the castrators – viewing them in effect as changing of their own volition – as well as the powerful figure in the center, who would become regenerated. By contrast, those who did not believe in this form of social change would first alter the kneeling men, making them assume a fighting posture, attacking the oppressors.

4)   One of the young women, besides showing the transformations to be the work of the kneeling men – who would free themselves, attack their torturers and imprison them – also had one of the figures representing the people address the other participants, clearly expressing her opinion that social changes are made by the people as a whole and not only by their vanguard.

5)   Another young woman made all kinds of changes, leaving untouched only the five persons with their hands tied. This girl belonged to the upper middle class. When she showed signs of nervousness for not being able to imagine any further changes, someone suggested to her the possibility of changing the group of tied figures; the girl looked at them in surprise and exclaimed: 'The truth is that those people didn't fit in! . . .' It was the truth. The people did not fit into her view of the scheme of things, and she had never before been able to see it.

This form of image theater is without doubt one of the most stimulating, because it is so easy to practice and because of its extraordinary capacity for making thought *visible*. This happens because use of the language idiom is avoided. Each word has a denotation that is the same for all, but it also has a connotation that is unique for each individual. If I utter the word 'revolution,' obviously everyone will realize that I am talking about a radical change, but at the same time each person will think of his or her 'own' revolution, a personal conception of revolution. But if I have to arrange a group of statues that will signify 'my revolution,' here there will be no denotation–connotation dichotomy. The image synthesizes the individual connotation and the collective denotation. In my arrangement signifying revolution, what are the statues doing? Do they have weapons in their hands or do they have ballots? Are the figures of the people united in a fighting posture against the figures representing the common enemies; or are the figures of the people dispersed, or showing disagreement among themselves? My conception of 'revolution' will become clear if, instead of speaking, I show with images what I think.

I remember that in a session of psychodrama a girl spoke repeatedly of the problems she had with her boyfriend, and she always started with more or less the same phrase: 'He came in, embraced me, and then . . .' Each time we heard this opening phrase we understood that they did in fact embrace; that is, we understood what the word *embrace* denotes. Then one day she showed by acting how their meetings were: he approached, she crossed her arms over her breasts as if protecting herself, he took hold of her and hugged her tightly, while she continued to keep her hands closed, defending herself. That was clearly a particular connotation for the word *embrace*. When we understood her 'embrace' we were finally able to understand her problems with her boyfriend.

[. . .]

Third degree: *Forum theater*: This is the last degree and here the participant has to intervene decisively in the dramatic action and change it. The procedure is as follows: First, the participants are asked to tell a story containing a political or social problem of difficult solution. Then a ten- or fifteen-minute skit portraying that problem and the solution intended for discussion is improvised or rehearsed, and subsequently presented. When the skit is over, the participants are asked if they agree with the solution presented. At least some will say no. At this point it is explained that the scene will be performed once more, exactly as it was the first time. But now any participant in the audience has the right to replace any actor and lead the action in the direction that seems to him most appropriate. The displaced actor steps aside, but remains ready to resume action the moment the participant considers his own intervention to be terminated. The other actors have to face the newly created situation, responding instantly to all the possibilities that it may present.

The participants who choose to intervene must continue the physical actions of the replaced actors; they are not allowed to come on the stage and talk, talk, talk: they must carry out the same type of work or activities performed by the actors who were in their place. The theatrical activity must go on in the same way, on the stage. Anyone may propose any solution, but it must be done on the stage, working, acting, doing things, and not from the comfort of his seat. Often a person is very revolutionary when in a public forum he envisages and advocates revolutionary and heroic acts; on the other hand, he often realizes that things are not so easy when he himself has to practice what he suggests.

[. . .]

Maybe the theatre in itself is not revolutionary, but these theatrical forms are without doubt a *rehearsal of revolution*. The truth of the matter is that the spectator-actor practices a real act even though he does it in a fictional manner. [. . .]

Here the cathartical effect is entirely avoided. We are used to plays in which the characters make the revolution and the spectators in their seats feel themselves to be triumphant revolutionaries. Why make a revolution in reality if we have already made it in the theater? But that does not happen here: the rehearsal stimulates the practice of the act in reality. Forum theater, as well as these other forms of a people's theater, instead of taking something away from the spectator, evoke in him a desire to practice in reality the act he has rehearsed in the theater. The practice of these theatrical forms creates a sort of uneasy sense of incompleteness that seeks fulfilment through real action.

Chapter 20

Antonio Gramsci

SELECTIONS FROM THE PRISON NOTEBOOKS

Quintin Hoare and Geoffrey Nowell Smith (eds and trans), *Antonio Gramsci, Selections from the Prison Notebooks*, Lawrence & Wishart *(1971, 2005)*, excerpt from pp. 9–13.

ALL MEN ARE INTELLECTUALS, one could therefore say: but not all men have in society the function of intellectuals.[1] When one distinguishes between intellectuals and non intellectuals, one is referring in reality only to the immediate social function of the professional category of the intellectuals, that is, one has in mind the direction in which their specific professional activity is weighted, whether towards intellectual elaboration or towards muscular-nervous effort. This means that, although one can speak of intellectuals, one cannot speak of non-intellectuals because non intellectuals do not exist. But even the relationship between efforts of intellectual-cerebral elaboration and muscular-nervous effort is not always the same, so there are varying degrees of specific intellectual activity. There is no human activity from which every form of intellectual participation can be excluded: *homo faber* cannot be separated from *homo sapiens*.[2] Each man, finally, outside of his professional activity, carries on some form of intellectual activity, that is, he is a 'philosopher', an artist, a man of taste, he participates in a particular conception of the world, has a conscious line of moral conduct, and therefore contributes to sustain a conception of the world or to modify it, that is, to bring into being new modes of thought.

The problem of creating a new stratum of intellectuals consists therefore in the critical elaboration of the intellectual activity that exists in everyone at a certain degree of development, modifying its relationship with the muscular-nervous effort towards a new equilibrium, and ensuring that the muscular-nervous effort itself, in so far that it is an element of general practical activity, which is perpetually innovating the physical and social world, becomes the foundation of a new and integral conception of the world. The traditional and vulgarised type of the intellectual is given by the man of letters, the philosopher, the artist. Therefore journalists, who claim to be men of letters, philosophers, artists, also regard themselves as 'true' intellectuals. In the modern world, technical education, closely bound to industrial labour even at the most primitive and unqualified level, must form the basis of the new type of intellectual.

[. . .]

The mode of being of the new intellectual can no longer exist in eloquence, which is an exterior and momentary mover of feelings and passions, but in active participation in practical life, as constructor, organiser, 'permanent persuader' and not just simple orator (but superior at the same time to the abstract mathematical spirit); from technique-as-work one proceeds to technique-as-science and to the humanistic conception of history, without which one remains 'specialised' and does not become 'directive' (specialised and political).

Thus there are historically formed specialised categories for the exercise of intellectual function. They are formed in connection with all social groups, but especially in connection with the more important, and they undergo more extensive and complex elaboration in connection with the dominant social group. One of the most important characteristics of any group that is developing towards dominance is its struggle to assimilate and to conquer 'ideologically' the traditional intellectuals, but this assimilation and conquest is made quicker and more efficacious the more the group in question succeeds in simultaneously elaborating its own organic intellectuals.

[. . .]

The relationship between the intellectuals and the world of production is not as direct as it is with the fundamental social groups but is, in varying degrees, 'mediated' by the whole fabric of society and the complex of superstructures, of which the intellectuals are, precisely the 'functionaries'. It should be possible to measure the 'organic quality' [*organicita*] of the various intellectual strata and their degree of connection with a fundamental social group, and to establish a graduation of their functions and of the superstructures from the bottom to the top (from the structural base upwards). What we can do, for the moment, is to fix two major superstructural 'levels': the one that can be called 'civil society', that is the ensemble of organisms commonly called 'private', and that of 'political society' or 'the State'. These two levels correspond on the one hand to the function of 'hegemony' which the dominant group exercises throughout society and on the other hand to that of 'direct domination' or command exercised through the State and 'juridical' government. The functions in question are precisely organisational and connective. The intellectuals are the dominant group's 'deputies' exercising the subaltern functions of social hegemony and political government.

These comprise:

1   The 'spontaneous' consent given by the great masses of the population to the general direction imposed on social life by the dominant fundamental group;

this consent is 'historically' caused by the prestige (and consequent confidence) which the dominant group enjoys because of its position and function in the world of production.

2 The apparatus of state coercive power which 'legally' enforces discipline on those groups who do not 'consent' either actively or passively. This apparatus is, however, constituted for the whole of society in anticipation of moments of crisis of command and direction when spontaneous consent has failed.

This way of posing the problem has as a result a considerable extension of the concept of intellectual, but it is the only way which enables one to reach a concrete approximation of reality. It also clashes with preconceptions of caste. The function of organising social hegemony and state domination certainly gives rise to a particular division of labour and therefore to a whole hierarchy of qualifications in some of which there is not apparent attribution of directive or organisational functions.

Notes

1 Thus, it can happen that everyone at some time fries a couple of eggs or sews up a tear in a jacket, we do not necessarily say that everyone is a cook or a tailor.
2 i.e. Man the maker (or tool-bearer) and Man the thinker.

Chapter 21

Majid Rahnema

PARTICIPATION

Wolfgang Sachs (ed.), *The Development Dictionary – A Guide to Knowledge as Power*, Zed Books (1999), pp. 120–9.

Popular participation

ACTIVISTS STRONGLY FAVOURING participatory development argue that they are fully aware of the reasons why politicians and development planners try to co-opt the concept of participation for their own ends. In their view, the types of interaction they propose are precisely intended to prevent all such hegemonistic and manipulative designs. They therefore believe the concept should be further refined – 'popular participation' being able to save development from its present crisis and give it new stamina for enabling the grassroots populations to regenerate their life spaces.

An UNRISD discussion paper defines popular participation as 'the organized efforts to increase control over resources and movements of those hitherto excluded from such control'.[1] For Orlando Fals-Borda, Anisur Rahman and many other PAR theorists,[2] the aim of such a participation is to achieve power:

> a special kind of power – people's power – which belongs to the oppressed and exploited classes and groups and their organizations, and the defence of their just interests to enable them to advance towards shared goals of social change within a participatory system.[3]

As a rule, participation is advocated by PAR theorists as the only way to save development from degenerating into a bureaucratic, top-down and dependency creating institution. They do not question the validity of the institution, *per se*, which most of them consider could be a powerful instrument in the hands of the oppressed. They do insist, however, that, for development to play its historical role, it should be based on participation. Genuine processes of dialogue and interaction should thus replace the present subject–object relationships between intervenors and the intervened, thereby enabling the oppressed to act as the free subjects of their own destiny.

The assumptions underlying the popular participatory approach can be summarized as follows:

(a)   Present obstacles to people's development can and should be overcome by giving the populations concerned the full opportunity of participating in all the activities related to their development.
(b)   Participation is justified because it expresses not only the will of the majority of people, but also it is the only way for them to ensure that the important moral, humanitarian, social, cultural and economic objectives of a more humane and effective development can be peacefully attained.
(c)   'Dialogical interaction', 'conscientization', 'PAR' and other similar activities can make it possible for all the people to organize themselves in a manner best suited to meet their desired ends.

When the concept of popular participation was initially advanced by its promoters as a key element in creating an alternative, human-centred development, it was intended to perform at least four functions: a cognitive, a social, an instrumental and a political one.

In *cognitive* terms, participation had to regenerate the development discourse and its practices, on the basis of a different mode of understanding of the realities to be addressed. It expressed the belief that the cognitive bases of conventional development not only belonged to an irrelevant *episteme*, representing an ethnocentric perception of reality specific to Northern industrialized countries, but were also no longer able to serve the objectives of a sound development. They had to be replaced by a different knowledge system, representing people's own cultural heritage, in particular the locally produced *techne*. Popular participation was to carve out a new meaning for, and a new image of, development, based on different forms of interaction and a common search for this new 'popular' knowledge.

The *political* function of participation was to provide development with a new source of legitimation, assigning to it the task of empowering the voiceless and the powerless and also, eventually, of creating a bridge between the Establishment and its target populations, including even the groups opposing development.

The *instrumental* function of the participatory approach was to provide the 're-empowered' actors of development with new answers to the failure of conventional strategies, and to propose new alternatives, with a view to involving the 'patients' in their own care.

Finally, in *social* terms, participation was the slogan which gave the development discourse a new lease of life. All institutions, groups and individuals involved in development activities rallied around the new construct in the hope that the participatory approach would finally enable development to meet everyone's basic needs and to wipe out poverty in all its manifestations.

The pitfalls of empowerment

The new methodologies of interaction inspired by the PAR and conscientization approaches did initially create waves of enthusiasm and hope, mainly amongst fieldworkers engaged in grassroots activities. The rush for the rapid creation of a 'popular knowledge', aimed at destroying the pernicious monopoly of the dominant paradigm, served as a contagious incentive to promote often inspiring activities in such fields as literacy and regeneration of traditional know-how. Particularly in a number of technical areas, it succeeded in denouncing the often dangerous and inhibitive impacts, on people's lives, of imported and irrelevant technologies. Here and there, but mainly at the local level, it served to keep alive the population's resentment against the most visible aspects of political and social discrimination. It also helped some bright elements to be recognized as local leaders, and gain a wider perception of their communities' possibilities of action.

Yet, there is not enough evidence to indicate that a new kind of knowledge did emerge from the process, 'in such a way that the dominated, underdeveloped societies can articulate their own socio-political position on the basis of their own values and capacities.'

While participatory thinkers do admit that all knowledge systems carry a number of values and biases,[4] they seem to exclude the possibility that, as products of a certain knowledge born out of the economic/developmental age, they could be, themselves, the carriers of very questionable values and biases. Neither do they pay enough attention to the fact that traditional or local knowledge systems suffer, too, from similar, sometimes even more inhibitive prejudices. The fact that the latter have been distorted and confused by the processes of change in the colonial and development eras does not change the picture. As such, any attempt to realize a mix of the two knowledges,[5] represented by local and outside persons interacting with each other, is not only a conceptually reductionist and patchwork type of exercise, but also may turn out to be a strange mix of very heterogeneous biases. The exercise tends, finally, to disregard the following very basic principle of learning – that no one learns who claims to know already in advance. Reality is the unknown which has to be 'dis-covered' together, free from all the presuppositions and influences of the known.

The notion of empowerment was intended to help participation perform one main political function – to provide development with a new source of legitimation. As already made clear in the first part of this essay, the intentions of the pioneers of participation were, indeed, pure and noble. They were right to consider that the tremendous abuses of power by oppressors had to be stopped, and the victims be provided with new possibilities of defending themselves. Yet, in practice, the empowerment discourse raised a number of important questions, both at the theoretical and practical levels. As some of these issues suggest that the discourse can eventually produce opposite results, the matter deserves to be more deeply explored.

When A considers it essential for B to be empowered, A assumes not only that B has no power – or does not have the right kind of power – but also that A has the secret formula of a power to which B has to be initiated. In the current participatory ideology, this formula is, in fact, nothing but a revised version of state power, or what could be called fear-power.

The crux of the matter is that the populations actually subjected to this fear-power are not at all powerless. Theirs is a different power which is not always perceived as such, and cannot be actualized in the same manner, yet it is very real in many ways.[6] It is constituted by the thousands of centres and informal networks of resistance which ordinary people put up, often quietly, against the prevailing power apparatuses. Amongst others, it manifests itself in the reality of 'tax payers cheating the state, young people evading conscription, farmers accepting subsidies or equipment from development projects and diverting them to their own ends, technicians or repairmen working without permits or licences, government paid teachers using the classroom to denounce government abuses of power.'[7]

As a result, there is little evidence to indicate that the participatory approach, as it evolved, did, as a rule, succeed in bringing about new forms of people's power. Instead, there are indications that the way many an activist interpreted their mission contributed to dis-valuing the traditional and vernacular forms of power. More often than not, they helped replace them with a most questionable notion of power, highly influenced by that of the leftist traditions in Europe. This vision of power did, in practice, prove useful to the development establishment. For it helps it to persuade its target populations that not only are economic and state authorities the real power, but that they are also within everyone's reach, provided everyone is ready to participate fully in the development design. . . .

Participation: boon, myth, or danger?

. . . Participation, which is also a form of intervention, is too serious and ambivalent a matter to be taken lightly, or reduced to an amoeba word lacking in any precise meaning, or a slogan, or fetish or, for that matter, only an instrument or a methodology. Reduced to such trivialities, not only does it cease to be a boon, but it runs the risk of acting as a deceptive myth or a dangerous tool for manipulation. To understand the many dimensions of participation, one needs to enquire seriously into all its roots and ramifications, these going deep into the heart of human relationships and the socio-cultural realities conditioning them.

As has already been noted, 'relating' is intrinsic to the very act of being and living. To live is to relate, or to participate in the wider living world of which one is only a part. To relate to that world, and to the human beings composing it, is an act of great consequence which cannot and need not be mediated. As such, one's inability fully to assume this vital necessity should only be *understood*. Only this understanding, by the subject and the others interacting with him, can enable one to overcome that predicament. No democratic or participatory panacea can give an ailing society of dead or conditioned persons what they individually do not have. Contemporary history is particularly rich in cases where induced participation in projects of an ideological national or ethnic nature had repeatedly led to frightfully self-destructive tragedies. After all, slogans of participation have accompanied the events which led to the physical or mental destruction of millions of innocent people in Germany, the USSR, Cambodia, India, Iran, Iraq and elsewhere.

All these difficulties point to a basic dilemma facing the participatory phenomenon. How to reconcile two facts: the fact that no form of social interaction or participation can ever be meaningful and liberating, unless the participating individuals act as free and un-biased human beings; and the second fact that all societies hitherto have developed commonly accepted creeds (religions, ideologies, traditions, etc.) which, in turn, condition and help produce inwardly un-free and biased persons? The dilemma is particularly difficult to resolve at a time when the old ways of socio-cultural conditioning have taken on new and frightening forms. The economization of life with all its implications (cultural, political and social) – is subjecting its participants, all over the world, to often invisible and structural processes of addictive manipulation. As a result, people are led to believe that their very biases, their conditioning and their inner lack of freedom, are not only the expressions of their freedom, but also of an even greater freedom still to be achieved.

Beyond participation

In real life, the dilemma is addressed differently, according to the great diversity of situations and cultures. In recent years, a number of grassroots movements have demonstrated particular creativity, both in bringing up new forms of leadership and 'animation', and in combining the inner and outer requirements of participation.

In relation to the first achievement, the presence within such movements of sometimes very sensitive 'animators', able to listen to their own people, to the world at large, and to the roots of their common culture, has enabled them to cultivate the possibilities of action and self-discovery dormant in the 'common man'. To take only the Indian scene, the Gandhian, the Chipko, the Lokayan and Swadhyaya movements are good examples of the way such inspiring animators have interacted with their fellow countrymen. Drawing on the most enduring and inspiring aspects of people's traditions, some of them have been able to use these as living instruments of socio-cultural regeneration. New ways of working, acting and hoping together have been found, which have also given new meanings and expressions to modernity, in its real sense of *belonging to the present*. The fact that specially trained change agents do not play a major role in these movements has not generally prevented them from being highly animated by their own members, most of them acting as their own agents of change.

In the second area of achievement, a new feature, common to most of these genuine grassroots movements, seems to be the substitution of various modern methodologies, project designs, organizational schemas and fund-raising constraints, by more traditional and vernacular ways of interaction and leadership. As a rule, the necessity for a spiritual dimension, and for the revival of the sacred in one's everyday relationships with the world, seems to be rediscovered as a basic factor for the regeneration of people's space. Wherever this spiritual dimension[8] has been present, it has, indeed, produced a staggering contagion of intelligence and creativity, much more conducive to people's collective 'efficiency' than any other conventional form of mass mobilization. In the above mentioned grassroots movements, this dimension has served as a most powerful instrument in reviving the old ideals of a livelihood based on love, conviviality and simplicity, and also in helping people to resist the disruptive effects of economization.

In that sense, to participate means to live and to relate differently. It implies, above all, the recovery of one's inner freedom, that is, to learn to listen and to share, free from any fear or predefined conclusion, belief or judgment. As inner freedom is not necessarily dependent on outer freedom, its recovery is an essentially personal matter, and can be done even in a jail, or under the most repressive conditions. Yet it enables one not only to acquire a tremendous life power for the flowering of one's own life, but also to contribute, in a meaningful way, to everyone else's struggle for a better life. As such, inner freedom gives life to outer freedom, and makes it both possible and meaningful. On the other hand, while outer freedom is often a great blessing, and a necessity to protect people from violence and abuse, it remains hollow and subject to decay, in the absence of inner freedom. It can never, *per se*, help alienated persons to flower in goodness, or live in wisdom and beauty. Anyhow, participation soon turns into a parody, and an invitation to manipulative designs, when it represents only a ritual amongst alienated persons acting as programmed robots.

To live differently implies, secondly, that change be perceived as a process which starts from within, and defines as one pursues one's creative journey into the unknown. It does not mean to conform to a preordained pattern or ideal designed by others, or even one designed by one's own illusions and conditioned ideals. For change to happen and to make sense, it should represent the open-ended quest and interaction of free and questioning persons for the understanding of reality.

In a situation where these crucial dimensions of change are disregarded, or artificially severed from it, organized forms of participation or mobilization either serve illusory purposes, or lead to superficial and fragmented achievements of no lasting impact on people's lives. Even when these seem to be beneficial to a particular group or region, their effects remain inevitably limited, in time and space, sometimes even producing opposite effects in many unforeseen and unexpected areas.

On another plane, planned macro-changes (which are generally the *raison d'être* of development projects) are more the indirect result of millions of individual micro-changes, than of voluntarist programmes and strategies from above. In fact, they often represent a co-option of the unplanned micro-changes produced by others and elsewhere. When these reach a critical mass, and appear as a threat to the dominant knowledge/power centres at the top, they are co-opted and used by their professionals as an input for planned changes, aimed at turning the potential threat posed to the top into a possible asset for it. Hence, major projects of change from above generally represent an attempt, by those very forces under threat, to contain and redirect change, with a view to adapting it to their own interests, whenever possible with the victims' participation. This is how the real authors of most revolutions are, sooner or later, robbed of the changes they have provoked, and ultimately victimized by the professional ideologues and agitators acting on their behalf. This is how the pioneering participatory mendicants of the early development years were also robbed of their participatory ideal, as the latter was transmogrified into the present-day manipulative construct of participatory development.

Should that mean that anything any free human being does for change, even in its genuine and holistic sense, will inevitably be countered and/or co-opted by vested interests? Or should such realities invite those who seriously want to remain free, to live and to relate as such, to continue partaking in the world, free from fears of all kinds, including the fear of co-option? If the participatory ideal could, in simple terms, be redefined by such qualities as attention, sensitivity, goodness or compassion, and supported by such regenerative acts as learning, relating and listening, are not these qualities and gifts precisely impossible to co-opt? Are they not, also, the same which always help flower, in others, their potentialities of inner transformation? To stay with this question could perhaps serve as a good companion to the activist looking for an answer to his or her life and to better ways of participating in other people's lives.

Notes

1   In a document produced by Matthias Stiefel and Marshall Wolfe. 'The Quest For Participation', UNRISD, Mimeographed Preliminary Report, June 1984, p. 12, the authors conclude that: 'The central issue of popular participation has to do with power, exercised by some people over the people, and by some classes over other classes . . .'

2   PAR — i.e. Participatory Action Research — is a methodology, or approach, to both action and research. It was introduced in the '70s, first in Asia and Latin America, by different groups of activists/theorists working in grassroots developmental activities. PAR seeks to set in motion processes of social change by the populations themselves, as they perceive their own reality. Orlando Fals-Borda, one of its founders, views it as 'a methodology within a total existential process', aimed at 'achieving power and not merely growth for the grassroots populations'.

3   Orlando Fals-Borda, *Knowledge and People's Power*, New Delhi: Indian Social Institute, 1988, p. 2.

4   'Any science as a cultural product has a specific human purpose and therefore implicitly carries those biases and values which scientists hold as a group'. See Orlando Fals-Borda, op. cit., p. 93.

5   The gist of this design can be found in the following statement by Orlando Fals-Borda: 'Academic knowledge combined with popular knowledge and wisdom may give, as a result, a total scientific knowledge of a revolutionary nature (and perhaps a new paradigm), which destroys the previous unjust class monopoly.' Ibid., p. 88.

6   The Gandhian movement was based on the assumption that Indian rural communities were invested with a much more forbidding power than that of the British administration. As such, Gandhi's persistent message to them was neither to oppose that illusory and corruptive power through violence, nor to try to seize it. Many of the present grassroots movements of India and elsewhere similarly believe that the narrow politics of capturing state power is often a last resort. For more on the question of power, see Majid Rahnema, 'Power and regenerative processes in micro-spaces', in *International Social Science Journal*, August 1988, No. 117, pp. 361–75.

7   Ibid., p. 366.

8   Short of a less controversial word, 'spiritual' is used here to express the following qualities: sensitivity; the art of listening to the world at large and within one, free from the hegemony of a conditioned 'me' constantly interfering in the process; the ability to relate to others and to act, without any pre-defined plan or ulterior motives; and the perennial qualities of love, compassion and goodness which are under constant assault in economized societies. The spiritual dimension has nothing to do with the so-called religious, atheistic or scientific perceptions of the world. It expresses mainly the belief that human beings, in their relations with the world, are moved not only by material, economic or worldly interests. It recognizes the sacred dimension of life which transcends the latter, giving a higher meaning to such awesome acts as living, relating and loving. The spiritual dimension, it may be said, is generally inhibited by fanatical beliefs in the superiority of one religion over another. As such, contrary to its promoters' claims, it is totally absent in religious fundamentalist movements based on hate and violence.

Chapter 22

Ananda Breed

PARTICIPATION FOR LIBERATION OR INCRIMINATION?

O NE OF THE ASSUMPTIONS MADE IN applied theatre is that participation is a good thing. This assumption will be supported by case studies of grassroots theatre practices in Rwanda that aid in the reconciliatory and justice phase post-genocide. The case studies illustrate how participation through theatre creates collaboration between perpetrators and survivors, forms associations that benefit the community economically, and stages the benefits of the participatory justice system used to try the perpetrators through the local *gacaca* courts. After initially supporting the benefits of grassroots theatre when viewed in isolation, I will then problematize the assumption that participation is a good thing when relating the dramas to other participatory practices in Rwanda. The genocide included the mass participation of the public in killing over one million Tutsi and Hutu moderates.[1] Likewise, the *gacaca* calls for the mass participation of the public, this time to bring the perpetrators to justice. The assumption that participation is good becomes problematic when juxtaposing the 'successful' case studies of *gacaca* with larger political dynamics in Rwanda. Several grassroots theatre productions enlist the local community to participate in the *gacaca*, to voice their stories and to bring to justice the accused. Participation may be used for liberation, but can also become a tool for imprisonment and persecution. The context of how theatre is being used in the light of larger political dynamics in Rwanda raises potential ethical concerns, both for myself as a researcher, and issues concerning representation and practice.

The question of participation for liberation or incrimination is derived from my own fieldwork in Rwanda from June through December of 2005.[2] Although in the beginning stages of my research, I could not find academic references regarding the use of theatre in post-genocide Rwanda, I ventured to Rwanda under the assumption that out of great suffering there is a need to create. As a practitioner, I believed theatre could aid in the reconciliation process. What I discovered was the complexity of justice and reconciliation in post-genocide Rwanda, and due to that complexity, that there are concerns regarding how and why theatre is utilized. The perspectives illustrated in this essay are in relation to this particular period in Rwanda, and may shift with the larger social and political dynamics of the nation. I have researched, through the lens of performance, how Rwanda is being reconstructed after the devastation of the genocide. Micro level cases of theatre for reconciliation are then related to the national campaigns for reconciliation and justice such as the *gacaca* courts. However, linking intimate moments of reconciliation between perpetrators and survivors to larger issues of nationalism is not to discredit the authenticity of those engagements, nor to undermine the courage of a country seeking to find its own solutions to create a united nation formerly torn by ethnic strife.

Ingando solidarity camp

Prior to discussing participation in the micro level grassroots associations or the macro level *gacaca* courts, I will initially place myself as a researcher within the context of theatre in Rwanda. While at first, I believed that I could use theatre as a tool to facilitate reconciliation through 'telling', what I discovered is that freedom of speech may be limited in Rwanda due to the national implementation of the *gacaca* court system in which 'telling' and participation is linked to justice. Although I had planned to use theatre in my practice, concerns were raised about how and why to use theatre in Rwanda from my experience conducting a month-long workshop in the *ingando* solidarity camps. Between July and August 2005, I worked with over twenty released *genocidaires* in an *ingando* solidarity camp. The word *ingando* is derived from *kuganika*, a Kinyarwanda verb 'which refers to a process in which the elders of a community would leave the distractions of their daily lives and retreat to places of isolation to solve problems of national concern'.[3] In an interview with the executive secretary of the National Unity and Reconciliation Commission (NURC), Fatuma Ndangiza explains:

> *Ingando* comes from Rwandan tradition; it means to make a temporary halt to a retreat. This was seen in pre-colonial Rwanda. If a disaster was threatening, Rwandans would come together to analyze the root of the problem. They would analyze the problem and come up with strategies to solve it.[4]

It is mandatory for university students, released *genocidaires*, and returned refugees to attend the *ingando* camps that range from two weeks to three months in duration. The *ingando* site that I attended in the Kichukiru region of Kigali was one of thirteen *ingando* camps that had been created to house the over 35,000 released *genocidaires* by Presidential decree in July 2005. The *ingando* camp of Kichukiru housed over 1,000 *genocidaires* at the site of a former high school. Daily, I attended lessons taught by government officials on themes such as the history of Rwanda, causes of the genocide, Kinyarwanda culture, peace and reconciliation, and justice and human rights. I sought to use participatory theatre as a method for the *genocidaires* to create plays based on themes of their choice. While at first utilizing forum theatre and image theatre in workshops, it became evident that the participants felt limited in what they could say. Participation had an uncertain side to it. One afternoon, the

1,000 residents of the *ingando* were called onto a nearby football field. The rehearsal stopped. The theatre participants waited anxiously as they listened to the names being called by *ingando* administrators. Several individuals were placed into the back of a pickup truck to be taken back to prison. The theatre workshop shifted, participants wanted to perform what they had learned at the *ingando*. History lessons are not taught in the schools, thus the *ingando* is the sole location in which history is presented, through oral narration by the government officials. The framework for the devised production that would be performed at the closing ceremony of the *ingando* for government officials was to encompass what the participants had learned at the *ingando*. After this initial experience, I began to question how theatre is used in Rwanda, and the limits of free expression.

There was one moment during theatre rehearsals when lessons taught at the *ingando* were challenged. It was in this moment that I began to question what may be performed as reconciliation or the new Rwandan identity (the former ethnic identities Hutu, Tutsi, and Twa are outlawed) on the surface, but that there may be undercurrents of the former ethnic identities underneath. I will share this observation as a lead in for further questions regarding the potential indoctrination of Rwandan Patriotic Front (RPF) ideology at the *ingando* camps and the limitations of my own theatre practice. The play that the released *genocidaires* wanted to create was based on the history of Rwanda. There was one scene based on the Hutu revolution. The group began singing some of the Hutu Power songs with hesitancy at first, looking around to see if anyone was listening or if there would be any reactions from the authorities. After the actors realized that because of the theatre rehearsal, they were free to perform the songs under the guise of 'performance', their behavior changed. I observed a lightening in mood and spirit, and exchanged glances that demonstrated a kind of in-group 'knowing'. There was a shift from what we were 'rehearsing' to what they were embodying during the rehearsal. At this moment, I began to question the effectiveness of a single nationalistic identity or 'rwandicity'.[5] While the objective of their play was to perform what they had learned in the *ingando*, it was in moments like this that identification of 'Hutuness' was allowed expression through theatre. Theatre provided an alternative space to perform repressed identities. In this way, there were two contrasting narratives; one in which events leading up to the genocide were illustrated in an overall theatrical structure that represented their crimes, the other in which the rehearsal itself allowed an outlet for expression of their former cultural identities.

The section that follows describes the use of theatre in grassroots associations as potentially a tool to forge new relationships between perpetrators and survivors, but perhaps also its function as a performance of government rhetoric as witnessed in the *ingando* solidarity camps.

Grassroots theatre

There are over 300 associations in Rwanda that have been created to foster reconciliation. Theatre, dance, and music are utilized to bring together genocide perpetrators, survivors, and community members. Several of the associations have been minimally funded through the National Unity and Reconciliation Commission

(NURC), but others emerged organically in the wake of the genocide. The two associations that I will exemplify, *Ongera Ureba* (See Again) and *Umuhanzi w'u Rwanda* (Rwandan Performer) provide examples of local participation in local association initiatives. The grassroots theatre, when observed in isolation on a micro-level, provides staggering narratives of reconciliation. The two examples do not typify associations throughout Rwanda, as each association has a different history, purpose, and relationship to both the genocide and post-genocide reconciliation. Some of the associations have been formed to aid development through community initiatives of beekeeping, building houses, and harvesting crops. However, both of the associations that I will demonstrate have utilized theatre as a tool for reconciliation and *gacaca* sensitization.

The association *Ongera Ureba* (See Again) was created in February of 1994, two months prior to the widespread genocide attacks. The initial objective was to create a cultural troupe for economic and entertainment purposes. Following the genocide, the troupe created the play *Ongera Urebe Ibyaya Mu Rwanda* (Once Again See What Happened in Rwanda). Originally, the play depicted the events leading up to the genocide, to instruct the population to prevent a future recurrence. The play has been adapted through the years, currently with the added scenes of the confession of a perpetrator to his daughter and a *gacaca* trial. The company started with 12 persons and now consists of 20 members. When asked how they devised the play, the director stated, 'The performances come from our inspiration. They are not funded from the outside, nor are we told what to create, but rather make plays about issues that concern us.' *Ongera Ureba* has devised four plays whose themes include AIDS, *gacaca*, street children, and reconciliation. The elected head of the association is a woman who is one of four Tutsi survivors in the region. During a rehearsal, a truck passed by filled with newly released *genocidaires* returning to the community. The survivor became emotionally distraught and began to shake. Several of the members from the association came to her side. In this state, she related that the association gives her some kind of meaning in her life, that her family had been killed during the genocide.

The second association, *Umuhanzi w'u Rwanda* (Rwandan Performer), was developed in 2002 by a returned refugee who had been trained in theatre while in exile. He created the association to make a space for community members to interact and reconcile without fear. Several survivors and perpetrators were approached to join the association. The day that I witnessed a performance, a survivor whose five children had been slaughtered, held the hand of the perpetrator while singing reconciliation songs. In a post-performance interview, the survivor explained that theatre gave her happiness. Prior to joining the association, she lived in fear. Participating in theatre helped her to momentarily be released from painful memories. Likewise, the perpetrator said that before joining the association he had frequent nightmares. After asking forgiveness and communicating with the survivor through theatre, his physical ailments subsided. Although the statements provoke awe regarding the human capacity to overcome the enormity of genocide, the following quote from the survivor links personal experience of reconciliation to state-driven campaigns of nationbuilding:

> This art and theatre gave me some kind of happiness. At first I would
> be discouraged; I would be lonely. As I associate and interact with people
> I begin feeling all right; I become happy. I can laugh. I can talk to people.

I feel liberated. When you are with others singing, acting, performing . . . the kind of ideas and fears that have been harbored in your heart will subside. I feel relaxed and I don't take time to think about them because much of my time is to interact and to laugh and to talk and to be happy with others. Another thing is when you are in this mission, it leads others to understand things which they didn't understand before. It makes you interact with a person you used to fear. Another thing is that there are other things that were hidden from you which you get to know. The good news is that when we are invited to say something or perform somewhere you find yourself participating in nation building. This leads to the success of unity and reconciliation as well as *gacaca* courts. It shows the people that have been antagonists, who have not been staying together well and we go as this group to give them an example of how people will live together.[6]

The next section challenges the assumption that participation is a liberatory tool by linking the grassroots theatre associations with the *gacaca* justice system and wider government campaigns of nation building.

Gacaca courts

The mandatory participation of all Rwandan citizens in the *gacaca* courts automatically affects any other form of participatory or community-based theatre practices. Once a week, on every cell level, *gacaca* court sessions are conducted. The whole of the community is requested to sit together during the daylong session, once per week. This includes perpetrators, survivors, witnesses, returned refugees, and all other citizens. The public is requested to 'tell what we have seen, admit what has been done, and move forward to healing.'[7] The *gacaca* trial phase began in 2002 as a solution to bringing to trial the over 120,000 perpetrators that had been imprisoned since 1994. At the current trial rate, it would have taken over 150 years to process the cases, thus the *gacaca* was implemented to speed up the trials. *Gacaca* is a Kinyarwanda word which refers to a pre-colonial mediation system in which conflicted parties would sit in the grass, usually underneath a tree, to have their problems mediated. The community members serve as witness, jury, and judge. Although the *gacaca* has been referred to as a pre-colonial system, it has been reinstituted specifically to resolve cases of genocide.

The format of the *gacaca* raises issues about participation, community building, and 'telling'. On the surface, there are several parallels between *gacaca* and theatre for development practices. The *gacaca* utilizes an established cultural form, integrates the community at large in finding solutions to their own problems, and involves a space for dialogue. The request for perpetrators and survivors to sit in the same location week after week is in itself an extraordinary event. However, the request of every citizen to move towards justice and reconciliation through *gacaca*, while ideologically admirable, does not address the concern that participation could provoke retribution. There is also the potential for grassroots theatre associations to parrot state-driven rhetoric, veiling a program of top-down enforcement rather than a societal healing that is organically created and sustained.

The *gacaca* has evolved from several stages, including a sensitization and mobilization campaign that used theatre and radio to introduce and instruct the nation regarding the *gacaca*. Several grassroots associations utilize theatre to illustrate the procedures of *gacaca*. In Rusagara, an association performed the *gacaca* play *Urubanza Rwa Gasaruhanda Alias Kigomeke* (The Trial of Gasaruhanda Alias Kigomeke). The performance duplicates the actual court proceedings. Eight judges, or *inyangamugayo* (elected persons of integrity), cross the field in single file. They are wearing the government *gacaca* sashes across their chests, of the same colors and symbols of the national flag. They stand behind a wooden table. The crowd stands for a moment of silence. The actor portraying the perpetrator denies all charges. The actors portraying community members stand as witness, offering their testimonies. The play concludes with the perpetrator being sentenced to 25 years' imprisonment. The *gacaca* coordinator in the district stated, 'We have a very big number of guilty pleas here as a response to the play, a large percentage of confessions.'[8] The use of theatre in Rusagara is common to several other associations researched. The rate of confessions was higher in the areas where theatre was utilized for sensitization and mobilization.

Gacaca versus Truth and Reconciliation Commission

The role of 'telling' through testimony, used as a cathartic tool towards healing and reconciliation in the South African Truth and Reconciliation Commission (TRC) hearings, may not have the same effect in the *gacaca* courts. While the TRC has implemented amnesty as a strategy for uncovering the truth of events during the apartheid, the *gacaca* aims for justice as well as reconciliation. Testimonies in the *gacaca* courts are inextricably linked to justice procedures including prosecution, while testimonies in the TRC are protected through amnesty. In Rwanda, due to a legacy of ethnic violence which in large part had been left unpunished, the *gacaca* sought to end impunity. The difference in responses to the atrocities of each country, impunity in South Africa and retributive justice in Rwanda may be due to the policies of the different post-conflict regimes. According to Katherine Lanegran, 'In Rwanda, where the Hutu forces were defeated, the government stresses retributive justice via prosecutions. In contrast, with South Africa simmering in violence, ANC leaders explicitly determined that they needed to use amnesty in order to convince authorities to negotiate the country's transition to democracy.'[9] The narrative that is created through the testimonial proceedings in each country, shape the 'new' nation. The *gacaca* documents the events of the genocide through data collection and testimonials. The judicial system memorializes and commemorates the genocide into the collective consciousness of the nation through the weekly *gacaca* courts. The TRC, on the other hand, promotes forgiveness as a collective response to the apartheid. Both countries seek to establish reconciliation, but with contrasting responsibility placed on the perpetrators to atone, the victims to forgive and the governments to punish. Different approaches to healing mass atrocity will affect how theatre or participatory practices will be utilized in national campaigns of justice and reconciliation.

Conclusion

The assumption that theatre can be used for political change against forces of oppression, like Augusto Boal techniques or theatre for development, can be questioned when one looks at the political context of where the theatre is being practiced. How or should one use theatre in a post-genocide context in which 'telling' can quickly lead from a personal action of testimony into a public act of incrimination? *Gacaca* was the theme for the 2006 commemoration of the genocide in Rwanda often referred to in government speeches. In an interview with the Minister of Sports, Youth and Culture, who was the main coordinator of the event, I asked if personal testimonies that were given publicly during the commemoration could be used as evidence in the *gacaca* courts. He replied by stating that the spontaneous testimonies during the commemoration are subject to justice proceedings and that, later, they could be used in the *gacaca* courts. Thus, personal acts of 'telling' that may momentarily be utilized for healing are subject to the broader national justice system. In Rwanda, 'telling,' in any form, whether through theatre or personal acts of public testimony, can be inextricably linked to the *gacaca* – the personal automatically becomes the political. Thus, participatory theatre practices associated with theatre for liberation can become a part of theatre for incrimination.

Bibliography

Mgbako, C. (2005) 'Ingando Solidarity Camps: Reconciliation and Political Indoctrination in Post-Genocide Rwanda', *Harvard Human Rights Journal* 18: 208.

Lanegran, K. (2005) 'Truth Commissions, Human Rights Trials, and the Politics of Memory', *Comparative Studies of South Asia, Africa, and the Middle East* 25 (1): 116.

Notes

1   See *Rwanda: Gacaca: A Question of Justice*, Amnesty International, December 2002. www.web.amnesty.org/library/index/engafr470072002.

2   The author has conducted further research in Rwanda during January 2005 and March through May 2006.

3   Mgbako, C. (2005) 'Ingando Solidarity Camps: Reconciliation and Political Indoctrination in Post-Genocide Rwanda'. *Harvard Human Rights Journal*. Vol. 18 p. 208.

4   Interview with Fatuma Ndangiza, Executive Director of the National Unity and Reconciliation Commission (NURC), conducted by author. Kigali, Rwanda. January 12, 2005.

5   The Rwandan newspaper *The New Times* described rwandanicity as, '. . . an idea and philosophy that guided the people's conduct and perceptions. As an ideology, therefore, it [rwandanicity] is what the people of Rwanda understood themselves to be, what they knew about themselves, and how they defined and related to each other and their country as a united people (Ubumwe). The new Rwandan identity is evoked through *ingando*, *gacaca*, and other 'pre-colonial' forms. Brig. Gen. Frank K. Rusagara, 'Gacaca: Rwanda's truth and reconciliation authority', *The New Times*, 16 May 2005.

6   Interview with grassroots association, Umuhanzi w'u Rwanda, conducted by author. Rwanda. July 18, 2005.

7   The slogan has been used in national sensitization and mobilization campaigns, in particular as a caption on *gacaca* billboards.

8   Interview with Gacaca coordinator of Rulindo. Interview by Author. Rulindo, Rwanda. July 13, 2005.

9   Lanegran, K. (2005) 'Truth Commissions, Human Rights Trials, and the Politics of Memory'. *Comparative Studies of South Asia, Africa, and the Middle East*, Duke University Press, Vol. 25, No. 1. p. 116.

Chapter 23

Paul Moclair

ALTOGETHER NOW?

Reconsidering the merits of participation in child-rights theatre

G UNS, GOATS, LIGHTNING strikes and vultures are all possible sources of interruption to a workshop in Sudan, but none proved quite as unsettling to this facilitator as the realisation that practice and theory had gone their separate ways.

In 2005 I was in Sudan with UNICEF redesigning a stalled children's theatre project, called *Theatre for Life*. The project, which operated in 450 villages across the country, had already been running for five years and had limited itself to basic health messaging. Participation was tokenistic, manipulative even. Plays were commissioned from professional writers in the cities. These scripts were then distributed to teachers across the country. The teachers would select a mere handful of 'talented' children as actors, and teach them their lines using the time-honoured pincer movement of rote-learning and corporal punishment.

Realising that the approach was chronically out of step with its own re-branding as a rights-based organisation, UNICEF decided to call in an evaluator.[1] He recommended that in future, *Theatre for Life* should concern itself less with health promotion, and more with child-rights. It was to be child-centred, rights-based and participatory. It was to involve the many and not just the few and children were to be the main creative force. Problem-posing plays were to replace message carrying ones, which were incapable of addressing the complex issues that arise when rights come into conflict with culture.

There already exist mountains of NGO literature providing off-the-peg arguments for children's participation. Commitment to participation by organisations is frequently formulated in a spirit of tough pragmatism. There are economic benefits: programme and project efficiency are enhanced when we choose to 'invest' in children's participation. There are political dividends: through participation, children learn a sense of responsibility and citizenship that can only result in a healthier, more stable democracy and an invigorated civil society. Finally, there are benefits in terms of personal development; children gaining enhanced communication and analytical skills and learning the advantages of dialogue over conflict, and a tolerance of diversity.

Convincing though these arguments may appear, they seem designed primarily for the consumption of donors whose perceptions of development remain dominated by products rather than processes, with the 'value for money' argument getting top billing. They may also betray a lack of confidence in emphasising the absolutist legal position that, independent of log-frames, children have a right to participate in decision-making processes that affect them, and in the cultural life of their own communities.

Formulating a defence of children's participation so as to render a project more palatable to donors is a strategic necessity. However, facilitators heading for the field may feel the need to chew the theoretical cud at greater length. Such leisurely meditations, hopefully, ensure that one embarks on a project with a sense of conviction and resolve and help one to fashion an appropriate workshop methodology. It is a valuable learning experience to watch the slow erosion of those cherished theories by actual field realities; the painfully illuminating and occasionally comical process of praxis. In the chapter that follows I will summarise some of the theoretical arguments I found helpful and discuss how workshop limitations prevented us from fully capitalising on them.

In the sterile calm of UNICEF's Khartoum office, I mapped out a nine-stage model designed to guarantee participation throughout the process. Each stage utilises games and drama-based exercises. The first deals with introductions and icebreakers. The second seeks to foster trust and teambuilding. In the third, we begin storytelling as a tool for teaching adults to listen to children without interrupting, criticising or judging them. In stage four the facilitator tries to help the group identify a shared or common problem. This problem will provide the workshop with its focus. It will be the subject of further scrutiny, and ultimately of the drama. In stage five, the group explores the problem and pools its knowledge through a series of extended, forum-style improvisations. In stage six the crude outlines of a plot are generated through circular story-telling games. In stage seven the devising work is refined and the facilitator may need to take a more overtly directorial role. Stage eight is the public performance of the problem-posing play. Immediately after the performance, the actors go into the audience and facilitate discussions about how the problem might be tackled at community level. Any resultant initiatives or action plans constitutes the ninth and final stage.

A central objective of the process outlined above was to ensure that all children got the chance to express a view, articulate their perspective and name their own world. The methodology favours drawing and oral exercises, much as PRA (Participatory Rural Appraisal) and PLA (Participatory Learning and Action) do, as a means of ensuring that girls are not drowned out by boys, that the poor are not suffocated by the rich, the shy not sidelined by the confident, the non-literate not eclipsed by the literate. Imperatives of equality and inclusion are at work throughout the process. In Stage six, for example, the group sits in a circle for story-telling games so as to generate a plot around the subject identified earlier in the drawing exercise. The game begins with the creation and naming of a protagonist. Working around the circle each child takes it in turn to contribute one or two sentences to the evolving story. In subsequent revolutions, the story is refined to develop characters, introduce dramatic turning points and ensure that the problem is left unresolved.

Both the drawing and story-telling exercises seek to avoid the dangers of what Timur Kuran has labelled 'preference falsification' whereby 'an unwillingness to engage with a more aggressively enforced dominant perspective restricts (people's) ability to express their true beliefs' (Rao and Walton 2004: 22). Paradoxically we are initially emphasising the collective approach as a means of safeguarding and guaranteeing individual input. As with herds of migrating animals, the primary function of the group is to protect each individual.

But there is much more going on here than simply being nice to children and ensuring that 'everybody gets a go'. While we are initially concerned with ensuring input from all individuals, it is the resultant recognition that the group amounts to more than the sum of its parts that is of greatest value to us and that best illuminates the empowering, educational and mobilising potential of this kind of participatory model. An analysis of this position might help expose the fundamental mechanics of a workshop, revealing the theoretical imperatives which underpin all the running about and fun and games. In contrast to a development debate frequently dominated by the economic perspective, a multi disciplinary approach allows us to listen to the otherwise neglected voices of anthropologists, social and political theorists, and ethicists who in turn draw heavily on the thought of feminists and environmentalists and the great battalions of the excluded. For within these disciplines we will find allies whose writing corroborates a central tenet of our methodology – the elevation of the group over the individual for reasons other than those of primary practicality. Considering participation in these terms will help us refine our rejection of the self-interested individual, directed unerringly by market forces, as some sort of moral exemplar canonised by neo-liberal theology. Our methodology then places us on one side of an ideological schism, placing us in opposition to neo-liberal philosophies.

The poorest, with whom we seek to work, owe their poverty in large part to neo-liberal economic policies thrust on them since structural adjustment. The architects of these policies, as Margaret Thatcher reminded us, elevate the self-interested individual above all else, even to the point of denying the existence of 'society'. Therefore participatory Theatre for Development's central emphasis on seeking community-led solutions has a political resonance from the moment we first invite participants to form a circle and sit on the floor, and to introduce their partners. When we move on to Stage Two and involve the group in a team-building exercise such as The Machine, we continue to attempt to wrest control of the development debate out of the hands of the neo-liberals. Robert Putnam refers to the 'long-standing interpretation of Anglo-American political thought' (1993: 87) that traces the elevation of individualism and individual rights over the community to the vanquishing of Nicolo Machiavelli by Hobbes, Locke and their liberal descendants. Anthropologist Mary Douglas helps us to regroup:

> Anthropologists see wants as defined collectively. The community itself defines its needs in the light of shared objectives, and of its accumulated knowledge and capabilities. This goes against the assumption from utility theory that wants arise in individuals and that there is enough uniformity among individual persons for generalizing.

> (Douglas 2004: 90)

This theoretical emphasis on the collective has immediate repercussions on methodology. It explains why unlike drama-therapy, with its focus on individual testimony, we engage the group in a collective exploration of shared problems then use the resultant drama to mobilise communities. Our emphasis in Sudan was on structural reform rather than on children's therapy (although such transformation is often a welcome secondary outcome). In the case of child soldiers, for example, the aim of drama is not to relieve individual children of painful emotions by acting out, but to persuade communities and people with authority over children to abandon the practice of recruitment. Our goal is to challenge cultural perceptions which are harmful to children. We want to guide children towards an appreciation of the commonality of suffering and an identification of its roots at a structural or cultural level within society. Our insistence on the collective approach places us alongside anthropologists who begin with the assumption that our behaviour is generated and regulated by a deep foundation of group norms.

> In other words, they adhere to 'methodological holism' where the unit of analysis is not an individual but a group. Individuals are so deeply conditioned by their group membership that one cannot really think of autonomous individual actors or identities
>
> (Rao and Walton 2004: 14)

Only within the context of group membership can we hope to comprehend our behaviour. If we wish to amend that behaviour we must involve the group in a kind of collective soul-searching. Consistent with our preference for group values and community culture, let us turn to social-theorist Pierre Bourdieu and his concept of *habitus*, referring to 'the set of durable principles – practices, beliefs, taboos, rules, representations, rituals, symbols, and so on – that provide a group with a sense of group identity' (Rao and Walton 2004: 15). *Habitus* is crucial because it determines the extent to which we accept our lot in life. These internalised perceptions of what is achievable, not only serve as endogenous restraints, they may be exploited and reinforced by a dominant social group for its own gain. We must help children redefine their own perceptions of childhood before they can begin selling that vision to adults.

However, it is incorrect to perceive *habitus* only as the source and repository of shackling values, as an inherited disability or genetic deficiency. Rather, it is within this same treasure chest of cultural and community legacy that we might locate the key that unlocks people's capacity to aspire; 'It is in culture that ideas of the future, as much as those about the past, are embedded and nurtured' (Appadurai 2004: 59). Because culture has the ability to determine our sense of the possible, it can be used to perpetuate social differentiations. Bourdieu therefore saw culture as a form of capital. Rao and Walton reflecting on David Swartz's interpretation of Bourdieu note; 'It [cultural capital] can also be used as a form of domination' (2004: 16).

To return to the workshop methodology used in Sudan: at stage five of the process, an issue previously identified as being of common concern to the participants is explored through open-ended, forum-style improvisations. The exercise starts with two characters brought into conflict through being given conflicting objectives. By 'rubbing these sticks together' we produce the 'spark' which will ignite the narrative or plot. With an improvisation on female genital mutilation (FGM), for example, the initial characters might be a mother and her older daughter with diametrically opposed views on circumcision. Participants are given the most cursory of character sketches. The mother is overjoyed because her youngest daughter is to be circumcised later that day. She locates the ritual within a long cultural tradition and is driven by pride. Her objective is to get the older daughter to help her prepare the celebrations for after the procedure. The older daughter is home on a visit. She herself has suffered as a result of her own circumcision and her objective is to persuade her mother to abandon her plans. Her motivation is fear or anger. Their initial confrontation inevitably brings into play an ever widening cast suggested by the audience; the grandmother urging the mother on, the imam who might stress the absence of any Koranic endorsement for female circumcision, the health worker who articulates the health concerns, the father who is conflicted over the issue, the midwife who has her own vested interests, community elders who are keen to see tradition preserved, the child herself.

The drama here acts like a flight simulator or virtual reality game, helping frightened children and marginalised people to transcend their experiential limitations. Furthermore, the powerful are demystified once we have acted out their roles. Appadurai (2004) talks of the capacity to aspire as a cultural capacity, and exercises like this can increase that capacity by allowing participants to experiment with the hypothetical. Participants, by experimenting with courses of action which they would deem too risky to undertake in real life, are free within these improvisations to explore alternatives, test boundaries and shadow-box authority. The bullied school-child can test the likely benefit of confiding in a parent. The young girl may gauge the extent to which a local imam may help villagers abandon FGM. By providing vicarious experience of new modes of behaviour the drama offers a way out of the impasse delineated by Bourdieu. It demonstrates to the group how the shackles of *habitus* might be broken, and it relieves the malaise of apathy.

As with the convention of structured forum pieces, the line between performers and audience disappears. The facilitator constantly asks the audience if what they are watching is realistic and true to local experience. Where there is disagreement, members of the audience replace actors. Conflicting perspectives are examined. Individual testimonies are absorbed. By working through the discord we seek to arrive at a deeper understanding of the problem, one capable of embodying contradictions even whilst approximating group consensus. The group is educating itself by pooling resources. Thus knowledge is treated as a group asset.

This empirical observation on workshop mechanics seems to chime and resonate with our political instincts. In her analysis of participatory politics, Hilary Wainwright (2003) makes use of similar observations on the nature of knowledge to undermine the Austrian economist, Friedrich von Hayek, a key neo-liberal influence. Hayek argued that 'practical knowledge is exclusively an individual attribute, not a social structure' (Wainwright 2003: 18) and this assertion led neo-liberals to argue against social engineering. If knowledge is individual and incomplete, and the status quo is the product of accident, then 'democracy and social change . . . become marginal and even redundant' (ibid.: 17).

When Wainwright ponders the implications of discrediting Hayek's ideas on knowledge as an individual attribute, she unconsciously articulates many of the achievements of our workshop process:

> If knowledge is a social product, it can be socially transformed by people who take action – cooperating, sharing, combining different kinds of knowledge – to overcome the limits on the knowledge that they individually possess. This view of knowledge as a social product opens up the possibility of people gauging, through exchange with others, the possible consequences of their intended actions, and therefore being able purposefully to influence social relations.
>
> (Wainwright 2003: 18)

This is entirely in synch with a workshop procedure that involves participants in the collective examination of a shared concern, that uses improvisations to map out a likely chain of cause and effect, and which then fashions those improvisations into a problem-posing play which seeks to transform harmful attitudes and kick-start community mobilisation.

Being aware that one's methodology is consistent with thinking in other disciplines is comforting to Theatre for Development facilitators and leaves them feeling less isolated in their lonely field. The potential for community mobilisation helps keep them motivated and inspired. But to leave matters there would be to ignore the problems that arise when you try and facilitate children's participation in the field. These can be summed up in one word – time. The old top-down *Theatre for Life* methodology that we sought to replace had been quick. It involved one adult producing a script, then individual teachers directing compliant children. By contrast, the new participatory approach of fishing for an issue, exploring it through improvisations then generating a plot through circular story-telling exercises is cumbersome and time-consuming. But you cannot have children's participation *and* speedy results if you are truly to honour the process.[2] There are times when a polished performance may have to be sacrificed on the altar of inclusion.

In a short workshop with children (and NGO restrictions on time and budget inevitably mean such workshops are short) you can often do little more than highlight an issue of common concern. Shifting stubborn cultural perceptions takes longer. Time and again as we moved around the compass points of the country, in Kordofan, Gedaref, Bahr El-Ghazel and Darfur, we were confronted with the same resilient double-thinks. Teacher violence is a good example. Invariably, children would use the drawing exercise at stage four to identify teacher violence as a problem. Yet when they began to devise their plays, a wholly contradictory narrative would emerge, with children portraying themselves as malicious and deserving of violent punishment. Children who had identified teacher violence as a problem in the morning were its most vociferous supporters in the afternoon. Untangling that knotty contradiction requires unhurried dialogue. We had raked over the topsoil of the children's experience without adequately mining the bedrock of *habitus*.

Nor had we taken time to adequately work through the collective cultural perceptions of the adult master trainers. After we had first witnessed one of the children's contradictory plays on teacher violence, I assembled the adults, hoping to rehearse with them some standard, rights-based arguments against the practice. 'Why', I asked them, 'are we opposed to teacher violence?' Heads lowered, gazes fixed on feet, the air thickened with silence and it dawned on me that many of them might not be opposed to it at all. We were training 120 master trainees and somewhere along the line we had recklessly assumed they would all share our progressive, NGO worldview.

The discrepancies between our and local communities' views on women and children were never far away. The very group dynamics and behaviour of the adult facilitators provided a constant, mocking reminder. At the end of a session on female empowerment we took a break, the men smoking and lounging whilst the women ferried refreshments. Another time we were sitting under trees discussing teacher violence when the nearby school opened its gates and disgorged its inmates. Immediately we were surrounded by hundreds of wide-eyed, noisy children, making the discussion difficult to continue. A sturdy female teacher, seeing what was happening reached up to a tree, tore off a branch and advanced on the children with the unhurried menace of a tank. They scattered. We laughed the incident off, then continued our discussion in peace, complicit in our unspoken gratitude to her.

We as adults must spend sufficient time exploring and transforming our own attitudes to children before a project like this can move forward,[3] and children must be given a similar space. Trainees themselves need a thorough grounding in rights if they in turn are to help children engage communities in dialogue over potentially divisive issues. If they are not equipped with strong arguments against practices such as teacher violence and FGM, and if they do not believe those arguments, the actor-facilitators will face real problems when they engage audiences in post-performance discussions. Participatory methodologies are about empowerment, not finding a cheap, quick-fix solution. That takes time. We wanted to leave our trainees holding the stick, but we risked leaving them holding the baby.

There is every reason to think that UNICEF's Theatre for Life project will succeed. However, success is contingent upon regular follow up and a steady, time-consuming emphasis on rights. UNICEF is to be saluted for its courage in adopting this innovative approach to theatre, so radically at odds with the didactic theatre beloved of many NGOs. Trying to persuade others of the benefits of a leisurely, process-driven, drama-based exploration of rights-based issues will not be easy. Shackled to deadlines and targets and the concept of product, they are unlikely to appreciate Philip Pullman's[4] remarks that 'It is when we do this foolish, time consuming, romantic, quixotic, childlike thing called play that we are most practical, most useful and most grounded in reality . . .'

Bibliography

Abraham, A. and Platteau, J-P., (2004) 'Participatory Development: Where Culture Creeps In' in V. Rao and M. Walton (eds), Culture and Public Action, Stanford, CA: Stanford University Press.

Appadurai, A. (2004) 'The Capacity to Aspire: Culture and the Terms of Recognition', in V. Rao and M. Walton (eds), Culture and Public Action, Stanford, CA: Stanford University Press.

Carmen, R. (1996) Autonomous Development: Humanizing the Landscape – An Excursion into Radical Thinking and Practice, London: Zed Books.

Douglas, M. (2004) 'Traditional Culture – Let's Hear No More About It' in V. Rao and M. Walton (eds), Culture and Public Action, Stanford, CA: Stanford University Press.

Putnam, R.D. (1993) Making Democracy Work: Civic Traditions in Modern Italy, Princeton, NJ: Princeton University Press.

Rao, V. and Walton, M. (2004) 'Culture and Public Action: Relationality, Equality of Agency, and Development', in V. Raoand M. Walton (eds), *Culture and Public Action*, Stanford, CA: Stanford University Press.

Wainwright, H. (2003) *Reclaim the State: Experiments in Popular Democracy*, London: Verso.

Notes

1   Alex Mavrocordatos, CDC Arts. http://www.cdcarts.org/.

2   Attempts at massaging outcomes so as to meet deadlines or manufacture appropriate 'messages', or otherwise manipulating the process, smack of what Ralph Carmen (1996) has labelled, 'participulation'.

3   'Indeed, if participatory development is seen as a new magic pill that can cure most of the present ills, and if existing community imperfections are not properly taken into account, serious future disillusionments are unavoidable' (Abraham and Platteau, 2004: page number).

4   Pullman, Phillip in *The Guardian*, 21 January 2005.

Chapter 24

Sarah Thornton

THE COMPLEXITY AND CHALLENGE OF PARTICIPATION
A case study of Collective Encounters' living place project

COLLECTIVE ENCOUNTERS IS A small professional arts organisation based in north Liverpool with a focus on using theatre as a tool for social change. Since early 2004 the company has sought interesting ways of bringing people together in creative, collective encounters to explore some of the key issues of our time. Through participatory and performance work with professional artists, local people and civic leaders the company uses theatre to challenge, entertain and stimulate debate, with the ultimate goal of contributing to the processes of democracy and change.

The area in which the company operates is one of extreme disadvantage and ranks in the top ten nationally in the Indices of Multiple Deprivation. Some communities in north Liverpool have illiteracy rates of up to 36 per cent, unemployment and poor health rank high above the national average and educational attainment is well below average. It is an area which has seen massive depopulation, the decimation of the industrial base and the fragmentation of communities initially through slum clearance and more recently through a plethora of urban renewal initiatives.

While these initiatives brought millions of pounds of European and government funding into the area throughout the 1990s, there were inadequate mechanisms for consultation and little visible improvement. The effect of this was that many residents believed the money was being misspent. They felt increasingly distanced from power and unheard by decision makers. By 2004 there was a recognition that Liverpool was living through a time of unprecedented change. With major new regeneration initiatives impacting on the area and massive amounts of European monies still coming in, and the build to Capital of Culture in 2008 pressing the agenda, the pace of change had quickened. While there was a renewed sense of optimism in some quarters, the confusion caused by conflicting information and the bureaucratic maze to be navigated in order to find out what the plans for the area were meant that most local people found it extremely difficult to find out what was actually happening. Many people were struggling to discover information fundamental to their lives such as whether or not their house was to be demolished.

Collective Encounters developed Living Place Project in response to this situation. Through a research and development (R&D) process the company identified an historical dearth of arts provision in the area, but a real interest among community leaders in the potential of arts activity. More importantly, the participants interviewed throughout the R&D process communicated a real sense of urgency of the need to find new and powerful ways of articulating local concerns, publicly. Living Place Project set out to explore and articulate the issues at the heart of the regeneration of north Liverpool. It was to be a multi-faceted programme of work which would involve broad-based research and consultation, the publication of reports, professional performances, community theatre training programmes and productions, and an international conference. The project grew directly out of local consultation and ran between March 2004 and October 2005 involving approximately 1,000 people.

An ethos of participation was at the heart of the project. Fundamentally this meant the participation of local people who were living through the changes and whose experiences, stories and viewpoints Collective Encounters hoped to platform. But, if the project was to have any real impact, the participation of key agencies and policy makers leading the regeneration process was also vital. This chapter explores some of the challenges faced by Collective Encounters in attempting to facilitate genuine participation from both constituencies and the complexities inherent in this kind of participative working.

Securing the participation of the people with real decision-making power was one of the greatest challenges of the project. The company hoped to be able to find some answers to local people's questions, to encourage the key players to listen to what local people had to say, to gain some understanding of the actual plans for the area's regeneration, and perhaps secure some financial support for the project which would indicate a willingness to listen and take local people's views on board. Initially this process involved extensive research to discover which private sector agencies and public sector departments had responsibility for the area: this was far from transparent and changed frequently as area boundaries were re-drawn, and city council departments re-structured. Once the relevant departments and agencies were identified it was extremely difficult to gain access to those in decision-making positions. Meetings with Community Liaison Officers proved fruitless as there was seldom a direct line between them and senior management, and many agencies were just uninterested in becoming involved in any way. Following much frustration and an overwhelming lack of success over many months; persistence, good luck, and vision on the part of some key individuals led to some success. Collective Encounters was able to secure the useful participation of three major agencies whose work was at the heart of regenerating north Liverpool.[1]

In terms of local participation, the first, key challenge was overcoming the barriers of scepticism and entrenched suspicion. Having lived through a myriad of unsuccessful short-term interventions, having explained their stories to a host of professional consultants and been offered empty promises, having built relationships with agency representatives only to have staff change and find themselves back at square one, local people were unsurprisingly wary of taking the time and trouble to expose themselves again. As a new company, Collective Encounters had no history in the area and as its artists did not live there, they were viewed by some as cultural missionaries with nothing really at stake and certainly no investment in the place. Surely the money raised for the project could be better spent re-fitting one of the local youth clubs? Surely the company would leave again as soon as the project was finished? Was Collective Encounters in cahoots with the regeneration agencies, taking money from them and so enabling them to tick their 'consultation' boxes? In the face of justifiable scepticism there was little to do but accept it, respect it, and maintain contact with those who articulated these feelings in the hope that over time (but probably not during the lifetime of this project) Collective Encounters could earn people's trust.

Fortunately there were still many people who were prepared to keep telling their story until someone listened, and others who were intrigued by the project and the idea of using theatre as a tool for change. But how to find them? Collective Encounters had worked hard during the R&D to build relationships with representatives from well-respected community groups, neighbourhood councils and community centres. By building partnerships with these agencies the company gained credibility and support, vital to the success of the project at local level. With their help, Collective Encounters began to find people who were prepared to take a leap of faith and show an interest in participating in the project. In order to earn the trust of these potential participants Collective Encounters considered it vital to be open and honest about the intentions and motivation behind the project, about its anticipated outcomes and benefits, and about its partnerships and funding streams. But with a company of six professional artists supported by sixty student researchers[2] transparency and clarity proved another challenge. The company worked closely with all its artists and researchers in advance of the participatory work to provide appropriate training, to develop collaborative working practices and ethical research processes and to produce an ethical research policy which everybody representing the company adhered to.

The next challenge was to find appropriate mechanisms for participation. The company was keen to offer a variety of ways in which local people could participate which would best suit their own circumstances, interests and needs; which would range from one-off encounters to longer-term and more sustained levels of engagement. In order to gain an honest, broad-based overview of the situation it was necessary for the company to speak with as many people as possible. But to build trusting relationships, reach a greater depth of understanding and facilitate any degree of empowerment, pockets of more intensive engagement with small groups were essential.

For broad-based research and consultation artists and researchers gathered experiences, stories and ideas from over 500 people of all ages. Methods included formal recorded interviews and informal anecdotal conversations, vox pops in popular locations and street-based questionnaires, public meetings, one-off arts workshops, short-term workshop programmes and psycho-geography trails.[3] The public meetings were the least successful of these methods. While they were well publicised through community centres, libraries and local media the turn-out was disappointing. Feedback from community leaders pointed back to scepticism and disillusionment, as they explained that attendance at all public meetings had plummeted over the previous two years. This was a real barrier to gathering significant numbers of people who were not already accessing community-based services. To combat this the company enhanced street-based research and found that the random encounters in markets, sports centres and public spaces opened new ways into the communities of north Liverpool and unearthed many fascinating stories. In addition Collective Encounters worked with more existing groups through adult education, children and family centres, youth clubs and pensioners clubs. A wealth of material was thus generated which provided the overview the company had hoped for. In keeping with the company's ethical research policy, all those who had participated in the research process were invited to an interim sharing of work, Living Place Live, which aimed to check the veracity of the research, identify gaps in understanding and provide an opportunity for the artists working on the project to begin exploring the subject matter creatively.

Living Place Live was an episodic, fragmented piece which presented aspects of the research through drama, multimedia and presentation. Actors multi-rolled a range of composite characters which were created by identifying common experiences and stories.[4] In some instances research was used verbatim and in others a more literary recounting was adopted. Through multimedia and audio-scape, edited extracts from interviews were presented integrating real people telling their own stories with the actor's performances. In addition, a formal presentation contextualised the research and the process. The performative aspects of the piece lasted 30 minutes and were framed by both formal and informal engagement with the audiences, some structured discussion and some chat over refreshments. Response from local residents was overwhelmingly positive; one man told the company 'you said in fifteen minutes what we've been trying to say for five years'. A less positive response came from a senior representative of Liverpool City Council who felt that the company did not have a full and clear picture of the situation and was presenting only the negative response of some residents. The company was able to use the criticism as a way to gain access to regeneration staff within the council who had previously been unwilling to meet with researchers; having spent over a year unsuccessfully trying to get to the heart of the council's policy and process, this was a very welcome development. Living Place Live pointed up other areas where further research was needed and informed the company's on-going participatory programme.

The more intensive participatory processes in Living Place Project included a Theatre In Education (TIE) initiative and two community drama training programmes. The TIE initiative was a partnership between Collective Encounters, Liverpool Hope University and a north Liverpool primary school. It involved a group of third-year degree students on a TIE module working over six sessions with a Keystage 2 class to explore the children's ideas and experiences of regeneration. Through drama workshops, song writing, discussion and painting the children created fictional characters and scenarios born of their own experience. The students used this material to devise an interactive TIE piece which they toured to primary schools in the area. Collective Encounters facilitated and directed this process, and followed it up with three workshops for each audience group. There were inevitable challenges inherent to this process, borne of tailoring the work to fit with the curriculum objectives of both the school and the university, and balancing the varying interests and needs of the three partner organisations. But the process offered a valuable insight into the experiences and perceptions of pre-teen children living through change.

The two participatory programmes provided theatre skills training while facilitating participants to explore the central issues and create their own performance pieces which articulated their own concerns in their own ways. In response to feedback during R&D the programmes were accredited to ensure that participants achieved lasting and formal recognition for their work. One of the programmes was delivered as a summer school initiative for young women and the other was delivered once weekly for a mixed third-age group.

Theatre of the Oppressed was the key tool for both participant groups, and both chose to use Forum Theatre as the mechanism for their performance pieces. The young women created a piece exploring issues around perceived anti-social behaviour and lack of provision for young people. This was performed at Arena Housing's Tenants' Conference to a group of housing officials and predominately retired residents. This was an extremely positive experience which resulted in heated debates and was described as a highlight of the conference. Twelve months later Arena reported that the event had had a significant impact on residents' meetings, with older locals more willing to take young people's needs seriously and less likely to perceive them all as anti-social troublemakers.

The third-age group explored compulsory purchase orders[5] and the idea that their city was being regenerated into something that didn't include or want them. Their piece was performed in Liverpool's Foundation for Arts and Technology centre to a live audience which included representatives from many of the older people's services. The event was transmitted live via webcast so Internet users could contribute ideas on line. Again, the piece was well received with a great deal of audience intervention and a stimulating debate.

These two programmes brought with them the traditional challenges faced in most participatory work; of securing commitment and attendance, accessibility, finding appropriate venues and timings, and finding non-threatening ways of documenting work for accreditation. But, along with the TIE initiative, there was a greater challenge inherent in these participatory programmes. Each needed to stand alone as separate projects with independent outcomes, performances and discrete groups who had a genuine ownership of their work. Evaluations of the projects indicate that this was successful. At the same time, however, Collective Encounters wanted them to be integrated into the broader Living Place Project, hoped that the groups would have an ownership of the project and that there would be clarity around the way in which each performance fitted into a wider body of work. This was not achieved. While Collective Encounters was able to draw stories, ideas and experiences from each of the three initiatives which fed into the wider research, there was little sense of genuine integration with the wider project. This was partly a staffing issue, as different artists delivered on the participatory project than on the wider scale research, and due to intensive activity there was little opportunity for a comprehensive sharing of work between the teams. Partly it was an organisational difficulty – the project was ambitious and at times stretched the capacity of a small company.

Living Place Project culminated in The Harmony Suite, a large-scale documentary theatre production. Its aim was to provide a high profile, theatrically exciting event which would recount the stories the company had unearthed for a non-traditional audience of local people and those involved in the regeneration of the area. All of the research from throughout the project fed into this production. While following a more traditional performance model, the piece aimed to engage the audience directly in its resolution and in exploring the future of north Liverpool.

Since many of the project participants lived either in or next to partially derelict streets the chosen performance venue was a derelict street in the heart of north Liverpool. The piece told the story of Lilly, an elderly resident and the last remaining tenant. Lilly was about to leave the street after a lifetime in the house, but having been an active community member she wanted to throw a final street party to mark the occasion. This naturalistic narrative enabled the company to address all the major issues which had arisen through the research, from anti-social behaviour to community engagement, from compulsory purchase orders to long term unemployment. Ten characters formed the basis for this story, each a composite of the many people who had participated in the research. Woven throughout this story was a more abstract narrative which illustrated the bigger picture: a local researcher set out to reach an understanding of regeneration and found himself embroiled in a Kafkaesque maze of confusion and absurdity. This second narrative drew on large chorus sequences, employing song and dance numbers, multimedia and documentary material. It enabled the company to contextualise the local experience (Lilly's story) within the national and global situation; and to contrast the experience of the individual with the perceived needs of the decimated urban populace.

Throughout the piece audience members were spectators with no opportunity for direct engagement in the action. The intention, however, was to invite them into the street to join in the party at the end of each show. The company had hoped that with food, drink, music and chat the audience of local people, regeneration professionals and more traditional theatregoers would sit down together and engage in discussion and an exploration of ideas. The biggest disappointment for the company was that neither the funds nor the appropriate license could be secured to enable this final participation. Instead the cast came out into the audience and joined with the small groups and individuals who hung around chatting about the piece and the issues informally. The actors were told many times 'that was my life on stage' and of how good it felt to have one's personal experiences validated through the performance. As with all Collective Encounters productions The Harmony Suite was performed free of charge. It achieved a 90 per cent capacity and approximately 90 per cent of the audience were local people. Senior representatives from each of the three major agencies who had been involved with the project attended the show as well as a handful of grass-roots representatives from other housing and regeneration companies. The project was followed up with an extensive evaluation and research report which was made available to all who had been involved with the project.

Since Living Place Project Collective Encounters has continued its work in north Liverpool and has secured the support of additional regeneration agencies and civic bodies. The company continues to explore the issues and concerns most pressing to local people and to contextualize them within a wider national and international frame. The participant base for the work is growing, with on-going youth theatre and third-age theatre groups established and a satellite workshop programme in operation. The company continues to try to contribute to positive social change within north Liverpool by providing opportunities for local participants to be active in their own transformations, by making work which provokes new thinking and stimulates debate, and by creating platforms for hidden voices to be heard by those who can make a difference.

Notes

1   Liverpool City Council (North Liverpool Neighbourhood Management Team); NewHeartlands, the organisation established to deliver Merseyside's Housing Market Renewal Initiative; and Arena Housing, the lead Registered Social Landlord for a significant portion of north Liverpool.

2   Liverpool Hope University was a key partner throughout Living Place Project, providing academic support and enabling over 60 students to be involved practically through their studies. For further information about student involvement in the project see *PRIME: Pedagogical Research in Maximising Education*, Vol. 2 No. 1 Feb 2007 'Once more with meaning: Strengthening the Links between Research and Teaching in Drama and Theatre Studies using Living Place Project as a Case Study', Sarah Thornton pp25–44.

3   An idea borrowed from the Situationists' Derivé where one walks somewhat aimlessly through city streets in order to understand the area in a different way. Often this leads to chance encounters and new discoveries.

4   These types emerged naturally through the process as many of the people we talked to were experiencing exactly the same frustrations and anxieties as each other. In effect we heard a handful of stories many times.

5   The Compulsory Purchase Order is an extreme measure which enables the city council to force the sale of a private property if it is in an area marked for regeneration once negotiations have been exhausted. It is a great fear for many people in north Liverpool, where it is common for only one or two houses to be occupied on an otherwise derelict street.

Chapter 25

Marina Henriques Coutinho and Marcia Pompeo Nogueira

(trans. David Herman)

THE USE OF DIALOGICAL APPROACHES FOR COMMUNITY THEATRE BY THE GROUP *NÓS DO MORRO*, IN THE VIDIGAL FAVELA OF RIO DE JANEIRO

> No one frees another. No one frees himself. People free themselves together.
>
> (Paulo Freire 1977: 58)

THE THEATRE GROUP Nós do Morro[1] represents one of the most important initiatives in the field of artistic and social activity in Brazil's marginalized communities today. Created in 1986, the group now counts on the participation of three hundred people including children, youths and adults who live in the 'morro' of Vidigal, in Rio de Janeiro. Over two decades, for the most part without financial support, Nós do Morro has entrenched itself within the heart of its home, Vidigal, and also gained recognition outside the community. Today the productions of The Actors' Company of Nós do Morro are staged in principal theatres in Rio de Janeiro and São Paulo. In 2006 their staging of Shakespeare's Two Gentlemen of Verona was presented in Stratford-on-Avon, England, at the invitation of the Royal Shakespeare Company's 'Complete Works' Festival.

The group's activities stem from a deep-rooted background: the history of the mother community, a story of struggle and accomplishment. The stability of the group's activities has been guaranteed through the active participation of the residents of Vidigal who learnt to organize themselves in the struggle to overcome various attempts to relocate the community.

The Vidigal community

Situated in one of the most valuable areas of Rio de Janeiro, Vidigal has always been a target for real estate speculation interested in the construction of houses and luxury hotels. The threat of removal, and in some cases the actual relocation of some Vidigal dwellers, was a problem faced not only by the population of Vidigal but also by dwellers in all Rio de Janeiro's favelas. In the 1960s, the mobilization of community leadership became a significant factor for Rio's favelas. With the military *coup* of 1964, the threat of removal increased. The authoritarian policies of the military regime adopted 'removalism' as a solution for the eradication of favelas from the urban landscape of Rio de Janeiro and began to invest in the construction of housing projects for the relocation of populations. These plans, however, met with strong resistance from the favela dwellers. Founded in 1967, the Vidigal Residents Association (Associação de Moradores do Vidigal – AMV) led the struggle in defence of the consolidation of the community. In general, the community associations became a place for debate and an instrument of political pressure; their aim, to communicate the peoples' point of view to the government and other power groups.

During the 1980s, transformations in the political situation at the end of the military regime that brought about the transition to democracy helped to create a dialogue between the authorities and community leaders. This resulted in benefits for the favelas, principally with regard to basic sanitation, water and power supply, the construction of day nurseries and schools, and the construction of local health care centres.

The origins of Nós do Morro

It is within this context, in the 1980s, that Nós do Morro came into existence. The initiative started in a modest way but gradually attracted an audience which, today, forms a faithful public, sustaining runs of up to four months in its home, the Teatro do Vidigal.[2]

In the 1980s, diverse groups lived in Vidigal. The artistic community was among those who lived in the apartment buildings at the foot of the slope, close to the wealthier traditional families. The poorer residents lived in shacks which were built on the middle and upper slopes; the favela, which began to extend itself climbing slowly up the hill.

Guti Fraga, Fred Pinheiro, Fernando Mello da Costa and Luiz Paulo Corrêa e Castro[3] are the central characters in the story of Nós do Morro. It was their friendship which engendered the embryo of the group. According to Corrêa e Castro, the community was a province where everyone knew each other and socialized freely, the bar 'Bar-raco' being the principal meeting point. There, met – using the words of Corrêa e Castro – the 'long-hair mob' from the apartment buildings, and 'the boys from the favela'. Guti, Fernando and Fred counted themselves as representatives for the 'long hairs' and Luiz Paulo, one of the 'boys from the favela'. From the interaction between the two 'tribes' Nós do Morro was born. The 'boys' were eager to imbibe the information brought by the 'long hairs', who, for their part, found it an opportunity for instigating an interaction between the groups that lived in the locality, and above all for creating an access to art for the disadvantaged residents. But the opportunity to fulfil the idea of a core group for theatre would only occur in 1986 when Fraga was invited to carry out a project in the Padre Leeb Cultural Centre.[4] It was in that year that the group began its activities counting on the collaboration of about twenty members, including Guti Fraga, now recognized as the 'legendary founder', who began to dedicate himself exclusively to Nós do Morro.

The origins of the group emerge therefore from a dialogue between those outside the favela culture, the 'long hairs', and 'the boys from the favela' who adopted and assimilated Guti's ideas. We cannot say therefore that the group emerged from a spontaneous development within the favela because the initial ideas came from external elements. We can, however, affirm that the artists who were bringing the innovation of theatre adopted a stance in relation to the favela dwellers which favoured and confirmed their participation.

This stance was established from the very start; a partnership of mutual exchange between those who were sharing their theatre experience and those from within the favela culture. In practice, what we see in the first productions of Nós do Morro is the staged manifestation of this dialogue between the artists, who were contributing the fruits of their theatre experience, and the community which was contributing with its culture, its language, its universe. With the play Biroska (Street Bar) (1989), for example, Nós do Morro chose to present the day-to-day life of the favela. The play represents an important moment in the strengthening of ties between the group and the community, due not only to the subject matter of the play but also to the artistic choices of the staging. The script, written by Luiz Paulo Corrêa e Castro[5] and developed from the actors' improvisations, tells the story of Neguinho,[6] a favela dweller who, believing he has won on the Jogo do Bicho,[7] buys beers for his drinking companions, not realizing until the end that it was all a joke. The plot has fun with the remote possibility of becoming rich overnight, with which the lottery tantalises the poor Brazilian. However, in Biroska, rather than use a dramatic tone to talk about poverty and the difficulty of real life for the favela dweller, the group treats Neguinho's dilemma with humour. Humour would become a fundamental ingredient in the creation of plays by the group, especially in those which deal with the day-to-day themes of the favela.

Biroska's scenery reproduced exactly a well-known bar in Vidigal, and real personalities of the community were introduced into the play's events. Music incorporating rhythms common to the culture of the favela, such as samba and pagode, were played and sung by the actors creating a strong appeal for the community audience. The lighting for the play was improvised using tin cans as reflectors, and the price of admission was symbolically set at the price of a beer.[8] By these means Nós do Morro conquered the affection of the community, which became from that moment on its dedicated ally.

The magic of this partnership between stage and audience helped to develop from within the group the skill of transforming quotidian themes into artistic material. Other examples of this approach are two plays, also by Luiz Paulo Corrêa e Castro. In Abalou – um musical Funk (Dazed – A Funk Musical) (1998) and Noites do

Vidigal (Vidigal Nights) (2002), the author again set his plots within Vidigal. The stories, conflicts, pleasures and sorrows of the community make up the backdrop of these plays. *Abalou* deals with the life of favela youths by means of funk dances, a popular entertainment for young adults in poor communities of Rio de Janeiro. In *Vidigal Nights* the samba universe, with its all important yearly carnival parade, permeates the plot which tells the story of a love affair between the Mestre-sala and Porta-bandeira (two traditional and important carnival figures) of the Vidigal Samba School.

This appreciation of the intrinsic worth of the community, of its culture, and forms of artistic expression together with the commitment to an aesthetic quality desired by the group's young actors, guided by Guti Fraga and his theatrical knowledge, were the determining factors in gaining the support of the favela. Accordingly, Guti Fraga, Fred Pinheiro, Mello da Costa and Corrêa e Castro guaranteed, from then on, the survival of the group and its activities within and, later, outside the community of Vidigal.

Nós do Morro as a Freirean perspective

The stages of implementation undertaken by Nós do Morro in its first years of activity allow us to establish points in common with Paulo Freire's approach. Freire is critical of approaches that rely on the imposition of issues established outside the community, part of which he aligns with the concept of 'banking education'. Banking education is based on the idea that one party has the knowledge and nothing is expected from the 'other' beyond their acceptance of 'deposits' of knowledge. His educational method is an important example for those critical of models of interaction in which people from outside see the community members as objects. For Freire, an educational relationship must be based on dialogue among subjects.

In *Pedagogy of the Oppressed*, Freire offers a dialogic model of interaction, which starts with informal talks between the educators and the target community that aim to find partners to generate information about life in the area. For Freire, 'their active presence in the investigation is more important than the collection of data' (Freire 1977: 122). The similarities of Nós do Morro's approach and that of Paulo Freire are easily perceived in how the two 'tribes' approached each other and how they took into consideration the favela's culture, its daily life and 'characters' as elements of the plays they devised and performed to the Vidigal community.

For Freire, the dialogical investigation of reality aims at developing a critical perception of reality. The method includes the step of identifying symbolic situations that express the community's problems; what he calls 'codifications'. The analysis of a codification – decodification – is proposed to unveil reality as part of the process of transforming reality.

> The only standpoint that the investigators should have within their area of investigation, which one expects to be shared with the people whose life themes are to be investigated, is a critical perception of their reality which will give rise to the correct method of approaching and revealing the concrete reality.
>
> (Freire 1977: 122)

Freire has influenced several theatre practices around the globe[9] most of which form part of Augusto Boal's 'Forum Theatre' framework. Similar to the Nós do Morro's approach, these practices include dialogic strategies related to the identification of the community problems that are analysed by means of theatrical strategies; aiming ultimately to organize a collective discussion as a step to solve the community's problems.

In the case of Nós do Morro, however, even though the inspiration for many of their presentations is the favela itself, the goal has never been to turn the stage into a space or forum to debate the problems of the community. The plays bring to the stage the past, the present, and the conflicts and the people of Vidigal; they possess surprising plots which are full of irreverence and humour using a lens which focuses on Vidigal from an artistic viewpoint.

Accordingly, we could affirm that the practices of Nós do Morro are in sympathy with a Freirian approach even though the main beliefs of the group are different from those whose principal focus is the use of theatre as a tool for the discussion of issues related to the reality of the communities. The foundation on which the development of Nós do Morro is based is the dialogic relationship established between the artists and the young favela residents in its first stages of existence. However, they include the creation of plays of artistic quality, as part of their main goal.

The distinctiveness of Nós do Morro approach

The phenomenon of Nós do Morro, whose beginnings stemmed from a cultural exchange between two groups, transformed itself little by little into a movement belonging to the favela community; produced by the community for the community, and by means of this, through the pact established between stage and audience, became the legitimate expression of the community. It seems important to dwell on the characteristics of the beginnings of Nós do Morro to enable us to understand its distinctiveness in relation to the many projects offered by Non-Government Organizations (NGOs), private enterprise and government agencies. In these initiatives the various artistic activities were seen as tools for keeping in check the social chaos and violence since they offered children and adolescents stimulating cultural alternatives with which they could identify and transform into a life option.

A study prepared by UNESCO entitled Cultivando Vida, desarmando violências (Cultivating life, disarming violence) brings to the forefront endeavours spread throughout Brazil aimed at youths in social risk situations and which have contributed to promoting a more peaceful society. The study recognizes that art, sport, education and cultural growth represent an: 'alternative and strategic element to confront and combat violence [. . .] an incentive for young people to distance themselves from dangerous situations [. . .]' (Castro 2001: 19).[10]

It is in fact evident that all of these initiatives, much featured in the Brazilian press, have brought about an improvement in the quality of life of children and adolescents by occupying their time in a healthful and creative way. But one needs to be attentive to the fact that some of these projects, by emphasizing to the news media the vulnerability of 'favela' youth with regard to a life of violence, may be 'selling' the idea that, if they did not exist, all the young 'favelados' would become criminals. The slogan 'Save children from a life of crime' has been adopted by some of these initiatives. Besides spreading the idea that favela dwellers are, for the most part, vulnerable to the influence of the drug traffic organizations, which is far from the truth, this attitude also exposes another mistake: that of considering the favela dweller as someone who needs to be 'saved' and the favela as a territory of the 'needy'. By embracing this slogan, these projects end up adopting the role of 'saviours' because, evidently, if there exist those who must be saved, there also exists those who can 'save'.

This viewpoint rules out the possibility of these initiatives approximating the experience of *Nós do Morro*. By seeing themselves as 'saviours', they will most likely harm their endeavours through adopting a posture which is in opposition to the Freirian approach. This is an ideological error that reveals itself in a paternalistic attitude, which, far from serving to free these historically oppressed people, can end up helping to prolong their situation of exclusion. For a social action to be in fact transforming, it is necessary that we believe in the oppressed as also capable of right thinking; in the words of Paulo Freire:

> If we lack this belief, then we abandon the idea or we lack it, of dialogue, of reflection, of communication and we revert to slogans, directives, teaching by rote, authoritarianism. This is the threat contained in the inauthentic collaborations to the cause of the liberation of man.
>
> (Freire 1977: 57)

A study conducted in 2002 by the dance teacher and critic Silvia Soter shows that projects in favelas do not always establish a relationship with their communities which resembles that developed between *Nós do Morro* and the Vidigal community. Soter traces thirty-two projects which offered free dance activities to youths from low-income families in Rio. According to Soter, the young people who participated in dance events which were staged by the projects tended to be identified in the news media as youths from the poorer sectors, needy children and adolescents or favela 'kids'. As stated by Soter:

> Often their lives are directly associated to exclusion and violence. Some newspaper headlines, like those that follow, illustrate the treatment they receive in the news media: *Youths dodge violence with dance; Between the drug wars and the glamour of dance.*
>
> (Soter, 2005: 9)

For Soter, '. . . in most cases, the participation of the young people does not constitute a real artistic collaboration. In general, they are dancers in pieces which they did not create' (2005: 10). Additionally, some of these initiatives, besides failing to establish a dialogue with their participants and with the communities involved, might be said to endorse the stereotypes that have impregnated the image of the favela populations for more than a century. According to the researchers Alba Zaluar and Marcus Alvito, escaping the stereotypes of being 'wanting' or a 'criminal' has been a problem faced by the favela dweller since the beginning of the twentieth century, when the poorer population began to occupy the 'morros'. Since 1908 the favela has represented in the popular urban imagination: 'a focal point of disease; a place of swindlers and rogues; a cradle for criminals and a stronghold of disorder.'

And, 'despite what is stated often in the literature of the favela, it had come to be perceived as a "problem"'(Alvito and Zaluar 2003: 10).

According to Zaluar and Alvito, looking upon the favela as a phantasm which haunts the city has created a division, a duality, which radically separates the 'morro' from the 'asphalt':

> With the arrival of cocaine trafficking in the city as a whole, the favela – where the gangs armed themselves to sell in the same commerce that was taking hold of the rest of the city, not to say the rest of the country – began to represent again a bandit's lair, a free zone for crime, a natural habitat for the criminal classes [. . .] in spite of different vestments, but always within a specific historical context, the 'favelado' was a phantasm [. . .]
>
> (Alvito and Zaluar 2003: 15)

The articles contained in this study contradict the common idea which for a long time has imprisoned the image of the favela in a context of disorder and neediness. The study demystifies them by saying that the hundred years of existence of the Rio favela is a history of attainments; where the residents' capacity to struggle has earned them improvements in urbanization. But above all, showing that in the favela there has been created 'what is most original in the city's culture: samba, the carnival, where books are written, verses are composed and plays are staged [. . .]'(Alvito and Zaluar 2003: 22).

Because of this, it seems necessary to single out the distinctiveness of the history and importance of *Nós do Morro* within the present panorama of initiatives in Brazilian communities. Primarily, this is because the group has pursued a *modus operandi* which started with the construction of its identity within the favela of Vidigal, and involved respecting the values of the local culture and developing a theatrical form capable of communicating with its community. The dialogical approach was present, not only in the process of implantation (given the relationship between the 'long-haired artists' and the 'boys from the community'), but also in the artistic choices which allowed them to establish complicity between the stage and the Vidigal audience; these choices recognized and presented on stage the socio-cultural characteristics of the community.

Afterwards, the group expanded its limits and succeeded in bringing down the barriers that separate the 'morro' from the 'asphalt' by the artistic merit of its plays. Theirs is a course of action pledged to the transformation of the social group (the favela) and to a dialogue with the other ('asphalt' and the news media). Inherent in this interaction is one of the most fascinating aspects of the phenomenon: the theatre's capacity to dissolve frontiers and instigate encounters. In the history of *Nós do Morro*, there are no 'saviours', nor those who need to be saved. The story was written by men and women who believe that *together* we are capable of transformations.

Bibliography

Abah, S.O. (1997) *Performing Life: Case Studies in the Practice of Theatre for Development*, Zaria: Bright Printing Press.

Alvito, M. and Zaluar, A. (2003) Um século de favela, Rio de Janeiro: Editora FGV.

Castro, M.G. (2001) Cultivando Vida, desarmando violências, Brasília: UNESCO, Brasil Telecom, Fundação Kellogg, Banco Interamericano de Desenvolvimento.

Coutinho, M.H. (2005) 'Nós do Morro: percurso, impacto e transformação. O grupo de Teatro da favela do Vidigal', Masters Dissertation at UNIRIO.

Freire, P. (1977) Pedagogia do Oprimido, Rio de Janeiro: Paz e Terra.

Kidd, R. (1984) From People's Theatre for Revolution to Popular Theatre for Reconstruction: Diary of a Zimbabwean Workshop, The Hague: CESO.

Mda, Z. (1993) When People Play People: Development Communication through Theatre, London: Zed Books.

Soter, S. (2005) 'Cidadãos dançantes – A experiência de Ivaldo Bertazzo com o corpo de dança da Maré', Master's Dissertation at UNIRIO.

Notes

1   'Morro' is a term synonymous with 'favela' or 'poor community' in Rio de Janeiro since the majority of early favelas were built on the steep slopes of the morros or mountains which are a marked characteristic of the Rio landscape. Nós do Morro means 'We of the Morro'.

2   The theatre, which accommodates an audience of 80, was built by the group members, in 1996, attached to the local Municipal School. In 1998 the group was offered the use of a large house which is used to hold rehearsals and classes for children and adolescents. Today, their work is divided between the house and the theatre.

3   From 1990 on, Maria José da Silva became part of this group.

4   The Padre Leeb Cultural Centre was founded by the Austrian Padre Humberto Leeb who arrived in Brazil in 1976. He created in Vidigal a Meeting, Social Aid and Cultural Centre. In 1995, alarmed by the violence, the missionaries brought to a close their activities in Vidigal.

5   For the two initial productions of the group, Encontros and Biroska, Luiz Paulo Corrêa e Castro was responsible for transcribing the improvisations created by the actors. In this way he developed his writing skills. Now he is the group's dramatist and dramaturge, recognized by theatre critics in Brazil principally for his own works Noites de Vidigal (2002) and Burro sem Rabo (2004). According to Corrêa e Castro the script Biroska no longer exists. This information about the plays is based on interviews with the author.

6   Diminutive of Nego (black male).

7   Informal and illegal lottery, similar to the American Numbers Racket, popular among poor Brazilians.

8   Nós do Morro had adopted the practice of a symbolic price of admission. From Biroska on, this amount has been based on the price of a beer in the local bars.

9   See: Abah, 1997; Mda, 1993; Kidd, 1984.

10   This study dedicates a chapter to the experience of Nós do Morro, and finds that, among the 30 projects traced in various Brazilian states, the group is one of the pioneers.

PART 5

Intervention

Chapter 26

Tim Prentki

INTRODUCTION TO
INTERVENTION

THE NOTION OF INTERVENTION implies the arrival of some outside
force to alter the dynamics of a static situation. Applied theatre, according to
this understanding, is the agency of intervention forcing its way into closed worlds
(schools, prisons, African villages, old people's homes, aboriginal communities) in
order to provoke changes, such as dropping a boulder into a stagnant pond. The
terms upon which the outsider enters the chosen community may well determine the
response offered by participants to the proposed project or workshop. Many
facilitators and companies only work by invitation as a point of principle, although
this stance raises the question: whose invitation? For instance, prison theatre is
normally undertaken in response to an invitation from the prison governor rather
than the prisoners; TIE companies enter schools at the request of teachers rather
than pupils; and international NGOs are typically invited by community-based
organisations which may or may not be representative of the participants in the
applied theatre project. The very idea of intervention is implicated in issues of power
and the right to speak on behalf of others. While practitioners may and, we would
argue, should be bound by democratic principles whereby the voice of each participant
has an equal right to be heard in the process, the context in which the practice
occurs may have predetermined inequalities structured into the formation of the
group or community. The playing field is never level but there may be some scope
for practitioners to elect whether to attempt to flatten the slope, to exacerbate the
incline or merely to accept the existing contours.

Despite these caveats, interventions on behalf of or with those whose voices are
not normally heard in the societies they inhabit are a vital feature of applied theatre
practice since they act as a counterweight to the myriad interventions of the dominant
into the lives of all of us. The power and reach of the dominant, neoliberal, economic
model in the lives of almost all the inhabitants of the planet is cogently attested by

Noam Chomsky. A sample of his writing is included here to remind readers of the macro context into which micro interventions of applied theatre are made. Those who are squeamish about the right of applied theatre workers to make exogenous cultural interventions might spare a thought for the multi-national corporations, government agencies and global media organisations that intervene thousands of times per day to interfere with our actions, beliefs and desires without incurring moral outrage. As Wolfgang Sachs points out:

> The worldwide simplification of architecture, clothing, and daily objects assaults the eye; the accompanying eclipse of variegated languages, customs and gestures is already less visible; and the standardization of desires and dreams occurs deep down in the subconscious of societies. Market, state, and science have been the great universalizing powers; admen, experts and educators have relentlessly expanded their reign.
>
> (Sachs 1992: 4)

In the face of this onslaught the interventions of applied theatre practitioners appear as very small beer, yet they constitute an important contribution to the antidote of the counter-culture. As a participatory, collective form of artistic and social engagement, theatre resists the isolating, passive modes of the dominant forms of screen culture. One of the socio-economic forces at work to induce passivity is colonialism and its legacy of neo-colonialism. In those nations or sections of nations where the people have been victimised by hundreds of years of propaganda into believing that their culture – the ways in which they make meaning of their lives – is second-rate or worthless, it is naïve to suppose that a move to self-empowerment and autonomy can always be made without the external involvement of a decolonising agent such as the facilitator of an applied theatre process. The people may have the will to decolonise but the generations of oppression may have robbed them of the means. An example of such an instance is offered by Ngũgĩ wa Thiong'o in the famous case of Kamĩrĩĩthũ Community Education and Cultural Centre where the force of peasants and workers allying their own forms of artistic expression to theatrical communication – finding and using their own voices – was deemed too severe a threat to the neo-colonial regime to be allowed to continue. This *locus classicus* of applied theatre intervention demonstrated what can be achieved when the will for change (and the invitation) came from the community itself and when the applied theatre process takes its place among a network of movements dedicated to the self-development of that community until the government determined on its own form of violent intervention.

Where applied theatre projects espouse the aim of transformation or social change, it might be expected that the practitioners would seek to work with those who are best situated to bring about change. But all too often there is an almost automatic assumption that applied theatre practices are to be located in the territory of the victims of personal or social oppression; empowerment for the disempowered. Such practices may serve the participants well in terms of confidence building and social skills but are unlikely to make much impact in terms of wider questions of structural transformation. It is, for example, commonplace for applied theatre processes to be used with female victims of domestic violence who may leave the workshop with heightened awareness of their rights and with the confidence of their new empowerment that puts them at even greater risk of abuse from unchanged men who were no part of the workshop process. Who needs to be changed? To whom should theatre be applied? In the next phase of its existence applied theatre needs to cast its net wider to include the power-brokers at both national and local levels if these are the people with the greatest opportunity to effect change. One innovative example of such a practice is the *Teatro di Nascosto* (Hidden Theatre), run by Annet Henneman from Volterra in Italy. Having researched and worked with the stories of refugees and asylum seekers, Henneman develops performances in which members of the national and European parliaments and relevant professionals recite these verbatim stories alongside actors and refugees. By bringing politicians into direct contact with the raw, very raw, material of actual stories, cases are transformed into people and the theatrical force of empathy is let loose upon those who have the power to make and unmake the legal framework.

There are many strategies for intervention; as many as the contexts into which a practitioner might intervene. 'Optimum intervention', to borrow Zakes Mda's phrase, is not achieved through a fixed formula but only through a dialectical inter-action of participants and facilitators who are practising a co-intentional approach to self-development and social change.

Bibliography

Sachs, W. (ed.) (1992) *The Development Dictionary*, London: Zed Books.

Chapter 27

Noam Chomsky

PROFIT OVER PEOPLE

Profit over People, 'Neoliberalism and Global Order', Seven Stories Press (1999), excerpt from Chapter 1, pp. 19–40.

Neoliberalism and global order

I WOULD LIKE TO DISCUSS each of the topics mentioned in the title: neoliberalism and global order. The issues are of great human significance and not very well understood. To deal with them sensibly, we have to begin by separating doctrine from reality. We often discover a considerable gap.

The term "neoliberalism" suggests a system of principles that is both new and based on classical liberal ideas: Adam Smith is revered as the patron saint. The doctrinal system is also known as the "Washington consensus," which suggests something about global order. A closer look shows that the suggestion about global order is fairly accurate, but not the rest. The doctrines are not new, and the basic assumptions are far from those that have animated the liberal tradition since the Enlightenment.

The Washington consensus

The neoliberal Washington consensus is an array of market oriented principles designed by the government of the United States and the international financial institutions that it largely dominates, and implemented by them in various ways – for the more vulnerable societies, often as stringent structural adjustment programs. The basic rules, in brief, are: liberalize trade and finance, let markets set price ("get prices right"), end inflation ("macroeconomic stability"), privatize. The government should "get out of the way" – hence the population too, insofar as the government is democratic, though the conclusion remains implicit. The decisions of those who impose the "consensus" naturally have a major impact on global order. Some analysts take a much stronger position. The international business press has referred to these institutions as the core of a "de facto world government" of a "new imperial age."

Whether accurate or not, this description serves to remind us that the governing institutions are not independent agents but reflect the distribution of power in the larger society. That has been a truism at least since Adam Smith, who pointed out that the "principal architects" of policy in England were "merchants and manufacturers," who used state power to serve their own interests, however "grievous" the effect on others, including the people of England. Smith's concern was "the wealth of nations," but he understood that the "national interest" is largely a delusion: within the "nation" there are sharply conflicting interests, and to understand policy and its effects we have to ask where power lies and how it is exercised, what later came to be called class analysis.

The "principal architects" of the neoliberal "Washington consensus" are the masters of the private economy, mainly huge corporations that control much of the international economy and have the means to dominate policy formation as well as the structuring of thought and opinion. The United States has a special role in the system for obvious reasons. To borrow the words of diplomatic historian Gerald Haines, who is also senior historian of the CIA, "Following World War II the United States assumed, out of self-interest, responsibility for the welfare of the world capitalist system." Haines is concerned with what he calls "the Americanization of Brazil," but only as a special case. And his words are accurate enough.

The United States had been the world's major economy long before World War II, and during the war it prospered while its rivals were severely weakened. The state-coordinated wartime economy was at last able to overcome the Great Depression. By the war's end, the United States had half of the world's wealth and a position of power without historical precedent. Naturally, the principal architects of policy intended to use this power to design a global system in their interests.

High-level documents describe the primary threat to these interests, particularly in Latin America, as "radical" and "nationalistic regimes" that are responsive to popular pressures for "immediate improvement in the low living standards of the masses" and development for domestic needs. These tendencies conflict with the demand for "a political and economic climate conducive to private investment," with adequate repatriation of profits and "protection of our raw materials" – ours, even if located somewhere else. For such reasons, the influential planner George Kennan advised that we should "cease to talk about vague and unreal objectives such as human rights, the raising of the living standards, and democratization" and must "deal in straight power concepts," not "hampered by idealistic slogans" about "altruism and world-benefaction" – though such slogans are fine, in fact obligatory, in public discourse.

I am quoting the secret record, available now in principle, though largely unknown to the general public or the intellectual community.

"Radical nationalism" is intolerable in itself, but it also poses a broader "threat to stability," another phrase with a special meaning. As Washington prepared to overthrow Guatemala's first democratic government in 1954, a State Department official warned that Guatemala had "become an increasing threat to the stability of

Honduras and El Salvador. Its agrarian reform is a powerful propaganda weapon; its broad social program of aiding the workers and peasants in a victorious struggle against the upper classes and large foreign enterprises has a strong appeal to the populations of Central American neighbors where similar conditions prevail." "Stability" means security for "the upper classes and large foreign enterprises," whose welfare must be preserved.

Such threats to the "welfare of the world capitalist system" justify terror and subversion to restore "stability." One of the first tasks of the CIA was to take part in the large-scale effort to undermine democracy in Italy in 1948, when it was feared that elections might come out the wrong way; direct military intervention was planned if subversion failed. These are described as efforts "to stabilize Italy." It is even possible to "destabilize a freely elected Marxist government in Chile" because "we were determined to seek stability." With a proper education, one can overcome the apparent contradiction.

Nationalist regimes that threaten "stability" are sometimes called "rotten apples" that might "spoil the barrel," or "viruses" that might "infect" others. Italy in 1948 is one example. Twenty-five years later, Henry Kissinger described Chile as a "virus" that might send the wrong messages about possibilities for social change, infecting others as far as Italy, still not "stable" even after years of major CIA programs to subvert Italian democracy. Viruses have to be destroyed and others protected from infection: for both tasks, violence is often the most efficient means, leaving a gruesome trail of slaughter, terror, torture, and devastation.

In secret postwar planning, each part of the world was assigned its specific role. Thus the "major function" of Southeast Asia was to provide raw materials for the industrial powers. Africa was to be "exploited" by Europe for its own recovery. And so on, through the world.

In Latin America, Washington expected to be able to implement the Monroe Doctrine, but again in a special sense. President Wilson, famous for his idealism and high moral principles, agreed in secret that "in its advocacy of the Monroe Doctrine the United States considers its own interests." The interests of Latin Americans are merely "incidental," not our concern. He recognized that "this may seem based on selfishness alone," but held that the doctrine "had no higher or more generous motive." The United States sought to displace its traditional rivals, England and France, and establish a regional alliance under its control that was to stand apart from the world system, in which such arrangements were not to be permitted.

The "functions" of Latin America were clarified at a hemispheric conference in February 1945, where Washington proposed an "Economic Charter of the Americas" that would eliminate economic nationalism "in all its forms." Washington planners understood that it would not be easy to impose this principle. State Department documents warned that Latin Americans prefer "policies designed to bring about a broader distribution of wealth and to raise the standard of living of the masses," and are "convinced that the first beneficiaries of the development of a country's resources should be the people of that country." These ideas are unacceptable: the "first beneficiaries" of a country's resources are U.S. investors, while Latin America fulfils its service function without unreasonable concerns about general welfare or "excessive industrial development" that might infringe on U.S. interests.

The position of the United States prevailed, though not without problems in the years that followed, addressed by means I need not review.

As Europe and Japan recovered from wartime devastation, world order shifted to a tripolar pattern. The United States has retained its dominant role, though new challenges are arising, including European and East Asian competition in South America. The most important changes took place twenty-five years ago [1973], when the Nixon Administration dismantled the postwar global economic system, within which the United States was, in effect, the world's banker, a role it could no longer sustain. This unilateral act (to be sure, with the cooperation of other powers) led to a huge explosion of unregulated capital flows. Still more striking is the shift in the composition of the flow of capital. In 1971, 90 percent of international financial transactions were related to the real economy – trade or long-term investment – and 10 percent were speculative. By 1990 the percentages were reversed, and by 1995 about 95 percent of the vastly greater sums were speculative, with daily flows regularly exceeding the combined foreign exchange reserves of the seven biggest industrial powers, over $1 trillion a day, and very short-term: about 80 percent with round trips of a week or less.

Prominent economists warned over twenty years ago that the process would lead to a low-growth, low-wage economy, and suggested fairly simple measures that might prevent these consequences. But the principal architects of the Washington consensus preferred the predictable effects, including very high profits. These effects were augmented by the (short-term) sharp rise in oil prices and the telecommunications revolution, both related to the huge state sector of the U.S. economy, to which I will return.

The so-called "Communist" states were outside this global system. By the 1970s China was being reintegrated into it. The Soviet economy began to stagnate in the 1960s, and the whole rotten edifice collapsed twenty years later. The region is largely returning to its earlier status. Sectors that were part of the West are rejoining it, while most of the region is returning to its traditional service role, largely under the rule of former Communist bureaucrats and other local associates of foreign enterprises, along with criminal syndicates. The pattern is familiar in the third world, as are the outcomes. In Russia alone, a UNICEF inquiry in 1993 estimated that a half-million extra deaths a year result from the neoliberal "reforms," which it generally supports. Russia's social policy chief recently estimated that 25 percent of the population has fallen below subsistence levels, while the new rulers have gained enormous wealth, again the familiar pattern of Western dependencies.

Also familiar are the effects of the large-scale violence undertaken to ensure the "welfare of the world capitalist system." A recent Jesuit conference in San Salvador pointed out that over time, the "culture of terror domesticates the expectations of the majority." People may no longer even think about "alternatives different from those of the powerful," who describe the outcome as a grand victory for freedom and democracy.

These are some of the contours of the global order within which the Washington consensus has been forged.

The novelty of neoliberalism

Let us look more closely at the novelty of neoliberalism. A good place to start is a recent publication of the Royal Institute of International Affairs in London, with survey articles on major issues and policies. One is devoted to the economics of development. The author, Paul Krugman, is a prominent figure in the field. He makes five central points, which bear directly on our question.

First, knowledge about economic development is very limited. For the United States, for example, two-thirds of the rise in per capita income is unexplained. Similarly, the Asian success stories have followed paths that surely do not conform to what "current orthodoxy says are the key to growth," Krugman points out. He recommends "humility" in policy formation, and caution about "sweeping generalizations."

His second point is that conclusions with little basis are constantly put forth and provide the doctrinal support for policy: the Washington consensus is a case in point.

His third point is that the "conventional wisdom" is unstable, regularly shifting to something else, perhaps the opposite of the latest phase – though its proponents are again full of confidence as they impose the new orthodoxy.

His fourth point is that, in retrospect, it is commonly agreed that the economic development policies did not "serve their expressed goal" and were based on "bad ideas."

Lastly, Krugman remarks, it is usually "argued that bad ideas flourish because they are in the interest of powerful groups. Without doubt that happens."

That it happens has been a commonplace at least since Adam Smith. And it happens with impressive consistency, even in the rich countries, though it is the third world that provides the cruel[sic]est record.

That is the heart of the matter. The "bad ideas" may not serve the "expressed goals," but they typically turn out to be very *good* ideas for their principal architects. There have been many experiments in economic development in the modern era, with regularities that are hard to ignore. One is that the designers tend to do quite well, though the subjects of the experiment often take a beating.

The first major experiment was carried out two hundred years ago, when the British rulers in India instituted the "Permanent Settlement," which was going to do wondrous things. The results were reviewed by an official commission forty years later, which concluded that "the settlement fashioned with great care and deliberation has unfortunately subjected the lower classes to most grievous oppression," leaving misery that "hardly finds a parallel in the history of commerce," as "the bones of the cotton-weavers are bleaching the plains of India."

But the experiment can hardly be written off as a failure. The British governor-general observed that "the 'Permanent Settlement,' though a failure in many other respects and in most important essentials, has this great advantage, at least, of having created a vast body of rich landed proprietors deeply interested in the continuance of the British Dominion and having complete command over the mass of the people." Another advantage was that British investors gained enormous wealth. India also financed 40 percent of Britain's trade deficit while providing a protected market for its manufacturing exports; contract laborers for British possessions, replacing earlier slave populations; and the opium that was the staple of Britain's exports to China. The opium trade was imposed on China by force, not the operations of the "free market," just as the sacred principles of the market were overlooked when opium was barred from England.

In brief, the first great experiment was a "bad idea" for the subjects, but not for the designers and local elites associated with them. This pattern continues until the present: placing profit over people. The consistency of the record is no less impressive than the rhetoric hailing the latest showcase for democracy and capitalism as an "economic miracle" – and what the rhetoric regularly conceals. Brazil, for example. In the highly praised history of the Americanization of Brazil that I mentioned, Gerald Haines writes that from 1945 the United States used Brazil as a "testing area for modern scientific methods of industrial development based solidly on capitalism." The experiment was carried out with "the best of intentions." Foreign investors benefited, but planners "sincerely believed" that the people of Brazil would benefit as well. I need not describe how they benefited as Brazil became "the Latin American darling of the international business community" under military rule, in the words of the business press, while the World Bank reported that two-thirds of the population did not have enough food for normal physical activity.

Writing in 1989, Haines describes "America's Brazilian policies" as "enormously successful," "a real American success story." 1989 was the "golden year" in the eyes of the business world, with profits tripling over 1988, while industrial wages, already among the lowest in the world, declined another 20 percent; the UN *Report on Human Development* ranked Brazil next to Albania. When the disaster began to hit the wealthy as well, the "modern scientific methods of development based solidly on capitalism" (Haines) suddenly became proofs of the evils of statism and socialism – another quick transition that takes place when needed.

To appreciate the achievement, one must remember that Brazil has long been recognized to be one of the richest countries of the world, with enormous advantages, including half a century of dominance and tutelage by the United States with benign intent, which once again just happens to serve the profit of the few while leaving the majority of people in misery.

The most recent example is Mexico. It was highly praised as a prize student of the rules of the Washington consensus and offered as a model for others – as wages collapsed, poverty increased almost as fast as the number of billionaires, foreign capital flowed in (mostly speculative, or for exploitation of cheap labor kept under control by the brutal "democracy"). Also familiar is the collapse of the house of cards in December 1994. Today half the population cannot obtain minimum food requirements, while the man who controls the corn markets remains on the list of Mexico's billionaires, one category in which the country ranks high.

Changes in global order have also made it possible to apply a version of the Washington consensus at home. For most of the U.S. population, incomes have stagnated or declined for fifteen years along with working conditions and job security, continuing through economic recovery, an unprecedented phenomenon. Inequality has reached levels unknown for seventy years, far beyond other industrial countries. The United States has the highest level of child poverty of any industrial society, followed by the rest of the English-speaking world. So the record continues through the familiar list of third world maladies. Meanwhile the business press cannot find adjectives exuberant enough to describe the "dazzling" and "stupendous" profit growth, though admittedly the rich face problems too: a headline in *Business Week* announces "The Problem Now: What to Do with All That Cash," as "surging profits" are "overflowing the coffers of Corporate America," and dividends are booming.

Profits remain "spectacular" through the mid-1996 figures, with "remarkable" profit growth for the world's largest corporations, though there is "one area where global companies are not expanding much: payrolls," the leading business monthly adds quietly. That exception includes companies that "had a terrific year" with "booming profits" while they cut workforces, shifted to part-time workers with no benefits or security, and otherwise behaved exactly as one would expect with "capital's clear subjugation of labor for 15 years," to borrow another phrase from the business press. [. . .]

[. . .] There is much more to say about these matters, but one conclusion seems fairly clear: the approved doctrines are crafted and employed for reasons of power and profit. Contemporary "experiments" follow a familiar pattern when they take the form of "socialism for the rich" within a system of global corporate mercantilism in which "trade" consists in substantial measure of centrally managed transactions within single firms, huge institutions linked to their competitors by strategic alliances, all of them tyrannical in internal structure, designed to undermine democratic decision making and to safeguard the masters from market discipline. It is the poor and defenceless who are to be instructed in these stern doctrines.

We might also ask just how "global" the economy really is, and how much it might be subject to popular democratic control. In terms of trade, financial flows, and other measures, the economy is not more global than early in this [sic] century. Furthermore, TNCs rely heavily on public subsidies and domestic markets, and their international transactions, including those mislabel[sic]ed trade, are largely within Europe, Japan and the United States, where political measures are available without fear of military coups and the like. There is a great deal that is new and significant, but the belief that things are "out of control" is not very credible, even if we keep to existing mechanisms.

Is it a law of nature that we must keep to these? Not if we take seriously the doctrines of classical liberalism. Adam Smith's praise of division of labor is well known, but not his denunciation of its inhuman effects, which will turn working people into objects "as stupid and ignorant as it is possible for a human creature to be," something that must be prevented "in every improved and civilized society" by government action to overcome the destructive force of the "invisible hand." Also not well advertised is Smith's belief that government "regulation in favour of the workman is always just and equitable," though not "when in favour of the masters." Or his call for equality of outcome, which was at the heart of his argument for free markets.

Other leading contributors to the classical liberal canon go much further. Wilhelm von Humboldt condemned wage labor itself: when the labourer works under external control, he wrote, "we may admire what he does, but we despise what he is." "The art advances, the artisan recedes," Alexis de Tocqueville observed. Also a great figure of the liberal pantheon, Tocqueville agreed with Smith and Jefferson that equality of outcome is an important feature of a free and just society. One hundred and sixty years ago, he warned of the dangers of a "permanent inequality of conditions" and an end to democracy if "the manufacturing aristocracy which is growing up under our eyes" in the United States, "one of the harshest that has ever existed in the world," should escape its confines – as it later did, beyond his worst nightmares.

I am only barely touching on intricate and fascinating issues, which suggest, I think, that leading principles of classical liberalism receive their natural modern expression not in the neoliberal "religion" but in the independent movements of working people and the ideas and practices of the libertarian socialist movements, at times articulated also by such major figures of twentieth-century thought as Bertrand Russell and John Dewey.

One has to evaluate with caution the doctrines that dominate intellectual discourse, with careful attention to the argument, the facts, and the lessons of past and present history. It makes little sense to ask what is "right" for particular countries as if these are entities with common interests and values. And what may be right for people in the United States, with their unparalleled advantages, could well be wrong for others who have much narrower scope of choices. We can, however, reasonably anticipate that what is right for the people of the world will only by the remotest accident conform to the plans of the "principal architects" of policy. And there is no more reason now than there ever has been to permit them to shape the future in their own interests.

Chapter 28

Zakes Mda

WHEN PEOPLE PLAY PEOPLE

When People Play People, Zed Books (1993), excerpt from pp. 177–89.

[. . .]

The efficacy of theatre in development communication

THE STUDY HAS ILLUSTRATED that theatre can be effective as a medium for development communication. The work of Marotholi Travelling Theatre analysed in this study has confirmed some of the assertions made by theatre-for-development and development communication practitioners and scholars on the relative efficacy of the medium in conscientising a rural population, and in disseminating development messages. The work particularly confirms the findings of the Telu Workshop in Sierra Leone, of which the workshop director writes:

> Today, Theatre for Development has been identified by many in the Third World as an effective two-way communication process predicated on dialogue and genuine participation on the part of the researchers and the researched. If properly used, it can perhaps be a most efficacious instrument for conscientising and enabling the masses and for propagating development messages using the people's language, idioms and art forms.
> (Malamah-Thomas 1989)

It is significant that Malamah-Thomas adds the qualification 'if properly used' to his statement on the efficacy of theatre. Like all other media, theatre's effectiveness in development communication depends very much on the proficiency of the practitioner. In theatre-for-development the proficiency should not only be in the creation of highly polished productions of great aesthetic merit; the practitioner must also have clarity of what development and development communication entail. [. . .]

The plays that evinced efficacy were those that concentrated not only on the artistic product, but also on the process of analysis from the rural community's perspective. The practitioner must find the balance between aesthetics and function. This study has shown that the two are not in opposition. Indeed, it was clearly illustrated that those works which were of high aesthetic quality in the utilisation of popular performance modes such as lifela were the most effective in drawing people to participate in a critical analysis process. In those plays, then, theatre-for-development was able to serve the following functions:

1   **Mobilisation in support of national development:** People were motivated into effective participation in programmes geared towards people's self-reliance. . . .

2   **Conscientisation:** In all the plays where there was community participation and catalyst intervention, the villagers were able to question some of the contradictions in society. The villagers examined the contradictions at local level . . ., at national level . . . and at international level. . . .

3   **A two-way communication process with inbuilt feedback:** Through the plays, dialogue was developed among the members of the community themselves, and between the community and extension workers from governmental and non-governmental agencies. Each side had an opportunity to express its views, and to learn the other side's perceptions and priorities. Government was able to have feedback on its policies, and the peasants had a say in their own development.

4   **Community discussion and community decision-making:** The plays gave the villagers the opportunity to discuss their problems, to decide solutions, and to implement the solutions.

5   **Intervillage and intravillage solidarity:** The performances fostered intravillage solidarity since community members were able to discuss their common problems, and to work out solutions together as a community, rather than as individuals. Intervillage solidarity was fostered with villagers from one village attending and participating in performances in other villages. . . .

6   **Revitalisation of the people's own forms of cultural expression:** The plays provided a stimulus for the villagers' cultural activity. . . .

This study's position is that of all these functions, the most important is that theatre-for-development gives the periphery access to the production and distribution of messages. It was shown that critical analysis, and therefore conscientisation, happens only when the periphery is able to produce and distribute its own messages. . . .

Indispensability of mass media

The study has made the following points:

*   Live theatre is not mass communication.
*   Some theatre is interpersonal communication, or has strong elements of interpersonal communication (for example, forum theatre, simultaneous dramaturgy, and to some extent participatory agitprop).

- Not all theatre is interpersonal communication (for instance, agitprop lacks the crucial characteristics of interpersonal communication. Agitprop can be best described as public address communication).

One major problem with theatre is that it is not multiplicative. Mass media, on the other hand, can multiply a message and make it available in many places. Radio, for instance, is much in use in Lesotho. Its advantage is that it can overcome distance and time. Radio signals reach the widely dispersed homesteads in the remotest areas of the country. At 62.2 per cent, radio-set ownership is high for a developing country. This means that the majority of the people in Lesotho can be reached through the radio. Theatre, on the other hand, can only be performed in one place at a time. This means that, in spite of its advantages over mass media, theatre can never replace it. . . .

Assets and liabilities of different methods of theatre-for-development

Agitprop: Its major disadvantage is that it engenders little or no conscientisation since the audiences do not participate in producing and distributing the messages. The theatre is produced by an outside agent, but is oriented towards the people. It is either diffusionist or persuasive communication (market approach). But until constraints of time and manpower have been solved, agitprop will continue to have a role in theatre-for-development. It was noted that the other methodologies take time since catalysts have to live with the community and create plays with them. In agitprop the spectacle is presented as a finished product, and then there are informal post-performance discussions. The theatre group is therefore able to tour from village to village within a very short time. However, all they will be doing is disseminating messages from development agencies without creating any critical awareness of the objective situation from the villagers' own perspective.

Agitprop is also well-suited for packaging for radio and television. Indeed Marotholi have produced many television films on such subjects as AIDS, TB, and breastfeeding, all using the agitprop method.

Participatory Agitprop: Compared to agitprop, participatory agitprop engenders a higher level of conscientisation. This is because of the interpersonal element, albeit in a predetermined product. Kamlongera notes in his study the advantages of opening up dialogue within performance time.

> The advantage of this is that issues are debated within 'play' atmosphere, while at the same time alternative courses are being looked at. The audience do not only sit to be entertained, but to participate in a debate for which theatre is only a catalyst. This dispenses with the 'cold' after-performance discussions common to more traditional uses of theatre.
> (Kamlongera 1989: 245)

Like agitprop, participatory agitprop is easy to tour from village to village. Since it is more effective than agitprop, it is probably the best method in those instances where there are constraints of time and manpower, and the catalysts are unable to stay with the villagers and create theatre with them. Participatory agitprop can meet the immediate communicational needs of extension workers, while a long-term theatre-for-conscientisation takes place at its own pace in the villages.

Theatre-for-Conscientisation (both simultaneous dramaturgy and forum theatre): Of all the methodologies identified and discussed, simultaneous dramaturgy and forum theatre are the most effective in conscientisation. The study has developed a new theatrical communication model explicating the interaction through messages between catalysts and audiences in theatre-for-conscientisation situations. In this method, the plays are produced by and for the people without spectators, since the spectators ultimately become actors. Improvisation happens throughout the play, and the direction the play takes is never pre-planned. Etherton's assertion that people need to learn the conventions of what he calls 'the well-made play' before they can improvise and create theatre-for-development is shown to be a fallacy.

By presenting two strongly conflicting views, the catalysts provoke the people to participate. Ideally, community participation and community control should increase as catalysts pull out. The ultimate goal is that villagers take over until there is no need for catalysts. This will be a point of convergence of forum theatre and comgen theatre.

Theatre-for-conscientisation is, however, a time-consuming process, which works over a long period. It therefore cannot deal with immediate country-wide communicational needs since resources (of personnel, for instance, who must stay in a single village for some time) are limited.

An adaptation of this method should be used in electronic media. For instance, in a situation where there are radio forums, radio plays can be left unfinished, and radio forum participants can then discuss how best to complete the story. The information is fed back to the production unit, and the next serial will reflect the ending that has been determined by the listeners. The same technique may be used for drama on small-format media and on television.

Comgen Theatre: [. . .] local communities in the villages may have the means of producing theatre, but without the guidance of catalysts in analysing the problems, the theatre does not become a vehicle for conscientisation. Villagers isolated problems and treated them as inherent and internally generated, for which they themselves were to blame. This indicates that although comgen theatre is the least expensive method – it does not involve a touring group of performers, but is created and performed by the locals – it does not serve as a vehicle for conscientisation. For comgen theatre to serve as a vehicle for critical analysis, and therefore critical awareness, catalysts must visit the village from time to time to enhance the level of analysis. This can be done through workshop sessions using the simultaneous dramaturgy and the forum theatre techniques. In this way comgen theatre and theatre-for-conscientisation will ultimately converge, as the villagers themselves ultimately become catalysts. The process is a time-consuming one, and the catalysts will have to make many visits. . . .

What Marotholi were doing, in order to have the theatre activity in all the villages of Lesotho, was to hold workshops for village health workers. All villages have village health workers, and workshops can be held only for a small group at a time. The village health workers then go back to their villages and create theatre with their fellow villagers. This becomes an 'each one, teach one' process, where those who have been trained in workshops train other village health workers from neighbouring villages. In this process catalysts should travel from village to village and work with the established groups there to enhance their level of analysis. In this way both grassroots control and grassroots participation will be maintained, while critical analysis will increase until comgen theatre becomes theatre-for-conscientisation.

Efficacy of popular and traditional media

The study has, through the analysis of the work of Marotholi in this area, illustrated that popular and traditional media can be effective in development communication. However, some modes of traditional performance do not lend themselves well to such uses, since they would be out of their social context in a theatre-for-development situation.

The practitioner of theatre-for-development and of development communication must take great care to ensure that, if and when traditional and popular modes of performance are used, they are used proficiently. It must be remembered that among the villagers there are people who have attained a high artistic standard in the practice of these performance modes. People know a mediocre product when they see one, and they will only be attracted to watch and participate in an event that evinces a high level of artistic merit. It is therefore important to pay particular attention to the aesthetics of the performance modes for them to have any effect.

Intervention

The study has shown that theatre is not a self-generative communication medium that automatically becomes effective. For theatre to be effective it needs informed intervention. Theatre-for-development practitioners may fall into the dangers of romanticising the democratic aspects of theatre-for-development, and the ability of peasants to identify and solve their problems. [. . .] Intervention by catalysts is essential in a theatre-for-development process. Peasants may identify their problems, but a solution will elude them if they have not gone through a process of critical analysis of the problems. It must be remembered that all forms of exploitation and domination have been heaped on the peasants – first by the colonialists, and then by the African ruling classes who took over from colonialists and perpetuated the structures of domination. As a result a number of peasants have internalised oppression and domination, and live in what Freire (1972) calls a 'culture of silence'. Intervention helps to extract them from that culture of silence, and unleashes in them a critical analysis that will lead to a critical awareness.

The study has evolved a new paradigm of intervention. The paradigm explains the relationship between intervention and participation. The two variables are dependent on each other in that if one increases, the other decreases. The paradigm further explains the relationship between participation and conscientisation. It places the various methodologies of theatre-for-development that have been identified on a curve. The curve portrays the rising level of conscientisation with the rising level of participation, until optimal participation is reached, then the level of conscientisation decreases as participation increases. From this point of optimal participation more participation engenders less conscientisation until a stage of maximal participation-minimal conscientisation is reached. Another curve portrays the relationship between intervention and conscientisation. The picture that emerges here is that minimal intervention engenders minimal conscientisation. Maximal intervention on the other hand also engenders minimal conscientisation. Optimal intervention is the ideal balance between intervention and participation that engenders the highest level of conscientisation.

The study concludes that for catalysts to play an effective interventionist role they must have a higher level of critical awareness than the villagers.

Domestication and other constraints

The study identified three traits of domestication: one is domestication that arises from an innocuous situation intended to liberate, the second is domestication that happens as a result of a conscious effort from an agent who seeks to domesticate, and the third happens through censorship and self-censorship. In all cases domestication's vehicle is intervention or lack of it. Writing on folk media, Lent made these observations:

> As Third World governments use folk media and interpersonal communication channels to transmit the developmental message to rural peoples, it becomes apparent that they have in their hands a truly grassroots propaganda machine capable of being harnessed to also promote non-developmental interests. Therefore, because the dividing line between developmental, governmental and political ends can be hair-thin, it is possible (and is happening) for folk media to be misused to promote the development of national policies and programmes. That, indeed, would be unfortunate in a world where governments already control so many mass media used to promote their own ends.
>
> (Lent 1982: 15)

Lent is writing of a situation where the government consciously uses the medium for the purposes of the domination and exploitation of the oppressed rural people. Governments are capable of enforcing domestication also by preventing theatre-for-development from being a truly democratic vehicle. In Malawi, for instance, practitioners have to go through the ruling political party structures in order to carry out their work in the villages. There will therefore be constraints of both censorship by the party hierarchy and self-censorship by the theatre practitioners.

It is all very well to talk of examining structural causes of problems. In some countries this may not be possible since it would invite the wrath of the rulers to descend upon the heads of the catalysts. Not many theatre practitioners and development communicators are prepared for martyrdom. Few of them have such a high commitment to social and political transformation that they would follow the path of exile taken by Ngũgĩ wa Thiong'o and Ngũgĩ wa Mĩriĩ of the Kamiriithu Educational and Cultural Centre. Others are just as highly committed as these two gentlemen, but prefer to explore various strategies that they can use in their theatre so that they may continue to work with the peasants while at the same time avoiding a confrontation with the ruling classes.

In the Kumba workshop (Eyoh 1987) a letter from the Presidency of the Republic of Cameroon authorising the workshop warned the participants against the development of themes of a political nature. The participants had to design strategies to negotiate this. Eyoh does not say what these strategies were. It is possible that they involved self-censorship, since that was what was demanded by the Presidency. Kidd, on the other hand, reports that in Zimbabwe the situation is different:

> Part of our success in this work was due to the particular political situation and historical experience of Zimbabwe and the receptiveness to this kind of work. The war's radicalization of the rural areas and the experience of people's theatre during the liberation struggle made fertile ground for the workshop. The Zimbabwe's government commitment to dialogue, consultation, conscientization, and mobilization provided a clear mandate and focus for the workshop.
>
> (Kidd 1985: 198)

In Lesotho the work of Marotholi has not been restricted through either censorship or self-censorship. The theatre group has even undertaken assignments from government ministries with a clear understanding on the part of all involved that in their mobilisation of the peasants for participation in development programmes, political and social structures will be analysed. However, there can never be any guarantee that this state of affairs will continue. Perhaps Marotholi has been fortunate in that, although the government often commissioned them to do campaigns in the villages, no one in the government really took a close interest in their work.

Since some governments are not very pleased with a conscientised peasantry, theatre-for-development practitioners who want to avoid the wrath of the authorities should use participatory agitprop. In participatory agitprop intervention will qualitatively and quantitatively control structural analysis of the problems to the level that the catalysts may deem safe. Other practitioners may prefer to devise subversive strategies in participatory agitprop. Theatre-for-conscientisation, the experience of Marotholi found, will undoubtedly open up the proverbial can of worms.

Another constraint on theatre-for-development, which may also have overtones of domestication, pertains to financial support. Theatre groups such as Marotholi Travelling Theatre depend on international donors, and on government sources when they undertake work in support of government development campaigns. Such financial support may compromise the liberating quality of the work. One of the questions posed at the Kumba workshop was on this very issue.

> Can workshops of the kind organised in Murewa and Kumba effectively take place without all sorts of support mechanisms from the state and international sponsors, and does the existence of such support mechanisms not compromise the liberating quality of the work, thus rendering the process domesticating?
>
> (Eyoh 1987)

[. . .]

Evaluation

Communication programmes need to be evaluated to find out what they have accomplished and how they can be improved. The work of Marotholi Travelling Theatre was very weak on evaluation. [. . .] The Marotholi explored ways of using *formative evaluation*. In this method all evaluation is integrated into the normal project activities. This allows the planner to change the course of the programme if early evaluations show that something is not working as planned. Often a theatrical performance is used to evaluate previous performances.

Whatever method of evaluation is adopted, it is crucial that projects of this nature should contain a constant evaluative component.

Bibliography

Etherton, M. (1982) *The Development of African Drama*, New York: Africana Publishing Company.

Eyoh, H.N. (1987) 'Theatre, Adult Education and Development: A Workshop at Kumba (Cameroon)', *IFDA Dossier* 60 (July/August): 3–16.

Freire, P. (1972) *Pedagogy of the Oppressed*, Harmondsworth: Penguin.

Kamlongera, C. (1989) *Theatre for Development in Africa with Case Studies from Malawi and Zambia*, Bonn: German Foundation for International Development.

Kidd, R. (1985) '"Theatre for Development": Diary of a Zimbabwe Workshop', *New Theatre Quarterly* 1 (2): 179–204.

Lent, J.A. (1982) 'Grassroots Renaissance: Folk Media in the Third World', *Media Asia* 9 (1): 9–17.

Malamah-Thomas, D.H. (1989) 'Innovative Community Theatre for Integrated Rural Development in Sierra Leone: The Telu Workshop Experience', *IFDA Dossier* 70 (March/April): 3–14.

Chapter 29

Dorothy Heathcote

DRAMA AS A PROCESS
FOR CHANGE

Drama as a Process for Change (1997, 2008).

[. . .]

LET US LOOK AT WHAT IS special about drama itself. The most important manifestation about this thing called drama is that it must show change. It does not freeze a moment in time, it freezes a problem in time, and you examine the problem as the people go through a process of change. If you want to use drama as education, you have to train people to understand how to negotiate so that the people go through a process of change.

[. . .] In drama activity, change must be seen to happen. Second, in drama, there must be interaction of people and forces. Third, these people, or these forces, must be given a framework within which they negotiate their change, their interaction. It might be a lifestyle or it might be a place. The playwright is not bound to one thing or another. A place need not be created by actual objects. It does not have to be two pictures of your Auntie Fannie or a candlestick for it to be located in a place, in a framework. It may be in limbo, but we have to be able to perceive where they are, and 'where they are' is going to contribute to the process of change. So, if we desire to train teachers to use drama as education, we have to be able to help them to structure so that the place where the people find themselves to be contributes to the process of change, contributes to the process of new awareness. And finally, teachers have to be able to trap the people into an agreement that for now they will believe in 'the big lie' in order that they will fight through to the process of change and not say, 'I don't like this, Miss', and go away. There is an awful lot of 'I don't like this, Miss' unless you train people to lure their classes into traps.

Now, because in drama we involve people in a situation, a circumstance, which pressurizes them and causes them to work through the problem, we have to at the same time understand what the final process is going to be. You cannot go on struggling forever; otherwise people say, 'I'll have to get out off here. I just can't cope with this any longer'. So, as you struggle through, you have to reach a stage in drama where there is some easement of the struggle. Some temporary feeling that, 'Oh, it feels a bit better now'. This is, for instance, when children reach a point in their struggle where they can say, 'I could leave it for a bit now. I understand it a bit, enough to know a bit about it'. Or, it occurs in a theatrical play in a conclusion where you know that they 'got married', or, 'he dropped dead'. The feeling of conclusion. That is not the same as easement. Sometimes the situation only brings easement and not conclusion. As teachers, we need to consider very carefully when a class needs conclusion because they are not ready to tolerate the more difficult easement of the problem. As well as conclusion or easement, there is a third area – to get a new view out of it, for us to learn that it did not solve anything, but at least we are looking at it differently. 'I'll never again think that about people like that' might be the new view we get out of the theatrical event. That is not necessarily the same as easement, and of course this new view may be very disturbing to us. Sometimes, in education, a new view is the most disturbing element that a teacher might set up: so risks must be calculated carefully.

A fourth response might be that we can perceive that 'there's a new start to be made'. It is not only the idea that the problem is concluded, but that there is a whole new beginning.

The fifth development from the struggle may be just a new awareness, not an understanding, but a slight feeling that 'There's something I haven't conceded before'. This is what the theatre can do for us. As a teacher, I ask myself if I want to use dramatics to help this happen to my students in my classrooms and if I want to do it constantly for myself.

In the past, there have been a minority of people (we call them actors!) who have been prepared through some alchemy in their make-up to spend their lives upon this struggle of humanity, within the framework out of which people can receive reflective energy. Actors are called by psychologists 'productive schizophrenics'. They productively live a double truth for other people, not for themselves only; they try to produce a change of view, attitude, awareness, and understanding in other people.

Common people, such as you and I, have only entered this kind of territory at times of festival, at times of mourning, and at times when public statements of feeling are symbolized through action, public action. All of us at some time have taken part in such things: and, for that brief moment of time, we have met with what the actor does. We haven't done it as the actor does it, but we have been privileged to enter this world of sharing in an experience and publicly finding the images whereby the meaning of the experience is spread about the community.

At times of enormous public presentation of a nation's idea, we enter this world of the actor, where not only do we feel something, but the statement is publicly made. Whether it is in the church, or in the marketplace, it seems to me everybody has this privilege. Every teacher must decide for him or her self whether there is any value in this.

If you do decide that you want to use this as part of your students' education, there are three very important things you may not abdicate from, I warn you, because if you try to abdicate from these, you not only cripple yourself, but you won't make any education out of drama.

One of these is that you must accept you are going to use human material, not fancy ideas, not cool abstractions of facts. You are using the human condition of your students, their attitudes, their philosophy, their ideas, and you have got to use them as they really are. You cannot pretend that they are different. So, you are going to be involved in human material and there are some teachers not born to be involved in human material. Am I still worthy of being involved with human material? is a question I have to keep asking myself. So, it is your human material and their human material that is going to somehow come together.

Secondly, you have to accept that you will be involved with distortion. You cannot examine all aspects of everything simultaneously. You are involved with distortion the minute you start to breathe. You are certainly involved with distortion as soon as you build a school, but it looks more respectable when called selection. What of the historian's distorted view of The Declaration of Independence? We are always concerned with distortion, but drama brings it to notice. Isn't it worrying when the distortion you are dealing with inside your classroom doesn't please the people who are walking past your classroom who would prefer another aspect of distortion? They would rather it wasn't so blatant, or they would rather it was pushed under the counter or made to sound more academic. You cannot make drama sound academic. The academic aspect is there, with all the bias, the distortion that people bring to it. Their readiness for change, of course, is part of this too.

The third area you are going to be involved with is fighting for form to give shape to these ideas, so that as the shape is fought for and crystallized there is more reflective energy available in your groups of students.

Now, of course, the 'freedom lovers' in art do not want you to fight for form. They want all people to do what they like. They do not want them all to do what they like in history, but they do want them to do what they like in art. Anything goes, you know. Don't interfere with little kiddies when they are thinking, and certainly don't do anything to check them when they are wrecking the joint or the drama.

So, these are the three elements you have got to train for and you have got to be prepared to accept. I use the human condition. I use distortion in order to examine, and I seek for form, so that in the examining I may create reflective force to consider what I am learning. I repeat, these three things you may not abdicate from.

Now, for my next point. There is, in any teaching situation, the inner structure of the teaching you create and there is the outer apparent look of the teaching you create. I have always planned, though I did not realize this until recently, for the internal structure of my lesson building. This week I had to teach a high school class. I wanted them to come to some understanding of loyalty within a feudal situation. I had been given a 'history brief', you see: loyalty within a feudal situation – this is an 'English' class. I did not, therefore, start thinking about how the place was going to look. I did not start thinking, 'Right, we need a Tudor mansion'. Instead I said to myself, 'How do I introduce the whole idea of loyalty? What strategy will I use whereby there shall be a slow realization that the choices between loyalty and disloyalty become available to the class? And, how do I do this within a Tudor framework? And what shall be the dilemma? What will make it possible for them to make that choice?' They were fifteen years old.

I call this 'classic form', the careful looking at the internal structure of how you bridge between one part of the learning and the next development. I find that teachers are not trained in this. It is not the pretty outer romantic form that teachers must examine. You have got to look at the internal form: What is the value of doing this? What is the purpose in doing this?

Drama particularly, and much of our teaching, has suffered desperately about this inner and outer structure, because somehow or other we have looked at the outsides of how other people look when they are teaching. We have never looked at the inside of what they are aiming at in any particular moment. A lesson changes from second to second. Often, others have torn my work apart and the work of each other by saying, 'Well, of course, I would never dream of teaching the way Dorothy Heathcote teaches'.

And so we get this manifestation in our profession, whereby people say, 'Well, I've looked at what she's doing and I don't like it'. They have not looked at what the teacher is doing at all. They have only looked at the outer manifestation, and they have decided, as people often judge my work, 'Oh, I wouldn't work in role like she does. She makes it too easy for them'; or 'Why does she have to make it so difficult?' These are all the external romantic forms.

The internal meanings are so important, for example when I say in the Tudor Mansion work, 'Good morrow. Have you walked from your homes today?' I am trying to establish, 'You had a life before you came into this room, and that is the attitude you will bring to my Tudor house'. I am changing my language slightly to limit the view and distort the world.

A child says, 'Yes, I walked all the way', and I reply, 'Is your hovel far from here?' If the onlookers look at the outside, they might say, 'There she is insulting him again, calling his home a hovel'. If they look at the inside, they see how I am upgrading whilst I am using the word hovel because in the act of saying hovel, I am actually starting to draw the house on the board to begin imagery with the class. The boy says, 'Yes, and it isn't a hovel, it's my home'. 'Forgive me. I had assumed you had all lived in rather poor circumstances.' I am slowly establishing in my class the ability to fight my own role attitude. The internal form is going to grow a strength in that class that will tell me where I am overstepping my rights because I am trying to build a group of people who are proud of their origins, and this demands training. And this demands much more careful training, a much more delicate training of this selective ear and tongue.

It demands the selective use of words, the selective use of gesture in the teacher. We have mistaken casualness for the ability to get on with people. Casualness gets you nowhere in teaching. A semblance of casualness might often be a useful strategy, but unselective casualness is death to the teacher. One of the most important elements in teacher training is high selectivity of the way we will signal our relationship to our classes. Every teacher in this world is functioning within a variety of roles. You know this. You know sometimes you fetch and carry for them, sometimes bully, and sometimes you don't let people 'off the hook', and sometimes you listen, and sometimes you give, and sometimes you share, and sometimes you dictate. All these roles we use, and many others beside, in our daily teaching. Drama demands we use them even more specifically and with a greater range of flexibility and consciousness for effect.

So I now reach my main question. Do you think this 'trapping of people within a life situation', however small or lengthy (because drama can be two seconds or it can be two months), has anything to offer you in the teaching concerns you have? Can it help you to draw attention to something? You have to answer it for yourself. And, try if you can, to put aside fear. Drama is such a normal thing. It has been made into an abnormal thing by all the fussy leotards, hairdos and stagecraft that are associated with it. All it demands is that children shall think from within a dilemma instead of talking about the dilemma. That's all it is; you bring them to a point where they think from within the framework of choices instead of talking coolly about the framework of choices. You can train people to do this in two minutes, once they are prepared to accept it.

Do you think this thing called drama offers you anything? Can it help you to extend the understanding about something by thinking from within a framework? Do you believe it might help you to help your classes bring about any behavioural change? It might be the behavioural change of 'stop chucking the books about' or it might be the behavioural change of 'notice the archaeology or the architecture of it more'. These are all different aspects of behavioural change for they are the beginning of perceptive changes. Do you think it is valuable to help you extend with your classes the range of attitudes they are capable of examining, and do you think it would help them to develop ordinary gumption?

The children in the Tudor mansion met their final moment when they had to make the choice of being loyal or not. They were raided by three men sent from her majesty, Elizabeth I, to look for hidden Catholic priests. They could betray me as Lady Norris, or they could keep me safe. I had done nothing to win their loyalty. We had only grown into a feeling for this building, this house, this responsibility for the Norris family. There had been no proselytizing. There had been no religious teaching. There had only been the furnishing of a mansion, ready for Lady Norris and her family to occupy. And, in the course of the furnishing, they discovered that there were certain spaces in the house that seemed unnecessary. As soon as the three soldiers arrived, with their pikes, seeking for evidence of popery, every child jumped to the conclusion that they were searching for the great Bible which I carried, and would not be separated from. Slowly, they had realized I valued the Bible. Children had kept coming up and saying, 'M'Lady, uh, do you want me to do anything with your book?' And I would say, 'Not yet. I think I would rather keep it with me until I have seen all of the house that you have created.' I do not think they ever realized it was a Bible I was carrying, but as soon as those troopers came, every one of those children realized that Lady Norris's book would give the whole game away if they were to find it. And from then on they hid it. It disappeared. I never saw where it went. They did not know they were going to have to choose whether to be loyal or disloyal. They just were caught in 'a moment of authenticity', of real choice and real concern. Drama gives us the opportunity as teachers to allow our classes to stumble upon authenticity.

What mattered then to me was that suddenly they were in a very real situation with their capacity to understand it being employed in the process of change. It is not for me as a teacher to dictate how they should go about choosing. I have set it up. It has a form. But how they choose is for them to decide. We can then all reflect together upon the choices they made. So a choice becomes consciously understood and pondered on. They were in a difficult position because the three soldiers who were teachers in role were very, very clever. They knew about priest holes and they searched every inch. I did not give those soldiers any orders about whether they should find or they should not find anything.

One of the things I must do as a teacher is know why I want to bring that class to that moment of choice. And this is the fourth element in using the arts. You must know why. You must not do them 'because they are fashionable'. You must do them because you have decided that they will efficiently teach the precise thing that at the moment you want. In my Tudor work, I wanted to introduce two things. One was something true, as far as there is any truth about history: the reality of the Norris family and Speke Hall which they built and they lived in and in which they hid thirty-four priests. They were fined constantly, 500 guineas, by the king for hiding priests and would eventually have gone to their deaths if their people had not been loyal. I also wanted to bring the children to the realization that a teacher and a class are in each other's hands. They were in my hands at that moment when the soldiers came, and I was in theirs.

And so, I have two reasons. The choice of the Tudor mansion was the curriculum choice – they were learning history. The choice of how to use the Tudor mansion was a teacher choice to do with my teaching ethics. You have the double choice. In the choice of the curriculum, you have bound yourself to try to further learning as meaningfully and as educationally as possible and in your personal teaching, understanding of the procedures, you want to set up for real learning to take place. What I want is the reflective energy that comes out of the experience – an examination of that condition we are now in, as people, because of how we handled the Tudor situation.

What I am always saying in the drama situation is, 'From where you are, how does this problem seem to you? And when it's been dealt with, let's look at where you now are.' Because what I am really saying is, 'It's where you are that makes you deal with your life. It's how you understand that makes you deal with your way of life so that all the time the growth you bring about is the reality of the class you've got.'

[. . .]

We have to set up a situation in our schools where all the time, every time, we introduce a new element to children, it has the effect of cracking all their previous understanding into new awareness, new understanding. This is what growing older is about. This is what being more mature is about. This is what being educated is about. The moment whereby all the understanding you had before is sharpened into a new juxtaposition. Drama is about shattering the human experience into new understanding. It uses the facts, but, in addition, it fuses the new understanding all the time.

[. . .] We have as our roots now the attitudes the child brings to school. Often we try to push those attitudes under in order to try to get some kind of conforming from our classes so that the curriculum can be taught, but the real roots of the inner attitudes are going to be there all the time. One of the big problems of teaching today is that as more and more cultural ideas become diffuse and people become their own experts, it is much harder for a teacher to handle the variety of different roots that the children bring into the school.

What are the roots of our tree of knowledge now? The first root is that children have already tried and failed a bit before they come to us. That is one of the roots they bring. And we have to keep that root of trying, failing, and picking yourself up and growing strong. That is a root to cultivate. The second root is they have already often faced the choice of whether they will, or will not, care about anything. And that also is a root that we have to keep growing. The third root is they have to decide for all their lives whether they will, or will not, get committed to doing things with quality. They have already at the age of five had a lot of experiences that have grown this root system. They already are beginning the process of reading, writing, and numbering skills. These are roots, not blossoms. These are keys to all our education forever. It is the means by which the trunk can get the sun, the person to mature.

Another root is the skill to look with perception. They have already learned to perceive. They have already learned to read people before they come to school at five: that is a root they bring. They already have begun a process of reflection about their experience. Every child we get in our classes has begun this to a greater or a lesser degree. So, a common root all teachers have to grow is reflective power. Another root is the business of accepting others and being accepted by others.

[. . .]

And what is the blossom of this tree? The blossom is high quality culture. That is the only blossom worth having at the top of our tree. I cannot make much effect in my small lifetime, but I am not settling for less.

Chapter 30

John Somers

THEATRE AS COMMUNAL WORK
Intervention in rural communities

> Neither human existence nor individual liberty can be sustained
> for long outside the interdependent and over-lapping communities
> to which we all belong. Nor can any community long survive unless
> its members dedicate some of their attention, energy and resources
> to shared projects.
>
> (Etzioni 1997: 7)

IN THE SPACE OF SIXTY YEARS, the fabric of rural English communities
has changed radically. These shifts have occurred due to a number of influences,
among them the changed nature of farming leading to fewer people being employed
in agriculture; the migration of the working classes to urban environments; the
move to the countryside by the middle classes; the decline of many of the rituals
of country living which only made sense in a community of shared experience and
interdependence; the impact of global cultural values; and the impact of television,
consumerism and the new technologies. Some of these influences have had positive
effects – young people's increased awareness of wider educational and occupational
opportunities and life styles, for example, and the freeing up of restrictive social
conventions which made rural communities uncomfortable for some who failed to
'conform'. Conversely, the decline of shared work, interdependency and significant
celebrations and rituals has led to the social fragmentation of rural communities.
There are many fewer opportunities for community members to meet and engage
with each other. Physical proximity is not enough; just because people happen to
live in the same place geographically, this will not necessarily create the circumstances
which can produce 'a community'.

One great loss in current rural communities is the knowledge of community
stories. This shared understanding can be as slight as knowing why an oak tree has

a large gash on its trunk (a milk lorry crashed into it in 1953 and Farmer Dickson pulled it out of the ditch with his tractor – a David Brown) or extend to intimate knowledge of families, scandals, achievements and shame.[1] Residents without access to these, often apparently inconsequential stories therefore lack a 'sense of place', a quality which is best achieved through absorbing the layered meanings accreted through centuries of, often oral, storytelling and shared experience.

Such stories have no forum for being shared unless, as Etzioni says, members of a community 'dedicate some of their attention, energy and resources to shared projects'. In writing about memory, A.C. Grayling (2001) says '. . . what makes a person the same person through life is the accumulating set of memories he carries with him. When these are lost, he ceases to be that person and becomes someone else, new and as yet unformed'. If we substitute 'community' for 'person', the statement still holds true, for if a community's collective memory is lost, it too has to be reformed. Theatre can be an important approach in building this new community identity and can, through its research and performances, ensure its development is based firmly on elements of the past. Such theatre represents a dynamic exploration and presentation of the defining narratives of a community.

Theatre in communities

We are well aware of the forms of theatre which existed in pre-industrial Europe.[2] Medieval Mystery Plays have survived and are still performed in parts of England, although their purpose of convincing a largely illiterate population of the power of Christianity is lost. These Christian dramas transformed into secular dramas, giving rise to Shakespeare and his contemporaries. Much other drama was a survival of ritual forms linked to the seasons – surviving morris dances and mummers plays are remnants of a greater body of work which entwined itself through the rural year. This phenomenon is still evident in rites of passage, community festivals and religious rituals in parts of the world where this cultural activity is still extant (Banham et al. 1994). Although there are vibrant English examples of this tradition – Padstow May Day, for example – many of these performances largely have become heritage events, detached from their roots and ritual purposes.

There was a revival of community-centred theatre in the inter-war years, The Unity Theatre[3] being one well-known example which was inspired by communist ideology (Chambers 1989). In the 1960s there was an upsurge of theatre fired by radical notions of social and political change. Political theatre initiatives often embraced the notion of community and the ambition of empowering its members to take collective action positively to change the circumstances in which they lived. John McGrath's work with 7:84 theatre company[4] is a prominent example (McGrath 1989). His play The Cheviot, the Stag and the Black, Black Oil not only played to Scottish rural community audiences, but impacted on the wider UK through its televised performance.[5] The company's website holds that:

> . . . in the early seventies, theatre in the heart of Scotland's remote communities was a complete innovation. Theatre that could actually address the direct concerns of those communities was a sensation.[6]

The person most strongly associated with Community Theatre in England is Anne Jellicoe (Jellicoe 1987). Jellicoe's first play, *The Reckoning*, developed and performed in Lyme Regis, involved over one hundred local people and a minimum of professional input. The defining characteristics of this work were unusual performance venues; promenade style performances; deep involvement of local people at all levels and at all stages of the process; and plays based on local events and stories. Subsequently she developed the concept of presenting performances of significant local stories through the Colway Theatre Trust, creating twelve other community plays, the majority of which took place in South West England communities. Although subsequently there have been a number of other community plays in Lyme Regis, the expected follow-through was dissipated when other communities became daunted by the enormity of creating such projects and a feeling that they did not possess the expertise and resources to involve such large numbers of people in creative endeavour.

The current state of theatre in community in England is that amateur theatre is alive and well, as is Youth Theatre, especially where a local theatre building has a commitment to its community. There are sporadic attempts at the kind of play described later in this chapter.

My work

I have worked in a university's education and drama departments and in schools. I specialise in Applied Drama,[7] the creation of dramatic experience which 'has a job to do'. Five years ago I founded a theatre company, *Exstream*, which specialises in Interactive Theatre and making theatre in communities. During the past five years I have engaged consistently in theatre making in rural communities. The projects have ranged from a celebratory millennium play, *Parson Terry's Dinner and other stories*, to an interactive theatre programme, *The Living at Hurford*, dealing with the struggle of small family farms to stay in business in the post foot and mouth disease countryside. I have obtained finance for and directed a community theatre school in which the skills of theatre making in a rural community were enhanced by the contributions of six theatre professionals. Two strong plays emerged from this initiative and one will be performed by community actors in a marquee pitched on the spot at which a dead German airman hit the ground in 1941. The descendants of this airman and his three dead colleagues who fell to the ground in three adjacent parishes, plus those who shot them down, will be invited to the performance as an act of reconciliation. My work has been heavily influenced by promenade performances such as the National Theatre's *The Mysteries* (1985), the 1978 production of *Lark Rise to Candleford*, the RSC's *The Dillon*, and documentary plays such as Peter Cheeseman's *Hands up for you the War is Over*, which I saw in the round at the Victoria Theatre, Stoke on Trent in the 1960s. During my various community theatre projects, I have come to see the processes as exercises which enable 'community work'.

The concept of theatre as communal work

As previously mentioned, sixty years ago, rural English communities were relatively closed and interdependent. At this time, the parish was a site for work. Perhaps

90 per cent of people worked in the community, with only the small number of professionals venturing outside it. Now it is probable that 90 per cent work outside the parish which is seen simply as a place to 'live'. Clubs, societies and more informal meeting points in the parish are largely structured on age criteria: the young mothers meet at the playgroup, older ones outside the school. Older community members meet at the 'lunch club', seen as a once-a-month social activity for widows and widowers. The short mat bowls club attracts the over 55s and the youth club caters for teenagers. I estimate that fewer than 15 per cent of the parish residents are active in such groups, most of which are small in numbers of adherents.

I decided that the theatre-making should be a challenge; not just dramatically, but in terms of the 'labour' needed to make it happen. I wanted to create a communal focus in the parish, a shared project that would bring the disparate elements of the community together. This was when I arrived at the concept of 'theatre as communal work'.

The community

Payhembury is thought to derive its name from the Old French 'pays' and the name of a chieftain 'Hembury'. Hence it means the 'country ruled by Hembury'. There is a nearby hill encampment that dates back to at least the Bronze Age known as 'Hembury Fort'. This was taken by the Romans who reinforced its defences and used it as a means to extend their occupation of this part of England two thousand years ago. The village and its environs are rich in history. Some of its sites are mentioned in the Domesday Book, that fascinating tally of property and people produced in 1086 following the Norman invasion.

Many village dwellers have little contact with parish organisations, some of which, such as the Women's Institute[8] and the annual crowning of the carnival queen, fête and sports day, have, in the last ten years, ceased to exist. The village retains its church (although it shares its vicar with two other parishes and attendance is relatively low), its school (built in Victorian times, but vibrant and popular), its pub (which forms a major focus for social activity), a Parish Hall (used for community social activity), as well as one garage and a shop. These institutions, particularly the school, are believed to be essential 'heartbeats' to rural community survival.

In 1999 I was invited to make a play to celebrate the coming of the new millennium in Payhembury which is my home parish. I accepted this task and set about devising the kind of drama which would work in this rural community. I quickly decided that the Parish Hall was too small to house anything which would involve large numbers of people. The parish was to publish a book in 2000 containing stories associated with the parish's history. In reading proofs of the book, I decided to find ways in which some of these stories could come to life.

The millennium play project

I chose seven stories from the millennium book which had dramatic potential. I decided on eight sites for the performance of scenes from the play and decided to use the centre of the village for the finale. The audience would gather in the village centre just before the start of the play, where they would be divided into seven equal groups. Each group would be led by its own storytellers to visit the seven scenes in an order different from the other six groups. This ensured that only one group was present at each scene at any one time. On the journey between scenes (one of which, to the cider mill, was taken in a minibus due to distance), the storytellers related additional stories about the village.

Each scene lasted around ten minutes and the finale twenty. With seven scenes visited, for the audience this led, with journey time, to a performance of approximately two hours. The actors performed each scene seven times a night and audience groups were limited to nineteen to allow each to enter the smallest space, the house kitchen. The play was performed for three nights to a total of three hundred and eighty nine people. We could have sold many more tickets had we had the capacity. The name of the play, *Parson Terry's Dinner and other stories*, was suggested by the events in scene one.

The scenes comprised:

1   The dragging from the pulpit, as he made his 1650, Christmas Day sermon, of Parson Robert Terry, Rector of the Parish of Payhembury.[9] Cromwellian soldiers who were in the Church (England was then a republic under the Lord Protector, Oliver Cromwell following the execution of Charles 1st) objected to the Parson's support for the Royalist cause. They dragged him to his parsonage where they ate his family's Christmas dinner in front of them and promised to return at a later date to turn him out of the parish. Performed in the Church and in the parsonage of 1650, now a private house.

2   An inspection in 1920 of the school children by a visiting inspector who tests the children on their skills in basic subjects. During the inspection (which was very important as, not least, it affected the teachers' salaries) a boy fools around wearing a wolf mask, and is beaten by the headteacher. An older girl, held down in the class through her inability to pass tests, finally achieves a pass. Performed in the School which was built in 1851.

3   The reception in 1941 in a village house of three child evacuees from London who were sent to the countryside to avoid Second World War German bombing. The scene examines the upset caused in the host family by the evacuees' arrival. Performed in the large kitchen of an ancient village house.

4   An old man runs to the street with scalded hands after children drop bricks down his chimney into his cooking pot. This leads to a drunken argument between this and another older man, in which the latter chops off his thumb. The doctor is too busy to tend to his problem and also requires payment, which the injured man does not have. Performed outdoors in front of an old village house.

5   A scene set in a cider mill in which the male hierarchy of the community in 1860 is established, prior to the entry of the young wife of one of the workers. She pleads with him to leave the cider making to fetch a doctor for their sick child. He is torn between fear of his authoritarian employer and his family responsibilities. Resolved through a confrontation between the wife and her husband's boss, which she wins. Her victory promises to endanger her husband's employment prospects. Performed in a cider mill dating from the seventeenth century.

6   The arrival of the first car in the village in 1920. There is intense rivalry between the car owner, a prominent local butcher and cattle dealer, and the owner of a horse and wagon who claims to have been cheated by the dealer in the past. After a further argument about which of them will get to market first, the scene ends with the farmer trotting away to market as the butcher tries unsuccessfully to start his engine. Performed in front of a garage which, until 1920, was a carriage-making business.

7   The unveiling of the Parish War Memorial in 1921 to commemorate the dead of the First World War, 1914–18. A family from the Second World War period (1939–45) arrives at the memorial in a kind of time travel. They learn by War Office telegram of the death of the man of the family in France. Ghosts of the two wars – soldiers and nurses – visit the memorial to ensure they are remembered.

8   The finale. This comprised a specially written song sung by a 14-year-old girl who symbolically, through the gift of a parchment declaration, gives the future of the parish to the youngest children of the community. She also gives to them the stories we have performed and urges them to live many more in the future. This was performed on a raised stage on the village green with a painted panorama of the village as a backdrop. The panorama included vignettes of each scene. The audience and cast, around 250 people each night, joined in the chorus of the song. Some pyrotechnics and dancing followed. The dance involved the cast and audience linking hands around the village green, after which all who chose adjourned to the Parish Hall where there was a bar, exhibition and more singing.

The process of the play

Early on, a musical director was appointed and we held three Saturday music workshops to bring together those with musical skills and interests. I held three evening drama workshops in the School at fortnightly intervals to get a nucleus of residents involved. They came from all sectors of the community and their ages ranged from five to seventy-nine. From the stories culled from the millennium book, I created and typed out seven scenarios that had dramatic potential. During the drama workshops, we experimented through improvisation with all seven scenarios, discussing each to explore how they might develop into scenes. Some participants volunteered to take away a set of scenarios and conducted historical research on them. Although numbers of participants at this stage were low,[10] those who did attend made valuable contributions to the decision making process. They also became committed to the project and pledged to enrol others.

The rehearsal process was concentrated into five weeks. Each of the seven scenes was rehearsed in the School for one and a half hours on three occasions. Individuals from the community and some students from the University of Exeter's Department of Drama costumed the scenes in period clothing. Singing and instrumental music were built into five of the seven scenes and the finale. Twelve days before the first performance, a Saturday morning rehearsal was held with each scene being performed in sequence so that the storytellers could see what each was like, and discover their part in it. This was the first occasion when the scenes were performed in their correct venues. In the afternoon of that Saturday, all scenes were run simultaneously three times to give their casts the experience of repeating their performances and to allow the storytellers to experience some of the journeys between scenes. Most of the instrumental musicians concentrated into a swing band that played Glenn Miller tunes as the audience approached the evacuees' scene. This band also played for the finale.

At 4.00p.m. the finale was rehearsed and the cast heard and sang the chorus of the song for the first time. This was the first occasion that cast from an individual scene had seen the casts from the other six scenes, all of whom were in costume. This generated huge excitement as each cast member realised they were part of a very varied and large project involving 120 people. We also practised the circle dance. We then adjourned to the Parish Hall for a debriefing. I stressed to the participants that I could now do no more for them and the play and there would be no more rehearsals directed by me before the first performance night. They were urged to take full ownership of their play and to ensure they were ready for the opening night. By their own choice, each group rehearsed its scene at least once in the remaining days. They also added additional properties, and perfected costumes and music.

Historical background

There was not time in the ten minutes each scene lasted to tell a story and give its historical context. Accordingly, an eighteen-page programme was produced containing two pages on each scene. One page explained the historical background to the scene, the other gave an outline of the scenario, words of songs with which the audience was invited to join in the singing, and a list of cast members. The programme was sold well in advance of the performances, also serving as an admission ticket.

The performances

In addition to the seven scenes, small incidents/stories were encountered by audience groups as they moved around the village – a man on a 1950s motorbike, dressed accordingly, stopped to ask directions; a man in a 1934 Austin Seven car did likewise as did a man and wife in a 1930s Bullnose Morris car. A woman who had sheep penned on the village green asked audience members if they had seen her husband who had gone off for help to mend their broken wagon in which they were taking their sheep to market; a clown fire-eater juggled and advertised a circus that would soon visit the village; two teenage girls fantasised about the US airmen who are stationed at a nearby airfield.

The audience groups were integral to the performance and took part in several of the scenes. At the War Memorial they merged with the celebrants and joined in the singing.

When the audience and cast gathered in the village centre for the finale, the sun was setting and the atmosphere was charged. The giving of the parchment scrolls to the smallest children formed an effective focus and the song chorus was sung with gusto. To open things out and to reinforce the international aspect, I introduced speakers from Korea, USA, Taiwan, Greece and Brazil. Cast members and audience spoke subsequently of being greatly moved by the finale. There was a collective count down from ten to zero at which point the pyrotechnics at the front of stage were fired. This brought great applause from audience and cast, who then mingled, joined hands and danced a circle dance around the Village Green.

Evaluation of the project

Questionnaires were distributed to the cast as a means of acquiring a first level of response. Forty-six were returned. Unsolicited written comment was received from twenty-three audience members and many more provided oral feedback. My main data source is my observations of the process, the live performance and the extensive video recordings.

Reflection and analysis

I have directed many projects in my forty years of professional involvement with drama and theatre, including community theatre projects. I have never experienced the overwhelmingly positive response, at several levels, that followed this play. I received many letters, cards, e-mails and verbal messages from audience members and cast. All had enjoyed the experience and many found it especially moving. Comments such as 'I wanted to write and tell you how fantastic I and everyone I have spoken to thought the play was. I felt very moved by the whole play, and the finale evoked real emotion in me' from an audience member were typical. There was also a very positive response from cast members. They spoke of the great satisfaction they found in working with others – often those they barely knew or had never met – to make the production. There was a widespread feeling that something significant had taken place, both in the life of individuals who had experienced it, and in the communal experience of the parish:

> The whole experience was magical – to see the whole village working together and proud of what they were doing was a seminal experience.
> . . .
>
> (Adult cast member, and resident of five years)

Why should this be so? My evaluation of the work identified several factors which were significant, among them:

- the nature of the stories;
- the unification of community;
- the use of fact and fiction;
- the performance venues;
- the audience experience;
- the actor experience;
- alternative theatre form;
- celebration;
- the social affect;
- the aesthetic quality;
- intergenerational participation;

- project structure;
- the project's style of leadership;
- international participation.[11]

The community engaged in real work to make this project successful. In doing so they amassed social capital, cultural awareness, historical insight and the satisfaction to be had by joining with others to make a unique event. Other projects have followed, all with large casts and demanding inventiveness, sweat and, eventually, celebration of being part of a community which can conceive of and mount unique theatrical events. Many in this community now see making theatre as part of their 'work'.

Bibliography

Banham, M., Hill, E. and Woodyard, G. (eds) (1994) *The Cambridge Guide to African and Caribbean Theatre*, Cambridge: Cambridge University Press.

Chambers, C. (1989) *The Story of Unity Theatre*, London: Lawrence & Wishart.

Etzioni, A. (1997) *The New Golden Rule: Community and Morality in a Democratic Society*, New York: Basic Books.

Grayling, A.C. (2001) *The Meaning of Things*, London: Weidenfeld & Nicolson.

Jellicoe, A. (1987) *Community Plays: How to Put them On*, London: Methuen.

McGrath, J. (1989) *A Good Night Out*, London: Nick Hern Books.

Notes

1   Just this morning, a man in my parish in Devon, knowing that I was directing a new community play which focuses on the crash of a German bomber in 1941, urged me to look in a field outside the village which still bore the groove of a roadway used to move Spitfire fighter planes which were brought out of Exeter Airfield to protect them from attack during WW2.

2   See, for example, Peter Woods (1997) *Hunting The Wren on the Dingle Peninsula*, http://www.dingle-peninsula.ie/wren.html.

3   The company's name is based on the notion that 7 per cent of the population own 84 per cent of its wealth.

4   For an explanation of the process Jellicoe adopted in developing a community play, see http://www.asha-foundation.org/women/women/ann_jellicoe.php.

5   See http://www.784theatre.com/index.cfm/page/2/.

6   I argue here and elsewhere that Applied Drama is the correct generic term for work which can range from workshop-based activity where there is no commitment to performance, to role-play exercises, to Interactive Theatre and straight performance. Just as the term 'dance' embraces various styles and approaches, so 'drama' creates the umbrella under which the various drama and theatre forms can shelter. Not least, 'Applied Theatre' conjures for the lay person notions of darkened auditoria, lights, applause, etc., which is counterproductive in encouraging an awareness of a panoply of dramatic approaches.

7   For more about this project, see <payhemburycommunitytheatre.org>.

8   An organisation of women, especially in rural areas, who meet regularly and participate in crafts, cultural activities and social work. Now worldwide, it was first set up in Canada in 1897 and in Britain in 1915.

9   Parish priests in the Anglican, Protestant Church are usually called 'parsons', 'rectors' or 'vicars' depending on the constitutional relationship of the church to the parish. A parson lives in a parsonage, a rector in a rectory and a vicar in a vicarage.

10   Although the maximum number was 18 at any one session, a total of 43 individuals attended music and drama workshops.

11   Contact John Somers j.w.somers@ex.ac.uk for a fuller account of this project and the research outcomes.

Chapter 31

Jenny Hughes with Simon Ruding

MADE TO MEASURE?

A critical interrogation of applied theatre as intervention with young offenders in the UK

> If a man does not keep pace with his companions, perhaps it is because he hears a different drummer. Let him step to the music which he hears, however measured or far away.
>
> Henry David Thoreau (1854)

I

THEATRE PRACTICE WITH OFFENDERS is historically linked to the emergence of applied theatre as a term in the UK.[1] Theatre with young offenders and young people 'at risk' of offending is an important category of this practice, increasing in prominence with the focus on young people in the Labour government's policies on social exclusion (following their election in 1997). This focus recognised that more young people in the UK face difficulties as a result of multiple social disadvantage than in comparable countries, and that social and economic changes are creating new uncertainties for young people making a transition to adulthood (fewer jobs open to those without qualifications, disappearance of traditional sources of employment, earlier exposure to risk).[2] This focus on social exclusion has had far reaching implications for socially oriented arts practices in the UK. Arts funding opportunities have become more tightly tied to targets relating to social inclusion and arts organisations are routinely asked to demonstrate the impact of their work in relation to such agendas. Most relevant to the concerns of this chapter, it has led to a close relationship between the Arts Council England and Youth Justice Board (the national bodies responsible for arts policy and funding, and youth justice provision respectively) that has stimulated a range of arts programmes in youth justice settings as well as a concern to evaluate the impact of the practice on challenging and reducing offending by young people (the key aim of the Youth Justice system).[3]

Applied theatre practice with young offenders and young people at risk of offending emerges in different settings across prevention, custodial and resettlement contexts, including formal institutional and informal settings: prisons, youth justice centres, pupil referral units, youth centres, schools, neighbourhood or community centres. Applied theatre projects have been seen as a means of supporting young people's transitions into adulthood by reinforcing protective factors (cognitive skills, creative and imaginative capacities, personal and social skills) and tackling risk factors (lack of access to engaging educational opportunities or positive adult role models) associated with young people's antisocial or offending behaviour.[4] This practice represents a continuation of youth, community, educational and social theatre practices that have a long history in the UK. More recently the discourses surrounding this practice have exhibited peculiar resonances relating to the contemporary social and economic context and it is these resonances and their implications for applied theatre practice and research that are of concern here.

This chapter explores applied theatre practice that has the explicit intention of changing a young person's attitude or behaviour. It challenges some of the prevailing orthodoxies of theatre as 'intervention' in a youth justice context and seeks to reflexively trouble assumptions about the capacity of theatre to change lives of participants. The arguments posed reflect the different perspectives of the two writers. Over the last six years we have worked together to develop research, evaluation and practice that is responsive to context as well as maintaining a self-critical perspective on accepted discourses in applied theatre research and practice.[5]

II

> The best bit was where we were planning out his robbery because everyone was talking and you was getting everyone's opinion, but I would have planned it different, that robbery just sounds fake doesn't it? It would have been more serious, it wouldn't have happened that way.

> When we came to do (the scene about the crime), it was like 'oh my god, I've done that', it's what actually does happen, it's not all made up, it's just what does happen to people . . . I know how to act it out because it's actually happened to me.

These two comments were made by a young man and young woman who participated in a theatre-based offending behaviour workshop (Blagg!).[6] Blagg! takes elements of a participatory drama workshop — warm up, creation and exploration of fictional characters and narratives, warm down — infused with elements drawn from a cognitive behavioural approach, for example, 'freezing' moments in time to explore thoughts, feelings and alternative responses to problems suggested in scenarios. The cognitive behavioural approach is the privileged theory base for interventions in the criminal justice system: this theoretical approach identifies poor thinking skills as a key factor in offending and focuses on developing the thinking and feeling patterns of offenders to improve their capacity to identify and solve problems in a pro-social way.[7] Blagg! developed from a realisation of a point of contact between cognitive behavioural approaches and participatory theatre methods (which also operate in cognitive and emotional modalities and can be applied to explore and analyse thinking and feeling states).

The comments made by young people participating in Blagg!, as with any kind of research 'evidence', can be interpreted in plural ways. An interpretation of the first comment might be that the workshop, in recreating an offence (albeit fictional or 'fake'), reinforced offending thinking by permitting the young man to consider more effective ways of committing future offences. Another interpretation might be that the workshop provided an opportunity to access previously obscured thoughts and feelings and generated useful material for ongoing one to one work. This latter interpretation was privileged in the evaluation report and is more palatable for youth justice audiences. The aim of creating a fictional character and offence is to provide reflective distance: young people can more freely and critically evaluate their responses and actions through the experience of an imagined other (and this also enhances perspective or role-taking and empathic capacities associated with reduced offend-ing). The creation of a metaphorical or fictional space to explore issues is the key contribution of the 'theatre' aspect of the 'applied theatre' equation and a basic principle of a wide set of applied theatre practices including dramatherapy and theatre-in-education methodologies. However, it is clear that both young people quoted above directly related the fictional offence – scenes from the fictional or metaphorical realm – to their own personal experiences of offending. This direct association troubles the assumptions by which the intervention is supposed to 'work' by challenging the distinction between the 'real', 'fictional' and 'fantastical' in how the workshop is experienced. What negotiation happens between the original, 'real' or remembered experience and the reconstructed and/or imagined experience in the workshop, and what is its relationship to future behaviour?

In the young man's statement there is a reconfiguring of self as a 'real' criminal – with the knowledge, capacity and power to carry out the robbery effectively as opposed to the rest of the group who were simply faking it. The young woman, in the second statement, expresses shock and a sense of powerlessness (the lack of ownership in the statement, 'it happened to me') that may be equally problematic – and equally constructed, imagined or 'unreal'. The young man's construction of self as a criminal and the crime in question as either real or fake may relate to notions of criminality influenced as much by his experience of mainstream Hollywood films as by a need to appear 'hard' as a young man growing up in an area known for problems with gun crime and gang culture. The young woman's performance of powerlessness may be linked to her experiences of abuse as well as awareness of the socially appropriate norms for young women in her specific social milieu. The relationships between the 'real', 'fictional' or fantastical in the ways young people construct or perform self in their daily lives, inside the theatre workshop and in accompanying research activities are extraordinarily complex.

Such realisations have led theatre practitioners working with Blagg! to question the usefulness of the re-construction and repetition of events that are similar to those that have been 'really' experienced by participants, even when played out in a fictional realm. This is in line with a wider shift in applied theatre practice in criminal justice settings that might be characterised as a move from the social realism of a cognitive behavioural approach to a more direct embracing and exploring of the metaphorical or fantastic.[8] In the construction of the fictional offence narratives of fantasy, desire and power are played out by participants – aspects of experience not easily explored within a cognitive-behavioural approach which seeks to challenge patterns of thinking and therefore may obscure rather than open up areas for exploration. A concern with the way Blagg! has been used by non-drama specialists (currently, youth offending teams are trained to run the workshop without specialist drama input) is that pressure to 'follow the programme manual' leads to challenging offending thinking negatively ('don't say that') and staying within the constraints of social realism as an aesthetic ('that's not a realistic response') rather than finding creative ways to explore the responses of young people. This can lead offenders to learn how to 'play the game' by constructing and performing the 'right' response, or refusing to play at all rather than generating opportunities for participants and leaders to explore and undermine fixed patterns of thinking and constructions of self and others that underpin offending behaviour.[9]

In practice these concerns have led to increased openness to working with fantasy – the exploration of worlds of meaning underpinning fixed beliefs and actions in scenarios suggested by young people. This can involve utilising the bizarre, surreal and fantastic as a means of challenge rather than directing young people to perform a morally correct and 'realistic' response to the constructed offence. For example, it was clear that for the young woman a focus on the offence was damaging efforts to support the development of a positive sense of self and capacity to control events in her life. The response of the workshop leader – in this case an experienced applied theatre practitioner – was to shift the focus from an analysis of the crime to devising scenes of the fictional character's ideal future – including scenes where the young woman played a supermodel being interviewed with members of her 'real' proud family on a chat show. This was an emotional moment at the end of the workshop which the young woman described as the most powerful part of the workshop, and, when meeting one of the writers six months later, could still describe in some detail.

Embracing the fantastic is a useful direction for practice and may help challenge negative aspects of self concept. However, it does not negate the need to challenge constructions and play with alternatives: fantasy can be a place where negative and destructive desires are played out and made 'real'. The important point is that these challenges can be made in a fantastic *as well as* socially realistic realm: fantasy can be useful in creating moments when something in the world might be revealed in new and surprising guises, and apparent certainties disrupted and transformed. A mass gangster shoot out leading to 64 gruesome deaths played out by a group of 15-year-old boys in a secure unit can be transformed through the introduction of the ghosts and angels who rise from the dead and by replacing the guns with fruit. Conversely, a scene of a young woman as a millionaire supermodel is brought into the 'real' by extending an invitation to her grandmother and aunt to join her on the star sofa. These are not planned interventions that can be written into programme manuals but derive from the awareness, imagination and tacit knowledge of the practitioner.

The realisation that realistic or naturalistic and fantastic portrayals of experience are linked in complex and unpredictable ways challenges practitioners to become more imaginative in their interventions in workshops and raises questions about how people and worlds might be transformed through theatre workshops. Theatre that challenges the thinking and behaviour of young people asks them to take an imaginative leap into a world that may have very different routines, roles, values from their familiar environment. Whilst it is important to avoid setting up a false opposition between the realistic and fantastic here, this imaginative leap might be facilitated by permission to 'forget' familiar habits of thought and behaviour and 'real' or remembered events rather than recreating and confronting them. Young people participating in theatre workshops often most powerfully express a sense of joy, surprise and excitement at the novelty of their experience rather than a clear sense of what they have achieved ('I never thought I'd be able to do anything like this'). The specific conceptualisation of 'intervention' in applied theatre with young people at risk that emerges here is that theatre may bring about new and temporary realities or perspectives on reality by providing spaces where connections between the fantastic and real can be re-imagined, embodied, experienced, focussed – rather than through the performance of 'pro-social' behaviour in an obvious way.

The skills and capacities needed by practitioners to facilitate these imaginative leaps have not been fully articulated by those working within applied theatre. Research and evaluation has focussed on identifying impacts within the narrow discourses of the criminal justice system (and in terms understandable to policy making agencies) rather than exploring how theatre and performance expertise might contribute in complex ways to personal and social change. There is an urgent need to research the skills and capacities of practitioners in order to support their confident engagement with the discourses of institutional environments they 'apply' their methodologies within as well as enhance the impact of the work. A cursory attempt to define these skills might be: recognition of a hyper-reality that can be played with, sensitivity to making obscure and unexpected connections between different ideas and experiences, amenability to working in non-linear ways, openness to following the direction of the group, willingness to take risks, ability to respond in the moment (spontaneity) and to work 'off manual'.

It is important to note that the cognitive behavioural model was initially adopted across numerous applied theatre projects inside the criminal justice system because there was uncritical acceptance of the evidence base to support its impact on reducing offending. These projects were therefore more marketable than others. However, the applicability of cognitive behavioural approaches to the offending of young people has been increasingly questioned from inside as well as outside of the criminal justice system. The approach is no longer seen as a 'blueprint' but as an exploratory method that may not work for all offenders.[10] Applied theatre's more recent preoccupation with articulating the value of creativity and the skills and capacities of creative practitioners is a timely response to this shift and its implicit invitation to explore new, more flexible methodologies. Moreover, the integration of the arts into mainstream youth justice provision has come about as a result of *discourses of creativity* that are becoming orthodox across complex institutions. In the youth justice context this can be deconstructed as follows: creative skills and capacities are linked to personal and social skills that make it more likely that a young person will successfully engage in mainstream educational and vocational opportunities and as a result avoid negative life trajectories. However, research into young people's offending continues to show that the causes of young people's offending are complex and experiences of social and economic disadvantage – rather than creative skills and capacities –

remain strongly correlated with offending by young people.[11] The concluding section of this chapter challenges the idea of creativity as implicitly radical and empowering for young people at risk by exploring its status in a capitalist context that creates the very social inequities associated with offending by young people.

III

> [I]s the modern project of (political) freedom a false appearance whose 'truth' is embodied by subjects who lost the last shred of autonomy in their immersion into the late capitalist 'administered world' . . . ?
>
> (Žižek 2002: 95)

The problematisation of the idea of the creative imagination as inherently radical comes from cultural and performance theory: Eagleton, for example, twins the idea of the creative imagination with the birth of capitalism[12] and McKenzie's notion of the '*liminal norm*' suggests that liminal spaces – moments where familiar order and routines are disrupted in a creative process of transition or transportation – have become the norm in a contemporary globalised world.[13] Risk, uncertainty and change are part of daily experience and the ability to be creative in the construction of self and perform flexibly in varied social contexts is integral to successfully negotiating contemporary networks of power. Late capitalism demands subjects and subjectivities that are flexible and amenable to reconstruction: imagination and creativity can be enlisted as part of this project and have achieved a new status in the contemporary social and political climate. The Labour government has been interested in the role of creativity in enhancing productivity since its election in 1997, born out of recognition that with the destruction of the manufacturing industry, imagination and creativity are essential to accessing new 'idea led' markets.[14]

As noted above, the accepted analysis of applied theatre practice that has emerged in such a context is that it can help young people build the capacities and resources – the ability to respond flexibly and fluidly – needed to survive and prosper in an uncertain world. When applied theatre 'works' it is said to develop the ability of individuals, groups and communities to engage with the world confidently, skilfully and with more awareness of the relationship of self to other(s). The experience of the applied theatre workshop – enjoyment and 'buzz' involved in actively exploring new ideas with other people in a temporary space – creates an energy that can help forge new conceptualisations of self and relationships with other people. It is even possible – and the growth of evaluation and research in applied theatre have shown how (especially if methodological problems with research in the criminal justice sector are ignored) – to measure or otherwise assess such 'shifts' and their associated programme mechanisms so as to bring about more effective interventions in the future.

Interestingly and provocatively, the ways in which applied theatre is described and legitimised in this context are mirrored by those agencies involved in the globalisation of markets and growth of capitalism. For example, the world of marketing has shifted away from the model of communicating 'messages' to consumers to providing 'experiences' of new products or brands. Brand experiences employ creative and participatory approaches and utilise fantasy, the bizarre and surreal to influence a consumer's construction of self and provide 'authentic' moments of connection between self and product (where the desire for the product becomes part of a reconceptualisation of individual identity).[15] Young people are often the primary target here and are more and more familiar with and competent at performing different aspects or presentations of self across distinct social contexts, relationships and audiences. These new realities for performance and creativity, and young people's familiarity with and ability to play across the blurred boundaries between reality and fantasy in their daily lives, have important implications for applied theatre practice with young people.

These points sound a warning against reifying the radical potential of creativity and the imagination and raise a number of crucial questions: do applied theatre interventions in youth justice settings simply help young people adjust more effectively to an oppressive reality that will continue to disenfranchise them? Are there possibilities in the practice for making more autonomous negotiations with power – opportunities to affect or bring about a social reality that might reflect young people's needs more adequately? Is the (re)turn to creativity and fantasy exemplified in applied theatre practice inside the criminal justice system an expression of powerlessness (of participants as well as practitioners) in the face of the complex and overwhelming institutional environments of late capitalism? An embracing of fantasy may simply help us negotiate an abusive and disempowering reality and is a mechanism for coping that suits those who already traverse social norms – offenders and artists. Is it possible to link personal development to more political objectives of social change in applied theatre?

The preoccupation of applied theatre practice and research through the 1990s was with establishing 'model' interventions that sought to resolve complex social problems together with a search for 'foundational' texts: evaluation reports with 'evidence' of impact and manuals setting down guidelines for good practice. These approaches risked uncritically participating in wider mechanisms of power and control. They were part of a search for more certain principles in a post Cold War era characterised by the globalisation of uncertainty and disorder; an era which, as Nicholson comments, coincided with the emergence of applied drama.[16] The return to the creative practices of theatre described in this chapter similarly mirror shifts in wider structures of power and knowledge.

The search for an empowering set of practices is an ongoing practical, methodological and philosophical challenge for applied theatre. Whilst this chapter does not offer any solutions, three areas for further analysis have emerged: exploration of the creative and imaginative skills and capacities of the applied theatre practitioner; increased attention to complexity in understanding the process and impact of applied theatre as an intervention; and more focus on the wider political and ethical questions relating to applied theatre interventions. Late capitalism's embracing of performance and creativity might be a more fruitful era for applied theatre with young people than the 1990s era of evidence led practice. However, that creativity and performance are playing wider roles in the drive for profit means that there is a need to more assertively ask, 'applied to whom, by whom, and for what purpose?': to return to questions of ethical and political commitment and to experiment with form, content and process rather than express absolute faith in learned methodologies and the inherent goodness of theatre when applied in complex social contexts.

Bibliography

Balfour, M. (ed.) (2004) *Theatre in Prison: Theory and Practice*, Bristol: Intellect Books.
Bial, H. (2004) *The Performance Studies Reader*, London and New York: Routledge.
Falshaw, L., Friendship, C., Travers, R., and Nugent, F. (2003) 'Searching for "What Works":
    An Evaluation of Cognitive Skills Programmes', Home Office Findings No. 206.
Hughes, J. (2005) 'Doing the Arts Justice: A Review of Research Literature, Practice and
    Theory', Department for Culture, Media and Sport, Home Office and Unit for the Arts
    and Offenders, available at www.culture.gov.uk (accessed 11 April, 2005).
Maguire, J. (ed.) (1995) *What Works: Reducing Offending*, Chichester: Wiley.
Maguire, J. and Priestley, P. (1985) *Offending Behaviour: Skills and Stratagems for Going Straight*, London:
    Batsford.
Nicholson, H. (2005) *Applied Drama: The Gift of Theatre*, Hampshire: Palgrave Macmillan.
Policy Action Team 12 of the Social Exclusion Unit in the Cabinet Office (2000) 'National
    Strategy for Neighbourhood Renewal – Report of Policy Action Team 12: Young
    people', Crown Copyright, Social Exclusion Unit.
Thompson, J. (1998a) *Prison Theatre: Perspectives and Practices*, London and Philadelphia: Jessica
    Kingsley Publishers.
Thompson, J. (1998b) 'Theatre and Offender Rehabilitation: Observations from the USA',
    Research in Drama Education 3 (2): 197–210.
Thompson, J. (2003) *Applied Theatre: Bewilderment and Beyond*, Bern: Peter Lang.
Žižek, S. (2002) *Welcome to the Desert of the Real*, London and New York: Verso.

Notes

1   A development that can be traced in the work of James Thompson and Michael Balfour (Thompson 1998a; Thompson 2003; Balfour 2004), and in the history of TIPP, a theatre organisation based at the University of Manchester. TIPP's work with young offenders is the inspiration for this chapter.
2   'National Strategy for Neighbourhood Renewal – Report of Policy Action Team 12: Young people' Crown Copywright 2000. Published by the Social Exclusion Unit.
3   See 'The arts and young people at risk of offending' (2005) published by Arts Council England for an account of the national strategy for the arts and young people at risk of offending. Available from www.artscouncil.org.uk.
4   See Hughes J. 2005 'Doing the Arts Justice: A Review of Research Literature, Practice and Theory' for a review of evidence for the impact of arts on young people at risk of offending. Available from www.culture.gov.uk.
5   Simon Ruding is the director of TIPP, an arts charity based in the University of Manchester. Jenny Hughes is Lecturer in Applied Theatre in the University of Manchester. For more information go to www.arts.manchester.ac.uk/catr and www.tipp.org.uk.
6   'Blagg!' was originally developed by James Thompson and Paul Heritage in 1992. After the establishment of the Youth Justice Board in 1998 a number of Youth Offending Teams across England were trained to implement Blagg! with young offenders. It is now used in more than 40 youth justice settings. Manchester and Bury Youth Offending Teams commissioned an evaluation in 2002 to explore the impact of the intervention on reducing and challenging offending behaviour by young people. This evaluation was carried out by Jenny Hughes.
7   See Maguire and Priestley 1985 and Maguire (ed.) 1995.
8   For an excellent example of a project that seeks to engage with fantasy in the self concept of offenders in order to challenge offending see Johnston in Balfour 2004.
9   See Thompson 1998b and Hughes in Thompson 1998a.

10   Falshaw *et al.* 2003 'Searching for 'What Works': an evaluation of cognitive skills programmes' Home Office Findings 206.

11   See 'Risk and Protective Factors' 2005 Research undertaken by Communities that Care for the Youth Justice Board. Available from www.yjb.gov.uk.

12   Eagleton T. (2006) 'The Death of Criticism' John Edward Taylor Chair in English Inaugural Address, University of Manchester, 26 September 2006.

13   McKenzie J. 'The liminal-norm' in Bial H (ed.) (2004) p.27.

14   See 'All Our Futures: Creativity, Culture and Education – Report to: the Secretary of State for Education and Employment and the Secretary of State for Culture, Media and Sport' by National Advisory Committee on Creative and Cultural Education (1999). Available from www.dfes.gov.uk.

15   For a provocative example see 'What's all the fuss about brand experience?' published by the brand consultants Enterprise IG. Available from www.enterpriseig.com. Also see www.brandexperiencelab.org.

16   Nicholson (2005) p.11.

Chapter 32

Kathleen McCreery

FLIGHT PATHS
Challenging racism in Sunderland and Newcastle

FOR MANY ASYLUM SEEKERS IN Britain regional dispersal has been a bitter experience. The harassment and racist attacks to which they have been subjected in Sunderland and Newcastle, Glasgow and Liverpool have compounded the traumas that led them to flee their homelands. *Flight Paths* was a theatre project which helped audiences in the North East of England understand why people become refugees, what it costs them, and what it feels like to arrive in a place where you may not understand the language or culture, and you are treated with suspicion and hostility. Intended as a TIE production for years six through eight, the play went far beyond its original remit, reaching 10,000 young people and adults.

Preparing the ground

In 2002 Margaret Ferrie of Sunderland LEA was charged with introducing Citizenship into the school curriculum. She enlisted the help of Flabagast Theatre Company who in turn asked me to write and direct a relevant play, one hour in length. 'We're good on emotional literacy,' Margaret said at our first meeting, 'not so good on racism.' Out went the cartoon characters originally proposed. I was given an open brief.

For me it's essential to get to know my audience. Margaret contacted four Sunderland secondary schools, Thornhill, Southmoor, Hylton Red House and Houghton Kepier, and Rosa Stourac McCreery and I spent three weeks running drama workshops with pupils in years seven, eight and ten. We weren't just researching. These sessions had their own validity, we were beginning the process of stirring, sharing, and sifting, of bringing the private into the public arena, of bearing witness.

Our Insider/Outsider game proved particularly effective. Everyone was given a number. A '1' meant you were an Insider, a '2' Outsider. We varied the ratio between the two groups during the exercise. Sometimes there was only one Outsider, sometimes very few Insiders. As Outsiders the young people said they felt:

> 'invisible', 'a target', 'alone', 'rejected', 'ridiculed', 'inferior', 'small', 'hurt', 'like a piece of dirt'. 'All you want to do is stay out of the way of people so that nobody says anything.' 'It feels like being locked outside the door.' 'It feels like you want to die.' 'It wasn't very nice but I don't think big groups of Insiders look much fun either.'

Insiders reported,

> 'You can say and do whatever you like, no one's going to stop you. Even if you sound stupid no one cares.' 'If someone dares to pick on you it's not so serious because you have back-up.'

They felt:

> 'powerful', 'important', 'big', 'cool', 'like a boss'.

However,

> 'You can be an Insider and still feel alone.' 'When you were an Insider you felt like you were wanted and liked for the person you were. When your label was changed, no one liked you for who you were anymore, but just thought of you as an Outsider, and didn't think it was the exact same person you were as an Insider.'

Bullying in and out of school, usually violent, was a recurring theme in the images and improvisations. Victims were targeted for their race, sexuality or weight. The prevailing view was that schools were not addressing the problem. Pupils had no confidence that if they reported the bullying, it would stop.

By contrast, the safe atmosphere generated in some of the workshops allowed pupils to talk about painful experiences. A boy whose black friend was killed while they were playing football in the street heard the hit-and-run driver yell, 'Nigger bastard!' as he drove away. His group were visibly moved. They created a powerful frozen image of the incident. A black lad beaten up at primary school had to change schools; one of several examples of the victim being treated as the problem. A top student who was bullied mercilessly several years earlier for being a swot suddenly burst into tears. His classmates were sensitive and supportive.

On occasion we were stunned by the casual racism we encountered, and taken aback by the ignorance that fuelled these attitudes. Pupils agreed their ideas came from the media, their grandparents and parents: 'My dad's exact words: "If you marry a blackie, you're not my daughter."' Some were cynical about Oxfam adverts on the telly and the 'stories' refugees tell. One girl told Rosa, 'I think you should do a play . . . that shows what it's like. But no lying, no exaggerating. Just the truth.' It was clear that racism among young people in Sunderland was focussed on asylum seekers and refugees. Margaret Ferrie and Flabagast agreed that was the play I had to write.

The response to the workshops was overwhelmingly positive. There was one exception: a group of year ten girls who announced that they hated drama. 'We're not kids!' Rosa returned to interview them. Towards the end of a lengthy, often heated, discussion a girl suddenly began to tell a story.

> 'This isn't racism, but there was a lass in my primary school and her mam's boy friend beat her up . . .'

They had had to leave London and ended up at a refuge in Sunderland.

> '. . . She says that they gave you like a tin of food and a bed, and they expected you to be so grateful . . . You still can't sleep at night, 'cos you know you've got to move on.'

This story gave me the idea for the opening scene of the play. It wasn't only asylum seekers who had to take flight in the middle of the night. Here was a bridge.

Our next step was to talk to people at the sharp end. We interviewed and got to know Turkish Kurds, a Rwandan, a Congolese, Zimbabweans, a Guinean and a family of Colombians. We talked with health workers, the police, a psychologist and with professionals and volunteers working with refugees in a range of organisations.

None of the asylum seekers or refugees we met were economic migrants. All asked us to stress this in the play. They had fled from persecution, death threats, war, torture, prison. Among them were a lawyer, a teacher, a multilingual secretary, a farmer, and a young man with a degree in Industrial Chemistry. They had left behind good jobs, houses, land, even servants, and their extended families. One had to leave children and her husband. They ached with loss, were scarred physically and emotionally. They wanted to work, study, contribute. They were not asking for handouts or pity, and they did not want to remain victims.

All had experienced racism since arriving in Sunderland and Newcastle. They were called names, spat at, and attacked with cans, bricks, fists, knives. F had been pelted with eggs. She was carrying her four-month-old baby at the time. The two A children were set upon outside their house immediately after our interview with their parents, they were in tears. Over a three-day period I witnessed the callous way the authorities dealt with Kurdish families too frightened to return to their homes on one of the toughest estates in Sunderland after an incident which the police described as an attempted burglary. The Kurds said there had been a racist mob outside.

Then on 28 August 2002 Peiman Bahmani, a 30-year-old Iranian asylum seeker, was stabbed to death in Sunderland by an 18-year-old shouting racist abuse. I participated in the marches, rallies, memorial services and vigils, and in angry meetings between the Iranian community and the police. By this time I was angry too.

Information and argument were not enough. If we were to challenge racist attitudes effectively and help prevent racist behaviour, our audiences had to be able to relate emotionally, viscerally, to the events and characters portrayed. We had to start from the situation of local people. It was vital to create characters they could empathise with before introducing other worlds, to explore the identity crisis, insecurity and powerlessness of the white working class.

We decided to hold auditions before I began writing. Two white female members of Flabagast, Beverley Quinn and Therase Neve, were included in the cast. We also employed Reza Kianpour, an Iranian asylum seeker who had studied drama at North Tyneside College, Kenyan/South African actress Yvonne Wandera, and Nitin Kundra, a Newcastle-born actor of Indian descent. Later we invited them back for an exploratory week. I still had no script, just ideas and tons of research material.

In facilitating the workshop week I began by asking: 'What do we think? What do we know?' This was an opportunity to risk daft questions, to lay our cards on the table without fear of censorship or judgement. We played with stereotypes, and created our own landscapes: 'This is my home, this is my street.' We drew characters from experience and our imaginations. Cross acting was especially productive: men played women, blacks played whites. We talked and argued and shared our stories.

None of the dramatic material generated fed into the play I went on to write. It did give me an excellent sense of the actors' range and qualities: I could hear and see them while I was writing. They got to know me and each other. We sorted out issues that might have led to conflict later on. We were able to start rehearsals with some common understanding and commitment. And I discovered that Reza had a phenomenal voice and a huge repertoire of traditional Persian songs.

The play

There is no easing into the serious nature of the drama. An actress enters, chalks 'Jenny's Story' on the blackboard flat. She briefly sets the scene and then transforms into Jenny's mother, a victim of domestic violence. She and Jenny pack and creep down the stairs in the middle of the night '. . . like criminals. Like it was us had done something wrong.' This sets the pattern for the play. Each actor plays a young person and that character's parent. Through Jenny we meet Lisa, a tough, rebellious kid who unexpectedly takes the shy new girl under her wing. The issue of race is barely mentioned in the first eight pages.

Then a black teenager stalks in, scrawls 'Anysie's Story' on the flat, and throws the chalk half way across the stage. Inspired by a report in the Annual Review of the Medical Foundation for the Care of Victims of Torture, I invented the character of a girl who has stopped speaking because of her experiences in Congo. One day the music therapist patiently working with her sings a hauntingly beautiful Persian song, without preamble or translation. It touches something deep inside her. When the release comes it is explosive. The actress tears across the stage delivering a page-long monologue about the soldiers, the prison, the torture. The actress transforms into her mother Harriet, struggling with the slow, inefficient and patently unjust and inhumane system for processing asylum seekers in Britain.

Anysie and her mother are moved to the North East and encounter Jenny, Lisa and their mate Omar. He's born and bred in England, wears the Sunderland (or Newcastle) football strip, he's 'a Makkem [or Toonie] with a tan,' says Lisa. But when she calls Anysie 'a black monkey' Omar is torn. He tells the audience about an incident in his dad Rashid's corner shop, and asks 'What if you can't go back to where you come from because you didn't come from there in the first place? You just look as if you did.'

Abbas' Story expresses the confusion and frustration of being catapulted into a country where you don't speak the language or understand the culture and are pushed and pulled back and forth between housing and benefit officers, solicitors, doctors and education authorities as you try to rebuild your life, having risked everything to get to this land of 'football, fish and chips and freedom!'

As the play progresses, the separate stories are interwoven against a backdrop of increasing racism. Anysie's mother is pelted with eggs at the bus stop by Lisa and a friend. A swastika appears on the wall of Rashid's shop. Lisa's mother Carol, a cleaner, is bitter at being passed over for promotion to supervisor by Abbas' father Siroos, and at waiting for years on the housing list. And then '. . . that lot come in and suddenly they've got plenty of houses.' Called to the school because Lisa's racist bullying is out of control, Carol defends her daughter in an impassioned, xenophobic speech. Lisa in turn lashes out at the people she blames for making her tired, defeated mother cry.

Lisa asks Jenny and Omar to help her put a firecracker through the letterbox of Abbas' home. They are torn between their loyalty to her, the desire to fit in, to belong, and their knowledge that Abbas and his family don't deserve this; it's dangerous and it's wrong. There's a tense stand-off. When both refuse Lisa does it herself. There's a fire and Abbas and his mother are killed. Anysie delivers a moving funeral oration.

The play is laced with references to birds and flight. I was struck by the long distances travelled by migrating birds and humans, and by the strength this requires. Rashid, an economic migrant, sighs, 'There was no future for us in Pakistan . . . we are like hungry birds, we must fly further and further away from our homeland if we are to survive.' Jenny, the newcomer, finds solace in birdwatching. Lisa overhears her calling 'Teacher, teacher,' to a great tit in the park and doubles up with laughter: 'They're all of them great tits, the teachers, the whole horrible lot of them.' Abbas' father Siroos has nightmares about the prison guard holding a knife to his throat and whispering, 'This is what happens to birds who sing about things they shouldn't.'

When I delivered the script Flabagast said it wasn't suitable for the target audience. It was too complex, emotional, heavy. They wouldn't understand or relate to it. These mutterings continued, culminating in pressure to do a trial run-through for a local youth theatre days before we were to open. We had battled over the amount of rehearsal time as it was. I knew that the play wouldn't work if it was under-rehearsed, and performing before we were ready would undermine the actors. We compromised on a preview the Saturday before our Monday launch for the youth group and adult guests.

The audience were moved to tears by Anysie's powerful monologue, shocked when Carol spat her gum on the floor and Siroos slowly bent over to pick it up, dismayed when Anysie's mother Harriet produced her egg-stained coat. They gasped and ducked when Omar simulated kicking his football in their direction, and laughed out loud at Abbas' disgusted encounter with school dinners. The lively discussion afterwards involved young people and adults on an equal footing.

It worked. Why? I believe that people under-estimate the young. By the age of 11, they know that life is serious. Art which respects this, which does not talk down to them or skirt round the issues, makes them feel *they* are being taken seriously. (There was an added bonus: *Flight Paths* appealed to older teenagers and adults as well as our target audience. Some schools invited parents, governors, community policemen, education students.) The intensely intimate and specific nature of the story-telling in the play, often using direct address, makes it possible for audiences to recognise and empathise with the characters. The fact that they are flawed and unpredictable, that the racist Lisa is sassy and strong and she and her mother are presented sympathetically, that Jenny and Omar are initially far from heroic, that the asylum seekers are not presented as victims, Anysie is bolshie and Abbas spirited means that audiences have to make difficult judgements just like the characters. The episodic framework and the juxtaposition of narratives encourage spectators to see the connections between characters and to see how these particular events relate to the wider world. The play demonstrates through its very structure the fact that human beings are interdependent.

The resource pack, training for teachers, workshops

The first *Flight Paths* resource pack was compiled by Elaine Marsden, a primary school teacher seconded to work with Margaret Ferrie and distributed to the 28 schools which booked performances. The pack contains 'thinking skills' activities, question-naires, legal definitions, case studies, post-play debrief/discussion suggestions, and a useful appendix. It provides material to stimulate exploration of the concept of human rights and the media portrayal of asylum seekers and refugees. The units are organised into core and optional categories to allow for flexibility.

Two preparatory workshops for teachers were offered by Sunderland Education, one on race awareness and issues surrounding asylum seekers and refugees, and a second on the use of the resource pack and hosting the play. The take-up was poor. This was partly due to limited promotion and organisation. The pressures on teachers and the low priority some gave to the subject were undoubtedly other factors.

The follow-up workshop was devised by me and the company for a maximum of 30 pupils. In secondary schools the actors returned in role and participants elected to speak to a character in a smaller group. Pupils were eager to confront Lisa. There were a few who agreed with her views, if not her actions. When she was on her own, the actress sometimes had to drop out of role to deal with this. At schools with Asian pupils Nitin Kundra was surrounded. They identified with football fan Omar's situation, torn between two cultures, and saw Nitin as a positive role model. However, the actor was racially abused in the corridor by a white pupil who had seen the play. She was suspended. Jenny too, with her stark moral dilemma, appealed to the pupils. Anysie and Abbas were chosen by fewer pupils, but the discussions in their more intimate groups were often profound. Pupils began to ask Reza if he would sing again. (At the start of the tour there was surprised laughter when he sang. The music and language were surprising, strange. As the actor became more confident, this rarely happened.)

We had more time in primary schools. Participants had to imagine they lived in a country affected by war, famine, a repressive regime, or in an economically sound, democratic country. Those in the first three groups were given a role card: soldier, journalist, politician, managing director, student, drug dealer, factory worker, child, etc. If they chose to leave their homeland they had to convince the prosperous nation to give them asylum. Meanwhile, that group decided how many they would allow in and on what grounds. When this exercise was facilitated properly, pupils loved it and learned from it.

Sunderland Education did not allow us to publicise the play. Evening performances at the Bangladeshi Centre were by invitation only. Plain-clothes policemen were in the audience. The British National Party's high level of activity in Sunderland during the 2003 local elections had led to security concerns. I disagreed with this approach, but understood their reasons.

2004

Nevertheless, word spread. Neil Denton from ARCH (Agencies against Racist Crime and Harassment), Rizwan Sheikh of WRAP (Working with Racist Perpetrators), and Fiona Evans, a freelance arts worker, came to see the play. They were so impressed they raised funds to bring the project to Newcastle. In 2004, a second production with a company of six and specially trained workshop facilitators gave 60 performances in Newcastle and Sunderland. Rizwan edited an attractive and comprehensive resource pack with material suitable for Key Stages 1 to 4.

Fiona, Neil and Rizwan were a determined and utterly committed team. *Flight Paths* helped roll out the ARCH 24 Hour Racist Incident Reporting Line. It was used in the training of play, youth service and city council employees. It toured community venues, youth centres, colleges, and a seniors' day centre as well as schools. Hundreds came to watch a celebratory performance at the Civic Centre in Newcastle.

The response to *Flight Paths* was humbling. A member of the youth theatre who had watched the preview performance wrote an intensely moving and well-researched story about a Bosnian refugee for which he received an award at school. Poems were composed in creative writing workshops led by me and by teachers, letters were written and feedback gathered by Fiona and the facilitators. Here are some of the comments:

- 'I am writing about when you came to our school and changed our lives for ever. The second story about Anysie broke my heart.'
- 'My dad doesn't like refugees or asylum seekers, he doesn't want anybody anymore to come in to this country, but maybe if I tell him this story it will make him think twice about refugees.'
- 'There's these children on my street, they started to laugh and call a little black boy from Africa. I stood up for the child and told them to leave him alone. Now I have got the courage to stand up to bullies.'
- 'I just want to say thank you because my four cousins are refugees and they are going through the same thing.'
- 'I also have got my confidence up in telling people not to be racist. The other day I was going to the shops with my sister and my cousin when she asked her to sing the song about Indians. I felt my anger burning then I told them to go home if they were going to be racist.'
- 'I've changed my opinion totally about asylum seekers I think now it's not the asylum seekers which is the problem it's Great Britain what's the problem.'

Chapter 33

Penny Bundy

THE PERFORMANCE
OF TRAUMA

VARIOUS GOVERNMENTS THROUGHOUT the Western world now recognise that many children who were raised in orphanages and other care facilities throughout the twentieth century were subjected to repeated physical, emotional and sexual abuse. The impact is often severe and continues to create problems for adult survivors. The types of problems experienced include the psychological difficulties often associated with complex post-traumatic stress disorder as well as poverty and low levels of literacy. Schwartz *et al.* (1995: 3–9) liken the ongoing impact to that experienced by torture victims. Briere (1996) draws similar conclusions also noting that adult survivors of childhood abuse often lack the ability to reflect. This emerges as a direct result of the dangerous childhoods they experienced. To stay alert to danger, one must continually focus away from internal experience to focus on the external world. The result of such learned response is a reduction in the development of both a sense of identity and self understanding. Adult survivors often lack self-awareness.

In Queensland, Australia the nature and impact of the experiences of former children in care was revealed to the public following a State Government Inquiry. Significant media attention followed release of the *Forde Report* (1999) and a number of groups and individuals submitted formal responses requesting action to redress the problems created. One of these responses titled *Healing or Horror* (2000) was submitted by ex-residents who claimed that survivors need 'to be empowered in order to experience and create more fulfilling lives'. Two of the specific requests made by ex-residents at this time were:

a   programs that promote creative expression
b   the opportunity to learn new living skills to replace learned survival skills.

In October 1999, the State Government established the Aftercare Resource Centre as a one-stop-shop to support ex-residents by offering counselling services, facilitating educational opportunities, providing advice and assisting in family reconciliation processes. In their quest to find innovative ways of assisting survivors to redress some of the ongoing problems experienced, the Aftercare Resource Centre approached a team of Griffith University researchers/applied theatre workers. The result of those discussions was *The Moving On Project*, a three-year Australian Research Council-funded drama based approach to change. The project was a response to the expressed needs of ex-residents as documented in *Healing or Horror* by attempting to provide:

- an opportunity to raise awareness of the reasons for and the findings of the Forde Inquiry in professional and community contexts
- an opportunity to acknowledge the similarities and differences of the experiences of ex-residents
- a program that would promote the creative expression of ex-residents
- an opportunity to learn living skills to replace learned survival skills
- an opportunity for ex-residents to experience empowerment and through this to experience and create more fulfilling lives.

The initial facilitators on *The Moving On Project* were Merrelyn Bates (a counsellor), Bruce Burton and myself (both drama educators and theatre practitioners). Since the commencement of the project we have worked together with Susan Kelly (an experienced counsellor and current PhD student) and other counsellors from the Aftercare Resource Centre as an interdisciplinary team to plan, conduct and evaluate the progress of the work. At various times throughout the project we have been joined by further undergraduate and postgraduate students who have taken an active role in the work.

The practical workshops

At the commencement of the project we ran a series of eight, three-hour drama workshops. The number of participants attending at this time varied from week to week with the maximum number in any session being 16 ex-residents, two to three drama facilitators and two to three counsellors. Our focus at this time was to build trust, build a sense of group cohesion, negotiate working guidelines that we hoped would meet the needs of all participants and explore different approaches to drama that might help us achieve these aims at this time.

Following this, all of the participants were interviewed and asked about their goals and reasons for participating. Some of the goals stated at this point included the development of self-confidence, self-esteem and feelings of self-worth. Some hoped that through the drama they would become more assertive and/or learn to trust others. Others wanted to gain a sense of achievement through either participating in the workshops or creating performance.

In the second year, guided by the stated goals of the participants and our analysis of the needs of the people who had participated to date, we planned a series of weekly two-hour drama workshops. In addition to the participants' stated goals, my approach was influenced by the work of Briere (1996) and by the need we all perceived to build safety, trust and self-resilience. We focused on offering the participants opportunities to "play" and also created a number of drama workshops that offered them opportunities to explore issues that appeared important in their lives. The exploration of power was a significant issue.

Throughout this time my planning was guided by the belief that everyday life and life history are the source of human role models. Healthy individuals have the ability to play many roles in everyday life and to switch between these with ease. However, life experience had stripped many of the participant group of the ability to experience themselves in multiple ways and encouraged them to define themselves by a limited range of roles. As Thompson (1999: 22–3) noted, drama offers people who have narrowly defined role perceptions the opportunity to extend the roles they play, and to switch between them in new, flexible and creative ways.

Towards the end of the second year, at the request of the participants, the focus of the work shifted away from process-based drama towards playmaking and performance. We worked with the participants to build skills in playbuilding using stories and ideas that allowed them to explore significant issues but without, at this stage, being in any way autobiographical.

In the final stage of the process (2006), the focus shifted again. Three years after commencing the project, the participants felt they were ready to begin to use performance to explore and tell their own stories. To allow the original facilitators the opportunity to view the work from another perspective and to give the participants the opportunity of developing a relationship with a different "teacher", we employed another drama facilitator. The original team continued to work with the group but as co-participants rather than facilitators.

In the following I offer two examples of people sharing their stories and reinterpreting them in performance in the later stages of the work. Although the two scenes discussed were actually explored in different sessions, I am drawing on these here because they offer slightly different approaches, meeting slightly different needs.

Exploring autobiographical stories

Following a warm-up exercise that focused on the themes and skills that would be explored in the session, Sarah (the facilitator) asked the group, "Who has brought a story today?" Two people signalled they had a story they wanted to share. Mary (who only joined the project recently) was offering her story to the group for the first time. Annie (who has been working with the group throughout the whole project) had shared and explored her story in previous sessions but wanted to continue with some new ideas she had developed. The group divided in two. A counsellor and a drama facilitator joined each of the groups. I joined Mary's group.

Playing Mary's story

A small group of us gathered our chairs into a close circle. The story Mary had chosen was a story of kindness, of change, of hope, of a new beginning. She told the story of a young "run away" teenager – spending her life drinking in bars, surviving by meeting sailors who would sneak her and her friend onto their ships as they travelled from port to port. She was usually intoxicated. One night, a nun found her in a park, drunk. She took Mary home to her convent room and offered the young girl her own bed for the night. In the morning, she realised that the nun had slept on the floor so that she herself could have a bed. The nun suggested she could make choices in life and offered her the opportunity to have a job and a place to call home. This was a turning point in her life.

After Mary told us her story she decided who she would like to play each part. I was given "her" part to play. Mary's friend was played by another group member. As a group we discussed how we might create the possible action, constantly deferring to Mary. As we did so, Mary's story became more and more detailed. It also appeared to become more emotionally distanced for the teller whose focus was on the actors getting the action right as they performed. As actors tasked with portraying the event, we asked questions such as: Should I do it this way or that? Am I feeling . . . ? What do I think about . . . ? The author and owner of the story thus had the opportunity to reflect on the feelings and attitudes she believed the various people engaged in the event actually experienced.

Under Mary's direction we set up the space physically and began to create the action. Mary directed and redirected me playing her. Like many of the participants, her attention as director was on the externals of the scene – who I look at, talk to, how drunk I should seem. Although the scene is not funny, there was a sense of playfulness in the portrayal and a sense of enjoyment for Mary as she saw her scene being acted out. We played the story through to its conclusion as she had given it to us. As director, she reworked us to try to get the "right" feeling in the characters and in their reactions to the circumstances. Later in the session (as we often do), we presented the scene to the other half of the group who had been working on a different story.

Over the following weeks, Mary stepped into the scene, first as the nun, later as herself. As she took roles as different characters in her own story, so she shared her reflections with us about it, about her beliefs about the world and herself in the world now.

Playing Annie's story

Annie brought a scripted piece in the form of a poem she had written and wanted to include. She explained her story to her smaller working group. Hers was also a story of change in circumstances. The group negotiated how they would work and how they might portray this scene to capture the feelings of it. Annie chose to play herself. She chose one of the counsellors and Glenda (another participant) to be her friends in the orphanage. Another participant, Trish took on the role of the nun. They decided to present the poem as a voice-over and set up the physical space. At first, Annie focused on the accuracy of the space and the detail of the story.

Her scene began with the children playing. The three actors focused on creating the excitement of the children and their happiness in the moment to such an extent that when the nun walked in, the actors failed to notice her entrance. Sarah (as facilitator and director) stopped the scene and asked the participants if this was accurate. Is this what would happen when the nun walks in? Is that what you want to show – that they are oblivious to her? They discussed a more accurate representation and remained focused and alert as they played the scene again.

The group reworked the scene but this time as the nun entered "the children" half froze, focused on the nun but not looking her in the eye. They appeared frightened. As a spectator I had a sense that something was going to happen. As the two subdued children remained relatively still, we saw the nun and Annie moving to the back of the stage. The nun was fierce, cold. "Annie" in role as herself as a much younger child was obedient, submissive and seemed oblivious to what would happen next. As the nun threw the child (Annie) to the ground the audience heard a voice-over (played by a counsellor) and earlier scripted by Annie.

VOICE-OVER: As sister threw me to the ground, she said, when you go out that door keep your eyes down, head down.

Trish, playing the brutal nun, continued from her script:

NUN: Go straight forward and don't look back.

Annie played the role obediently and with great conviction and concentration. Once again the director stopped the scene and suggested they replay it, slowing it down, stylizing it further. The actors were attentive, focused, concentrating on the task of portrayal. They resumed the scene. The actors continued the action silently while the voice over continued.

VOICE-OVER: Those words still linger with me today and feel so sad in everyway . . . falling down, tears in my eyes as I turned around, her head in the air as though she couldn't care.

The actors stopped and looked to Sarah, the director. The question seemed to be: well, what did you think? Their focus seemed to be on the presentation of the play, not the content of the story. The director said, "That was lovely". The actors beamed, happy with the praise and with their own sense of achievement in the scene. The director continued, "As you keep working, concentrate on the physicality to highlight the scene".

Performing traumatic autobiography

I find this a fascinating example of how the rehearsal (for performance) of potentially traumatic autobiographical story offered opportunities for growth for the people sharing their stories with the group. It also appeared to offer other group members (who have their own traumatic stories) an opportunity to engage empathically and responsively in the process.

Several key aspects of this process appear to impact on the way participants experience the creation of autobiographical performance in the workshop space. These include risk balanced against the level of trust and safety felt, acceptance, the level of power and control experienced and the role of emotional distance in offering participants an appropriate balance between engagement/protection and the possibility of reflection.

Both of the participants who shared their stories felt sufficient safety and trust within the group to do so at this time. For Mary though, as a relative newcomer, there was a risk in revealing her past to the group for the first time. In the debrief following the drama she revealed how nervous she had been about what people would think of her, how they might judge and reject her. No one in the group censured her. Rather they appeared understanding and more willing to welcome her in.

Although the participants have not used the term "power and control", my observation is that in both of the events described, the storyteller experienced elevated status and a sense of power and control in the telling and creation process. This sense of power and control over their own lives has not always been available to them. It appears to arise because of a number of factors. Firstly, the tellers own their stories and the way they choose to present them in this context. Again, and in particular for this participant group, "having ownership" over their own narratives had been absent in the past. Some had been denied knowledge about who they or their parents and siblings were. Prior to the Forde Inquiry, others had not been believed when they did tell their stories.

At the beginning of the project, many of the group members claimed to lack self confidence. The status roles they assumed in everyday life were often low and life experiences afforded them little opportunity to experience themselves in other ways. By electing to tell their story in the workshop, they become the centre of attention. The focus of others on them and their story raises their status and their sense of power and control over the story they tell. The attention of the listeners is quite different to the attention that might be present if the stories were shared in a social context. Here, there is a degree of emotional distance created because those listening are focused on a specific task – gaining sufficient knowledge and understanding in order to be able to re-enact the event. The storyteller, too, is focused on this.

The emotions normally attached to the story are portrayed in the scenes but (in these two examples) did not appear to be experienced by the tellers as they recounted and staged their past experiences. In the presentation of Mary's story, the actors' need for sufficient detail in order to portray the event forced the storyteller to think, to reflect, recall. In both these instances, this search for more depth seemed to increase the emotional distance of the storyteller. Mary even referred to herself in the third person as she did this. In the case of her story, further emotional distance seemed to be achieved (or maintained) as she became designer (creating the physical space) for re-enactment.

Unlike Mary who had taken the role of storyteller and then designer/director, Annie had chosen to play herself in the scene she was creating. While electing to play oneself potentially reduces the necessary distance (for emotional protection and possibilities of reflection), this didn't appear to happen here. At least three particular aspects of how her scene was created struck me as positive and significant. Firstly, Annie has worked with the group since it first began and had explored the same story several times in the previous sessions. Each time it was told and explored in a slightly different way. The group were familiar with her story and its importance to her. Some, who had lived in the same orphanage, had undergone similar experiences and feelings. Creating the story for public performance is important to Annie and she enjoys performing. She also enjoys writing and was proud of the poem she had written and wanted to incorporate. The focus as the group worked was on the performative aspects, rather than the story itself. This was reinforced by the facilitator who directed the scene. The questions she asked and the comments she made (e.g. her seemingly ironic statement "That was lovely" after the child is thrown to the ground) forced their attention to the dramatic detail – timing, focus, use of space, vocal portrayal, etc. rather than relating to the personal story directly. Although the scene portrayed fear, pain and powerlessness, the working mood of the group was in direct contrast. They were in control and were having fun. Thus here too, the rehearsal offered the storyteller and performers an opportunity to experience emotional distance in order to explore an autobiographical event safely.

In both instances, giving form to one's story in this way alters the emotional response that the person might normally feel if they were to reflect on this story as a past event outside a dramatic context. Although the stories may have previously been painful to the tellers, the mood of engagement of the storyteller/director and storyteller/performer as they work these stories in the drama is focused enjoyment. The distance created through this process opens the way for reflection that might not otherwise be available. This seems to be the case for others who perform in the scenes too.

Earlier in the chapter I suggested that risk balanced against the level of trust and safety a participant feels, their experience of acceptance, the level of power and control they experience and the role of emotional distance all influence how a person experiences the drama in this context. While the workshop events described here did appear to offer an appropriate balance between engagement/protection for all participants, there have been other workshops where the participants have felt less protected.

Quite often, as described here, we have worked (and then presented) two different stories separately in one session. As time moves on and as the individual members of the group feel greater trust and safety in the context, so the stories told increase in horror. It appears that those involved in creating the scenes have a degree of protection afforded to them by their active engagement. Those who witness the scenes (and who have not worked on their creation) do not always experience sufficient emotional distance and can suffer as a result. One presumes, quite glibly perhaps, that a feature of applied theatre practice is that the participants identify as a community with a shared purpose. While the participants of *The Moving On Project* share the fact that they are all adult survivors of institutional child abuse, their specific experiences, difficulties, values, beliefs and responses to the work are individual. Each has particular needs that must be met in a group context and this is not always easily achievable.

Bibliography

Briere, J. (1996) *Therapy for Adults Molested as Children: Beyond Survival* (2nd edn), New York: Springer Publications.

Commission of Inquiry into Abuse of Children in Queensland Institutions (1999) *Report of the Commission into Abuse of Children in Queensland Institutions* (The Forde Report), Brisbane: Queensland Government.

Network for Ex-residents of Queensland Government and Church Institutions and Former Children in Care. (2000) *Healing or Horror*, Brisbane: Esther Trust in collaboration with Micah Inc and the Network for Ex-residents of Queensland Government and Church Institutions and Former Children in Care.

Schwartz, M., Galperin, L., Masters, W. (1995) 'Sexual trauma within the Context of Traumatic and Inescapable Stress, Neglect, and Poisonous Pedagogy', in M. Hunter (ed.), *Adult Survivors of Child Sexual Abuse: Treatment Innovations*, California: Sage Publications, pp. 1–17.

Thompson, J. (1999) *Drama Workshops for Anger Management and Offending Behaviour*, London: Jessica Kingsley Publishers.

Chapter 34

Jonathan Fox

PLAYBACK THEATRE
IN BURUNDI
Can theatre transcend the gap?

FROM THE AIR, FLYING over the rolling green hills, their color so rich and uniform, it is difficult to imagine the bloodshed that has stained the earth below—over 300,000 dead in a 30-year conflict now inching towards settlement. We are flying to Ngozi, Burundi, to conduct training in playback theatre sponsored by the NGO Search for Common Ground (Search). It is 2003 and my second time to this country. My face is pressed against the window in anticipation. This chapter reflects the hope that enticed me onto that airplane in the first instance; of using theatre for trauma recovery and dialogue-building, and reveals the profound, ethical questions that the project uncovered. By mid-2006, as I write this account, it is by no means clear if our program has been a success or what the next steps will be.

The background

A white American raised in cosmopolitan New York City, I am a founder of the theatre method being introduced to predominantly rural Burundian people as a conflict resolution tool. Playback theatre has theoretical roots in the oral tradition— we use no set texts in our work—and it was born of frustration with modern conditions of elitism, alienation, and art. Could such a theatre approach emerging out of the ferment of American experimental theatre in the 1960s have any relevance for the social conditions in Burundi, where there has been so much civil disruption and where the per capita income is $700?[1]

Playback theatre is based on a simple idea: audience members share thoughts, feelings, memories—stories—and a team of performers enact them on the spot.[2] Nothing is prepared beforehand. The actors and musicians come before their audiences with no memorized play; they have only their skills at improvisation, their ability to listen deeply, and their humanity. Naturally each performance of playback theatre is different, depending on the audience. In the course of a playback theatre event, a kind of tapestry is woven of stories told and embodied on the stage. The pattern on the tapestry reflects what is important for the community, made up as it is of tellers 'restorying' their experience.[3]

Our sponsoring agency in Burundi was Search for Common Ground, a conflict resolution NGO. We were invited to Burundi to train the actors of Tubiyage, a mixed Hutu-Tutsi theatre group founded by Michel Ange Nzojibwami. In the first training (2001) the Tubiyage performers received five days of instruction in playback theatre. They learned the most basic short and long forms, the structure of a performance, and took part in three performances. The second training (2003) consisted of 10 days. New actors received the basic training, and the experienced actors deepened their knowledge of the playback theatre improvisational process, including a special focus on enacting traumatic stories. The Tubiyage actors reported that in the 17 months between the first and second trainings, they had performed playback theatre 72 times, a high number in any setting.[4] Accustomed to utilizing Theatre of the Oppressed, the actors reported that with playback they did not have to prepare scenarios beforehand, the theme of which, they said, in any case often failed to connect with the audiences. Similarly, if there is no rapport between actors and audience, a playback theatre show will fail, because no one will want to come forward as a teller. However, as I witnessed in Burundi, tellers did not hesitate to raise their hands and willingly told stories; in public performances mostly about family issues, and in more intimate settings, such as the training workshops, about love relationships, domestic violence, and death.

Potential

Why would playback theatre find a positive response from audiences in war-torn Burundi? A first reason has to do with what Judith Herman calls the transformation of experience from traumatic to narrative memory; she writes: 'Remembering and telling the truth about terrible events are prerequisites both for the restoration of the social order and for the healing of individual victims,' (Herman 1992: 1). Playback Theatre is a gentle way of lessening social amnesia in that tellers tell only what they want to when they want to. A second reason comes from playback theatre's ability to avoid oversimplifying or instrumentalizing experience. Its story approach and improvisational nature, even while bringing the essentializing focus of an aesthetic sensibility to what the teller has narrated, allows actors to capture many layers of a story.[5] A third reason has to do with the sharing of perspectives embodied in different tellers' stories. 'To be in a viable culture is to be bound in a set of connecting stories, connecting even though the stories may not represent a consensus,' writes Jerome Bruner (Bruner 1990: 96). Playback theatre inspires divergent yet connecting stories on a very local level.

We saw many examples of this positive process at work during our time in Burundi. In groups large and small, tellers offered stories with eagerness. The Burundian actors brought them to life on the stage with commitment and were joyous at the success of the performances. My colleague Karin Gisler and I flew home full of optimism. Yet three years later we have almost completely lost contact with the Tubiyage theatre actors. As far as we could tell—until a recent surprising communication—they had stopped using playback theatre. In addition, Search for Common Ground has ceased sending us to Burundi or any other of their site countries. The playback theatre project appears not to have been sustained. What went wrong?

Problems and learnings

Upon reflection there seemed to be four kinds of problems: transmission of the method, issues of congruence, the challenge of sustainability, and cultural differences. The discussion that follows reflects on these problems and identifies learning useful for future programs of Playback training.

Transmission

Developing skills in deep listening, improvisational acting, and ensemble work necessary to capture people's stories takes time. The skills of the playback theatre conductor, or emcee, are even more demanding.[6] In a totally unplanned situation anything can happen at any time, especially when the stories become serious—so the conductor must know how to hold the ritual space. At the School of Playback Theatre in New York our maximum class size is 15 and after the basic training, consisting of about forty days of intensive classroom work over a minimum of two years, students often express a humble sense of incompletion. This is appropriate, since pursuit of playback theatre is in many ways like an Eastern spiritual practice, and we are always learning. Furthermore, playback theatre demands a very high level of maturity and integrity from its practitioners. In brief, you have to know where your own self ends and the other begins. This is often a deeply challenging task and takes years to master. It can be especially difficult when one's moral education has been truncated by adverse social conditions.

   In the context of development, however, there is pressure to transmit knowledge as efficiently and inexpensively as possible. The trainings in Burundi consisted of two short workshops more than a year apart. The participants included not only Tubiyage actors but others the NGO wanted to bring together, and numbered over 25. With such a group size, it was hard to achieve the intimacy and cohesiveness necessary for deep learning. During the second training the Tubiyage actors responded to a traumatic story with an inadequate portrayal because, despite their good will, they had not had enough training to be able to handle very serious stories. So they hid behind the short, abstract form we call a 'fluid sculpture.' How do we persuade 'Search' or any other NGO, which must raise funds for each program and is under pressure to achieve positive results, to support the necessary small group work, an ongoing laboratory program of training lasting many years, and performances for small audiences? Admittedly, playback theatre has not yet fully proven itself as a tool for peace-building, but it does hold significant promise.

   In developing playback theatre training programs for the future in regions like Burundi it would be necessary to enter into realistic talks with funding partners about expectations and results, trying to find a compromise between the need for extensive exposure and support and practical concerns of time and money. Effort would need to be made to ally with local institutions that could offer the playback group(s) logistical and personal support. I would promote the idea that by studying playback theatre the cohort groups of performers would receive an extensive education in personal development, listening non-judgmentally to others; and teamwork, which would be a significant human resource for their communities in addition to the playback theatre skills. I would argue for the training to be in-depth enough for students to acquire the skills of the playback theatre method as it has developed over 30 years before adapting it to the needs of their societies.

Congruence

The period of political colonization may be over, but globalization perpetuates the dominance of the Western countries. No matter how deep my respect for the people I met, the fact remains that I, a white American, with commensurate stature and authority, was the teacher. My colleague on the second trip was a white Swiss. Looking back we might have deliberated more before sending two white trainers to Burundi and considered a person of color, preferably of African descent, instead. It is only in recent years that we have gained awareness that it might be important, firstly, to reach out to those interested African-Americans and other people of color from our own communities. If our own unconscious racism, lack of social awareness, and failure of commitment to redress social injustice keeps us from including people of color in our playback theatre work at home, then our desire to spread the work in Africa may well be questioned.

On its part, no matter how admirable its objectives of assistance and peace building, Search for Common Ground in Burundi potentially has tremendous power. Its funding comes from US and European sources. Under the direction of an American, it sent me, another American, to teach local people a new technique, one of a series paraded before them. Knowing they are poor, the organization pays them transportation money and feeds them. The actors are professional only insofar as Search and other NGOs employ them. Ethical questions arise: are they coming to learn theatre, to learn tools for change in their country, eat a good meal, to make a connection that will someday take them to the developed world? Who is benefiting most? Personally, I get a trip to Africa, a tremendously stimulating new experience, and a new item for my resume. I even get paid. To the extent that I may be successful, the work will become 'fodder for the imperialist international gaze' (Edmondson 2005: 473). Even my writing this chapter becomes suspect, since it will appear in a book not readily available to my Burundian colleagues, or written in a language they can understand.

Since our training trips to Burundi, and following several years of determined effort, we have made big strides as US playback theatre practitioners in attending to issues of congruence. In 2006 we were able to respond to the devastation in New Orleans from Hurricane Katrina by sending playback teams to act out the stories of evacuees. On this occasion the teams consisted primarily of persons of color to match the demographic of our audiences. We are now in a stronger position to employ experienced playback theatre trainers of color for future trainings in Africa.

Sustainability

The issues raised above become starker when we fail to secure the means for the work to continue after we have left. NGOs are continually addressing themselves to problems of sustainability, yet aid project after aid project has failed the test. Is it ethical for me to agree to a training program that is not adequate to the task and cannot be sustainable? Actors new to playback theatre performed in a village during my second trip in an attempt to gain an accelerated performing experience. An audience member told a serious story from her seat in the audience (in our customary theatre ritual, we invite the teller to a chair on stage, where she and her story can be held in safety and respect). The audience, an entire village, was so big and unruly that I suspect the teller's isolation was increased, not decreased, by her revelation. The purpose of the playback was subverted, but more important, the actors failed because they had not learned enough. In such a context, tellers might hesitate to tell, and the performers will sense keenly their lack of positive impact. Eventually, they will give up.

Sustainability cannot ever be guaranteed, but at least it can from the outset be a paramount objective. In the future, we would include the issue of sustainability throughout the planning process. Important considerations are the depth of initial training and ongoing support over time.

Cultural difference

The philosophical values embedded in playback theatre encountered local Burundian cultural values in problematic ways, some of which seemed amenable to solution, some not. Let me cite a few examples. As a culture still embedded in the oral tradition, Burundians often communicate through stories. But the stories have a different flavor than playback theatre stories which champion open revelation and a kind of spontaneous freshness before the experience. Burundian stories are circuitous and often allegorical; the meaning has to be interpreted; communication through stories can be a battle of wits with often much at stake. At first the Tubiyage actors balked at asking direct questions to the audience. Instead of asking the simple start-of-show question asked by playback theatre practitioners all over the world, 'How was your day today?', they tended to ask a long, complicated conditional query, such as 'Suppose you were walking down the street and you bumped into your boss, how would you feel?' After considerable dilemma, I urged them to try out the direct method. One reason was my allegiance to the integrity of playback theatre; the direct way of telling was essential to what playback theatre is. A second reason, however, had to do with the history of the civil conflict in Burundi, the breakdown of the system of justice, and the politicization of truth. Each side had it own version of every atrocity. Until both sides could accept the revelation of those who suffered without judgment, I felt there was little hope for coexistence in Burundi. When I returned to Burundi the Tubiyage actors excitedly told me about a man who recounted a story in a performance about his struggles with the local town officials regarding a deserved subsidy, and how the town official, also in the audience, had stood up, acknowledged his new understanding of the situation, and promised him his grant. The direct approach works, they had decided.

A second, related cultural issue is not so easily solved, however. To date in Burundi, it is not socially acceptable to be open about ethnicity. Because of years of intermarriage, especially before the period of conflict, one cannot accurately tell a Hutu or a Tutsi by sight. Often people know, but it is not publicly acknowledged. In playback theatre stories in Burundi, the ethnic background of the teller will often be an essential element of any story, but if it cannot be brought to the stage, the actors suffer under a restriction that limits greatly their ability to portray truth with artistry. The potential of playback theatre to further peace in Burundi depends on the willingness of its citizens to acknowledge each others' ethnic identity.

A third issue concerns the Tubiyage model of including a large number of actors, so that as many as possible can benefit from the group's opportunities. To learn playback theatre, however, actors must rehearse extensively in a small ensemble. This aesthetic demand seemed impossible to meet with Tubiyage's membership of over 30.

A fourth cultural issue concerns the concept of participatory democracy. Playback theatre, spawned in resistance to cultural hierarchies in North America, is a people's theatre valuing the unheard voice. Its aim is to give space for anyone, even one of lowest rank, to speak and have their story heard. We proclaim that everyone has a story and deserves to tell it. How to position such an approach in a cultural context that has no democratic tradition? Are we promoting a human right, or are we perpetuating on the level of theatre exchange what so often takes place on the political level, where the rich democracies use their economic and military power to try and impose their own system?

In future trainings I would raise cultural differences between trainers and trainees as an ongoing part of the training, working with local institution and the students themselves to develop experimental applications for solving problems in the applicability of the method taught. Thus the training itself would be accompanied by dialogue about difference and a search for solutions.

In conclusion, one feels suspended between Fanon, with his vision of a world irrevocably split (Fanon 1963: 32), and Desmond Tutu's Ubuntu-inspired vision of all humanity embraced in the same 'bundle of life' (Tutu 1999: 31). Despite discouragements, I see playback theatre as a potentially effective vehicle for promoting individual agency and communal dialogue. I also share Tutu's spiritual conviction of the presence of a feeling that is 'not to be achieved but to be received as a gift freely given' (Tutu 1999: 85), a condition that transcends cultural, economic, and political differences. The gap caused by history, economic disparity, race, politics, and culture seems wider than the ocean. Yet while preparing this chapter, I received an email from one of the Tubiyage actors, Melchiade Ngendabanyikwa. This is what he wrote:

> Playback theatre does not cease operating its cures even in prison to give a fresh memory to those which lost it because of these ceaseless wars. I have just lived a beautiful experiment in central prison of Bujumbura where I spent a small moment with prisoners who cannot even appear before the judges because they actually forgot what happened. After a funny story of one of the prisoners that they played themselves—without artistic perfection of course—a second arose to also tell his funny story as a history of the insane. But he started to add elements which referred to his cause of arrest. Suddenly he made a *volte face* and found the true memory of the events. The second day he asked me to seek a lawyer to report all that occurred. With the end of this meeting I distributed some soaps according to my small means.
>
> (Personal communication 27 July 2006)

Such a story gives me new hope. From it I learn of a new possibility for playback theatre, discovered by Melchiade, in helping repair a 'broken narrative' (Lederach 2005: 147). But I also find that to my surprise, even without any ongoing support, playback theatre in Burundi remains alive.

Bibliography

Bruner, J. (1990) *Acts of Meaning: Four Lectures on Mind and Culture*, Cambridge, MA: Harvard University Press.

Edmondson, L. (2005) 'Marketing Trauma and the Theatre of War in Northern Uganda', *Theatre Journal* 57: 451–74.

Fanon, F. (1963) *Wretched of the Earth*, New York: Grove Press.

Fox, J. (1992) 'Defining Theater for the Nonscripted Domain', *The Arts in Psychotherapy*, 19: 201–7.

Fox, J. (1994) *Acts of Service: Spontaneity, Commitment, Tradition in the Nonscripted Theatre*, New Paltz, NY: Tusitala Publishing.

Herman, J. (1992) *Trauma and Recovery*, New York: Basic Books.

Lederach, J.P. (2005) *The Moral Imagination: The Art and Soul of Building Peace*, New York: Oxford University Press.

Salas, J. (1993) *Improvising Real Life: Personal Story in Playback Theatre*, New Paltz, NY: Tusitala Publishing.

Tutu, D. (1999) *No Future Without Forgiveness*, New York: Doubleday.

Notes

1   2005 statistic. *CIA the World Factbook*. Available: <https://www.cia.gov/cia/publications/factbook/geos/by.html>.

2   Playback theatre was founded in 1975 in the Hudson Valley of New York and is now practiced in about 50 countries. For more information see www.playbackcentre.org and www.playbacknet.org.

3   Telling one's story in playback theatre is an act of conscientization. 'This is the challenge of restorying: It continuously requires a creative act . . . to live between memory and potentiality is to live permanently in a creative space' (Lederach 2005: 149).

4   See 'Representations En PlayBack Par L'association « Tubiyage»' (2003) Report on playback theatre training in Burundi, March, submitted to Search for Common Ground, November 21, 2005, Appendix II.

5   See Cohen, Cynthia (2005) 'Creative Approaches to Reconciliation,' in *The Psychology of Resolving Global Conflicts: From War to Peace*, Mari Fitzduff and Christopher E. Stout (eds) Westport, CT: Greenwood Publishing Group Inc.

6   See Hosking, Bev and Hutt, Jenny (2005) 'Playback Theatre: A Creative Resource for Reconciliation.' Working paper of Recasting Reconciliation through Culture and the Arts fellowship program, Center for Ethics, Justice & Public Life, Brandeis University, 35. Available: <http://www.brandeis.edu/programs/Slifka/vrc/papers/index.html>.

PART 6

Border crossing

Chapter 35

Tim Prentki

INTRODUCTION TO
BORDER CROSSING

S INCE THE PUBLICATION OF Henry Giroux' *Border Crossings*[1] there
has been a growing interest in the concept, not only in the discourses of education
but also among those who are concerned with cultural work in its broadest sense.
The notion has powerful resonances for applied theatre which is itself frequently
concerned with strategies of self-empowerment that enable communities and individuals to move from one place to another; a transition which may involve crossing
one or more borders. These borders may appear in many guises: psychological; racial;
sexual; sociological; professional; as well as geographical. Paradoxically, the border
may be at once what provides us with some security about our identity, demarcating
ourselves from others, while also being the barrier that prevents us from developing
new capacities or trying on new identities. Theatre processes, on the other hand,
depend upon the willingness of the actor to cross borders not only to impersonate
the dress, manner and speech of another but also to achieve, temporarily, the ultimate
expression of border-crossing, empathy.

But before the crossing can occur the border has to be recognised. Many of the
research activities of applied theatre practitioners are directed towards enabling the
participants in projects to identify where they draw their own borders; where they
have erected the razor wire around their 'comfort zones' to keep out the threats to
a stable, if fossilised, identity and to discourage adventurous attempts to stray onto
the territory of another. Not all borders, however, are of our own making. In most
situations where applied theatre is practised, the participants, if they wish to alter
their starting position, have to negotiate their way across borders designated by other
people; people who organise the world either to suit their own ends or out of a desire
to do what is best, according to them, for others. So the chief executives of multi-
national corporations ensure that there are no borders to interfere with the movement
of their financial assets around the world while being at the forefront of pressure to

restrict the movements of people, thereby guaranteeing the preservation of zones of cheap labour to maximise profit. It is part of a facilitator's role in applied theatre processes to assist the participants in distinguishing between those borders which have been created by the external world so that they can be controlled or oppressed (to use Freire's term) and those which they have put up around themselves out of fear, selfishness or lack of imagination. This is broadly the distinction which Boal makes between his Theatre of the Oppressed methods designed to combat external, social oppression and the devising techniques of *The Rainbow of Desire* that seek to liberate the individual from the guard-posts and search-light towers of self-consciousness. Without delving into the domain of the mind, however, there are a whole variety of external borders, some of which may be susceptible to change and others beyond the scope of an applied theatre practice. For instance, an applied theatre practitioner working with a group of peasants in an African village needs to distinguish between those aspects of the community's material conditions which are susceptible to being changed from within the community, such as gender relations or local corruption, and those which are the direct or indirect consequence of the structural adjustment programme – the 'conditionalities' – to which their national government has subscribed in return for World Bank and International Monetary Fund loans.

When working with those groups who hold power in particular communities, police, politicians, doctors or whomever, it is often the border between the professional and the human being that is hardest to cross. The prospect of being stripped of the protective shell of the social role can induce fear and evasion among those for whom professional habits have shut off access to the wellsprings of imagination and creativity. The underlying principle in all these various applications of the theatre process is fundamentally the same: to enable the participants to (re)discover their innate capacities for play, for imagining, for creating, for relating to others by exploring the self in the other and the other in the self. Theatre is being applied to a world where being human has been reduced to a set of transactional economic relations. It is therefore an activity of resistance, of crossing the border between objectification and subjectivity. Participants are invited to recreate themselves in ways which the daily business of economic existence constantly thwarts.

Where practitioners come into a community or context to which they do not normally belong, they also undertake an act of border crossing. They move temporarily into other, unfamiliar worlds where, as outsiders, they will see some things less clearly than the participants and others, perhaps, more clearly with the benefit of distance. They are guests or visitors who will do their work, then leave; recrossing the border back into their known worlds. Although qualities such as humility and sensitivity, combined with thorough research and preparation, can mitigate the dangers of misunderstanding and inappropriate actions, it is important that facilitators do not mislead participants into seeing them as bearers of solutions or messianic figures who can take away the sins of their world. Responsibility for acting upon the discoveries unearthed by the process rests with the community of participants and the decision about whether to cross a border, and which one to cross, belongs with them, not with the external agents.

Besides the border-crossing into and out of a particular community, the facilitators are also border crossers as part of the theatrical process. They are, in common with the tricksters who inhabit all cultures and mythologies, the figures who move between two worlds, whether this be Boal's Joker who negotiates the stage fiction for the 'real' world of the audience, or Jesus Christ who commutes between the human and divine worlds. The application of theatre to the social realities of its audiences and actors is an ancient, popular tradition from which contemporary applied theatre draws its inspiration. The applied theatre facilitator, in the European tradition of the stage fool, is not only adept at crossing borders but also plays along the edges of art and life to expose contradictions and invite reflections upon the theatrical in life and the lively in theatre. In moving from *a play* to *play* the foolish facilitator draws participants back into the carnival of the human senses. This is the process which Brecht depicts through the character of Azdak, the fool and facilitator of the play in which he is also a participant, *The Caucasian Chalk Circle*.[2]

Any applied theatre process is likely to involve multiple border crossings in which the facilitators assist the participants in making the transition without falling foul of the border guards whether actual or in the head. But the facilitators, themselves, are not exempt from the pitfalls of moving into unfamiliar territory. Crossing the border may well be liberating but is rarely accomplished without difficulty.

Notes

1   Giroux, H. (1992) *Border Crossings*, London: Routledge.
2   Prentki, T. (2006) 'Fooling with Social Intervention: Azdak, Brecht's Dialectical Joker', in M. Balfour and J. Somers (eds), *Drama as Social Intervention*, Concord: Captus University Publications.

Chapter 36

Henry Giroux

BORDER CROSSINGS

Border Crossings: Cultural Workers and the Politics of Education, Routledge (1992), pp. 168–176.

The politics of voice and difference

> So, if you really want to hurt me, talk badly about my language. Ethnic identity is twin skin to linguistic identity – I am my language. Until I can accept as legitimate Chicano Texas Spanish, Tex-Mex and all the other languages I speak, I cannot accept the legitimacy of myself . . . and as long as I have to accommodate . . . English speakers rather than have them accommodate me, my tongue will be illegitimate. I will not longer be made to feel ashamed of existing. I will have my voice: Indian, Spanish, White. I will have my serpent's tongue – my women's voice, my sexual voice, my poet's voice. I will over come the tradition of silence.[1]

> Difference must not be tolerated, but seen as a fund of necessary polarities between which our creativity can spark like a dialectic. Only then does the necessity for interdependency become unthreatening. . . . Within the interdependence of mutual (nondominant) differences lies that security, which enables us to descend into the chaos of knowledge and return with true visions of our future, along with the concomitant power to effect those changes, which can bring that future into being. . . . As women we have been taught either to ignore our differences, or to view them as causes for separation and suspicion rather than as forces for change. Without

community there is no liberation, only the most vulnerable and temporary armistice between an individual and her oppression. But community must not mean a shedding of our differences, not the pathetic pretence that these differences do not exist.[2]

THE DISCOURSE OF DIFFERENCE AS USED by both Gloria Anzaluda and Audre Lorde provides a glimpse of the multiple and shifting ground that the term suggests. Defined in opposition to hegemonic codes of culture, subjectivity, and history, a number of social theorists have begun recently to use a discourse of difference to challenge some of the most fundamental dominant assertions that characterise mainstream science. [. . .] Theorists writing in anthropology, feminism, liberation theology, critical education, literary theory, and a host of other areas firmly reject mainstream assumptions regarding culture as a field of shared experiences defined in Western ethnocentric terms; in addition, critical theorists have rejected the mainstream humanist assumption that the individual is both the source of all human action and the most important unit of social analysis; moreover, many critical theorists reject the view that objectivity and consensus are the privileged and innocent concerns of dominant social science research. Reading in opposition to these assumptions, the notion of difference has played an important role in making visible how power is inscribed differently in and between zones of culture, how cultural borderlands raise important questions regarding relations of inequality, struggle and history, and how differences are expressed in multiple and contradictory ways within individuals and between different groups.

While theories of difference have made important contributions to a discourse of progressive politics and pedagogy, they have also exhibited tendencies that have been theoretically flawed and politically regressive. In the first instance, the most important insights have emerged primarily from feminist women of color. These include "the recognition of a self that is multiplicitous, not unitary; the recognition that differences are always relational rather than inherent; and the recognition that wholeness and commonality are acts of will and creativity, rather than passive discovery".[3] In the second instance, the discourse of difference has contributed to paralyzing forms of essentialism, ahistoricism, and a politics of separatism. In what follows, I first want to explore the dialectical nature of the relationship between difference and voice that informs a discourse of critical pedagogy. I conclude by pointing to some of the broader implications that a discourse of difference and voice might have for what I call a liberatory border pedagogy.

It is important for critical educators to take up culture as a vital source for developing a politics of identity, community and pedagogy. In this perspective culture is not seen as monolithic or unchanging, but as a site of multiple and heterogeneous borders where different histories, languages, experiences, and voices intermingle amidst diverse relations of power and privilege. Within this pedagogical cultural borderland known as school, subordinated cultures push against and permeate the alleged unproblematic and homogenous borders of dominant cultural forms and practices. It is important to note that critical educators cannot be content merely to map how ideologies are inscribed in the various relations of schooling, whether they be the curriculum, forms of school organization, or in teacher–student relations. While these should be important concerns for critical educators, a more viable critical pedagogy needs to go beyond them by analysing how ideologies are actually taken up in the voices and lived experiences of students as they give meaning to dreams, desires, and subject positions that they inhabit. In this sense, radical educators need to provide the conditions for students to speak so that their narratives can be affirmed and engaged along with the consistencies and contradictions that characterize such experiences. More specifically, the issue of student experiences has to be analyzed as part of a broader politics of voice and difference.

As bell hooks has pointed out, coming to voice means "moving from silence into speech as a revolutionary gesture . . . the idea of finding one's voice or having a voice assumes a primacy in talk discourse, writing and action. . . . Only as subjects can we speak. . . . Awareness of the need to speak, to give voice to the varied dimensions of our lives is one way [to begin] the process of education for critical consciousness."[4] This suggests that educators need to approach learning not merely as the acquisitions of knowledge but as the production of cultural practices that offer students a sense of identity, place, and hope. To speak of voice is to address the wider issues of how people either become agents in the process of making history or function as subjects under the weight of oppressions and exploitation within the various linguistic and institutional boundaries that produce dominant and subordinate cultures in any given society. In this case, voice provides a critical referent for analyzing how students are made voiceless in particular settings by not being allowed to speak, or how students silence themselves out of either fear or ignorance regarding the strength and possibilities that exist in the multiple languages and experiences that connect them to a sense of agency and self-for-mation. At the same time, voices forged in opposition and struggle provide the crucial conditions by which subordinated individuals and groups can reclaim their own memories, stories, and histories as part of an ongoing collective struggle to challenge those power structures that attempt to silence them.

By being able to listen critically to the voices of students, teachers become border-crossers through their ability to not only make different narratives available to themselves and other students but also by legitimating difference as a basic condition for understanding the limits of one's own voice. By viewing schooling as a form of cultural politics, radical educators can bring the concepts of culture, voice, and difference together to create a borderland where multiple subjectivities and identities exist as part of a pedagogical practice that provides the potential to expand the politics of democratic community and solidarity. Critical pedagogy serves to make visible those marginal cultures that have been traditionally suppressed. [. . .] Moreover, it provides students with a range of identities and human possibilities that emerge among, within, and between different zones of culture. Of course, educators cannot approach this task by merely giving equal weight to all zones of cultural difference; on the contrary, they must link the creation, sustenance, and formation of cultural difference as a fundamental part of the discourse of inequality, power struggle and possibility. Difference is not about merely registering or asserting special, racial, ethnic, or cultural differences but about the historical differences that manifest themselves in public and pedagogical struggles.

[. . .]

Resisting difference: towards a liberatory theory of border pedagogy

[. . .]

To take up the issue of difference is to recognize that it cannot be analyzed unproblematically. In effect, the concept has to be used to resist those aspects of its ideological legacy used in the service of exploitation and subordination as well as to develop a critical reference for engaging the limits and strengths of difference as a central aspect of a critical theory of education. In what follows, I want to look briefly at how the concept of difference has been used by conservatives, liberals and radicals in ways that either produce relations of subordination or undermine its possibility for developing a radical politics of democracy.

Conservatives have often used the term difference in a variety of ways. To justify the relations of racism, patriarchy, and class exploitation by associating difference with the notion of deviance while simultaneously justifying such assumptions through an appeal to science, biology, nature, or culture. In many instances difference functions as a market of power to name, label, and exclude particular groups while simultaneously being legitimated within a reactionary discourse and politics of public life, i.e., nationalism, patriotism, and "democracy."

[. . .]

Liberals generally take up a dual approach to the issue of difference. This can be illuminated through the issue of race. On the one hand, liberals embrace the issue of difference through a notion of cultural diversity in which it is argued that race is simply one more form of cultural difference among many that make up the population like the United States. The problem with this approach is that "by denying both the centrality and uniqueness of race as a principle of socio-economic organization, it redefines difference in a way that denies the history of racism in the United States and, thus denies white responsibility for the present and past oppression and exploitation of people of color."[5] In this view, the systems of inequalities, subordination, and terror that inform the dominant culture's structuring of difference around issues of race, gender, and class are simply mapped out of existence. On the other hand liberals often attempt to appropriate and dissolve cultural differences into the melting pot theory of culture. The history, language, experiences, and narratives of the Other are relegated to invisible zones of culture, borderlands where the dominant culture refuses to hear the voice of the Other while celebrating a "white, male, middleclass, European, heterosexuality [as] the standard of and the criteria for rationality and morality."[6] Under the rubric of equality and freedom, the liberal version of assimilation wages "war" against particularity, lived differences, and imagined futures that challenge culture as unitary, sacred, and unchanging and the identity, as unified, static, and natural.

On the other hand, radical educational theorists have taken up the issue of difference around two basic considerations. First, difference has been elaborated as part of an attempt to understand subjectivity as fractured and multiple rather than as unified and static.[7] Central to this approach is the notion that subjectivities and identities are constructed in multilayered and contradictory ways. Identity is seen not only as a historical and social construction, but also as part of a continual process of transformation and change. This position is of enormous significance for undermining the humanist notion of the subject as both unified and the determinate source of human will and action. As significant as this position is, it is fraught with some theoretical problems.

By arguing that human subjectivities are constructed in language through the production and availability of diverse subject positions, many radical theorists have developed a theory of subjectivity that erases any viable notion of human agency. [. . .] Lost here is any understanding of how agency works within the interface of subject positions made available by a society and the weight of choices constructed out of specific desires, forms of self reflection, and concrete social practices. There is little sense of how people actually take up particular subject positions, and what the conditions are that make it impossible for some groups to take up, live, and speak particular discourses.[8]

The second approach to difference that radical educational theorists have taken up centers on the differences between groups. [. . .] In the most general sense, identity politics refers to "the tendency to base one's politics on a sense of personal identity - as gay, as Jewish, as Black, as female."[9] The politics of identity celebrates differences as they are constructed around the categories of race, class, gender and sexual preference. [. . .]

Initially identity politics offered a powerful challenge to the hegemonic notion that Eurocentric culture is superior to other cultures and traditions by offering political and cultural vocabularies to subordinated groups by which they could reconstruct their own histories and give voice to their individual and collective identities. This was especially true for the early stages of the feminist movement when the slogan, "the personal is the political," gave rise to the assumption that lived experience offered women the opportunity to insert themselves back into history and everyday life by naming the injustices they had suffered within a society constructed in patriarchal social relations. A number of problems emerged from the conception of difference that informed this view of identity politics. [. . .] To accept the authority of experience uncritically is to forget that identity itself is complex, contradictory, and shifting and does not unproblematically reveal itself in a specific politics. Second, the emphasis on the personal as a fundamental aspect of the political also results in highlighting the personal through a form of confessional politics that all but forgets how the political is constituted in social and cultural forms outside of one's own experiences.

[. . .]

Another problem with the radical notion of difference is that it sometimes produces a politics of assertion that is both essentialist and separatist. [. . .] In this case, racial and class differences among women are ignored in favour of an essentializing notion of voice that romanticizes and valorizes the unitary experience of white, middle class women who assumed the position of being able to speak for all women. Moreover, forms of identity politics that forego the potential for creating alliances among different subordinated groups run the risk of reproducing a series of hierarchies of identities and experiences, which serves to privilege their own form of oppression and struggle. All too often this results in totalizing narratives that fail to recognize the limits of their own discourse in explaining the complexity of social life and the power such a discourse wields in silencing those who are not considered part of the insider group. [. . .]

Far from suggesting that critical educators should dispense with either the notion of difference or an identity politics, I believe that we need to learn from the theoretical shortcomings analyzed above and begin to rethink the relationship among difference, voice, and politics. What does this suggest for a liberatory theory of border pedagogy? I want to end by pointing briefly to a number of suggestions.

First, the notion of difference must be seen in relational terms that link it to a broader politics that deepens the possibility for reconstructing democracy and schools as democratic public spheres. This means organizing schools and pedagogy around a sense of purpose and meaning that makes difference central to a critical notion of citizenship and democratic public life. Rather than merely celebrating specific forms of difference, a politics of difference must provide the basis for extending the struggle for equality and justice to broader spheres of everyday life. This suggests the discourse of difference and voice be elaborated within, rather than against, a politics of solidarity. By refusing to create a hierarchy of struggles, it becomes possible for critical educators to take up notions of political community in which particularity, voice, and difference provide the foundation for democracy. [. . .]

Second, critical educators must provide the conditions for students to engage in cultural remapping as a form of resistance. That is, students should be given the opportunity to engage in systematic analyses of the ways in which the dominant culture creates borders saturated in terror, inequality, and forced exclusions. Similarly, students should be allowed to rewrite difference through the process of crossing over into cultural borders that offer narratives, languages, and experiences that provide a resource for rethinking the relationship between the center and margins of power as well as between themselves and others. In part, this means giving voice to those who have been normally excluded and silenced. It means creating a politics of remembrance in which different stories and narratives are heard and taken up as lived experiences. Most importantly, it means constructing new pedagogical borders where difference becomes the intersection of new forms of culture and identity.

Third, the concept of border pedagogy suggests not simply opening diverse cultural histories and spaces to students, but also understanding how fragile identity is as it moves into borderlands crisscrossed with a variety of languages, experiences and voices. There are no unified subjects here, only students whose voices and experiences intermingle with the weight of particular histories that will not fit into the master narrative of a monolithic culture. Such borderlands should be seen as sites for both critical analysis and as a potential source of experimentation, creativity, and possibility. This is not a call to romanticize such voices. [. . .] There is more at risk here than giving dominant and subordinated subjects the right to speak or allowing the narratives of excluded differences to be heard. There is also the issue of making visible those historical, ideological, and institutional mechanisms that have both forced and benefited from such exclusions. It is here that the borderland between school and the larger society meet, where the relevancies between teachers and cultural workers come into play, and where schooling is understood within the larger domain of cultural politics. [. . .]

Fourth, the notion of border pedagogy needs to highlight the issue of power in a dual sense. First, power has to be made central to understanding the effects of difference from the perspective of historically and socially constructed forms of domination. Second, teachers need to understand more clearly how to link power and authority in order to develop a pedagogical basis for reading differences critically. Difference cannot be merely experienced or asserted by students. It must also be read critically by teachers who, while not being able to speak as or for those who occupy a different set of lived experiences, can make progressive use of their authority by addressing difference as a historical and social construction in which all knowledges are not equally implicated in relations of power. [. . .] Teachers and cultural workers must take responsibility, as Stuart Hall points out, for the knowledge they organize, produce, mediate, and translate into the practice of culture.[10] At the same time, it is important for teachers and cultural workers to construct pedagogical practices that neither position students defensively nor allow students to speak simply by asserting their voices and experiences. A pedagogy of affirmation is no excuse for refusing students the obligation to interrogate the claims or consequences their assertions have for the social relationships they legitimate. [. . .]

Fifth, border pedagogy also points to the importance of offering students the opportunity to engage in the multiple references and codes that position them within various structures of meaning and practice. [. . .] This suggests providing students with the opportunities to read texts as social and historical constructions, to engage texts in terms of their presences and absences, and to read texts oppositionally. This means teaching students to resist certain readings while simultaneously learning how to write their own narratives.

Finally, border pedagogy points to the need for educators to rethink the syntax of learning and behavior outside of the geography of rationality and reason. For example racist, sexist, and class discriminatory narratives cannot be dealt with in a purely limited, analytical way. As a form of cultural politics, border pedagogy must engage how and why students make particular ideological and affective investments in their narratives. [. . .]

[. . .] It is within this shifting and radical terrain that schooling as a form of cultural politics can be reconstructed as part of discourse of opposition and hope.

Notes

1   Glora Anzaldua, *Borderlands/ La Frontera: The New Mestiza* (San Fransisco: Spinsters/Anuntlute Press, 1987), 59.
2   Audre Lord, *Sister Outsider* (Freedom, CA: The Crossing Press, 1984), 111–12.
3   Angela P. Harris, 'Race an Essentialism in Feminist Legal Theory,' *Stanford Law Review* 42 (February 1990), 581. . . . I am deeply indebted to Linda Brodkey for bringing this literature to my attention. Also see Linda Brodkey's excellent piece 'Towards a Feminist Rhetoric of Difference,' (University of Texas at Austin), 1990.
4   bell hooks, *Talking Back* (Boston: South End Press, 1989), 12.
5   Paula Rothenburg, 'The Construction, Deconstruction, and Reconstruction of Difference,' *Hypatia* 5:1 (Spring 1990), 47.
6   Ibid. 43.
7   Julian Henriques, Wendy Hollway, Cathy Urwin, Couze Venn, and Valerie Walkerdine, *Changing the Subject: Psychology, Social Regulation, and Subjectivity* (New York: Methuen, 1984).
8   Lawrence Grossberg, 'The Context of Audience and the Politics of Difference', 28.
9   Diana Fuss, 'Lesbian and Gay Theory: The Question of Identity Politics,' in D. Fuss, *Essentially Speaking: Feminism, Nature, and Difference* (New York: Routledge, 1989), 97.
10   Stuart Hall, 'The Emergence of Cultural Studies and the Crisis of the Humanities,' *October* 53 (Summer 1990), 11–23.

Chapter 37

Ngũgĩ wa Thiong'o

DECOLONISING THE MIND

Decolonising the Mind, James Currey (1986), pp. 34–61.

I

EARLY ONE MORNING IN 1976, a woman from Kamĩrĩĩthũ village came to my house and she went straight to the point: 'We hear you have a lot of education and that you write books. Why don't you and others of your kind give some of that education to the village? We don't want the whole amount; just a little of it, and a little of your time.' There was a youth centre in the village, she went on, and it was falling apart. It needed group effort to bring it back to life. Would I be willing to help? I said I would think about it. In those days, I was the chairman of the Literature Department at the University of Nairobi but I lived near Kamĩrĩĩthũ, Limuru, about thirty or so kilometres from the capital city. I used to drive to Nairobi and back daily except on Sundays. So Sunday was the best day to catch me at home. She came the second, the third and the fourth consecutive Sundays with the same request couched in virtually the same words. That was how I came to join others in what later was to be called Kamĩrĩĩthũ Community Education and Cultural Centre.

II

Kamĩrĩĩthũ is one of several villages in Limuru originally set up in the fifties by the British colonial administration as a way of cutting off the links between the people and the guerrillas of the Kenya Land and Freedom Army, otherwise known as Mau Mau. Even after independence in 1963 the villages remained as reservoirs of cheap labour. By 1975 Kamĩrĩĩthũ alone had grown into a population of ten thousand.

[. . .] the peasants and the workers, including the unemployed, were the real backbone of the centre which started functioning in 1976.

[. . .] what is important, for our discussion on the language of African theatre, is that all the activities of the centre were to be linked – they would arise out of each other – while each being a self-contained programme. Thus theatre, as the central focus of our cultural programme, was going to provide follow-up material and activities for the new literates from the adult literacy programme, while at the same time providing the basis for polytechnic type activities in the material culture programme.

But why theatre in the village? Were we introducing something totally alien to the community as the Provincial Commissioner was later to claim?

III

Drama has origins in human struggles with nature and with others. In pre-colonial Kenya, the peasants in the various nationalities cleared forests, planted crops, tended them to ripeness and harvest – out of the one seed buried in the ground came many seeds. Out of death life sprouted, and this through the mediation of the human hand and the tools it held. So there were rites to bless the magic power of tools. There were other mysteries: of cows and goats and other animals and birds mating – like human beings – and out came life that helped sustain human life. So fertility rites and ceremonies to celebrate life oozing from the earth, or from between the thighs of humans and animals. Human life itself was a mystery: birth, growing up and death, but through many stages. So there were rituals and ceremonies to celebrate and mark birth, circumcision or initiation into the different stages of growth and responsibility, marriages and the burial of the dead.

But see the cruelty of human beings. Enemies come to take away a community's wealth in goats and cattle. So there were battles to be fought to claim back one's own. Bless the spears. Bless the warriors. Bless those who defend the community from its enemies without. Victorious warriors returned to ritual and ceremony. In song and dance they acted out the battle scenes for those who were not there and for the warriors to relive the glory, drinking in the communal admiration and gratitude. There were also enemies within: evil doers, thieves, idlers; there were stories – often with a chorus – to point the fate of those threatening the communal good.

Some of the drama could take days, weeks, or months. Among the Agĩkũyũ of Kenya, for instance, there was the Ituĩka ceremony held every twenty-five years or so that marked the handing over of power from one generation to another. According to Kenyatta in his book Facing Mount Kenya, the Ituĩka was celebrated by feasting, dancing and singing over a six-month period. The laws and regulations of the new government were embodied in the words, phrases and rhythmic movements of the new songs and dances.[1] How Ituĩka came to be was always re-enacted in a dramatic procession. Central to all these varieties of dramatic expression were songs, dance and occasional mime!

Drama in pre-colonial Kenya was not, then, an isolated event: it was part and parcel of the rhythm of daily and seasonal life of the community. It was an activity among other activities, often drawing its energy from those other activities. It was also entertainment in the sense of involved enjoyment; it was moral instruction;

and it was also a strict matter of life and death and communal survival. This drama was not performed in special buildings set aside for the purpose. It could take place anywhere – wherever there was an 'empty space', to borrow the phrase from Peter Brook. 'The empty space', among the people, was part of that tradition.[2]

IV

It was the British colonialism which destroyed that tradition. The missionaries in their proselytising zeal saw many of these traditions as works of the devil. They had to be fought before the bible could hold sway in the hearts of the natives. The colonial administration also collaborated. Any gathering of the natives needed a licence: colonialism feared its own biblical saying that where two or three gathered, God would hear their cry. Why should they allow God above, or the God within the natives to hear the cry of the people? Many of these ceremonies were banned: like the Ituīka, in 1925. But the ban reached massive proportions from 1952 to 1962 during the Mau Mau struggle when more than five people were deemed to constitute a public gathering and needed a licence. Both the missionaries and the colonial administration used the school system to destroy the concept of the 'empty space' among the people by trying to capture and confine it in government-supervised urban community halls, schoolhalls, church-buildings, and in actual theatre buildings with the proscenium stage. Between 1952 and 1962 'the empty space' was even confined behind barbed wire in prisons and detention camps where the political detainees and prisoners were encouraged to produce slavishly pro-colonial and anti-Mau Mau propaganda plays. [. . .]

V

Kamīrīīthū then was not an aberration, but an attempt at reconnection with the broken roots of African civilization and its traditions of theatre. In its very location in a village within the kind of social classes described above, Kamīrīīthū was the answer to the question of the real substance of a national theatre. Theatre is not a building. People make theatre. Their life is the very stuff of drama. Indeed Kamīrīīthū reconnected itself to the national tradition of the empty space, of language, of content and of form.

Necessity forced the issue.

For instance, there was an actual empty space at Kamīrīīthū. The four acres reserved for the Youth Centre had at that time, in 1977, only a falling-apart mud-walled barrack of four rooms which we used for adult literacy. The rest was grass. Nothing more. It was the peasants and workers from the village who built the stage: just a raised semi-circular platform backed by a semi-circular bamboo wall behind which was a small three-roomed house which served as the store and changing room. The stage and the auditorium – fixed long wooden seats arranged like stairs – were almost an extension of each other. It had no roof. It was an open air theatre with large empty spaces surrounding the stage and the auditorium. The flow of actors and people between the auditorium and the stage, and around the stage and the entire auditorium was uninhibited. Behind the auditorium were some tall eucalyptus trees. Birds could watch performances from these or from the top of the outer bamboo fence. And during one performance some actors, unrehearsed, had the idea of climbing up the trees and joining the singing from up there. They were performing not only to those seated before them, but to whoever could now see them and hear them – the entire village of 10,000 people was their audience.

Necessity forced a commonsense solution to the issue of language. Ngũgĩ wa Mĩrĩĩ and I had been asked to script the initial outline of a play that later came to be called *Ngaahika Ndeenda* (*I will marry when I want*). The question was, what language were we going to use? [. . .]

The use of English as my literary medium of expression, particularly in theatre and the novel, had always disturbed me. In a student's interview in Leeds in 1967 and in my book *Homecoming* (1969) I came back to the question. But I kept on hedging the issue. The possibility of using an African language stayed only in the realm of possibility until I came to Kamĩrĩĩthũ.

It was Kamĩrĩĩthũ which forced me to turn to Gĩkũyũ and hence into what for me has amounted to 'an epistemological break' with my past, particularly in the area of theatre. The question of audience settled the problem of language choice; and the language choice settled the question of audience. But our use of Gĩkũyũ had other consequences in relation to other theatre issues: content for instance; actors, auditioning and rehearsals, performances and reception; theatre as a language.

Ngaahika Ndeenda depicts the proletarisation of the peasantry in a neo-colonial society. Concretely it shows the way the Kĩgũũnda family, a poor peasant family, who have to supplement their subsistence on their one-and-a-half acres with the sale of their labour, is finally deprived of even the one-and-a-half acres by a multi-national consortium of Japanese and Euro-American industrialists and bankers aided by the native comprador landlords and businessmen.

The land question is basic to an understanding of Kenya's history and contemporary politics, as indeed it is of twentieth century history wherever people have had their land taken away by conquest, unequal treaties or by the genocide of part of the population. The Mau Mau militant organization which spearheaded the armed struggle for Kenya's independence was officially called the Kenya Land and Freedom Army. The play, *Ngaahika Ndeenda*, in part drew very heavily on the history of the struggle for land and freedom; particularly the year 1952, when the Kĩmaathi-led armed struggle started and the British colonial regimes suspended all civil liberties by imposing a state of emergency; and in 1963, when KANU under Kenyatta successfully negotiated for the right to fly a national flag, and to sing a national anthem and to call people to vote for a national assembly within every five years. The play showed how that independence, for which thousands of Kenyans died, had been hijacked. In other words, it showed the transition of Kenya from a colony with the British being dominant, to a neo-colony with doors open to wider imperialist interests from Japan to America. But the play also depicted the contemporary social conditions particularly for workers in multi-national factories and plantations.

Now many of the workers and peasants in Kamĩrĩĩthũ had participated in the struggle for land and freedom either in the passive wing or in the active guerrilla wing. Many had been in the forests and the mountains, many in the colonial detention camps and prisons; while some had of course collaborated with the British enemy. Many had seen their homes burnt; their daughters raped by the British;

their land taken away; their relatives killed. Indeed Kamīrīīthū itself was a product of that history of heroic struggle against colonialism and of the subsequent monumental betrayal into neo-colonialism. The play was celebrating that history while showing the unity and continuity of that struggle. Here the choice of language was crucial. There was now no barrier between the content of their history and the linguistic medium of its expression. Because the play was written in a language they could understand the people could participate in all the subsequent discussions on the script. They discussed its content, its language and even the form. The process, particularly for Ngũgĩ wa Mĩrĩĩ, Kĩmani Gecaũ, and myself was one of continuous learning. Learning of our history. Learning of what obtains in factories. Learning of what goes on in farms and plantations. Learning our language, for the peasants were essentially the guardians of the language through years of use. And learning anew the elements of form of the African Theatre. [. . .]

They were also particular about language which, of course, is another element of form. They were concerned that the various characters, depending on age and occupation, be given the appropriate language. 'An old man cannot speak like that' they would say. 'If you want him to have dignity, he has to use this or that kind of proverb.' Levels of language and language-use and the nuances of words and phrases were discussed heatedly.

But what gives any form its tautness and special character and shape is the content. This is even more true in drama. Drama is closer to the dialectics of life than poetry and the fiction. Life is movement arising from the inherent contradiction and unity of opposites. Man and woman meet in a united dance of opposites out of which comes a human life separate from the two that gave it birth but incorporating features of both in such a way that it is recognisable at a glance that so and so is really a product of so and so. The growth of that life depends on some cells dying and others being born. Social life itself arises out of the contradiction between man and nature. But man is part of nature. Karl Marx has said: 'He opposes himself to nature as one of her own forces, setting in motion arms, legs, head and hands, the natural forces of his body, in order to appropriate nature's production to his own wants. By thus acting on the external nature and changing it, he at the same time changes his own nature.'[3] Drama encapsulates within itself this principle of the struggle of opposites which generates movement. There is in drama a movement from apparent harmony, a kind of rest, through conflict to a comic or tragic resolution of that conflict. We end with harmony at a different level, a kind of temporary rest, which of course is the beginning of another movement. The balance of opposing ideas and social forces, of all the contending forces is important in shaping the form of drama and theatre. [. . .]

The results of all this effort to evolve an authentic language of African theatre were obvious when the play opened to a paying audience on 2 October 1977. Once again the performances were timed for Sunday afternoons. Evenings would have been too cold for everybody. Ngaahika Ndeenda was an immediate success with people coming from afar, even in hired buses and taxis, to see the show. Theatre became what it had always been: part of a collective festival. Some people knew the lines almost as well as the actors and their joy was in seeing the variations by the actors on different occasions to different audiences. There was an identification with the characters. Some people called themselves by the names of their favourite peasant and worker characters like Kĩgũũnda, Gĩcaamba, Wangeci, Gathoni. But they also used the names of such characters as Kĩoi, Nditika, Ikuua, and Ndugĩre, to refer to those, in and outside the village, who had anti-people tendencies. The Language of Ngaahika Ndeenda was becoming part of the people's daily vocabulary and frame of reference. There were some touching moments. I remember one Sunday when it rained and people rushed to the nearest shelters under the trees or under the roofs. When it stopped, and all the actors resumed, the auditorium was as full as before. The performance was interrupted about three times on that afternoon but the audience would not go away. The people's identification with Kamĩrĩĩthũ was now complete.

Later they were driven away, not by rain, not by any natural disaster, but by the authoritarian measures of an anti-people regime. On 16 November 1977 the Kenya government banned any further public performances of Ngaahika Ndeenda by the simple act of withdrawing the licence for any public 'gathering' at the centre. I myself was arrested on 31 December 1977 and spent the whole of 1978 in a maximum security prison, detained without even the doubtful benefit of a trial. They were attempting to stop the emergence of an authentic language of Kenyan theatre.

But that was not the end of Kamĩrĩĩthũ's search for an authentic language of African theatre in form and content.

In November 1981 they regrouped for another effort, the production of Maitũ Njugĩra (Mother sing for me). Auditions were set for 7, 14 and 15 November 1981, almost as if Kamĩrĩĩthũ was resuming the search from the very date and month it had been stopped. I have narrated the fate of this second production in my book, Barrel of a Pen: Resistance to Repression in Neo-Colonial Kenya. Here I would like simply to point out that all the elements of theatre developed in 1977 were employed and further extended. Maitũ Njugĩra depicted the heroic struggle of Kenyan workers against the early phase of imperialist capitalist 'primitive' accumulation with confiscation of land, forced labour on the same stolen land and heavy taxation to finance its development into settler run plantations.

Dance, mime, song were more dominant than words in telling this story of repression and resistance. The visual and the sound images carried the burden of the narrative and the analysis. The medium of slides was also introduced to give authentic visual images of the period of the twenties and thirties. And at every stage in its evolution more people from many of the Kenyan nationalities were involved. Maitũ Njugĩra (Mother sing for me), a drama in music, had more than eighty songs from more than eight nationalities in Kenya all depicting the joy, the sorrow, the gains, the losses, the unity, the divisions, and the march forward as well as the setbacks in Kenyan people's struggles.

Kamĩrĩĩthũ was due to put on the musical drama at the Kenya National Theatre on 19 February 1982 after more than ten weeks of strenuous work by what had now become an important alliance from all nationalities of workers, peasants and progressive teachers and students. By going to perform at the Kenya National Theatre the alliance was going to make the point that an authentic language of African theatre, no matter in what specific African tongue it found expression, would communicate to people of all nationalities. It was also going to prove that this trend had the support of people of all the nationalities. Where else to prove this than on the premises of the so-called Kenya National Theatre. It was booked to be the longest run ever even though it was during the off theatre season, at the beginning of the year after Christmas.

The peasants and workers were about to bring national theatre to the capital city. But this was not to be. This time the authorities would not even deign to give a licence, instructions were sent to the management to padlock the doors, and the police were sent to ensure public peace and public security. Our attempts to continue with open rehearsals at the University premises – the famous Theatre II – were again frustrated after about ten such 'rehearsals' seen by about 10,000 people! The University authorities were instructed to padlock the doors of Theatre II. That was on Thursday 25 February 1982. On Thursday 11 March 1982 the government outlawed Kamīrīīthū Community Education and Cultural Centre and banned all theatre activities in the entire area. An 'independent' Kenyan government had followed in the footsteps of its colonial predecessors: it banned all the peasant and worker basis for genuine national traditions in theatre. But this time, the neo-colonial regime overreached itself. On 12 March 1982 three truckloads of armed policemen were sent to Kamīrīīthū Community Education and Cultural Centre and razed the open-air theatre to the ground. By so doing it ensured the immortality of the Kamīrīīthū experiments and search for peasant/worker-based language of African theatre. [. . .]

There has been an interesting twist to the Kamīrīīthū story. In February 1984 President Moi made 'a surprise visit' to Kamīrīīthū and he shed tears at the poverty he saw around the centre: how can human beings live in such conditions? On 'an impulse', 'an unrehearsed' act of 'personal' generosity, he there and then gave a donation towards the building of a polytechnic where the open air theatre used to be. No mention of the Kamīrīīthū Community Education and Cultural Centre. But the people were not deceived. A polytechnic was what they were hoping to build. They would welcome one built by the government for after all it was their money. But the regime had different hopes. By its wanton act of destruction of Kamīrīīthū Theate in 1982, it had shown its anti-people neo-colonial colours and it had become further alienated from the people. Its intensified repression of Kenyans in 1982 – through detentions without trial or imprisonment on trumped-up charges, particularly of university lecturers and students – did not improve its image and its further alienation from the people. It hopes that people can forget the alternative vision, even though unrealised, but embodied in the Kamīrīīthū experience. Kamīrīīthū must not be allowed to become a revolutionary shrine. People have to be taught the virtues of subservience and gratitude to a gallery of stars.

But can an idea be killed? Can you destroy a revolutionary shrine itself enshrined in the revolutionary spirit of a people? [. . .]

Notes

1   Jomo Kenyatta Facing Mount Kenya, London 1938.
2   I am indebted to Wasambo Were for the comparison between The Empty Space of Peter Brook's title, and the practice of African literature during a discussion I had with him on Theatre in Kenya in London 1983.
3   Karl Marx Capital, Vol. I, Chap. VII, p. 177.

Chapter 38

Helen Nicholson

RE-LOCATING MEMORY
Performance, reminiscence and communities of diaspora

> All theatre . . . is as a cultural activity deeply involved with memory and haunted by repetition.
>
> (Carlson 2003: 11)

MEMORY PLAYS AN AMBIGUOUS ROLE in contemporary social life, serving both to fuel conflict and to support co-operation. Collective memory has a part to play in constructing historical knowledge, in determining values and creating a shared sense of identity. What is included as history and whose memories are recalled is, of course, contentious and highly problematic. Acts of remembrance may be institutionally shaped in ways that reproduce the prevailing social and political order, resulting in the closing of boundaries and fixing attitudes. On the other hand, the process of embodying and sharing memories can create the conditions for new ways of thinking and feeling. This means that memory has particular significance to applied theatre; memory is invoked in acts of testimony and witness, it is integral to the processes of learning and embodied memories have an important role in everyday experience and social interaction.

The performance of memory is inevitably a political act. Mnemonic communities are sustained through repeated institutional enactments, including those evident in commemorative ceremonies, festivals, courtrooms and other public rituals designed to legitimate and reproduce a specific social order. In this conceptualisation, memory acts as a form of self-regulation, a way of achieving stability and maintaining a particular political economy. Conversely, memory is also required to envisage social change, to challenge official accounts of history by raising awareness of alternative perspectives. Michel Foucault described this form of historical representation as 'counter-memory', in which the popular memories embedded in the experiences of everyday life might be exhumed, and the voices of the subordinated or silenced might be heard (Foucault 1977). Foucault's insights into how representations of the past might be unfixed has held wide appeal for radical historians interested in reconstructing public histories and who have recognised the dynamic and political interplay of remembrance and forgetting in creating a sense of the present. One consequence of this way of thinking about memory draws attention to its instability and fluidity, and acknowledges the different ways in which memories are shaped and reshaped performatively. Furthermore, rather than harking back to an imagined community in which homogenisation, unity and shared values served as a basis for social interaction, counter-memory highlights both the shared experiences and the discontinuities and differences inherent in contemporary social life.

One of the social functions of memory is to contribute to shaping the future by providing people with insights into the past and by offering symbolic frameworks through which to interpret contemporary experiences. Applied theatre is, as all forms of theatre, intimately connected with the performance of memory. Because memory is deeply involved in creating communities and a sense of belonging, its expression and representation has particular significance for applied theatre practitioners and perhaps especially for those who work in communities of diaspora. There is, of course, a long history of honouring the voices of the marginalised in applied theatre contexts, and more mainstream practices such as documentary and verbatim theatre have generally been regarded by audiences and theatre-makers as counter-cultural and politically oppositional.

This chapter is concerned with the symbolism of memory in applied theatre, in questioning how memory contributes to self-affirmation, and how it might be employed to encourage reflection on personal experiences and to extend contemporary notions of social justice. Two case studies of companies working with elders in Britain will illustrate the implications of sharing autobiographical narratives in community contexts, and the chapter will consider how the public representation of memories in performance might contribute to the collective formation of community. This process not only values the memories of elderly participants by relocating them in time and space, but also respects what remains secret and unsaid.

Embodiment and reminiscence theatre

Those of us who work in applied theatre tend to be alert to our motives for engaging in practice and research, and I am aware that I came to reminiscence theatre through grief. I vividly remember the moment when I decided to work with the elderly. It was shortly after my father's death and I had begun the process of sifting through his belongings, deciding what should be kept, what might be given away, and what would be thrown out. His smart white shirt, rarely worn, had been washed and ironed and was hanging up to dry. It looked empty, swaying slightly in a draft of air, offering a lifeless imprint of a person like a scarecrow without stuffing. The image caused me to reflect on the embodied memories that had been lost, on stories never told, and on the familiar anecdotes that I would never hear my father rehearse again. I realised that, at the moment of his death, I had become guardian of my father's stories, and that the only material possessions I really wanted to keep were those that would prompt my fading memories. The hanging shirt reminded me of the French philosopher Henri Bergson, who recognised that memory relocates 'the past into the present' and that the flow of memories from one person to another transcends individualism by uniting the past with the future (Bergson 1996: 210). Perhaps more painfully, the unworn shirt symbolised the increasing sense of uselessness my father felt with age. My interest in work with the elderly, therefore, was not only a response to personal loss, it became part of a bigger impulse to make an active contribution to their creative and social experiences, and to explore my own cultural responsibilities as archivist of the memories of the elderly, the dying and the dead.

Reminiscence theatre has its roots in health and social care, where reminiscence therapy has been used to encourage the social and psychological wellbeing of older citizens (Gibson 1998). It is also indebted to the traditions of the theatre in education movement, where participatory performance practices have been used to explore historical themes and social issues. Age Exchange Theatre Trust, founded in 1983 by Pam Schweizter, is a company that specialises in reminiscence theatre, and their pioneering work has influenced practice throughout the world.[1] They describe their ethos as follows:

> Reminiscence work is essentially a person centred approach to working with people. The aim is to understand the individual person's view of their own life-experiences, and to give them opportunities to share this to wider audiences in the form of arts and educational products.
>
> (Arigho 2006: 3)

Age Exchange's philosophy seeks to value people's life experiences and to affirm their identities and life choices by inviting them to share their stories with others. This way of working, although often built on improvised storytelling, contrasts with Boal's forum theatre where the aim is to resolve social problems through deconstructing narratives and dismantling fixed identities. Age Exchange's work is explicitly intended to be non-judgemental in attitude, empathy is encouraged and the work values the everyday and domestic experiences of elderly participants. This ethic of care means that participants are able to choose what stories they will share, and with whom, and what they prefer to withhold. As practitioners, company members stress the importance of researching the community context, befriending the participants and planning collaboratively with professional carers, volunteers and the elders themselves. Taking time with people, rather than rushing into the drama, encourages people to listen to each other and build relationships of trust. In Age Exchange's 2003–4 reminiscence project with ethnic minority elders, *Mapping Stories*, project co-ordinator Meena Khatwa found that trust between participants came slowly but, as elders from the African, Caribbean, Asian, Chinese and Vietnamese communities gradually began to share their stories, Khatwa noted that 'a deeply-buried sense of value had returned to these elders' memories' (Khatwa cited in Schweitzer 2004: 41).

The process of relocating memories in space and time is necessarily a creative act, requiring imagination. In reminiscence theatre, participants are supported by practitioners skilled in both theatre techniques and in offering support to elderly people who wish to share their stories. In order to help participants to remember, Age Exchange has developed the use of the memory box, a collection of objects, music and artefacts that are chosen for their ability to trigger stories. These are selected both for their relevance to the experiences of the group, and for their different sensory qualities — the smell of a herb or medicine remembered from childhood, the weight of a coin in the hand, the taste of food, the sounds of birdsong or machinery, for example, can evoke powerful images and stimulate non-verbal memories as well as prompt stories. Using these artefacts and images, participants are encouraged to describe their memories by focusing on particular scenes from their lives, or by mapping special places they remember or by rehearsing games or crafts they know. Focusing on the memory triggers to support the narrative imagination illustrates social psychologist Barbara Misztal's theories of memory. She argues that the process of social remembering is constructed from cultural forms and is most readily accessed in relationship to others (Misztal 2003). This emphasis on somatic memory recognises the role of the body in the process of reminiscence, acknowledging that the body as well as the mind is integral to the poetic process of recalling memories as well as to the aesthetics of storytelling.

Although reminiscence theatre is motivated by a seriousness of purpose, the practice frequently incites a lot of shared humour as well as, on occasion, generating painful emotions. Memories are felt and experienced physically, and in reminiscence theatre it is not unusual for events that were once emotionally difficult or challenging to be represented through humour, as participants laugh at the absurdity of life or at the actions of their younger selves. Henri Bergson, writing about the significance of laughter, argues that it has a social function, enabling individuals to be 'freed from the worry of self-preservation', and by gaining self-awareness, leads them to relate more fully to others (Bergson 1996: 220). Humour can be a way of coming to terms with difficult life events, therefore, where the act of recollection and self-reflection creates an aesthetic distance between the event itself and the present.

A good example of the use of humour is found in *A View From The High Beech*, a project based in Cromer, Norfolk in 2003 as part of the Creative Ageing project funded by UK government's Department of Health. Now a wheelchair-user from a stroke, Bob Parish performed the story of racing home-made speedway bicycles on makeshift tracks constructed on London's bomb sites during the Second World War. Bob startled and amused his audience by telling reminiscence practitioners David Savill and Bernie Arigho, acting as the young Bob and his mate, that the bikes had no brakes. The actors amplified the story as it unfolded, questioning and repeating Bob's words for comic effect, and supporting him by creating a lively atmosphere in the performance. The audience's laughter was both empathetic and that of recognition. Perhaps most importantly, Bob's obvious pleasure in the performance signalled the dynamic between time present and time past in reminiscence theatre. Not only was he enjoying the funny side of his own reckless history, he obviously also relished the moment of performance and recognised his ability to entertain.[2] In a different context, I have witnessed an elderly woman from the British Asian community tell a story about her experiences of working in a biscuit factory as a recent arrival in England in the 1960s. She told the story about crying as the biscuits mounted up on the conveyor belt as if it were comical, possibly masking the pain of the memory through humour. Most of the story was told in her home language of Punjabi, but she offered a commentary in English which stressed the kindness of the factory supervisor — perhaps for the benefit of non-Asian people in the room — thereby uniting the past with the present.

All storytellers are vulnerable because stories, once told, have a life beyond the immediate context in which they were heard. This is particularly the case when personal stories are revealed; my secrets say more about me than those stories I reveal easily, and I am selective about what I tell to whom, and in what situation. Age Exchange stress that, in the process of editing, structuring and rehearsing autobiographical stories, participants should be in control of both the form and content of the performance and this is negotiated with the group. Moving from the safe space of the reminiscence workshop to the more public forum of performance involves a process of negotiation and is intended to be informal; the performance event is designed to be open and fluid, enabling everyone to participate comfortably. Participants are often invited to share the performative re-telling of their stories with the assistance of actors, who are entrusted to perform the roles of those who are part of their memories – family members, friends, sweethearts – whose photographs may be projected for the audience to see. As actors physically inhabit different roles in the story, their representations become part of their own lived and embodied experience. Phenomenologist Merleau-Ponty described this dialogic process as *inhabitation*, a term he used to indicate how the body is implicated in perception, knowledge and understanding.

> I am not in space and time, nor do I conceive space and time; I belong to them, my body combines with them and includes them . . . The space and time which I inhabit are always in their different ways indeterminate horizons which contain other points of view.
>
> (Merleau-Ponty 1962: 162)

Resituating memories in the context of the community makes them available for retelling, and open for re-interpretation through the performative qualities of gestures, movement, tones of voices and accents of the performers.

Sharing stories changes their ownership, moving from the storyteller to the reminiscence actors and to the audience. This means that the act of witnessing autobiographical performance not only invites reflection, it is also good practice for the emotional significance of treasured and guarded memories to be valued and actively recognised whether they are pleasurable or painful. This is perhaps most sensitively illustrated by reminiscence theatre practitioner David Savill's gentle prompting of an elderly woman who told a painful story about her father in the Great War that had remained a family secret for over 90 years. Although her father's work as a shoemaker meant that he was exempt from military service, she remembered his terrible sense of shame when given a white feather as a symbol of cowardice, and how he immediately enlisted in the army and left home. It was a powerful story, told with courage. She ended the performance with the words, 'so now you know', and with the reminder to the audience that, having witnessed her story, it now belonged to them as well as to her.[3] Reminiscence theatre practitioners have not only a duty of care for participants' emotional and physical wellbeing, but also an ethical responsibility to ensure that they have chosen which stories to tell, and how they will be told.

Memory and the performance of diaspora

When memories are re-told, they transgress the original boundaries of the individual storytellers' space, time and body and are relocated in the bodies and minds of performers and audiences. Connecting to the past through recalling personal memories is also a process that invites people to make sense of the present, to locate their lives in relation to public events, and to share and re-evaluate their cultural beliefs, values and aspirations. In this way, memory is intimately connected with the complexity of personal and cultural identities. For those who have experienced geographical mobility and displacement in their lives – particularly through migration – issues of location, home, identity and belonging are often particularly acute.

One motivation for undertaking reminiscence work is to honour and safeguard the culture, wisdom and experiences of the elderly. Rifco Arts is a theatre company whose cultural ambition is to reflect and celebrate the experiences of the South Asian community.[4] The company straddles the divide between professional theatre and community arts by commissioning new theatre that reaches audiences who are not habitual theatregoers, and by encouraging members of the local community to participate in creative and cultural activities. These activities are mutually embedded; artistic director Pravesh Kumar has close and sustained relationships with British Asian communities and it is their stories and experiences that are dramatised in the company's professional theatre output, using artistic forms that are accessible and entertaining to this sector of society. Kumar speaks of the trust he has developed with communities by 'opening a dialogue with grass-root audiences, who like to be part of the performance'.[5] Audiences see their own experiences translated on to the stage, join in familiar songs, and it is this basis of trust that also enables the company to raise social questions within their work. The play Meri Christmas (2006), for example, was developed as a result of the company's workshops in care homes with British Asian elders, and gently asked why elderly people were abandoned 'like old dustbins' by sons and daughters who are too busy to visit.[6] By relocating stories from individuals in care homes to the professional theatre, Rifco highlighted the situation of many South Asian elders in contemporary society.

Meri Christmas celebrates elders as the custodians of tradition and heritage, a response, as Kumar suggests, to 'the loss of culture and loss of belonging' experienced by many members of British Asian communities. In one scene Agnes, a young carer, is taught to cook a potato dish by the elderly, vulnerable and cantankerous Malkeet (played by playwright Harvey Virdi). Sharing this secret recipe symbolised the importance of passing on Asian crafts and customs, and although the play acknowledges that cultures evolve and change, it also implies that a secure sense of identity is fostered through intergenerational dialogue. The play poses questions about belonging, and about where 'home' is for elderly South Asian characters who had lived much of their lives in England. Rauf, a widower in his seventies (played by Rashid Karapiet), decides to return to his homeland of Pakistan, whereas Malkeet chooses to stay in England in the hope that her son will eventually visit. The complexity of emotional attachments in communities of diaspora, and the experience of belonging simultaneously to more than one place, has been eloquently theorised by social commentator Avtar Brah. Brah recognises the significance of both collective and personal histories in identity formation, asking, 'when does a location become "home"?' (Brah 1996: 197). This question resonated both in the play and in the reminiscence workshops that ran alongside Meri Christmas. In these workshops, applied theatre practitioner Lucy Bradley and playwright Samina Baig encouraged elders to share their stories of arriving in England as immigrants from South Asia in the 1960s. Listening to their stories of shameful discrimination in housing and employment, of their first experiences of cold weather, their difficulties in celebrating religious festivals without Temples or Mosques, and their homesickness prompted by food parcels from home, I was struck by the fortitude of people whose geographical location had repeatedly asked them to negotiate the tensions between the local and the global, and to renegotiate their cultural identities and sense of self in their everyday and domestic lives.

Applied theatre has an ambiguous relationship to the professional stage, which some practitioners regard as an elitist institution. There is, however, a strong tradition of popular theatre in Britain and in South Asia that is accessible to specific communities, that questions cultural and social change and that educates and entertains a wide audience. Theatre, for Rifco, whether it takes place in community settings or on the professional stage, has a role in developing cultural awareness and extending social justice by telling stories that need to be heard. By inviting audiences and participants to share and engage empathetically in domestic narratives and stories of everyday life, they are able to make the 'ordinary' extraordinary by exploring deeper questions of culture, heritage and belonging. As successful British Asian theatre-makers, who remain firmly rooted in the community in which they grew up, they have the authority to speak with compassion about the changing social landscape as cultural insiders.

Encountering counter-memories

Except for the powerful few, all memories of personal experience are counter cultural, and it is this interest in the domestic and the everyday that lies at the heart of reminiscence theatre practice. In his discussion of counter memory, Michel Foucault accepts that passion, instinct and intimacy are deeply embedded in images of the past. Not only do these remembered images stand as testimony to remarkable lives that are often hidden from official accounts of history, they also illustrate the political imperative of hearing stories that might be lost as communities fragment and as the memories of individuals fade and die.[7] In reminiscence theatre, and in theatre practices that celebrate counter-memory, there is the opportunity to extend, in Foucauldian terms, an empathetic understanding of the past that transgresses and challenges established or prejudicial perceptions of history.

In a society where elderly people often feel insignificant or lonely, persuading elders that their memories are interesting and their lives important is often a difficult but crucial part of the process. Amplifying and celebrating their lives in performance not only brings a personal sense of self worth and affirms cultural identities, it also offers a political challenge for the future by relocating the past in the present. It is a form of theatre-making that acknowledges the messiness of everyday lives, accepts the mistakes that are made, and resists neat resolutions to social problems. It does, however, speak about the values of contemporary society, and holds the promise for a more equitable future.

Bibliography

Age Exchange Theatre Trust (2003) *View from the High Beech*, DVD produced in association with Benjamin Court Day Centre.

Arigho, B. (2006) How to Help Reminiscing Go Well: Principles of Good Practice in Reminiscence Work, London: Age Exchange Theatre Trust.

Bergson, H. (1996) Mind and Memory (trans. N.M. Paul and W.S. Palmer), New York: New York Books.

Brah, A. (1996) Cartographies of Diaspora, London: Routledge.

Carlson, M. (2003) The Haunted Stage: The Theatre as Memory Machine, Ann Arbour, MI: University of Michigan Press.

Foucault, M. (1977) 'Nietzsche, Genealogy, History' in D.F. Bouchard (ed.), Language, Counter-memory, Practice: Selected Essays and Interviews by Michel Foucault, New York: Cornell University Press, pp. 139–64.

Gibson, F. (1998) Reminiscence and Recall, London: Age Concern.

Merleau-Ponty, M. (1962) Phenomenology and Perception (trans. C. Smith), London: Routledge and Kegan Paul.

Misztal, B. (2003) Theories of Social Remembering, Maidenhead: Open University Press.

Nicholson, H. (2005) Applied Drama: The Gift of Theatre, Basingstoke: Palgrave Macmillan.

Schweitzer, P. (ed.) (2004) Mapping Memories: Reminiscence with Ethnic Minority Elders, London: Age Exchange Theatre Trust.

Schweitzer, P. (2006) Reminiscence Theatre: Making Theatre from Memories, London: Jessica Kingsley Publishers.

Wan, W-J. (2006) 'The Subversive Practices of Reminiscence Theatre in Taiwan', Research in Drama Education 11 (1): 77–87.

Notes

1 The Taiwanese theatre company Uhan-Shii is a good example of this intercultural exchange. See Wan, Wang-Jung (2006) 'The Subversive Practices of Reminiscence theatre in Taiwan' Research in drama education Vol. 11. No. 1 pp. 77–87. Pam Schweitzer has also offered a vivid account of her experience of reminiscence theatre in Schweitzer, P. (2006) Reminiscence Theatre: Making Theatre from Memories London: Jessica Kingsley Publishers.

2 DVD (2003) View from the High Beech Benjamin Court Day Centre in Association with Age Exchange Theatre Trust.

3 DVD shown at Age Exchange Theatre Trust, 26 November 2006.

4 British Asians refer to Pakistan, India, Sri Lanka and Bangladesh collectively as South Asia.

5 Pravesh Kuar, personal interview with the author, 20 December 2006.

6 Meri Christmas was written by Harvey Virdi and directed by Pravesh Kumar, and toured venues across England in 2006.

7 I have written elsewhere on how memories move from individuals to the community. See Nicholson, H. (2005) Applied Drama: The Gift of Theatre, Basingstoke: Palgrave Macmillan, Ch. 5.

Chapter 39

Caoimhe McAvinchey

'IS THIS THE PLAY?'
Applied theatre practice in a pupil referral unit

IT'S A PARENTS' EVENING IN A South East London Pupil Referral Unit (PRU). The corridors are thick with anxiety and anticipation as people politely nod at each other, sipping cups of tea. Teachers wait in classrooms for students to reluctantly introduce their parents and discuss their academic progress. Other students hover by the biscuits, eating the pink iced ones, leaving the plain ones, and wishing the next hour away.

But tonight's parents' evening has an added element. For the past six months a group of students have been working with Yun Jung Ko, a visual artist, and myself, a theatre practitioner, to create a piece, *What We Think*. This is being launched tonight so that the young people who participated can show their families and other students what they have been working on. There is a poster on the wall stating that *What We Think* will take place in Room 6.

The door to Room 6 lies open. This is the room where Personal, Social and Health Education (PSHE) is taught. A mother peers inside the door. There are no desks, no chairs, no books, no sign of anything resembling a formal teaching space. Instead, she sees another room, a chamber, built within the classroom. The woman looks to her daughter who is standing beside her in the doorway for reassurance. The daughter nods and grins. Cautiously, the woman enters the room . . .

[. . .]

This chapter reflects on an Applied Theatre and Visual Art project with Year 10 students at a PRU. It asks, what can be understood about the possibilities and limitations of Applied Theatre practice by working in PRUs? And, through Applied Theatre practice, what can be understood about PRUs and the wider political and cultural climate they evidence? The chapter addresses these questions by focusing on moments within the project which reveal the particularities of working in a PRU with young people who are excluded. Before considering the specifics of the project, I will consider our working context.

Contexts

In England, over 9,000 children and young people are excluded from school each year. Thousands more are temporarily excluded and have alternative educational provision through PRUs and Learning Support Units (LSUs). Under Section 19 of the Education Act 1996, local authorities have a duty 'to provide suitable education for children of compulsory school age who, because of illness or exclusion from school for example, will not receive a suitable education without these arrangements'.[1] There are currently more than 421 Pupil Referral Units in England and this number is set to rise as the government reiterates its commitment to find alternative ways to engage young people in learning.

Children and young people attend a PRU for a range of reasons. Often this will have to do with their exclusion from mainstream school because of behavioural or emotional issues. Many of the students in PRUs will have been 'statemented'.[2] Mothers of a school-age, pregnant schoolgirls, 'school-phobics' and pupils awaiting placement in a maintained school many also continue their education at a PRU. PRUs do not have to teach the full National Curriculum but they must offer a broad and balanced curriculum in accordance with guidelines from the Qualifications and Curriculum Agency (QCA). There is no set time frame: students might attend a PRU for weeks, months or years. The ultimate focus of the PRU is the facilitation of the students' return to a mainstream school.

Over the last fifteen years there has been a growing understanding of the positive impact of participation in the arts on the lives of people who identify, or are identified, as being excluded or marginalised.[3] This understanding is reflected in government policy and Arts Council England's funding strategies which increasingly support work addressing issues of social exclusion.

The term 'social exclusion' is, according to the Cabinet Office, 'a shorthand term for what can happen when people, or areas, suffer from a combination of linked problems such as unemployment, poor skills, low incomes, poor housing, high crime environments, bad health and family breakdown' (Jermyn 2001: 2). Within this context, disengagement from school leads not only to poor academic achievement in the short term, but plays a fundamental role in long-term issues of low aspiration, decreased opportunity and, potentially, an increased risk of being in conflict with the law. By identifying young people who are considered to be at risk of exclusion and by finding ways to encourage their participation in the arts, it is hoped that this will have an impact on the way in which they engage and participate in other aspects of their lives.

Charitable organisations such as the Calouste Gulbenkian Foundation not only focus on the funding of arts projects in PRUs, engaging young people in learning, but also commission research which surveys, evaluates and disseminates this work, so that it can be used to encourage and persuade others of its value (Ings 2002; Ings 2004; Wilkin et al. 2005). In *Serious Play: An Evaluation of Arts Activities in Pupil Referral Units and Learning Support Units*, the study examines the effects and effectiveness of arts activities in PRUs and LSUs for pupils, teachers and artists. For pupils they identify a number of impacts including:

> Increased knowledge and skills in the particular art form; improved
> listening and communication skills and ability to interact in group settings;
> increased confidence and self-esteem, leading to positive change in
> behaviour; the 'buzz' of participating; pupils gained a sense of achieve-
> ment, satisfaction and, above all, enjoyment from the projects.
>
> (Wilkin *et al.* 2005: 92)

It is also suggested that the skills, knowledge and experience that the pupils
develop through participation in the arts are transferable beyond the specific arts
project and encourage a further engagement with other aspects of learning. So, it
is within this context, that Yun and I developed a programme with the PRU,
commissioned by a local authority arts department. The following section considers
specific moments in the project which address the possibilities and limitations of
Applied Theatre within a PRU and what this reveals of the context within which
we were working.

Practice: expectation and adaptation

The PRU had agreed that we could work with a group of students for two and a
half hours each Thursday afternoon for an initial period of six months. The brief
from the PRU staff was open. They were keen to find an opportunity through the
project for students to find alternative ways to both engage with the world around
them and to express themselves within it. The PRU acknowledged that the students'
participation in the project would impact on how they related to each other within
and beyond the project and they hoped that it would have a positive impact on
their learning in other classes. There was a strong expectation that there would be
an event of some kind to mark the end of the project. We proposed to develop a
programme of visual arts and theatre workshops that would equip the students with
skills to both investigate and present ideas that they would develop throughout the
residency.

We planned on using the first three workshops as introductory sessions: for us
to get to know the students and their expectations; for the students to get to know
us; to introduce and try out some ways of working; and to explore and establish
the themes that would be most appropriate, relevant and interesting for the group
to explore.

We planned each workshop rigorously. We addressed the specific aims of each
class, the fundamental skills that we wanted to develop with the group and how
we hoped to facilitate this. The skills learned during one week's session would be
developed by the work we anticipated doing the following week. There was a strong
sense of cumulative, developmental learning. However, by the end of the first session
it was apparent that nothing was going according to any plan. Every week, we
worked with different people. We were lucky if two of the group were the same
from week to week. Only one person had attended the first four sessions. We
reconsidered all our expectations and instead had to focus on being increasingly
flexible and adaptable in our practice to ensure that the project could continue. Each
week we tried to introduce different visual arts and theatre techniques to engage
the students and develop particular ideas. Because we were never sure who was

going to be in the session we had to structure the work in a way which meant that we could introduce and integrate new people within it – it was a series of beginnings.

The behaviour of the group was trying. They had a very limited concentration span. Even those individuals who were more focused were constantly being distracted by the others. They were continually talking to and over each other, winding each other up, demanding a response. Chairs were weapons to hold high above the person who initiated the goading. Sometimes chairs were thrown as a student ran from the room, shouting obscenities. We were constantly trying to find ways to divert tension within the group before it erupted.

There were rare occasions when the group worked together. In these moments it was as if they had forgotten, or were too exhausted, to keep fighting against themselves and each other. In one of these moments, we had a conversation about the things that were important to each person. There were many responses: family, money, music, everything and nothing. We tried to keep these ideas in play throughout the workshops, constantly referring things back to the group, to what they said, to what they declared that they cared about.

What quickly became apparent was that this group of fourteen- and fifteen-year-old boys and girls had great difficulty in representing themselves. Everything was masked with an aggressive stance. Discussions were riddled with references to gangs, drugs and guns. Many of the group, both girls and boys, played out the image of 'youf' promoted in rap videos and London street fashion: low slung trousers revealing a pair of tracksuit trousers and the designer stamped waistband of underpants. Hooded tops and baseball caps were banned but constantly worn as an act of defiance and provocation towards the authority of the school.

The group offered less resistance in the art workshops than in the theatre ones. In the art sessions, they were working at a distance from themselves, making something with materials that could stand alone, apart from themselves. The objects were made by them but separate from them. Each of the objects or images made was marked with a tag. Once something was made, Jun and I had to move quickly to engage the student in a discussion about their work as, once completed, they often defaced or destroyed their work, saying 'this is crap', before someone else could say that of their work.

The theatre workshops were difficult. When encouraged to do something more physical than sitting in a chair there was utter resistance. The playing of a simple game – standing in a circle, making eye contact – was an enormous feat. When we introduced new games there was mayhem yet when we suggested that we move on, the students complained and wanted to play the game again. When we played it again, chaos descended once more.

In one of the sessions, we planned two storytelling exercises. In one, the students would create stories through a guided writing exercise and in the other, the Alphabet game, the students would build images and harvest ideas from these images.

We struggled through the guided writing exercise: Curtis wouldn't write, the only way he would participate was if I transcribed what he said; Joseph would only write his name; Charles presented a piece of writing riddled with dark and violent imagery. When I asked him if he had written this just now or if it was something that he had already written, he looked furious and said sarcastically, 'No, I just opened my book and it was there'.

The only moment of focus was when Travis prepared to read his story and it became clear that he was making it up on the spot. There was absolute stillness as everyone fell silent, wanting to know where his words would lead us. His story revealed his fantasy of becoming a pimp.

Later, we introduced the Alphabet game.[4] In this game, small groups choose a letter of the alphabet and then find a way to represent it with their bodies. The others in the group look at the image and identify the letter. We then look at the image again, with fresh eyes, to see if this still image can yield other ideas and stories. It is a very simple but powerful game which encourages a group to read abstract and possible readings from material they have generated without the pressure of having a predetermined meaning. We asked the students to organise themselves into groups of three. Initially they wouldn't get up off their seats. When they eventually formed small groups and chose a letter, they refused to sit or lie on the floor to make the shape of the letter with their bodies. I offered to join one of the groups, to be the one on the floor whilst we made the shape of the letter L. Travis stepped out of the image, directed us in how to make the image clearer and then, amidst the laughing and banter whilst making and adapting the representation, the group suddenly dropped the image and wouldn't reform it to move on to the second part of the exercise. Travis suggested making the shape of the letter with chairs. The group did this, dragging chairs into the middle of the room and laying them out in the shape of the letter P. Yun stepped into the loop of chairs that formed the top part of the letter P and said 'If you saw this picture what could it be?' There was a tentative response: 'A cage'. We made another letter image with the chairs, E. Yun and I stepped into the image. 'What is the story now?' 'A train'. 'Love'. Despite this leap of faith and imagination none of the students would step into the scene being created. Rather they would create the frame with chairs and only respond when Yun and I stepped into the picture. They couldn't put themselves in the picture. They could not allow themselves to be represented, to be any more vulnerable than they already were. The stillness evaporated. Two of the girls plaited each other's hair. Another rocked in her chair. The group had made an imaginative leap but, at this moment, were not prepared to go any further.

These examples evidence how the group would not allow themselves the opportunity to take themselves, or each other, seriously. They continually tested our limits. They were trying to push us to the moment when we would throw up our hands and say 'I give up. I give up on you'. To do so would allow them to say, 'I told you so. I knew you'd walk out. I knew you'd leave us behind so why should we bother?' The group was daring us to repeat a familiar cycle of disappointment. In order not to fulfil this expectation, Yun and I had to keep changing strategies, deflecting situations between us, working with individuals who were on the cusp of falling out of the group, constantly demonstrating that we were not going to give up, walk away or watch them self-destruct.

Much of what emerged, in small flashes through the work, was that this group of individuals felt lonely, desperate and hopeless. They frantically wanted to find some sense to things yet they had given up so much hope already that they were not prepared to give anything a chance. Or, if they were individually prepared to give something a chance, the moment was dashed by someone else who wasn't ready at that time.

In time, it became increasingly clear that the resistance we met and the apparent obstacles we faced throughout the project revealed both the nature of working within many PRUs and the pragmatic tools we needed to develop as applied arts practitioners in this context.

Adaptations

Because of the fluctuating attendance and temperament of the group we had to rethink our approach. Rather than developing a project that built upon knowledge and skills from one week to the next we had to plan a series of one-off workshops. Each one needed to be coherent and complete within the two and a half hour session, and each one needed to find ways to refer back to what had been learnt whilst not assuming that everyone had participated in the previous workshop or had the same skills or knowledge. This way of working informed how the project developed and, ultimately, the final piece that the group made. Paradoxically, the group was adamant that they wanted to make something to show to others. We had to find a way to support, develop and present the students' work in a way which illuminated what had been possible and achievable rather than highlighting the difficulty of pursuing our initial ideal.

It became very clear that any sort of traditional play or performance would be inappropriate. Not only was the students' attendance sporadic but when they did attend, they had demonstrated great difficulty in representing themselves, in physically standing up in front of others, in articulating something as themselves let alone representing someone else. We had to find a way to work with the students, to help them represent themselves in a way which didn't expose them or set them up for failure.

Because of their reluctance to perform, live, in front of each other, we experimented with video and sound recording. We taught the students how to use the equipment and gave them the responsibility to film each other. All of the conversations about what the material for the final event could be focused on the idea of the young people sharing their thoughts with other people, about letting other people inside their heads just for a few minutes. Through this conversation, they came up with the idea of creating a space, their head space, a space that didn't already exist. They wanted to build a new space inside the PRU. The head teacher agreed to let us take over the PSHE room. The final piece would be an installation and it would be launched on parents' evening.

We found a carpenter who helped design the space and we set about building it together. Suddenly this gathering of individuals became a group. Throughout the construction there were continual verbal jousts but none which escalated into a physical fight or with people storming out of rooms. In the days before parents' evening, the group was excused from all other classes, and worked in quiet concentration measuring, sawing, drilling. We discussed the material that had been made over the past six months: collages, clay objects, soundscapes of songs about every day life, a video about the things that were important to them. We had conversations about how this material could be arranged so that a visitor coming into this space would be guided through it in a way that best represents their inner world. Everything was laid out. The video was on a loop. The soundscape echoed through the space. A shopping list was drawn up of particular biscuits to buy for the visitors. A programme was made. Everything was ready. We left the room. The parents arrived.

[. . .]

Abi, one of the girls who participated throughout the project, and her mum are standing in the doorway of Room 6. Outside, the poster advertises *What We Think*. Abi's mum asks, 'Is it in here?' Abi nods and grins at her mother who cautiously enters the room. She walks along the outer walls of the inner room in the PSHE classroom. She finds a hole in the wall of this inner chamber. It is in the shape of a human body, suspended, whilst jumping in the air. She looks around to see if it is ok to go in. She steps through the body and into another world with a soundscape of young voices describing thoughts, dreams and concerns. There is a large collaged face on one wall. Words of hope and promises for the future dangle suspended from the ceiling. A suitcase lies open in the corner. Inside there is a teddy, a photo, a padded birthday card. 'Is this the play?' Abi's mum asks, 'Where is everybody?' Abi grins at her mum's confusion, 'Yes' she says, 'This is the play and we are all around you but you just can't see us.'

Bibliography

DCMS (1999) *Policy Action Team 10: A Report to the Social Exclusion Unit*, London: DCMS.

Ings, R. (2002) *The Arts Included: Report of the First National Conference on the Role of the Arts in Pupil Referral Units and Learning Support Units.* Calouste Gulbenkian Foundation and Arts Council England, Birmingham, 29 October 2001, Pershore: Nick Randell Associates.

Ings, R. (2004) *Creating Chances: Arts Interventions in Pupil Referral Units and Learning Support Units*, London: Calouste Gulbenkian Foundation.

Jermyn, H. (2001) *The Arts and Social Exclusion: A Review Prepared for the Arts Council of England*, London: Arts Council England.

Matarasso, F. (1997) *Use or Ornament: The Social Impact of Participation in the Arts*, Stroud: Comedia.

Wilkin, A., Gulliver, C. and Kinder, K. (2005) *Serious Play: An Evaluation of Arts Activities in Pupil Referral Units and Learning Support Units*, London: Calouste Gulbenkian Foundation.

Notes

1   Department for Education and Skills website, www.dfes.gov.uk/exclusions/alternative_provision_policies/pupil_referral_units.cfm (accessed 20 October 2006).

2   'Statementing' is the word used to describe the process where a local education authority (LEA) assesses a child's Special Educational Needs (SEN) with the intention of making and maintaining a Statement of their needs.

3   The Policy Action Team 10 (PAT 10) report to the government's cross-departmental Social Exclusion Unit and Francois Matarosso's *Use or Ornament: The Social Impact of Participation in the Arts* are two pivotal publications which evidence this.

4   Ali Campbell taught me this game.

Chapter 40

Josie Auger and Jane Heather

MY PEOPLE'S BLOOD

Mobilizing rural aboriginal
populations in Canada around
issues of HIV

JULY 6, 2005. IT'S RAINING. Inside the school gym the staff from the
women's shelter are setting up the food on long tables. There's a raised stage at
one end, screwed together by volunteers from pieces of discarded building scrap.
The stage has a few flats standing on it; masks decorate the flats. The lighting guy
and the sound guy have set up their equipment. Round tables fill the gym floor;
the walls are hung with drawings and lists, written on big sheets of newsprint.

People are beginning to arrive. A group of Aboriginal youth is preparing to
perform their play *My People's Blood* for their community. They are nervous and excited
and so are we; Josie Auger and Jane Heather, co-writers of this chapter.

We had arrived in the community 10 weeks earlier. We came to this small
Northern Alberta indigenous community to facilitate a popular theatre/action research
process with youth, focused on HIV/AIDS. Studies have shown that HIV incidence
among Aboriginal people in Canada is increasing at twice the rate of non-Aboriginals
(Baldwin *et al.* 1999; Craig *et al.* 2003). Josie is a PhD candidate who is originally
from this community. She planned the project to help her community begin a public
discussion of this urgent health issue and ideally, take action on prevention. Jane is
a popular theatre worker; she came to help.

Usually popular theatre and action research projects begin with a group's
identification of a key issue. The topic for this project was determined by Josie and
offered to the community. A small group of youth chose to become involved
and slowly became public advocates of HIV/STI education and prevention. During
the course of the project they learned about HIV, examined factors that impact the
spread of the infection, reflected upon their own lives and sexual behaviour, created
characters and scenes based on their own experience, got tested at the local hospital
and performed for their community. Josie's dissertation will be based upon the
research she conducted during the project.

Josie's plan involved hiring a popular theatre practitioner, recruiting young (18–25) indigenous people to form a core group of co-researchers and actors, and provide honorariums to elders who would support the core group. The youth met several times a week and worked with us to create three scenes, two of which were performed for a large community audience. After each scene the audience members were invited to discuss what they had seen. At the end of the evening, the audience was invited to a conference to be held in the community later in the summer. Our goals, of working with the indigenous youth to create a drama that named and discussed the issue publicly and to prompt further action, were accomplished.

In addition to the approximately 200 community members who attended the performance (many of whom spoke in the discussion), the Chief of the Nation, Elders, and health professionals spoke in support of the youth and endorsed the intention of the project. At every step of the process some group or individual was asked to move from the known into the unknown, from safe to dangerous, from silence to speaking out. Everyone confronted complex difficult obstacles. Some chose silence and safety, some risked the danger of speaking out. All community-based applied theatre projects are difficult. This chapter will examine three factors at work in this project:

1   the social, historical and economic context of the community;
2   the topic itself and related issues of sexuality;
3   the dramatic process.

It will also identify three turning points in the process:

1   HIV testing;
2   the Canada Day parade;
3   community mobilization for the show;

and it will speculate on some factors that assisted the participants and the project to succeed.

Community: context

Colonization has had catastrophic effects on indigenous people in Canada with a toxic fall out which lingers to the present day. Indigenous communities in Canada (and around the world) have endured the long-term effects of colonization by Church and State. The destruction of cultural, spiritual, political, family and economic structures has resulted in a plethora of social, economic and health problems.

However, there has also been a movement toward healing the intergenerational impact of abuse, specifically sexual abuse. It is widely known that residential schools were a construct of the federal government's colonial policies that, coupled with the Church's practice, aimed at the assimilation of Aboriginal people into the dominant culture. That any indigenous people survived this colonial agenda is a testament to their tenacity, endurance and astonishing ability to keep themselves, along with their cultural and spiritual traditions, alive.

Youth participants: context

The participants were all employed or in school, all with some high-school or post-secondary education and all living in relatively stable circumstances. Nevertheless, each one had personal or family experiences with alcohol and drug abuse, suicide, sexual and physical abuse, multi generational poverty, absent parents, unemployment, racism and violence.

Their jobs, income, cars, possessions, social status, in some cases family support and family status in the community helped each participant construct an overlay of 'normalcy'. The participants could appear in any public urban setting and would be indistinguishable from the mass of other young urban dwellers. No race, class, language or behaviour markers are evident on the surface. This is a thin veneer stretched over personal and inherited experiences of brutality. During the process this veneer was regularly breeched, both in the story and scene building activities in the drama and the personal one-on-one interviews that Josie conducted with each participant.

This sub-text of pain manifested within the project (and their lives) in a variety of ways. Some participants were volatile, angry and emotionally chaotic, some disappeared, some were sullen and withdrawn. The context of the project, the historical and contemporary oppression, everything the participants carried in their memories, their bodies, could not be transcended. Often, it was a struggle just to get to the room, then it was a struggle to do anything as a group. Participants were paid a very good hourly wage, there was always food and when they did come, it could be fun. These enticements were insignificant. The central reason to come, to come on time, to stay, to commit to the group and the work had to come from within. And it did, eventually.

The project did not transcend their pain nor did it give respite from it. Because the participants were creating fictions from their own experience they had to face it, draw on it and embody it. To the pain of old and current injuries was added a new fear, a new pain, 'do I have it?'

Turning point

One of the group members raised a personal concern and we decided to get tested for STI/HIV. The group agreed to be tested together in order to ensure no one person was stigmatized. We also agreed that our test results would be kept private and personal. After this discussion we were extremely concerned about the group and how this would impact the process. The choice the group made, the action they took, did have impact although it was hard to see at the time. They tested their own courage and the strength of the group that day and each accepted that HIV was a social and health issue that belonged to them.

The topic

Small rural communities in Alberta tend to be very conservative and some indigenous people within these regions are no exception. Generally people do not discuss their sexual behaviour and there is a great silence around STI/HIV. The experience of colonization along with the influence of mainstream and fundamentalist churches, plus other less direct factors such as language and cultural loss, make for little understanding or discussion of traditional roles of Cree men and women much less sex. HIV/AIDS is particularly taboo because it is considered a death sentence. Some also view it as proof of aberrant sexual behaviour.

We heard both from video documentaries and personal stories that local people living with the virus were afraid to come out publicly. AIDS workers from around the world would tell a similar story. Fear of community shunning is a great silencer. Discussion and scene creation around the topic forced the group to examine their own lives and sexual practices. At times there was resistance to the process; avoiding the topic was safer.

Although the stories on STI/HIV prevention that they created and performed were not personal stories, they all came from a true place. We created the stories by first drawing them on long rolls of newsprint. Each participant drew characters and events in a central character's life. We then improvised the events. It was decided that one female character had attempted suicide when she was 13. 'How?' asked the popular theatre practitioner. 'Butcher knife' one participant said, 'that's how I did it.'

All the participants had the support of their families. One mother, also a local leader, attended the first meeting and was publicly supportive of her daughter and the project. But as the project went on and it began to sink in that they would be performing publicly, the possible reaction from others in the community began to have impact. I (Jane speaking) speculate that this pressure and the fear of disapproval was at the root of the complete disappearance of two very committed participants late in the process. Sadly, these two had created a scene that focused on STI/HIV prevention, by expressing the need to use condoms, get tested and be monogamous or at least alert your partner to an infidelity. Of the three scenes that were created this one was the closest to home for the participants, so perhaps the most difficult to perform.

Turning point

As the performance drew near, the remaining participants became more and more determined to perform despite having lost two actors. They recruited their friends and siblings to fill the roles. They wore the masks they had made and paraded on Canada Day, gleefully handing parade watchers little bags containing an invitation to the show, a red ribbon and two condoms. The group was becoming bolder and more visible in the community but their fears did not dissolve, they escalated. They continued to be fractious, volatile and very difficult to work with. Rehearsals were chaotic and short, but they kept on.

A significant moment in this period was a confrontation between a high-ranking official and the two of us. A front-page article, with an extensive interview with Josie about the project, appeared in the local newspaper describing epidemic proportions of HIV. The Chief and Council and Health Center had been tremendously supportive of the project. The grant money Josie had raised was managed by the Health Center; they gave us office space and saw us everyday. Perhaps the high-ranking official had not fully taken in what the project was about. He articulated a point of view that we knew existed in the community but that no one had named. A play about HIV/AIDS would not be received well in the community. People would be outraged, and feel they were being stigmatized again. The national press would pick it up and one more bad news story would appear. Chief and Council would throw us off the reserve. I (Josie speaking) suppose he was concerned about us but at this point we needed encouragement not fear-based warnings. I (Jane speaking) suggested to him that someone in his position should try to be at least as courageous as the youth in his community. It was possible that there were people who would be upset by the play, but what about the ones who were waiting in silence? Waiting for someone to speak and bring this issue into the light? We asked him to come to a rehearsal, we asked him to take a role and we invited him to the show. He did none of these things but then none of the things he warned us about happened either.

However, the issue he raised was crucial. Even before the performance we needed concrete public support from the community. The actors had stepped up; ragged and under-rehearsed but was the community ready to follow them? We needed an audience, of course, but before that we needed a million things: a space, a feast, a sound system, lights, a technician, a truck, a set, a stage, builders, posters, radio ads, slide show, projector and lots of expert advice. All of these things had to be found or created in the community. We had money in the budget to offer for work, groceries and materials but if community members were opposed to the project, if they felt this was some foreign imposition with little or no relevance to them, if they feared being seen to support it, we would be unable to go on.

Turning point: community mobilization

Despite some reluctance on the part of some community members, things began to move. We went to see the men at public works and they agreed to donate materials plus design and build us a stage. A woman at the Health Center got us in touch with a carpenter. He built us some flats and someone lent us their truck to pick them up. We got the name of a guy who could run the lights and sound. The secretaries at the Health Center did a poster and a program. Josie hired the staff at the women's shelter to cook the feast and we advertised the event. We drove down muddy reserve roads in the pouring rain to get a trunk load of smoked fish for the feast. So many people helped and by becoming involved declared their desire to make a change in their community.

We were ready, but would they come? And if they did come, would they speak? They came. Parents, babies, elders, teenagers, health workers and band council members showed up. Before the performance the Chief addressed the audience and spoke in support of the project. After their performance the group spoke passionately and eloquently about STI/HIV prevention. Several audience members also spoke about the issue and committed to supporting a follow-up conference.

The popular theatre process

Any dramatic process builds self-esteem and self-confidence. The co-operative and collaborative nature of the work builds strong human bonds, and supportive, positive groups. Everyone who has ever done a show knows that combination of intense, creative, joyful work and the explosive high of performance. The participants in this project achieved the latter but rarely the former. Quite often, not only did they not come but when they did, they did not want to do drama. They were usually happy to be together and enjoyed painting, mask making, drawing and craft projects. Context and the topic explain most of the resistance but not all.

The making of theatre requires two things: you have to be there and you have to work with others. The popular theatre process requires more. Those who create and perform must take ownership, take responsibility and take power in every aspect of the work. Each participant wanted to take that power but each was weighted down by fear. There would be a performance and something to perform only if they felt able to put themselves in a dangerous place. For many long weeks they chose to stay safe while we tried to give them courage. The desire to create and perform, to be in the spotlight, to stand up and speak about the topic was in constant tension with the fear of public failure, public exposure, public censure.

We pushed them, pulled them, cajoled them, lost our tempers, lost our minds. We made them do drama; hard, emotionally draining work on an ugly disease, saturated in death, when they just wanted to goof around or zone out on painting. Why? For two reasons: the value for the participants and the community of experiencing completion and success and the hint of 'yes' that was always present. They kept attending, sporadically, they went to ceremonies, recruited, wrote a letter to the newspaper, got tested, and walked in the parade. Finally, they stood up together to speak to their community. Those who stayed with the project, helped out, spoke about this disease, and the terrible impact on humans, made change. At some point each decided they had to, they wanted to. Change is terrifying but not as terrifying as no change.

What helped?

Many factors made it possible to begin talking and taking action about STI/HIV prevention in this community.

Elders

The inclusion of elders was a key component of the project and a significant factor in the young people's success. Elders attended sessions and worked with the youth, introducing them to traditional cultural and spiritual concepts and ways of living. Some group members attended sweat lodge ceremonies with the elders and some attended a round dance to mark the demolition of the residential school. The elder's support of the youth and the project, along with their wisdom and blessings, strengthened and elevated the group. The project brought two generations together; each committed to not letting the other down.

Facilitator background

Since Josie was born in the community (although she did not grow up there and had not lived there for a long time), her family connections and familiarity with the community opened many doors. The participants' connection to Josie and their desire to support her and her research was another element. For some periods of time it seemed that the participants were attending solely because they thought that without them, she might not complete the research for her PhD. Aboriginal PhD candidates are rare and Josie's achievements were a great source of pride to the participants and the broader community. They felt honoured that she chose to come home to do her research.

Before starting the project Josie presented cultural protocol to many elders for good blessings. The prayers of those elders, the elders who were involved in the group, and of the group members helped her and group members transcend all doubt and go beyond some adverse conditions.

Jane had worked in the community in the mid 80s facilitating a number of theatre projects with youth. Many things had changed in 20 years but familiarity with the basic historical, economic and social conditions meant less time lost to culture shock. Jane was not a complete stranger to the community and this was likely an asset.

Theatre process

Although the process was difficult, it was also paradoxically, a key component in helping the group and community take a step towards addressing the issue. Popular theatre demands honesty, courage, collectivity. It demands it of performers and of audiences. Unlike a mural or a video there is no place to hide in this kind of art-making process. Everyone could see what it took for the performers to get there. The stakes were very high for the performers because of the topic, the history and context of the community, and because it was theatre. Their vulnerability and courage convinced their community to be courageous too.

After the performance, Josie led a discussion. We saw single mothers hesitate, then stand up to ask: how do I talk to my son about HIV and sexuality? An adult woman wondered how she could talk to elders about this topic. Someone said they knew someone who has HIV, what should they do? The health nurse (and others) gave some advice. Listening, speaking, questioning – everyone in the room had a moment of full engagement. Because of this project, youth, adult and elder publicly acknowledged that HIV is in their community and that silence, denial, was no longer an option.

Did this project mean the HIV rate in this community has dropped? Or that more people are getting tested? Practicing safer sex, abstinence or monogamy? It would be naïve to imagine that one 10-week project could make this kind of change but the conversation has begun, the words have been said out loud in a public place, the question has been asked. In a small local way another step toward decolonization, self-determination and health has been taken.

References

Baldwin, J.A., Trotter, R.T., Martinez, D., Stevens, S.J., John, D. and Brems, C. (1999) 'HIV/AIDS Risks among Native American Drug Users: Key Findings from Focus Group Interviews and Implications for Intervention Strategies', *AIDS Education and Prevention* 11 (4): 279–92.

Craig, K.J.P., Spittal, P.M., Wood, E., Laliberte, N., Hogg, R.S., Li, K., Heath, K., Tyndall, M.W., O'Shaughnessy, M.V. and Schechter, M.T. (2003) 'Risk factors for Elevated HIV Incidence among Aboriginal Injection Drug Users in Vancouver', *Canadian Medical Association Journal* 168: 19–24.

Chapter 41

Jan Cohen-Cruz

TRANSGRESSING BORDERS
IN PORTLAND, MAINE

PLAYWRIGHT AND THINKER Bertolt Brecht, whose aesthetics developed during the dark times of fascism in the 1930s and 1940s, favored white theatrical lights and actors speaking directly to audiences, so spectators never forgot they were in the theatre. Rather than provide cathartic release *within* the drama, Brecht wanted spectators to let their emotional responses loose on the *off-stage* injustices his plays presented. Brecht transgressed the boundary between theatre and activism in his generation by allowing political concerns to shape aesthetic ones.

Marty Pottenger's *home land security* (*hls*), a contemporary play precipitated by the attack on the World Trade Center and subsequent passage of the US Patriot Act, features performances by people impacted by the January 2004 "border raids" targeting immigrants and refugees in Portland, Maine. It is in the tradition of first-voice artmaking, e.g., professional artists using their craft to amplify the voices of people seldom heard in public. Radical theatre in the 1960s/early 1970s, while seen as a viable form of political activism, typically entailed middle class actors speaking for the poor and oppressed. In contrast, Pottenger and other grassroots artists draw on storytelling traditions to facilitate people speaking publicly for themselves. Self-articulation of their own concerns is a step toward resolving them.

Pottenger directed attention to off-stage injustices that spawned *hls* not only through first-voice performance but also via workshops for city political and educational leaders so as to engender new policies supporting diversity. This model of art, conjoining aesthetics and activism, transgresses mainstream aesthetic norms even beyond Brecht, aiming to concretely better the lives of people most adversely affected.

The border raids

In January 2004, US patrollers stationed on the Maine/Canada border staged a raid several hundred miles south in Portland, Maine. They staked out a Latino grocery store, a halal butcher, an interstate bus station, the international jet port, and a homeless resource center, demanding to see people's identification papers. Ten people were jailed for alleged immigration violations and then either sent back to their country of origin or to out-of-state Department of Homeland Securities detention facilities. The Border Patrol withheld the names of detainees, but reports confirmed that they did not come from countries associated with contemporary terrorism (Albright 2004). Portland's border raids, while legal, were transgressive in a different sense than Pottenger's theatrics: the violation of human rights.

The circumstances that led to the raids emerge from September 11, the subsequent, speedy passage of the US Patriot Act, and the doubling of patrollers at US international borders. Bau Graves, artistic director of Portland's Center for Cultural Exchange (CCE), which had partnered with local immigrant communities for twenty years, was skeptical of the increase of border patrollers in the north. People illegally crossing the US/Mexican borders – though largely unrelated to 9/11 – probably provide enough work to keep even the expanded forces busy. But in Maine, says Graves, patrollers "didn't have enough work to do already and all of a sudden there were twice as many of them with not enough work. Since Portland is the biggest population hub in the state, that's where they came looking for illegal residents" (2005b).

Graves avows that laws meant to be anti-terrorist have in fact become anti-immigrant. He estimates that 2,500 Latinos and 2,000 Somalis reside in greater Portland, out of a population of 66,000 in the city proper and a quarter of a million in the metropolitan area. Portland's City Council passed a resolution condemning the Border Patrol's action; state officials, including Governor Baldacci, made speeches, calling for balance between security against terrorism and protection of individual rights. Nevertheless, the raids greatly agitated Portland's refugees and immigrants, particularly Latinos and Somalis who were among those targeted. As a result of the January raid, many immigrants and refugees barely left their homes; parents feared that if they went to work, they might be snatched by the Border Patrol and their children would return from school not knowing where they were. They also avoided contact with anyone official, including doctors when they were ill and police when they were victims of crime.

Cultural response

The CCE staff wanted to respond to the raids as an institution, as Graves explained: "We wanted to artfully address some of the issues. The main point that was sticking in my mind was that we'd adopted the US Patriot Act because some Islamic fundamentalists attacked the WTC; well, none of the Somalis or Latinos in Portland had anything to do with that. It felt like unintended consequences of the Patriot Act, or maybe opportunism" (2005b). The kind of response the CCE staff felt was called for was not within their aesthetic vocabulary. They typically raised money and collaborated with local ethnic communities to design culturally specific artist residencies, multicultural performances, and educational programs. Audiences mainly attended events from their own culture.

Graves had met Obie-award winning playwright Marty Pottenger through the Animating Democracy Initiative (ADI), a program that "fosters arts and cultural activity that encourages and enhances civic engagement and dialogue" (www.artsusa.

org/animatingdemocracy). With *Abundance* (2003), funded by ADI, Pottenger traveled across the US gathering stories and holding "civic dialogues" – facilitated conversations in which a broad spectrum of participants express a range of views about a contemporary concern. Meeting with people all along the economic spectrum, from multi-millionaires to welfare recipients, Pottenger made a play about the role of money in our lives. Impressed with her work, Graves invited Pottenger to Portland.

Why, a year and a half later, make a theatre piece about the raids, for and with Portlandians? Although politicians spoke sympathetically on their behalf, they did not think to provide a platform for the astonishingly diverse residents to speak for themselves. After the Vietnam War, thousands of Southeast Asian refugees were resettled in the US, with the relatively liberal city of Portland one of the more welcoming homes (Graves 2005a: 1–2). Global tragedies and quests for economic opportunities brought refugees from Afghanistan, Russia, several African nations, and Bosnia, and scores of Mexicans and Latin Americans. As Graves and his wife and partner Phyllis O'Neill attest, "Twenty years ago, people of color were rarely seen on the streets; today students at Portland High School speak 57 native languages" (Graves and O'Neill 2004: 7). In *home land security*, a very diverse cast of six epitomizes the richness of widely divergent cultural experiences and points-of-view.

The process

Pottenger emphasizes how rarely people have the chance to converse about subjects on which they hold various points-of-view, such as *hls* provided, citing her own experience:

> I have always been intrigued by how people of various points-of-view find "common cause." As an adult I have worked on progressive causes, yet always mindful of the honest questions citizens ask on all sides. But where are the opportunities to converse civilly across these differences? At our annual family reunion, my Rear Admiral sister greets my brother who runs a Legal Aid clinic. My born-again brother breaks bread with my French Socialist brother-in-law as my radically-Conservative Republican father sits down with his second wife, a died-in-the-wool Southern Democrat. Yet we don't have models to take on topics that stir our passion and pain.
>
> (Email from Pottenger, June 23, 2005)

Pottenger spent one week per month in Portland from January through October 2005, conducting individual interviews. She brought potential performers together for group story circles – formal gatherings in which an artist/convener poses questions and each person answers by recounting relevant personal experiences. Participants in the July circle that I attended, for example, told engrossing stories related to life post-9/11, the US war in Iraq, and the Portland raids. That 2½ hour session included an 82-year-old French Canadian retiree, a leader of the local Somali community, a homeless man, a Cambodian classical dancer, a Chicano contractor with ties to the labor movement, a middle-aged Afghani businessman, a politically active African-American working-class Muslim, and the president of Portland's chapter of the NAACP.

At the heart of Pottenger's aesthetics are three components: 1) questions and how she decides which questions to ask; 2) listening; and 3) creativity, having people make art as another way of responding to the questions. Pottenger states, "To ask a better question moves things forward and gets to the next and then the next question." Being listened to actively, she asserts, is so rare and deep as to affect us "physiologically." In making art together, she finds, "something different gets engaged; a lot of confusion drops away." That is, sometimes poems or drawings expressing how people feel about a topic are more eloquent than what they've said.

Performance theorist Dwight Conquergood asserts that marginalized people need spaces "for 'public discussion' of vital issues central to their communities, as well as arena[s] for gaining visibility and staging their identity" (2006: 360). Self-representation frequently contrasts with mainstream images, such as those of dangerous aliens propagated by the border patrol raids. From such source material, Pottenger fashioned *home land security*, which a core cast of six who had participated in interviews and story circles performed in November 2005 as readers' theatre, i.e., actors on-script but nevertheless rehearsed and emotionally engaged.

The production

Part I, "Home," begins with the sounds of moose, wolves, crows, birds, and wind, abruptly muted by the roar of a chainsaw. Lights come up on the core cast wearing hunter caps with earflaps. Three musicians stage right – a North American fiddler, a Bolivian guitarist, and a Somalian drummer – intersperse richly diverse music throughout the production, supporting the actors' words. A seventh actor plays the radio announcer, reporting high state productivity in areas that rely on immigrant labor – toothpicks, sardine tins, lobsters, and low-bush blueberries. The Department of Homeland Security has declared an "orange" alert for the third month in a row. The temperature, she tells us, is dropping.

Native American Heather Augustine, a college student and president of the Micmac Nation, steps forward and articulates a feeling about home: "We have lived on this land for tens of thousands of years. Our biggest battle was a half mile down the hill. . . . I struggle not to be ashamed of the half of me that's white." Somali Oliver Albino shares a sobering view of his old and new homes: "When we came to the United States in the mid-1990s, we expected a welcome from black people. You must not be teaching history very well. Some of them said to us, 'You are the ones who sold us to them.' I replied with the truth: 'We are still running away ourselves.' Today in Sudan, my people are being killed, captured, and sold as slaves."

After each core actor talks about home, Rachel Talbot Ross, director of the local NAACP chapter, appears, the first of three cameo appearances. Relating stories of the astounding nine generations of her family in Maine, she gets to her father, the first African-American to serve in the Maine State Legislature:

> One of his greatest legacies was removing all geographical markers, place names, titles, and landmarks in the state that had the word "Nigger" in their name: Nigger Bridge, Nigger Lane, Nigger Lake, Nigger Ridge, Nigger Mountain. If I remember correctly, there were 24 instances.
> (Pottenger 2005)

Overcome with emotion, she is horrified to be crying in public. For civic leaders, making complicated personal feelings public is taboo. But the audience is riveted. Ross describes what she loves about Maine but adds, "I don't necessarily feel like a Mainer." The ninth generation in this state and she feels like an outsider? Another core actor, Reverend Virginia Marie Rincon, a Mexican/Mayan/Aztec Episcopalian priest who works with undocumented Latinos, spontaneously brings Ross a tissue and stands beside her. In that act, Ross perhaps experiences the possibility that she is not a solitary outsider.

The cast paints a broad picture of Maine, "a working man's state" with the highest percentage of home ownership in the nation that, in the 1920s, had the largest Ku Klux Klan chapter and the smallest population of African-heritage people. A state where Protestants once ostracized Catholics, forbidding French to be spoken in public, including in the schools. French-Canadian retiree Lucien Mathieu adds, "Teachers pulled your ear if they caught you speaking French; I have the pulled ears to prove it."

The second cameo performer, State Senate President Beth Edmonds, who is also a librarian, takes the stage. She reads the audience one of her favorite children's books, Click Clack Moo, pausing to show us the pictures. The cows in a drafty barn use an old typewriter to ask the farmer for some electric blankets. At first the farmer refuses to comply, so the cows stop giving milk. Soon the chickens, also refused blankets, join the cows and stop providing eggs. Finally, a duck intercedes and an agreement is reached – the cows and chickens will get blankets. The book ends with the ducks' letter to the farmer – click clack quack – about how boring the pond is and their request for a diving board. The reading is interspersed with Edmonds' comments and questions about leading and following, building off the book's recognition of class conflict and the power of the strike. Edmonds then shows us the last picture in the book, a duck gleefully leaping off the tip of a diving board.

Act II, "The Land," opens with the radio announcer reporting on traffic (so backed up that the Portland High principal was late to school), economics (skyrocketing bankruptcies), and agriculture (about the state insect, the honeybee). We're warned, "Wind picking up tonight as heavy rains head this way. Get ready to hunker down, cover your woodpiles, close all your windows, and pull in the laundry."

Now we hear the sounds of the airplanes hitting the twin towers. Billy Woolverton, a homeless man and budding writer/actor, describes where he was and how he learned about the attack. The others tell fragments of their 9/11 stories, too, ending with a sobering reminder of how a few people's actions typecast whole groups in the popular imagination:

Lucien:	All I thought was, "Dear God, don't let it be a Vietnam vet."
Jill Duson:	(the African American mayor of Portland): A black man.
Oliver:	A Sudanese.
Rev. Virginia Marie:	An undocumented Mexican.
Billy:	Some poor person.
Heather:	An Indian.

The actors share their divergent opinions about and experiences with war. This leads to the story of the Portland "border" patrol raid itself, and the fear that followed. The auditorium goes dead silent, as Portlanders listen to what their neighbors went and continue to go through.

Act III, "Security." The actors are dressed for a storm, with yellow rain hats. The radio announcer reports that "Temperatures continue to fall as Mainers prepare to welcome another long winter." The musicians, holding flashlights and wearing baseball caps, portray Maine border patrollers. We hear a range of views, from discomfort to pride in dealing with "criminal activity": "You think you know where you're living but believe me – it's a whole new ball game."

The last cameo performer is Fred LaMontagne, Portland Fire Chief and head of Maine's First Responders Team. He tells us that at least once a week, he's woken by a middle-of-the-night call about possible danger. He describes how Mainers would be notified about evacuation in case of emergency. He lays out Portland's vulnerability with its "100PSI gas lines, an electrical grid, major arteries and institutions; it's the largest port in the country for oil, gasoline, and liquid propane . . . We have a choice to either be a greater police state or a state that is more vulnerable." Then he describes the personal toll his position takes: thinking about his kids' school as the location of a hostage crisis; "looking around my church in the middle of a prayer wondering where a terrorist might place a bomb." The core actors then speak their fears – someone will blow up a small quiet town, Bush will start another war, social security will go bust.

The cast articulates where they find hope: for Jill, making a difference as a black female mayor; for Rincon, in her faith and from the people to whom she ministers. The radio announcer marks the seventh anniversary of a terrible ice storm during which people took care of each other. Jill sings "America the Beautiful," with Lucien joining in. The play ends with:

Jill: You meet Lucien, you meet Maine.
Lucien: You meet the Mayor, you meet Maine.
Oliver: You meet Reverend Virginia Marie, you meet Maine.
Reverend: You meet Oliver, you meet Maine.
Billy: You meet Heather, you meet Maine.
Heather: You meet Billy, you meet Maine.

Some of the strongest moments in the play are the unexpected juxtapositions. Augustine expresses pride in her Native American father and in the same monologue, thanks her white mother for getting her out of the reservation, rescuing her from pervasive drugs and alcohol, and possibly saving her life. The cast members themselves are an unlikely combination, seemingly so dissimilar, but as the play unfolds, clearly linked in deep ways. For example, Augustine, Woolverton, and Duson speak with equal passion about their relationship to nature. And all the cast members are joined by their bravery as first-time actors, vulnerably standing on a stage just a foot above the spectators. As witness/spectators, it's sobering to see so much about each person in a real reality show, not set in some other place and time but here and now; about a struggle that is not over. So the jury is not in and we who watch may intercede in the very events as they continue to unfold, off-stage. But to do so requires an artist who also sees herself as an activist.

Follow-up

hls requires concerted follow-up to achieve its potential – assisting in the protection of civil liberties – not an easy task given the habit of seeing art and politics as separate and self-contained. Not even all applied theatre practitioners approve of artmaking that morphs into activism. Many avow that their training is in art, not politics. But the use of performance to address a concrete social concern justifies the very idea of applied theatre, particularly when artists collaborate with people of other expertise. Pottenger, though trained in both disciplines and partnering with local leaders, transgresses borders between community organizing and not so much a play with its requisite technical virtuosity as a cultural performance, a public expression of group meaning. Indeed, the first words the actors say are, "This is not a play. Or a concert. It's more like snapshots – of a journey. A scavenger hunt. To discover Portland, Maine, 2005."

Anthropologist Victor Turner saw cultural performance's potential as an active agent of change, a form for communal reflection, and a space in which to imagine a better way of living together. This paradigm is made possible by paying attention not just to the performance itself but also to the development phase and follow-up, providing time for in-depth involvement. For audiences, the emphasis on follow-up positions them as witnesses rather than spectators per se, with an invitation to participate in local efforts to protect civil liberties. The project's success ultimately relies on spectators and actors doing so.

First-person accounts affect audiences differently than political speeches. Albino reminds us of how much immigrants contribute to the US. Homelessness is personalized through Billy's gentle, gaunt face and soft Texan drawl. Even well-positioned African-Americans like NAACP leader Ross are seen to experience isolation because of race. While Conquergood emphasizes that such performance brings "poor and marginalized people denied access to middle class 'public forums' into civic life," it just as significantly creates a space for political figures to say what they do not usually have license to make public.

The project functioned as informal leadership training. For example, during the *hls* process, a search was conducted for a new Police Chief. The city's Acting Chief and Florida's police captain, an African-American, were the short-listed candidates. Mayor Duson, deciding along with city council members, was the only one supporting the Floridian and the only African-American voting. Although Duson's choice for police chief was defeated, she contends that participation in *hls* emboldened her to speak her mind and also jump-started conversations about instituting diversity training for city councilmen.

Reverend Rincon was called to the apartment of a recently deceased undocumented person, where family and friends were grieving. Police arrived, demanding to see people's papers. Rincon told them that this was illegal harassment according to Portland's resolution following the border patrol raids. She got the police to leave, and later told the cast that her ability to be firm was the result of what she described as "getting her voice back" through participation in *hls*.

The play also re-inforced intra-community ties. Hearing Rincon's remarks at a meeting about the new Police Chief hire led Albino to endorse her point-of-view. Other cast members reported that, before *hls*, they were less likely to have listened so openly to a woman, let alone a Latina. Albino's, and through him the Sudanese community's, embrace of Mayor Duson was manifested at an event in her honor sponsored by the NAACP, at which he was asked to present her with a bouquet of flowers. As a result of learning about the Sudanese situation through Albino, Beth Edmonds reversed her vote against the Maine Senate's economic sanction of Sudan.

Given *hls*'s theme of civil liberties, Pottenger invited the local library to display banned books in the lobby at each performance and sign up people for library cards on the spot. The initiative was so successful that the library instituted mobile registration, e.g., providing library cards at other events where people congregate. At a benefit performance on their behalf, the NAACP also invited lobby displays, particularly from local activist groups. The materials of one of them, the National Organization of Women, included their pro-choice stance. This was difficult for one of the participating librarians, who is strongly anti-abortion. Pottenger visited her in the library, explaining the initiative and encouraging her to participate. Just co-existing, side by side, was a significant step in learning tolerance.

Although under 400 people in total attended the performances, they included two of the four local high school principals, who asked Pottenger to expand the initiative. With support from members of the Board of Education and city government, Pottenger devised a larger frame, the Arts&Equity Initiative (AEI), which uses highly structured facilitated dialogue, incorporating story and creativity, to address issues of racial, economic, and gender equity. The school superintendent signed on to the idea of a joint city/schools' partnership with AEI to address issues of race, racism, and multiculturalism. Three more *hls* performances took place in spring 2006, building support for a subsequent school-wide series of performances and workshops. The cast was expanded to include a local Cambodian leader and two Muslim high school students (replacing the radio announcer) who shared their perspective on the play's issues with each other and the audience.

Pottenger is planning workshops for school, city, and community leaders to address equity issues identified by Portland's educational and government leaders. She is prepared to live in Portland the next two years to train and place artists in the schools and in government departments (police, fire, parks, etc.). As public Artists-in-Residence, they would make art and lead workshops with the people there about their work lives, continuing after Pottenger leaves. Having developed the tools and built a great deal of local credibility, the remaining tasks are raising enough money and building even more support.

[. . .]

The front page of the *New York Times* on December 24, 2005 featured an article about Representative Tom Tancredo, Republican of Colorado. Though previously even the Bush administration considered his efforts to curtail immigration too right wing, Tancredo has become the Republican Party's rallying point in the production of the most restrictive immigration legislation in more than a decade. Spring 2006 witnessed a phenomenal outpouring of immigrants and citizens resisting such punitive measures. *Home land security* expresses the belief that only by knowing and caring for each other, expressed through participation in the struggle for social and economic justice, will there be any real security for any of us. At the end of the play the radio announcer warns that we may be headed for more snow and ice, "making this as good a time as any to get your storm windows in, load up on supplies, call a friend or neighbor." *Home land security* and the AEI may well raise support for people adversely affected by the Patriot Act once the house lights come up. When those who patrol aesthetic borders value such crossings between art and politics, art can play a greater role in keeping physical borders open as well.

Bibliography

Albright, C. (2004) 'Border Control', Maine Public Radio archive: 1/27.

Animating Democracy Initiative, available at ww3.artsusa.org/animatingdemocracy/about/.

Conquergood, D. (2006) 'Rethinking Ethnography: Towards a Critical Cultural Politics', in D.S. Madison and J. Hamera (eds), *The Sage Handbook of Performance Studies*, Thousand Oaks, CA: Sage Press.

Graves, J.B. (2005a) *Cultural Democracy*, Urbana, IL and Chicago, IL: University of Illinois Press.

Graves, J.B. (2005b) Interview with the author.

Graves, J.B. and O'Neill, P. (2004) '20 Years and Counting', publicity.

Pottenger, M. (2005) 'Home Land Security', Unpublished script.

Swarns, R. (2005) 'Capitol's Pariah on Immigration is Now a Power', *New York Times*, December 24: A1.

PART 7

Transformation

Chapter 42

Sheila Preston

INTRODUCTION TO TRANSFORMATION

One of the strong connotations of the neoliberal discourse ... is a systematic refusal of dreams and of utopia, a refusal which necessarily sacrifices hope. [...]

Recognising that the current system does not include everyone is not enough. It is necessary, precisely due to this recognition, to fight against it, and to not assume the fatalistic position forged by the system itself, according to which 'nothing can be done; reality is what it is'.

(Freire 2004: 110)

In cultural invasion, the actors draw the thematic content of their action from their own values and ideology; their starting point is their own world, from which they enter the world of those they invade. In cultural synthesis, the actors who come from 'another world' to the world of the people do so not as invaders. They do not come to *teach* or to *transmit* or to *give* anything, but rather to learn, with the people, about the people's world.

(Freire, Chapter 44, this volume)

PAULO FREIRE WAS COMMITTED to the human imperative and potential of the oppressed to transform the limiting situations and structures they found themselves in. From this standpoint a transformative vision represents a counter project; existing dialectically with material reality (articulated here as the neoliberal discourse) and the resulting inequity and exploitation of the majority of the population in the world. On another, no less crucial plane, Freire indicates how transformation might be effected at the local level; where the learning environment might potentially be transformed from one of cultural invasion (where one party assumes the power to 'transform' the other), to 'cultural synthesis' where a climate of dialogue and reciprocity enables people to realise their capacity to discover their own transformative possibilities.

In this sense, the concept of transformation is *not* forced or born out of some romantic, metaphysical or religious notion *onto* vulnerable people; but rather, has a political function which reminds us that our human presence and agency (and that of others) in the world is not a neutral one. The possibilities of transformation are therefore understood as a material, cultural and social vision for change. The concept of transformation can be understood as multi-valent, operating at the political, the geographical and the individual level; transforming the public sphere of material circumstances, the pedagogical environment and the personal mindset.

Transformation is not a neutral concept. Developing countries have been 'transformed' economically and 'mentally' by global capitalism with devastating impact. Constantino's chapter in this section demonstrates the impact of contemporary capitalism and the influence of 'transnationalization' on Philippine culture.[1] Akin to the development discourse, 'transformation' carries contradictory ideological connotations, and needs therefore to be contextualised critically against a social, cultural and historical backdrop. Like the concept of development, the notion of transformation has been hijacked, misused and subjected to grand claims at all levels from cultural workers to governments. Any critique of the term must take account of its 'magical' connotations where the idea of transformation conjures images of 'saving' and 'rescuing' people from their impoverished situations. This romantic notion taps into our impulses and liberal need (or guilt) to 'do good' (or perhaps to 'feel good') but plays into the hands of a benevolent and civilising ideology where people are seen as, the 'poor unfortunates' who are 'underdeveloped' and need to be redeemed by those more privileged in the West. Critiques of development and transformation, while necessary, are not intended, however, to lead to a point of stasis or inaction. Such fatalism would play into the hands of the neoliberal ideologues whose vested interests resist transformation. One can, instead, begin by considering the injustice of the 'impoverished' and the 'privileged' contrast as real material circumstances in urgent need of transformation. Such an approach, however, needs to be multi-faceted; engaging local knowledge and action with wider critical awareness of the historical, cultural and economic causes of 'underdevelopment' and inequity.

There is a need to analyse critically and carefully the impact of projects as they happen in their contexts.[2] All too often there is an absence of such an analysis; an incongruity between the 'vision' of a project and the 'reality' occurring within the challenges of a specific cultural setting, leading to grand claims being made about its effectiveness. The reality is that positive transformative intentions may encounter all kinds of conflict in a cultural context where competing, multiple agendas and power relations are present. For example, those in a cultural setting who have (perhaps subconsciously) benefited from a power imbalance may resent any attempts to take power and to be self-determining on the part of those who were previously the victims.[3] Also, the 'success' of small-scale applied theatre projects, sometimes delivered as a 'one off', may be valuable, but limited by their scope. While recognising that many projects have a natural lifespan (perhaps appropriately so), there is a need for applied theatre projects to think through issues of sustainability, the possibilities for long-term change and the potential barriers to achieving it.

Each of the practitioners contributing in this section offers a different approach to the question of transformation and sustainability, outlining a variety of projects which are in some way concerned with supporting change and transformation. In their different ways, they reveal how creating a climate or ethos of working, which has structured within it *possibilities* of community change, requires the support of those representing the structures within any setting whose interests may or may not be served by a transformative agenda. Still, the question remains, how do we measure, assess or evaluate the transformative impacts of applied theatre in all their different manifestations?

Etherton and Prentki in their editorial on Impact Assessment usefully distinguish between 'monitoring and evaluation', and 'impact assessment'.[4] The former happens within the scope of a project design and is concerned with assessing its immediate impact, whereas the latter is concerned with measuring impact months and years after a project has ended (Etherton and Prentki 2006: 139–40). Assessing the long-term impact of an intervention on individuals and communities is difficult and rarely achieved by organisations unless there are tangible 'hard' indicators such as in a prison context where evidence of a reduction in re-offending might be claimed to 'prove' the success of a project; or the sustained use of an agricultural strategy might demonstrate that an intervention had been 'effective'. Similarly as Etherton and Prentki put it, applied theatre may be easily evaluated and measurable when it is message-based if the appropriate indicators are devised (Etherton and Prentki 2006: 147), and the project has incorporated into its design possibilities of gathering appropriate quantitative and qualitative data to gloss an evaluation. However, they go on to raise the problem of assessing projects with less 'measurable' and tangible features:

> Where there is no message or issue at the heart of the process but rather the encouragement to the community to develop self confidence and assume control over their own lives, to transform themselves, in other words, from the objects into the subjects of their development, it is much more difficult to assess whether such a personal transformation has led, in the long term, to the wider social impact envisaged.
>
> (Etherton and Prentki 2006: 147)

The challenge, therefore, for a contemporary applied theatre practice that is committed to engaging meaningfully with the current social and political reality is, at least, threefold. Firstly, there is a need to be alert to the useful and sustainable features of a project for participants and organisations involved. This might well not be predetermined or expected but emerge within a project. Secondly, practitioners need to develop effective strategies for evaluating that which is not easily measurable; the development of people's consciousness and agency long after a project has completed. In order that such research is not extractive (and contrary to the aims of the programme), this needs to be a fully people centred process. Finally, there is a need for practitioners to have a clear distinction between 'ideals' of transformation and the 'reality' in a given setting and to develop critical analyses of applied theatre interventions and their impact. Such analyses involve measuring *negative* impacts alongside positive interventions and considering what was *not* effective alongside analysis of competing agendas and power relations. (This may require two evaluations: one for the funding agency and one for the practitioners.) If critical awareness is not developed *by* cultural workers themselves, they limit their own transformative possibilities as well as the potential impact of applied theatre.

Bibliography

Etherton, M. and Prentki, T. (eds) (2006) Special edition 'Drama for Change? Prove it! Impact Assessment in Applied Theatre', *Research in Drama Education* 11 (2): 139–55.

Freire, P. (2004) *A Pedagogy of Indignation*, Boulder, CO: Paradigm Publishers.

Notes

1   Renato Constantino's historical–political critique of the American 'colonisation' of Philippine culture was a seminal influence on the renowned theatre company PETA (Philippine Educational Theatre Association). See Eugene Van Erven (1992) *The Playful Revolution*. Indiana University Press.

2   According to Etherton and Prentki the difference between these strategies has also been recognised by development agencies such as Oxfam and Save the Children. Also, see the journal *Research in Drama Education* where, generally, there is a growing number of researchers and practitioners attempting 'deep' analysis of the quality of projects they undertake.

3   See Preston (2000) Theatre for Development in Context. Unpublished PhD thesis which is held in the British Library.

4   For more information on impact assessment consult the following volume: Etherton, M. and Prentki, T. (eds) (2006) Special edition 'Drama for change? Prove it! Impact assessment in applied theatre' *Research in Drama Education* Vol. 11, No. 2.

Chapter 43

Edward Bond

THEATRE POEMS
AND SONGS

Theatre Poems and Songs, Methuen (1964), pp. 5, 59–60, 138.

Lear
On Leaving the Theatre

DO NOT LEAVE the theatre satisfied
Do not be reconciled
Have you been entertained?
Laughter that's not also an idea
Is cruel

Have you been touched?
Sympathy that's not also action
Corrodes
To make the play the writer used god's scissors
Whose was the pattern?
The actors rehearsed with care

Have they moulded you to their shape?
Has the lighting man blinded you?
The designer dressed your ego?

You cannot live on our wax fruit
Leave the theatre hungry
For change

The Fool
Culture

All men must answer in their lives
Those questions whose answers are enormous
Because when one man decides how he lives
  He changes all men's lives

There are no small questions for small men
All men are Hamlet on an empty street
Or a windy quay
All men are Lear in the market
  When the tradesmen have gone

No man eats sleeps or loves for himself alone
Harvest and dreams and teaching the young
Don't take place in a small room
  But in the spaces of other men's lives

How we eat decides justice

Our homes measure the perversion of science
Our love controls the meaning of words
And art is whatever looks closely
  In the human face

If there were only irrational ways
To make the world rational
Art would still be reason
  And so our race not left to rot in the madhouse

Reason is the mark of kin
Poetry destroys illusions – it doesn't create them
And hope is a passion that will not let men
  Rest in asylum's peace

The Bundle
Poem

They run the clinic in which you're born
Christen you in their church
Teach you the rules of their school
Examine your minds
Mark them
Donate your playing field
Teach you the rules of their games
Employ you and pay you
Pay you when there's no work

Print your money
Marry you in their church or their registry office
Christen your children
Censor your television
Let you listen to their radio
Share their newspapers with you
Sweep your street
Train your police
Give you medals
Encourage you with bonuses
Punish you when you're a nuisance
Put you in hospital when you're sick
Take you into care when you're old
Burn you in their crematorium
And scatter your ash on their grass

No wonder some of you fight for them
When the rest start to ask
What the hell they're doing!

Chapter 44

Paulo Freire
(trans. M. Ranos)

PEDAGOGY OF THE
OPPRESSED

Pedagogy of the Oppressed (trans. M. Ranos), Penguin Books and Continuum International Publishing Group (1972), pp. 160–4.

CULTURAL ACTION IS ALWAYS A systematic and deliberate form of action which operates upon the social structure, either with the objective of preserving that structure or of transforming it. As a form of deliberate and systematic action, all cultural action has its theory which determines its ends and thereby defines its methods. Cultural action either serves domination (consciously or unconsciously) or it serves the liberation of men and women. As these dialectically opposed types of cultural action operate in and upon the social structure, they create dialectical relations of *permanence* and *change*.

[. . .]

Dialogical cultural action does not have as its aim the disappearance of the permanence–change dialectic (an impossible aim, since disappearance of the dialectic would require the disappearance of the social structure itself and thus of men); it aims, rather, at surmounting the antagonistic contradictions of the social structure, thereby achieving the liberation of human beings.

Antidialogical cultural action, on the other hand, aims at mythicizing such contradictions, thereby hoping to avoid (or hinder insofar as possible) the radical transformation of reality. Antidialogical action explicitly or implicitly aims to preserve, within the social structure, situations which favour its own agents. While the latter would never accept a transformation of the structure sufficiently radical to overcome its antagonistic contradictions, they may accept reforms which do not affect their power of decision over the oppressed. Hence this modality of action involves the *conquest* of the people, their *division*, their *manipulation*, and *cultural invasion*. It is necessarily and fundamentally an *induced* action. Dialogical action, however, is characterized by the supersedence of any induced aspect. The incapacity of antidialogical cultural action to supersede its induced character results from its objective: domination; the capacity of dialogical cultural action to do this lies in its objective: liberation.

In cultural invasion, the actors draw the thematic content of their action from their own values and ideology; their starting point is their own world, from which they enter the world of those they invade. In cultural synthesis, the actors who come from 'another world' to the world of the people do so not as invaders. They do not come to *teach* or to *transmit* or to *give* anything, but rather to learn, with the people, about the people's world.

In cultural invasion the actors (who need not even go personally to the invaded culture; increasingly their action is carried out by technological instruments) superimpose themselves on the people, who are assigned the role of spectators, of objects. In cultural synthesis, the actors become integrated with the people, who are co-authors of the action that both perform upon the world.

In cultural invasion, both the spectators and the reality to be preserved are objects of the actors' action. In cultural synthesis there are no spectators; the object of the actors' action is the reality to be transformed for the liberation of men.

Cultural synthesis is thus a mode of action for confronting culture itself, as the preserver of the very structures by which it was formed. Cultural action, as historical action, is an instrument for superseding the dominant alienated and alienating culture. In this sense, every authentic revolution is a cultural revolution.

The investigation of the people's generative themes or meaningful thematics described in chapter 3 [of *Pedagogy of the Oppressed*] constitutes the starting point for the process of action as cultural synthesis. Indeed, it is not really possible to divide the process into two separate steps; first, *thematic investigation*, and then *action as cultural synthesis*. Such a dichotomy would imply an initial phase in which the people, as passive objects, would be studied, analyzed, and investigated by the investigators – a procedure congruent with antidialogical action. Such division would lead to the naïve conclusion that action as synthesis follows from action as invasion.

In dialogical theory, this division cannot occur. The Subjects of thematic investigation are not only the professional investigators but also the men and women of the people whose thematic universe is being sought. Investigation – the first moment of action as cultural synthesis – establishes a climate of creativity which will tend to develop in the subsequent stages of action. Such a climate does not exist in cultural invasion, which through alienation kills the creative enthusiasm of those who are invaded, leaving them hopeless and fearful of risking experimentation, without which there is no creativity.

Those who are invaded, whatever their level, rarely go beyond the models which the invaders prescribe for them. In cultural synthesis there are no invaders; hence, there are no imposed models. In their stead, there are actors who critically analyze reality (never separating this analysis from action) and intervene as Subjects in the historical process.

Instead of following predetermined plans, leaders and people, mutually identified, together create the guidelines of their action. In this synthesis, leaders and people are somehow reborn in new knowledge and new action. Knowledge of the alienated culture leads to transforming action resulting in a culture which is being freed from alienation. The more sophisticated knowledge of the leaders is remade in the empirical knowledge of the people, while the latter is refined by the former.

In cultural synthesis – and only in cultural synthesis – it is possible to resolve the contradiction between the world view of the leaders and that of the people, to the enrichment of both. Cultural synthesis does not deny the differences between the two views; indeed, it is based on these differences. It *does* deny the *invasion* of one *by* the other, but affirms the undeniable *support* each gives *to* the other.

[. . .]

Cultural synthesis (precisely because it is a *synthesis*) does not mean that the objectives of revolutionary action should be limited by the aspirations expressed in the world view of the people. If this were to happen (in the guise of respect for that view), the revolutionary leaders would be passively bound to that vision. Neither invasion by the leaders of the people's world nor mere adaptation by the leaders to the (often naïve) aspirations of the people is acceptable.

To be concrete: if at a given historical moment the basic aspiration of the people goes no further than a demand[1] for salary increases, the leaders can commit one of two errors. They can limit their action to stimulating this one demand or they can overrule this popular aspiration and substitute something more far-reaching – but something which has not yet come to the forefront of the people's attention. In the first case, the revolutionary leaders follow a line of adoption to the people's demands. In the second case, by disrespecting the aspirations of the people, they fall into cultural invasion.

The solution lies in synthesis: the leaders must on the one hand identify with the people's demand for higher salaries, while on the other they must pose the meaning of that very demand as a problem. By doing this, the leaders pose as a problem a real, concrete, historical situation of which the salary demand is one dimension. It will thereby become clear that salary demands alone cannot comprise a definitive solution. The essence of this solution can be found in the previously cited statement by bishops of the Third World that 'if the workers do not somehow come to be the owners of their own labour, all structural reforms will be ineffective . . . they [must] be owners, not sellers, of their labor . . . [for] any purchase or sale of labor is a type of slavery.'

To achieve critical consciousness of the facts that it is necessary to be the 'owner of one's own labor,' that labor 'constitutes part of the human person,' and that 'a human being can neither be sold nor can he sell himself' is to go a step beyond the deception of palliative solutions. It is to engage in authentic transformation of reality in order, by humanizing that reality, to humanize women and men.

In the anti dialogical theory of action, cultural invasion serves the ends of manipulation, which in turn serves the end of conquest, and conquest the ends of domination. Cultural synthesis serves the ends of organization; organization serves the ends of liberation.

This work deals with a very obvious truth: just as the oppressor, in order to oppress, needs a theory of oppressive action, so the oppressed, in order to be free, need a theory of action.

The oppressor elaborates his theory of action without the people, for he stands against them. Nor can the people – as long as they are crushed and oppressed, internalizing the image of the oppressor – construct by themselves the theory of their liberating action. Only in the encounter of the people with their revolutionary leaders – in their communion, in their praxis – can this theory be built.

Note

1   Lenin severely attacked the tendency of the Russian Social Democratic Party to emphasize economic demands of the proletariat as an instrument of the revolutionary struggle, a practice he termed 'economic spontaneity.' 'What is to be done?' in *On Politics and Revolution, Selected Writings* (New York, 1968).

Chapter 45

Renato Constantino

SYNTHETIC CULTURE AND DEVELOPMENT

Synthetic Culture and Development, Foundation for Nationalist Studies (1985), excerpts from pp. 33–43.

MAN IS BORN INTO A CULTURAL SYSTEM that is historically evolved. He is permeated by symbols, traditions, perceptions and value orientations that become mediating forces between himself and society just as society is the mediating agency between himself and his material environment. In much of the Third World today, this cultural heritage is in peril.

The transnationalization of communications has almost completely shattered the cultural defenses [sic] of developing nations. The very existence of indigenous cultures is threatened with massive modifications as Western culture is presented as the culture which every modernizing state must emulate. Aspects of indigenous culture are preserved in bastardized, "touristic form" to attract dollars while the local population consumes popular Western cultural fare or local films, TV, radio, and comics which ape the styles, techniques and content of Western cultural products. The incursion of Western informational and cultural commodities is constant and widespread. They are also technologically superior, therefore admired and enjoyed.

In the course of the worldwide invasion of its cultural and informational infrastructures, contemporary capitalism has fabricated a synthetic culture that has become the matrix of perceptions and orientations of masses of people both in the industrial world and in the newly independent states within the capitalist orbit. Indeed even the socialist world has not been spared from the incursion of some aspects of this synthetic culture.

Perhaps the most important feature of this synthetic culture is its consumerist ideology. That is not surprising since the capitalist dream society is one where everybody buys everything. While consumerism is directly promoted by advertisements, a more effective, because subtle, approach is the consistent presentation in media, particularly TV, of the concept of the good life in an affluent society. What should be regarded as luxuries in the Third World are perceived as needs – Western food and fashion, modern appliances, a TV set, a car, etc. – thus creating pressures for importation or local production and in the process distorting social priorities. Thus, we may see the latest car models in a poor country where public transport is woefully inadequate.

Reordering reality

In industrialized states where the period of initial accumulation is long past, the emphasis on such values as "prudence, restraint, thrift and saving" has waned. In an economy characterized by high productivity and ever threatened by the prospect of glut, the values which media nurtures are those of impulse buying and asset acquisition. Products are no longer bought for their sturdiness and durability but for their style or for some claimed innovation. In an economy that reaps handsome profits from planned obsolescence, the idea that certain articles could be bearers of tradition and continuity from one generation to the next would hardly be promoted. Instead, the highest value is attached to the newest and the latest. . . .

Standardization of culture

The standardization of popular culture provides the dominant classes with happy, exploited people whose minds are sedated with entertainment featuring comic strips, mindless music, and soap operas and comedies revolving around situations that distort reality and ignore basic problems of society. At the other end of the spectrum are the stories about sex and violence, the movie and TV mayhem, which brutalize and desensitize and hardly provide useful social insights because the emphasis is on individualistic solutions effected by cops, detectives, supermen and wonderwomen who are the equivalents of the cowboys of yester-years fighting bad guys in defense [sic] of the law, women, and private property.

Social relations are not dynamically presented. Instead, there is an atomization of society, individuals without relation to the society they live in. The hero fights the forces of evil as an individual. Social relations become abstract. This is hardly surprising since the fragmentation of oppressed classes – or better still, their unawareness of their status – is a condition of the hegemony of the dominating class.

Colonizing life experiences

Reality is reordered and class conflicts and other political questions are glossed over. The ruling class colonizes the life experiences of other classes in order to give its own values and objectives the appearance of universality. Thus, the culture disseminated is one that ignores class conflicts, and is not part of the political struggle. According to a study conducted in Venezuela, the "*marginales* or bottom segment of the population lost their perception of class differences. They think that there are, to be sure, rich and poor, but all have access to the same consumer goods they hear about on the transitor or see on the TV."[1]

Today's so-called popular music, in its various manifestations, reflects even more extremely both the emphasis on technology and the mindlessness that afflicts the majority of film and TV productions. Rock music with its ear-splitting volume, its empty repetitive lyrics, generates nothing more than a purely physical excitement. It is incapable of saying anything meaningful about human life. Instead, it simply erects 'walls of sound' behind which its consumers exist in an unreal world where the violence done to the senses becomes an opiate for the mind.[2]

It is said that when the generals took over in Chile they blasted rock music through loudspeakers into the streets of Santiago – cultural violence reflecting political and economic violence. Under Allende's government, Chilean musicians had rediscovered indigenous music and developed it to express the people's sentiments and aspirations. Song became a great mobilizing agent. The generals arrested and killed the artists to silence their music.

Means of social control

Cultural domination is facilitated by the fact that Third World audiences have been reduced to passive recipients of inputs from information monopolies. Cultural experience is limited to seeing, hearing, and to a lesser extent reading pre-digested and packaged products of the information industry that also controls entertainment. People now think that being informed is simply knowing the latest news: they are habituated to learning about the newest development or event and forgetting what happened the day before. This is especially true of a growing majority who rely on the TV news coverage rather than on newspapers.

In the Philippines, for example, the daily newspaper has become too expensive for most families. A TV set has higher priority since it provides both news and entertainment for a growing population of non-readers. But TV offers each day's events simply as a passing show: images flash on the screen, words assault the ear and fade away. Who, what and where are its staples; why is hardly its forte.

At least newspapers offer an occasional intelligent analysis, but a TV-habituated generation has no time or patience to be intellectually provoked – indeed, does not even miss such an experience. This does not imply that a non-analytical presentation is non-judgmental. Value judgments are incorporated in how news is presented, in what is considered newsworthy, in what is ignored. Unknowingly, most viewers will absorb these value judgments as part of the factual packages.

The extent of technological progress especially in the realm of communications has resulted, ironically enough, in the erosion of the individual's opportunity to arrive independently at an awareness of his environment. Instead, media, particularly TV, provide him with a mediated or synthetic environment which takes the place of personal sensory experience of the world he lives in. He is presented with a reconstructed world and his perceptions of the real world are defined and delimited by the images he sees on the TV screen from day to day, from one newscast to the next.

The viewer becomes a mere receiver, not only of the facts of the event but also of the value judgments implicit in the telling of the apparently factual account.

With information and opinion neatly packaged together and bombarding the viewer every waking hour, he hardly has the time to sort it all out and actively form opinions of his own. He has become simply a passive consumer of information and ideas in an environment recreated – one could even say manufactured – for him by the communications industry.

Ideological dependence

The analytical mind is exercised and honed through interaction. Popular culture as dispensed by television and video tapes is generally consumed in isolation and has produced a fragmented, escapist, pliable, largely unthinking audience. The isolated individual who lives within the recreated environment is ready for mental colonization. New needs are implanted through the medium of advertising which is an important means for homogenizing people. It trains them to regard commodities as the be-all and end-all of life. Possessing or enjoying them becomes life's sole meaning. The individual is given new images of himself and pressured to live up to that image – one which places the highest value on his consumption capacity thus making him an asset to the corporate society in which he lives. While the upper and middle classes constitute the more faithful market for Western cultural commodities, the relatively inexpensive transistor is fast becoming an indispensable fixture in the countryside and doles out, though not as graphically and with a more local accent, more or less the same pap as the television set.

This is not to say that television and radio are a complete cultural wasteland but certainly, good, serious, solid programs are the exception rather than the rule. As for material that addresses a problem in a people-oriented manner, that is scarcer than a hen's teeth on radio and TV. At least, the much maligned because administration-controlled newspapers, manage once in a while to print research findings and exposes [sic] from a progressive, Third World perspective. True, the occasional talk-show sometimes tackles controversial subjects but time constraints and commercial interruptions usually preclude thorough discussion.

The communications industry is now the main agent in the manufacture of a synthetic culture which promotes the concept of a universal and permanent economic system that is not to be challenged in any fundamental way. With the monopoly control of the television networks, the information systems, the record industry, video recorders, etc., culture itself has become a commodity. It has also become a means of social control. While a variety of cultural products give the illusion of freedom of choice, practically all of them aim to standardize men and women into acceptable types of citizens and consumers who do not question the system. . . .[3]

Standardization of consumption and culture

The standardization of both consumption and culture begins with the adoption of new products and styles (cultural or material) for the consumer markets in the imperial economies. These are disseminated to and readily appropriated by the upper and middle classes of developing countries. However, since wider markets are needed for more profits, the product is further promoted either as is, or in a less expensive version to be consumed by a larger public. This destroys its value of exclusivity. The upper classes must then be provided with completely new products or the old ones are restyled. Thus begins a new cycle in the inexorable process of premature obsolescence and frantic modernization.

From the exclusivity of the centers of modernity, consumption items are adopted by the elite in the Third World. Eventually, they seep down (though in cheaper versions) to the mass, thus "democratizing" these items. This leads the elite to pursue new items of exclusivity which are dictated from the centers of modernity. Modernity is little more than changing the forms of consumption within an unchanging social structure. Thus the appearance of change masks the fact that there is no real change.

This standardized culture with its international appeal is essentially anti-nationalist. At a time when Third World peoples need all the resources at their command to help them attain economic and political independence, the cultural products they consume divert their attention from such goals and promote cultural dependence. The Trans National Corporations and the governments that represent them correctly regard nationalist movements as threats to their economic expansion and political control. Cultural penetration has proven to be an effective tool to impede such movements or at least to tame them. . . .

Notes

1   R. Barnet and R. Mueller, *Global Reach*, New York, Simon and Schuster, 1974, p. 185.
2   Leon Rosselson, 'Pop Music: Mobiliser or Opiate?' in Carl Gardner, ed., *Media, Politics and Culture*, London, Macmillan Press, 1979, pp. 40–50.
3   Michele Mattelart, 'Notes on "Modernity": A Way of Reading Women's Magazines,' in A. Mattelart and S. Siegelaub, eds, *Communication and Class Struggle*, New York, International General, France, IMMRC, 1973, pp. 158–78.

Chapter 46

Jan Selman with Shaniff Esmail, Brenda Munro and Jim Ponzetti[1]

ARE WE THERE YET?
On the road to safer sex through interactive theatre

> When I thought about it more, I was really grateful for the play. I already knew everything in it, but seeing my peers give those people support helped me make a HUGE decision I would have otherwise been scared to make.[2]
>
> (A teenager after seeing and participating in *Are We There Yet?*)

A RE WE THERE YET?[3] is a remarkable play and workshop combination, created by artists and health educators out of a sense of urgency about the need for more effective sexuality education for teens. In Canada, teens are far more likely than three decades ago to engage in sex before they finish high school; now, approximately 25 per cent of Canadians will have had sexual intercourse by the age of 16 (McKay 2000), with the majority initiating sexual intercourse between 16 and 19 (Maticka-Tyndale 1997). More to the point, increasing numbers are engaging in risky sexual intercourse, which can lead to sexually transmitted diseases, including HIV/AIDS (Moore *et al.* 1998). Adolescents with multiple sexual partners are compounding their risks because they are more likely to have had sex for the first time before the age of thirteen, and more likely to have not used a condom and to have consumed alcohol or drugs during their most recent sexual encounter.[4] Long-term repercussions caused by these choices affect physical and mental health. And all this despite the fact that youth have more information on sexual issues than ever before. While the majority of teens in North America hold values consistent with responsible, healthy sexual conduct, many are unable to translate these attitudes into positive personal behaviours (Zabin *et al.* 1984; Christopher and Cate 1984; McCabe and Killackey 2004). Further, most programs aimed specifically at reducing sexual activity are found to be ineffective (Franklin *et al.* 1997).

So what to do? *Are We There Yet?* is one answer. It is a powerful program, and this chapter will focus on some of the elements that we think are key to it going beyond the 'well meaning' and towards contributing to 'transformation'. We want to make a difference to teens' health; this is urgent.

But first, what is *Are We There Yet?* (*AWTY?*). It started as a play and workshop combination, and this remains its core. It was developed by Concrete Theatre and Planned Parenthood in Edmonton, Canada. The play, written by Jane Heather, was based in research with teens, sexuality educators and teachers; it has developed further over time with input from other theatre artists. It focuses on building teens' agency and self-efficacy around naming and communicating their sexual boundaries, overcoming barriers to talking about and using birth control for safer sex, and renegotiating boundaries. The workshop, which gives teens extensive information about methods of safer sex in addition to a chance to define and name their sexual boundaries, has also changed over time in response to teen knowledge and school conditions. Both parts of this program have an underlying message; they say without saying, 'you have the power to decide for yourself what is right for you and you can ask and expect others to respect that.'

So what is special about this play? Many plays focus on sex education, but *AWTY?* stands out on a number of counts. First, it is funny. Students arrive, rightfully suspicious, thinking that this play will be 'good for us'. They plunk down on the classroom floor. Body language says, 'what are they laying on us today?' or 'at least I am missing chemistry'. Within two minutes of starting the play, they are laughing, having fun. The play uses the metaphor of learning to drive (thus the title) to highlight sexuality and sexual decision making. People laugh, the ice is broken.

Instructor One: Lesson One: know your vehicle. What you need to know before you start the car. Mechanics and equipment.

Parent-Instructor: *uses two cartoon diagrams of the human body, one male and one female, and points to different body parts through the demonstration.* The engine (*points to heads*): the control centre, everything is routed through here including the gas pedal and the brake pedal. Signal lights (*mouth*): to signal to others when you want to slow down, stop or change direction. The windows and mirrors (*ears and eyes*): must be kept clear to hear and see incoming messages and signals. Other standard equipment includes: headlights (*breasts*), gearshift lever (*boy parts*), glove compartment (*girl parts*), and various other knobs, buttons, dials, gauges, etc., scattered through the vehicle (*whole body sweep*). Drivers should be thoroughly familiar with their own equipment before starting the car. Drivers should also become familiar with the equipment of other models.[5]

The value of entertainment – and humour is central to 'having a good time' – is too often lost in discussions of popular and educational theatre. Laughter opens people up. In this case, students leave the classroom behind for awhile, and enjoy laughing with the actors and their classmates. An embarrassing topic becomes one they can admit to finding funny. They laugh together. Defences are down – this may be 'good for them' but they'll also enjoy themselves.

Second, *AWTY?* presents characters and serious situations that students recognize. The humorous use of the driving metaphor, presented in various elevated theatrical styles, is inter-cut with realistic scenes and direct address. Characters who could be someone the audience members know grapple with situations that have, or could happen to them. Students find characters to identify with and care about.

> The play showed me that there is sexual education out there other than the standard nurse. It really was 'open' and comfortable for everyone to talk, and it was interesting to see and play out the situations.
>
> (Participant, *Are We There Yet?*)

The other key element which sets this play apart from many others in terms of making a difference in its audience's lives is its highly participatory form. *AWTY?* is an interactive play which creates meaningful dialogue about safer sex. Half of the 90-minute performance is engaged in interaction with the audience. Characters who are 'like the audience' find themselves in dilemmas relating to sexual activity, boundaries, protection and the embarrassment we experience in talking about these things. Stakes are high: Marcel and Delphi really like each other, but keep bumping into their desire for different levels of physical intimacy. They are angry and stuck. Mac and Carol Ann nearly have intercourse without protection. In the last part of the play, the audience creates two of their own characters, one male and one female; the actors are 'living clay' which the audience moulds into characters. Then their characters are set in action: they meet, date, and have sex. When one of the characters wants to renegotiate their relationship he or she avoids dealing with it. It is the audience who takes the couple through their fears, confusion, shyness, anger, and worries. They engage with the stakes; 'their clay' could lose someone important and they grapple with resistance and the other blockades to building safe and respectful situations.

Throughout the play, students strategize on behalf of the characters. They care about the characters and try to come up with things they can do to achieve what they want. The first answers are usually easy. Students suggest 'communicate,' 'be yourself,' 'just tell her,' and 'be honest'. But the characters need more help than that. For example,

> Carol Ann is told to just tell her boyfriend to use a condom. She says 'sure, ok, thanks,' and goes to do so. She goes up to him, she opens her mouth, she can't do it. She comes back to the audience.

Now the teens have to face that doing the 'right' thing is just not that easy. They recognize this, we all do. Our brains know what we should do but nevertheless we avoid, stay silent. So they move forward and tackle tougher issues.

> The audience helps Carol Ann grapple with her embarrassment, her fears that Mac won't accept this from her, the fact that they parted last night on bad terms and he is angry, all sorts of things that make 'just tell him what you want' good advice, but too hard to actually do.

Like many of us, the characters know the right answers, but nevertheless may make the 'wrong decision' – wrong for them, wrong in terms of danger to their health, and wrong for them in terms of respecting themselves. It falls to the audience to coach the characters, characters who could be them, through these land mines. Audience ideas are taken in, challenged and tested. In these interactions they get to see their ideas tried, and, of equal importance, they hear what their peers think. Dialogues amongst audience members happen through their advice to characters. Girls hear boys' points of view. Disparate values are expressed and debated. Strategies that may work in one context are challenged in the current context. They discover that what is good for one person may not work for another.

Why is all this important to the project of change, of transformation? People involved with theatre for change discuss its power to make issues personal, to reach people on emotional levels, to increase empathy and identification with characters. Greater emotional engagement creates higher stakes; audiences feel that these things matter to people they care about. So why don't we simply present plays (and films) which engage people, get them all worked up about an injustice and leave it at that? Brecht and others have helped theatre artists, educators, and activists see that while emotional engagement is a major theatrical power, we must also create opportunities for the audience to distance themselves so they can consider options, assess the situation, and think about alternatives. The play and the actor contribute here. Brecht describes the actors' work in this kind of theatre:

> . . . it is a matter of two mutually hostile processes which fuse in the actor's work; his performance is not just composed of a bit of the one and a bit of the other. His particular effectiveness comes from the tussle and tension of the two opposites, and also from their depth.
>
> (Brecht 1974: 278)

This complicated approach is certainly asked of the actors in *Are We There Yet?*. On one hand, the *character* is in need of help and advice. She turns to the audience. The character is upset, mixed up, in a crisis, wonders what to do. She receives advice. The *character* wants ideas, and urgently seeks solutions to a dilemma. The *actor* playing the character, on the other hand, wants to be sure the audience explores the issues in depth, deals with issues of sexual health. She wants to draw out audience members who have not yet spoken, mediate discussion so many voices are heard, find contrasting ideas, and hear from the males and the females. Actors are both characters and educators, simultaneously in need of receiving help from the audience (as characters) and animating the audience (as educators). As half the play is strategically improvised and new each day, this multiple theatrical position requires special preparation and a major commitment of time, in rehearsal and throughout the performance run.

There are lots of approaches to interactive theatre. It is an exciting and theatrical form, very attractive to those who are interested in using theatre for social and educational purposes. It is more democratic than more closed theatrical forms, and the performance fully engages and initiates the processes of the audience taking on new behaviours – action begins within the performance space. However, in watching and reading about many kinds of participatory theatre, I am struck with the importance of some principles that colleagues and I, through creating many interactive performances over the years, have established. These principles are grounded in trial and error. They are not always adhered to in participatory theatre performances; I think they should be if the creators are actually committed to transformation. The dramaturgical principles are simple, but deceptively so:

1   Scenes are constructed so that characters who are *like the audience* ask for help and advice. 'Like the audience' has to be defined: who is the audience? Consider age, life circumstance, race, gender, lived experience, etc. This principle builds on the understanding in popular education and community development that top down answers seldom work and seldom take into account the lived reality of participants. In *AWTY?*, teens assist teens to embrace their full selves as they sort through sexually charged dilemmas, where the brain may know what is safe, but the body and heart may not want to listen.

2   Characters are based in current, relevant community research with people like the intended audience. Actors in *AWTY?* must be immersed in local teen culture and language.

3   Characters go out to the audience after hitting a point where they do not know what to do – they have to really need assistance. If a character actually knows the right answer (and how to enact it) then the participation becomes false; it is not theatrical, and why should audience members bother to engage and help?

4   Characters ask for help in ways that are true to their character. Some ask for help directly; others engage with the audience from a position where they 'know they are right' (even if they are wrong). For example, in *AWTY?* Mac confidently tells the audience that he and his friend do not need to use a condom because neither person has had another sexual partner. In every case, the emotional life of the characters, their biases, vulnerabilities, desires, bravado and rationalizations all need exploration if audience members are to dig into the social and emotional barriers to safer sex.

5   Characters interact with the audience and test out 'good' and 'bad' ideas theatrically, with emotion and high stakes, in direct interaction with the audience and in improvised scenes where ideas are tested and considered.

There is much to say about what it takes to be a great participatory actor. However, in this project, I believe there are two key qualities, curiosity and commitment, to teens' wellbeing and growth. When *characters* have high stakes and when they really need help to sort out their dilemma, *actors* find a clear path for drawing out many ideas, asking teens to dig deeper into the easy answers, challenging cut ups to focus, and encouraging shyer, more reticent audience members to share their thoughts and insights. Need and curiosity give the interactive sequences a strong spine, energy, theatricality and a high level of contact.

Are We There Yet? is about building teenagers' transformative agency. It suggests, deeply within its structure and performance, 'you have the power to decide for yourself how to be safe, and respect yourself and others'.

> It helped me realize that people have to respect my body and boundaries.
> (Participant, *Are We There Yet?*)

But, one of the obstacles which face theatre artists and community educators who seek to use theatre to create social change is the tendency for theatre events and programming to be delivered as 'one offs'. Theatre is usually practiced as an event, a 'performance'. Even projects which focus on theatre as *process* typically occur over several weeks, culminate in a presentation and then usually the theatre and its artists move on, to another venue, another community, another issue, another project. How can we best use the power of theatre and the skills of theatre artists in education and change processes, many of which require long-term and sustained community organizing and public education?

The *Are We There Yet?* project is attempting to develop and use a model in which theatre can do what it does best – provide intensive, holistic engagement in a concentrated process and event – yet also have a sustained impact. Here is where the other part of the play–workshop combination comes into action. I have described at length how the play *AWTY?* works, but there is another key aspect to discuss. Within the play, a sexual health educator is introduced and set up as an advisor about safer sex practices. This educator is available after each performance, particularly for any students who feel the need to disclose a difficult situation they face, or to seek advice on any safe sex matter. Within a week, the audience also participates in a workshop led by the health educator who is associated with Planned Parenthood, an ongoing support and education agency which remains available as a resource to kids long after the theatre group has moved on.

In 2004, Concrete Theatre, Planned Parenthood, and Jane Heather joined with me and a variety of other stakeholders to launch a national *AWTY?* project in order to make a substantial difference to teens in a wide variety of communities. With the support of Canada's Social Science and Humanities Research Council, the AWTY community–university research alliance links artists, health educators and social scientists from across Canada who are concerned with community health and development: four theatre companies, two playwrights, three health organizations, and social science and theatre researchers from three universities form the core of this alliance. This consortium will:

1   assess and evaluate whether and how *AWTY?* helps teens develop and improve sexual decision making;
2   create new, culturally appropriate versions of the play for rural, urban and Aboriginal communities across Canada;
3   encourage and assist others to use and benefit from *AWTY?*, nationally and internationally;
4   investigate, demonstrate, assess and disseminate information about the strengths and value of using theatre in community and educational programming;
5   contribute to prevention science; and
6   develop, assess and promote culturally and socially effective community partnerships and mobilization models.

Community partners joined the alliance from a variety of sectors, believing that this alliance could make a difference in their communities. For example, Saskatchewan Native Theatre Company and Native Counselling Services of Alberta are working with *AWTY?* to create culturally specific and appropriate interventions in their Aboriginal communities. 'There is a need to unlearn self-destructive and unhealthy behaviour, learned from school, society and parents, and to deal in healing ways with the legacy of residential schools.'[6] neworld Theatre Company wants to explore ways to reach some of Vancouver's culturally diverse teens, and Nova Scotia's Mulgrave Road Theatre and Guysborough Youth Health and Services Centre see the need for substantial adaptations in order to effectively reach youth in their rural communities.

In moving *AWTY?* away from its original community it is vital that we maintain all of the elements which build identification for the audience. Recognition and authenticity are key to teens' engagement with the stakes of the characters and the connections they make with the play. The more they believe that they and their peers are advising 'someone like me' the more impact the play will have on what they take forward into their own lives. So, how do we keep identification high yet share a great project? In the field of popular theatre, and often in the name of reflecting the local, projects run their course and are not heard of again; we hope that this one will transform and alter to sustain its strengths while maintaining the original commitment to reflecting teens with specificity and respect. As the project moves to other centres and cultures, we are committed to a full process of adaptation which is grounded in participatory, community-based research.

I write from the middle of these journeys, with many discoveries and decisions yet to come. However, a few ideas have emerged already from the work with partners from varying communities. For example, in the adaptation process with Saskatchewan Native Theatre we have found, surprisingly, that only a few character stories need revision; these are key, and authenticate the characters. Beyond that, however, the rhythm and cultural expression is primarily held in the Aboriginal actors' characterizations and vocal nuance. What will change significantly are the back stories of the characters; these emerge within the unscripted participation, and it is vital that the Aboriginal actors develop histories which can embrace both reserve and urban Aboriginal teen experience.

While the fixed script will alter only slightly, two significant changes did emerge from this collaboration. Both involve adaptations of the program model itself. As mentioned, the original version has a play and workshop for teens, both delivered in schools via a partnership between a theatre company and sexual health organization. To date, it appears that the Aboriginal version will work with a variety of locally based health organizations rather than one. These will work in association with an elder and a health worker who is hired and trained specifically for the theatrical tour. This adaptation speaks to the apparent lack of a consistent health system which serves Saskatchewan Aboriginal communities as well as the key role an elder plays in the theatre company's activities. In addition, community leaders have proposed that a community meeting which includes interactive scenes aimed at parents and elders be added for reserve and isolated community settings so that the wider community is alerted, included and encouraged to support its teenagers.

The rural Nova Scotia adaptation will also require outreach and training for local health nurses and educators in a way that has not been necessary in urban Alberta. The goal is to build resources, knowledge and supports for teens within each community. So, while we entered into the adaptation processes thinking that the script may change quite substantially, and it may yet in some of the adaptations, to date we are finding that the program model needs considerable revision, while the play will be most transformed by engaging, preparing and training the local actors in the form of improvised participation which the script initiates. It is in all of these levels of participation that the specificity and ownership will reside.

Transformation. Change. How do we know if it happens? Often in this field of theatre for change we work on faith. We have faith in the power of theatre. Faith in participatory research and theatre creation. Faith in community knowledge. We know some things work, or believe we do. We 'prove it' through meaningful anecdotes of reaction to the theatre work. We believe it because we observe people who are moved, angry, determined, and eloquent as a result of a theatre project. We write evaluation reports justifying our existence, and the costs. With *Are We There Yet?* we make testimonials, and tell stories from teachers and students and actors. We see the impact with our own eyes; students start cool and wary; soon the huge majority are leaning forward, calling advice to a character, or later in the play, clustered around a character giving her or him vital advice about handling a difficult crisis.

This community–university alliance will add to these important, impressionistic beliefs about the power of theatre. Artists and educators are collaborating with qualitative and quantitative researchers from the social sciences to evaluate the impact of the play. How to do this well is key to this alliance's work, and while initial findings show that some significant change is occurring for some groups of teens, we have much to learn yet about how to assess the impact of theatre-based programs. For applied theatre to continue to be supported, we believe that we should contribute to the field's still nascent capacity to demonstrate its impact and effectiveness. The social dollar, no matter where we are and what issue we are tackling, gets harder to come by, and foundations, governments, NGOs and education systems, however much they may wish to support this work, will only continue to do so if we can demonstrate, as richly as possible, that theatre of this kind is indeed transformative.

Bibliography

Brecht, B. (1974) *Brecht on Brecht* (trans. and ed. J. Willet), London: Methuen.

Calzavara, L.M., Bullock, S.L., Marshall, V.W. and Cockerill, R. (1999) 'Sexual Partnering and Risk of HIV/STD among Aboriginals', *Canadian Journal of Public Health* 90: 186–91.

Christoper, F. and Cate, R. (1984) 'Factors Involved in Premarital Sexual Decision-making', *Journal of Sex Research* 26: 363–76.

Franklin, C., Grant, D., Corcoran, J., Miller, P. and Bultman, L. (1997) 'Effectiveness of Prevention Programs for Adolescent Pregnancy: A Meta-analysis', *Journal of Marriage and the Family* 59: 551–67.

Health Canada (1996) *Towards a Common Understanding: Clarifying the Core Concepts of Population Health, a Discussion Paper.* Ottawa: Health Canada.

Heather, J. (1998) *Are We There Yet?* An interactive play, available at www.ualberta.ca/awty/theatre (revised 2006).

McCabe, M. and Killackey, E. (2004) 'Sexual Decision Making in Young Women', *Sexual and Relationship Therapy* 19: 15–28.

McKay, A. (2000) 'Common Questions about Sexual Health Education', *The Canadian Journal of Human Sexuality* 9 (2): 129–37.

Maticka-Tyndale, E. (1997) 'Reducing the Incidence of Sexually Transmitted Disease through Behavioral and Social Change', *Canadian Journal of Human Sexuality*, 6 (2): 123–32.

Moore, K.A., Manlove, J. and Glei, D.A. (1998) 'Nonmarital School-age Motherhood: Family, Individual and School Characteristics', *Journal of Adolescent Research* 13 (4): 433–57.

Waldram, J.B., Herring, D.A. and Young, T.K. (1995) *Aboriginal Health in Canada: Historical, Cultural, and Epidemiological Perspectives.* Toronto: University of Toronto Press.

Zabin, L., Hirsch, M., Smith, E. and Hardy, J. (1984) 'Adolescent Sexual Attitudes and Behavior: Are they Consistent?', *Family Planning Perspectives* 16: 181–85.

Notes

1   The author recognizes the contributions of all *Are We There Yet? Community–University Research Alliance* partners to this chapter, in particular Shaniff Esmail, Brenda Munro, Jim Ponzetti, the playwright Jane Heather, Anne Bailey, and two graduate students, Elizabeth Ludwig and Cortney Lohnes. See our website: www.ualberta.ca/awty.

2   Quotes by participants are taken from transcriptions of one-to-one interviews conducted by Dr Shaniff Esmail, a member of the AWTY CURA, May 2006.

3   Information about how to access the interactive play *Are We There Yet?*, by Jane Heather, can be found at www.ualberta.ca/awty/theatre.

4   *Canadian Association for Adolescent Health.*

5   J. Heather, *Are We There Yet?*, unpublished play script, 2006 performed version, p 5. Contact awty@ualberta.ca for script information.

6   Donna Heimbecker, interview with Jane Heather and Jan Selman, June 2004.

Chapter 47

Anna Herrmann

'THE MOTHERSHIP'
Sustainability and transformation in the work of Clean Break

WHEN WOMEN FIRST ATTEND Clean Break we ask them to think about what a clean break means for them in their lives. Unsurprisingly, the list is long; women talk of wanting a new beginning, safety, a space free from drugs and alcohol, where they feel free to express themselves, where they are understood, a second chance, an open door, a place to learn, a non-judgemental space, new opportunities, a sense of belonging, and so on. Each time we ask this question with a new group the women articulate a vision for themselves and for their futures which is fuelled by a huge amount of hope and optimism rising out of past experiences of failure and disappointment. The fear of repeating past cycles is an unspoken presence. We set ourselves the challenge to support their desired transformation.

In this chapter I offer an insight into what takes place at Clean Break which enables women to realise and sustain these ambitions. I have focused on the journeys of five women who have made and sustained positive changes in their lives. Importantly, I want their voices to emerge in this chapter; women's lack of representation and lack of opportunity for voice contributes significantly to their continuing marginalisation within the criminal justice system.

Prison theatre?

It is liberating to be able to contribute to a chapter without having to define our contribution as prison theatre.[1] Although Clean Break is firmly rooted within the criminal justice system, having been founded by two women prisoners in 1979, much of our current work takes place with women in the community. Some of the women are serving prisoners on day release, some have been in prison, some are or have been on probation and others are defined 'at risk' of offending because of mental health needs and/or drug and alcohol use. All of the women come together to participate as students in our arts education and training programme which is run from our purpose-built studios in Kentish Town, north London. This is clearly not prison theatre. Perhaps it is more community theatre, although the focus on learning and skills could make it better placed in the world of educational theatre. In a similar way in which the women we work with talk of the disabling effect of labels on their lives, Clean Break has also found labels of theatre practice limiting.

An overview of Clean Break

Clean Break's work comprises two distinct but complementary arms; one which produces theatre to tell the stories of women's experience of crime (the annual production), and the other which works with the women themselves to provide opportunities for expression, personal growth and professional development (the education and training programme). The annual production involves the commissioning of an established female playwright to research issues facing women offenders and to run playwriting workshops in a women's prison over a period of a few months. Following this experience, she writes a play which the company dramaturges, produces and then tours nationally to women's prisons and theatres (including the Arcola in London, York Theatre Royal, Birmingham Rep, Traverse in Edinburgh). Past plays have examined issues ranging from foreign national drug mules (by Winsome Pinnock, 1996), young women and crime (by Rebecca Prichard, co-produced with Royal Court, 1998) and coping with life on release (by Tanika Gupta, 2002). This strand of the company's work fulfils an aspect of our mission which is to challenge audiences about perspectives of women and crime. In order to do this, we place women's experience centre stage and draw from the professional world of female writers, directors, actors and designers to write, produce and perform the work.

The education and training programme fulfils another aspect of the Company's mission which is founded in the belief that theatre and the arts are powerful tools for the personal, social, professional and creative development of women with experience of the criminal justice system. This work is far more rooted in an intention for participation and empowerment. There is a tension within the company of whether the goals of empowerment would be better achieved if the annual production was written and performed by women with experience of the criminal justice system themselves. Whilst this tension is challenging, addressing it is a vital part of keeping our practice healthy and alive, especially for a company which is twenty-eight years old. It has been a driving force behind a number of newer initiatives including the fast-tracking of students into auditions for the annual production and a forthcoming tour by ex-students which assist the company in moving forward and exploring new models and ways of working. We are striving towards a dynamic exchange and interrelationship between the two strands of the Company's work, and this ambition gives us direction and challenge.

Education and training

Established in the early 1990s, the education and training programme has grown, matured and adapted to meet the diverse interests of the women we work with and the changing expectations of the world we live in. What has remained constant throughout is the provision of a women-only space where women are not judged but are valued and appreciated whilst encouraged to make the changes they are striving to make in their lives. Underpinned by this culture of respect, a belief which is carried by every member of staff, women are able to take risks, participating in a range of writing and performance-based courses as well as self development, anger management, literacy and life-skills training. Many women come with no theatre experience, perhaps just to pass the time or to create a much needed routine and structure in their lives following release from prison or drug rehabilitation. Here, they can gain skills and qualifications whilst receiving emotional support, advice and guidance on a one-to-one basis, provided by our student support service. Progression on to University, following completion of the year-long Access to Higher Education Course (accredited by Open College Network), or work experience through TAPS (The Arts Placement Scheme) are two of the formal routes for women beyond Clean Break. The provision of financial support in the form of travel expenses, contributions for food and child care is a significant factor in attracting the seventy women who come to us each year, aged from 18–60 years. It removes the acute financial barriers which can stand in the way of women accessing opportunities elsewhere. Women are recruited through referrals from prisons, probation, bail hostels, drug and alcohol centres and other community settings. Extensive partnership working with these agencies as well as outreach visits from our staff who go to talk to women, run drama workshops and begin the process of listening and engagement precedes a woman's decision to enrol.

What works?

Each of the five women I interviewed for this chapter first came into contact with Clean Break between six to eight years ago. Two women, Nadine and Diane,[2] are currently employed part time, one running drama workshops, and the other as a drugs worker. Jess is in her third year at University, Sandra has completed her University degree and has since set up her own company, and Edith is volunteering in a range of different settings with vulnerable adults. Each one attributes a significant aspect of their personal transformation to the intervention of Clean Break. So, what in their view were the key contributing factors?

It was good to know that a theatre existed for people like me

For four of the five women, the initial motivation for coming to Clean Break was the chance to participate in theatre. This was because theatre had been an unexplored passion and interest of theirs in their childhood or because they saw it as something accessible and fun to try out. More specifically, they were attracted to it because it was theatre exclusively for women ex-offenders. It interested me that this was so significant for each woman, as there is a flip side to this exclusivity, about whether it further reinforces the 'ex-offender' label society places on the women. For a woman to say she has studied at Clean Break she immediately discloses something of her past, which she may well want to keep private in a prejudiced world. Some women have chosen not to put Clean Break on their CVs for this very reason. There is a concern that 'Clean Break' as a label itself could do women a disservice as they strive to re-integrate into mainstream society. However, for these five women and others like them, it was clear that being exclusive was a compelling aspect of Clean Break not only because it gave them an entitlement to participate in theatre but more importantly it automatically implied that the space would be safe.

It was a safe-haven. We understood each other

This safety was cited in all the interviews as a major contributor to why women benefited from Clean Break. For three of the women, the safe space was rooted in the knowledge that all participants had similar past experiences and personal issues to deal with. This meant they didn't worry about being judged and there was an unspoken sense of equality in the group and of being understood by the others. Sandra described this as being 'evident in the atmosphere'. Nadine and Jess said it felt 'safe to be broken' at Clean Break; there was no need to hide behind a mask – they could be themselves. Diane spoke of 'warmth and acceptance – I didn't feel alone – the only one – I felt understood here.' For Sandra the women-only nature of the space supported this feeling of safety, but she says she would still have come to Clean Break had it been mixed. For the four other women interviewed, the women-only space was at the heart of feeling safe. Diane and Edith both talked about their negative past experiences of violent relationships and abuse which led them to distrust men.[3] For Edith, she was emphatic that when she first came along to Clean Break she did not feel confident enough to be herself in front of men and felt the women-only space helped her to build her confidence and self esteem. Diane talked of 'getting strength from being here, being able to be me'. Jess described it as 'a feminine fraternity, a place of empowerment. You can see women more clearly here, not through the eyes of men.' This expressed need for women-only provision is not often heeded within the criminal justice system. Making up only 6 per cent of the prison population, women offenders are often recipients of services without specialist design or delivery to best meet their needs.

I felt powerful performing my own poetry

Within this safe space, each woman spoke of the importance of being able to create a new identity, an identity to be proud of, built on achievement and success. For many of them it was the first time they started to feel worth something. Sandra said 'on release from prison, coming to Clean Break I was able to build my new identity. The drama enabled me to express myself, improve my self esteem and rebuild myself.' Edith acknowledged the role of performance in affirming her new identity, providing her with reward and encouragement to progress further in this direction.

At Clean Break most courses culminate in a performance, either to staff and students, or to a wider audience. The audience recognises the huge achievement that is made for each performer and genuinely delights in affirming this. Being recipients of applause can have a powerful effect on women who may not believe that they are worth anything.

> You are not good enough in the world, and at Clean Break you are always good enough. Without that you would not be able to move on

or take the next step. You would give up. It is very important to encourage the next step.

Jess

However, performing can also be very stressful and for some women, particularly those who experience mental distress, this can be detrimental to their wellbeing. Our challenge is to strike the right balance between creating performance opportunities yet ensuring that individuals progress at the level that is right for them. This demands a high degree of flexibility which is not always possible within the structures of an accredited course.

I have no intention of going back to crime, drugs and drink

For many women their new and positive sense of identity is an identity free from crime or drug use. Jess directly attributed being allowed to excel and achieve as the key to her not returning to crime. Edith felt that Clean Break has shown her own potential that she never recognised before: 'For rehabilitation of offenders, prison doesn't work. There is not enough fresh air in prisons to allow minds to breathe.' All the women commented that they have not re-offended since coming to Clean Break. As Nadine reflected:

> I have changed in leaps and bounds. I don't do things that hinder me anymore. That is amazing in itself. It is like there have been two of me; part one and part two. Part two is where I am at now, and it challenges the negative thoughts I still get. For example if you are that bad how can you come away from crime, finish a course? I have created a history that I am proud of.

Outcomes such as new-found confidence, self expression, raised aspirations, new skills, and team work form part of our understanding of the benefits of making theatre in these settings. However, less is known about how or whether these outcomes are sustained in years to come. The question remains; what are the requirements to sustain long-term change?

Moving on

My journey has been hard and slow

Each woman commented on how their journey of transformation had been complex and lengthy. Two out of the five women had experienced further trauma and breakdown since their initial contact with Clean Break, which had led to them withdrawing from courses and retreating into despair. What was particularly significant for them was having the opportunity to come back. Diane spoke of how she felt on coming out of hospital:

> I had thought that doors would be closed when I left hospital. I had deep feelings of undeservedness and failure. I didn't think I would get

another chance. I felt really welcomed coming back. I didn't feel judged. Like coming back to the mothership I felt nurtured, safe and protected. It is comforting to know that Clean Break is here – the consistency is really important. I really need to know it is still here.

This sentiment was echoed by each woman for different reasons and the term 'mothership' was used independently in a number of interviews to summarise how they perceived Clean Break. Jess said she felt loyal to Clean Break, knowing that Clean Break had been loyal to her. Sandra spoke of how positive she felt knowing that she has a good relationship with the organisation and that the feeling was mutual. The belief that Clean Break is there unconditionally was of central importance for the women, some of whom have never known unconditional love and acceptance. The fear of rejection was voiced by a few of the women and the realisation that they were able to return was pinpointed as a significant moment of change.

Coming from a background where you never got anything for nothing, you think you are going to get to a point when you are going to be told 'we've got no more cake', but that hasn't happened. I've not been shamed by anyone for asking for more.

Nadine

The importance of reciprocal relationships in assisting women to desist from crime is supported by an early study by Mary Eaton (1993). She interviewed thirty-four female ex-prisoners who had managed to transform their lives, and surmised that housing, employment and health facilities although vital were on their own insufficient. She concluded that women offenders need to feel that they are people of worth who have something to contribute, and the key to this recognition is reciprocal relationships. As Jess says, 'At first you join Clean Break then you become part of what Clean Break is.'

Enabling women to come back over a period of years and to have ownership of their own journeys of rehabilitation, rather than expecting them to fit into what society views as an acceptable pathway, is an important principle at Clean Break. All the women interviewed spoke of the time it has taken them to arrive at a point where they have turned their lives around. Edith said that she had been in the depths of despair for twenty years, so how could she be healed overnight? There was a sense that building a relationship and investing in someone takes time and that this might mean five to ten years.

The transformation has been very slow and very real. It is a commitment I have had to make to myself to live and try to be a part of society. To explore, to take risks, to grow, to change, to help other people. It's been a rewarding journey. I have put a huge amount of work in and I couldn't have done it alone. I have turned my life around and Clean Break has been instrumental in that.

Diane

For Nadine, the very fact of knowing that the door is always open has enabled her to go off and do other things:

> I come back to Clean Break because I have a sense of belonging here
> . . . It is so important to come back. We all need places we can come
> back to, where we are seen. Clean Break sees each woman.

There are drawbacks to this 'open door' policy. As Nadine asked, 'why wouldn't you want to be here?' The creation of a safe, supportive and nurturing environment can make the outside world less appealing and exacerbate the difficulty for women to move on. There is a tension between long-term accessibility and independence which we are seeking to nurture in the women. In light of this, although women can always come back, our courses are time-limited, rather than continuous, with a natural two-year cycle at the end of which we hope many women will be ready to move on. However, the reality is that for some women even small gaps between the courses can be problematic and they feel the classes should be ongoing. Also, some women are not ready to move on and have not yet built up the necessary skills to be able to do so.

> For those, like me, who don't want to go to University where do you
> tell them to go? Go get a job? I don't think so. Come and work here?
> Not easily. I didn't feel employable when I first left. I could get any old
> job but I wanted to follow my dreams. The rest of the world isn't like
> Clean Break.
>
> Nadine

Our arts work placement scheme was set up in 2003 in direct response to comments like Nadine's, as well as to the external environment which has placed increasing importance on moving women into employment as a measure of success. The possibility of dependency is heartfelt by the women I spoke to:

> A few years back, I was probably quite dependent – I felt like a small
> child. I needed to come for affirmation, protection and care. I am learning
> to give it to myself now.
>
> Diane

Limiting dependency is a key reason why we do not offer ongoing counselling onsite but refer women to other organisations who can provide this elsewhere, building up women's network of resources and support systems outside of Clean Break. Although we have made improvements in preparing women to leave Clean Break there is still a considerable way to go to assist this transition.

To be able to give something back has been a joy and a privilege

Another recurring theme for all the women was about giving back. The changed role from receiver to giver was seen unanimously as having a major part to play in their journey. Coming back and talking to new students or being an Ambassador for the Company has rewarded the women with heightened feelings of fulfilment and self worth. As Diane described 'It is important to feel that I am contributing something now. Before, I was on the receiving end. [There] comes a time when you want to give back.' Edith spoke of wanting to be a role model and inspiration for others. 'It is very important for me to be able to give back. I am living walking proof that you can survive the system. It's the final part of the healing process.'

These five women tell powerful stories of success, built on belonging to a place which feels safe and non-judgemental, where they learnt to trust, to give and receive support, and where they could redefine themselves as students and artists. Their journeys have not been straightforward but lengthy and difficult, and have demanded a huge amount of strength and risk-taking on their behalf. At Clean Break we can learn a lot from their journeys, learn how to better prepare women, avoid the pitfalls of a dependency culture and provide skills that are suited to the real world. There are many other women who are part way through their journey with the support of Clean Break and many more who do not have access to these opportunities at all. We must continue to be there for generations of women to come to celebrate more successes and to make sure that the door continues to stay open.

References

Eaton, M. (1993) *Women After Prison*, Milton Keynes: Open University Press.

Notes

1   There is a significant body of work which falls under the category of prison theatre, including theatre for prison audiences, theatre devised and performed by prisoners and theatre workshops. A wealth of companies specialise in working within prisons and meeting artistic, rehabilitative and educational goals through their work.
2   Names have been changed to respect the anonymity of the women interviewed.
3   Over half of women in prison have suffered domestic violence and one in three has been sexually abused (Smart Justice for Women Campaign, 2007, www.smartjustice. org/indexwomen.html).

Chapter 48

Liselle Terret

WHO'S GOT THE POWER?
Performance and self advocacy for people with learning disabilities, London

THIS CHAPTER BRINGS TOGETHER THE reflective voices of three people who worked together for a period of eight months within the context of a newly formed drama group in South East London. The group was self-initiated, by the members of a (leisure) service-provider for young people and adults with learning disabilities, primarily run by a committee consisting of parents of the young people and adults with learning disabilities. The drama group consisted of twelve people between fifteen and thirty years of age (approximately). Following an interview with the groups' key worker, notably, without the actual members being present, I was invited to work with the group.

From October 2005 until May 2006 we staged two very different performances in two very different spaces, however, there were important similarities in terms of intention, ethos and process.

The first production, entitled *Who Stole the Beautiful Octopus?*, was performed at a popular arts venue in South East London in December 2005, as part of Heart 'n' Soul's live performance/night club called The Beautiful Octopus Club. Heart 'n' Soul is one of the UK's leading musical theatre companies run by and for people with learning disabilities.[1] In May 2006, a second production was created called *Who's Got The Power?* and was performed as part of the organisation's annual general meeting. Guests to this performance included the Mayor of the borough, representatives from social services and care services, parents and other members of this service-provider organisation.

Two key voices in this chapter are Ian David Roberts and Emma Selwyn, who were two of the twelve collaborators and performers involved in the project. My voice represents the perspective of the drama facilitator. I conducted and documented several discussions with Ian and Emma with the intention for each of us to reflect on our experiences. Through consultation with Ian and Emma I have structured and edited their responses (and mine) into the material that follows which forms the basis of the six key questions that were asked.

How did we work as a group?

Liselle: My approach was informed by a self-advocacy model, based on People First, a national organisation founded in 1984 as People First London Borough (Buchanan and Walmsley 2006). It is a self-advocacy organisation led by people with learning disabilities with the overall aim to enable people with learning disabilities to have choice and control over their own lives. I wanted to work collaboratively with the participants to ensure that they had a genuine ownership of the intention, process and outcome of the project. In order for this to happen it was important to establish methods of communication that embraced the different ways that the participants interacted and communicated (which proved to be crucial in providing a clear and sturdy foundation for the devising process). We had to make sure that our working methodology would enable everyone to find a 'hook-in' for themselves.

Emma: We had creative freedom and choice. The facilitator used simple language but never patronising and was part of the group as much as we were. There was independence because we weren't ordered about, because that's what people get all the time.

Ian: I felt on an equal level, something I don't often feel outside of the group.

The first production – *Who Stole the Beautiful Octopus?*

Performed December 2005 as part of The Beautiful Octopus Club (Heart 'n' Soul).

What was the play about?

Ian: It was a dark musical comedy play that was set in a nightclub where we all played famous comedy TV characters. I played Johnny Vegas who owns the nightclub and he has a pet octopus that lives in a very small cage in his office. One day, the janitor Seymour secretly lets the octopus free.

Emma: Johnny Vegas then hires Pet-Detective Ace Ventura and he takes everyone on a musical dancing journey to find the octopus. Each of the characters represented different people, but could also represent the different sides to one person as well. For example, Stan Laurel represented how people can be very nervous and confused and have their own innate sense of humour; Johnny Vegas had power, Seymour was bullied, Ace Ventura was resourceful, Bart Simpson (the club bouncer) was calm and chilled, Janet Jackson helped to hide the octopus, and the pink octopus represented freedom.

Ian: I chose Johnny Vegas because I think people who act like him in front of the public eye have lots of guts.

Liselle: There were many layers to the play and each was told through a different medium; dance, song, music, slapstick comedy, large photographic images projected behind the performers of the famous characters they were portraying, and a brief step-by-step outline of the story as it developed through words and symbols.

What did we want to say?

Emma: For me the play was saying don't trap us, give us the opportunity to speak and to have freedom but at the same time protect us when necessary.

Ian: It's about when people become awake and aware they become quite frightened, but it can make them stronger. If you try to hide and move away from frightening situations then it's more dangerous for you because you will be less cautious and let people be not good to you.

Liselle: For me it was a story about being trapped by someone with power, and this is then juxtaposed with the idea of being able to not just survive in that situation but change it. It was also about the responsibility of others. In addition to this, the actual staging of this performance was also about celebrating equal opportunity by the mere fact that this production was watched by over 500 people with learning disabilities.

Who was it for?

Emma: The audience were lots of people with learning disabilities at the nightclub, and judging by the audience's reactions, there were lots of people laughing, clapping and cheering throughout the play.

Ian: It was something very different for the audience at The Beautiful Octopus Club to see. A lot of plays I have watched are about standing up for yourself, and I think that we wanted to put something comical but with a serious message underneath into it. If we just had the fear and dark without the comedy then the audience might be scared, but if it is a dark comedy play, then they will be less scared and they will want to see it.

How we made the performance

Liselle: During the first several weeks it was essential to establish a strong foundation for the devising process. We achieved this through participant-led drama games and exercises as well as exploring what type of performance the participants wanted to create, and indeed what they wanted to say through their performance. I brought in questions that we used as a basis to stimulate material for devising. The group were adamant that they did not want to create a serious piece about their lives as people with learning disabilities. They were interested in comedy and wanted to use humour, dance and song to perform a story.

Ian: We were asked to bring in something that we found funny and something that made us angry. I said that when people stand too close to me and shout at me that makes me angry; another person in the group said that he knows someone is being bullied at his school and that makes him angry. But we wanted to concentrate on what made us laugh. Most of the group brought in our favourite funny TV characters and decided to be those characters. It worked because no-one was telling us who to be. I liked it because the characters we played were funny; they were a little bit eccentric. We made the story to fit the characters' personalities.

Liselle: We took the concept of the actual nightclub where the play would be performed (The Beautiful Octopus Club) and created a storyline about the fictitious characters who worked for and ran the nightclub using the comedy characters and celebrities brought in by the participants.

Ian: The character I played was Johnny Vegas. He could be a little rude and cheeky sometimes, and sometimes when I feel like being cheeky to people I feel like I'm having a Johnny Vegas. I'm probably the opposite of Johnny Vegas but I try to imagine if I was him how I would pull him off. If Les Dawson was a little younger and still alive, I would choose to be him but it was important that Johnny Vegas is alive as he comes on TV a little more so I can observe him.

We rehearsed, analysed and discussed things, balanced them out and negotiated them. We didn't not do people's ideas [sic]; we just made more different ideas rather than getting rid of some. If someone forgot their lines, then someone else could ad-lib and step in and improvise to help the person out. I took my ideas forward that were the basis for the play. I felt respected.

What did we get out of making the play?

Ian: The production let me show a little bit of myself that other people wouldn't normally see. I wouldn't normally be allowed to make those jokes in front of people if I wasn't on stage because I don't think people would understand them. Someone would say not to do it but if you are on stage then you are appreciated.

Emma: There was an escapism from real life because although real life is good most of the time, there are problems sometimes as well, people need to retreat to their own world – it depends on the person though.

The second production – *Who's Got the Power?*

Performed in May 2006 at the organisation's annual general meeting.

What was this play about?

Liselle: The play took the form of a montage of short stories told through sound and wordscapes; live song, dance, dialogue, narration, visual images and words projected behind the actors onto a large screen. The overall performance raised the question, *Who's Got The Power* within these young people's lives? Within the performance there were two scenes where the protagonist in each experienced a loss of power. We used an adaptation of Augusto Boal's Forum Theatre to explore various options that the protagonist could use in order to overcome the misuse of power that they were experiencing.

Ian: We took off the comedy mask to show what was underneath in a serious piece which was about letting people speak out.

Emma: It was about asserting yourself, and having a voice. It showed different stories about solving problems, but also about things that are important to us, and ultimately about having power.

What did we want to say?

Emma: We wanted to say to these important people who have more privileges in life usually, that sometimes they need reminding that not everyone is as fortunate as them, although everybody can be fortunate if given the chance to speak out about what they want and need. I think the play showed sides of us that people don't want to normally see. A lot of people in the group find it hard to talk about their feelings, for example when you get stressed, you get a feeling inside of you and I think that everyone can only hold so much feeling and after a while they need to let it out. I wanted to say, accept us all for who we are, and myself as an individual with special needs and for people to be more tolerant please.

Ian: The short plays were about speaking up for yourself. We also decided to perform our inner characters. Mine was fire and explosive. Our inner characters are parts of us that other people never see. We also performed what we would do if we ruled the world.

Who was Who's Got The Power? for?

Liselle: The audience consisted of the Mayor of this London borough, residential care managers and other people who work in the care services, and other people with learning disabilities and their parents. When I suggested to the group's key-worker that perhaps the group might want to use this as an opportunity to use performance to raise some key issues and concerns, I was gently informed 'Don't be too political'. When I put this suggestion to the group, their answer was that they wanted to make a play that showed the audience things about themselves that they might not know about; which then led to the creation of Who's Got The Power?.

Emma: We made it especially for the AGM because we wanted to show them that given the chance special needs people have more of a voice than they originally think – as they are quite prone to being excluded.

Ian: It was important for the audience who watched it because they could see what those people go through everyday. People don't see what goes on in care homes and they only see the nice bits when they get welcomed into the house. It was important for me to perform in it because I wanted to have the power. I could see the audience engaged in the performance, and some of the clients could probably picture themselves in that situation and that could help them. It could show the parents and committee that we can express ourselves and our experiences.

How we made this performance

Emma: We discussed things we did and didn't like and how we would like things to be. We did this through games and role plays. We brought in ideas that we thought made our lives better. We didn't have to speak out necessarily as the person we are in real life. It's easier saying what you want or need to say as someone else because people who know the real you, have decided already what they think the real you is, and not all of them will take your real view seriously as their real view [sic]. I think we did it by giving the ones that did hold back a push, and they weren't ever actually told what to say.

Liselle: I tried to ensure that the outside-directing-eye was shared and negotiated with the group. I achieved this by structuring in time for us to critically reflect upon our choices, ask questions and ultimately make group decisions about the devising process and the blocking of the play. We had some new members in the group with more severe learning disabilities who communicated mainly through gesture and sound rather than through the spoken word. I remember some of the participants actually saying that they had spent most of their lives learning to 'know-their-place' and to only talk when told. Other participants said that they had learned to be silent and that it was less confrontational to just say yes. Therefore ethically speaking, a self-advocacy model had to be our guiding principle.

What did we get out of making the play?

Ian: I played the nasty carer. It let me release a lot of bad feelings I have that I didn't like towards the carers in my house. I felt I wanted to strangle them but you can't do that, and the play looked at different ways of standing up for yourself. One particular carer kept coming into my room without knocking and I tried to tell him to go away. He had army instincts in him. I think he probably reckoned I needed the discipline which I got quite annoyed about. The danger is I become weaker as a person if I don't react to it in any way. We wanted to say that those carers like that should not work in care homes and that also that people should have the right to speak up for themselves. Putting this on stage meant I could express how I was feeling. I wanted to get my own back on people, how they had upset me personally.

Liselle: In *Foucault and the Government of Disability* (2005) Scott Yates examines the forms of power that operate in community care accommodation. The author researched how people experience this power and how they understand themselves as subjects in relation to it and how these power relationships are institutionalised and normalised. He also interviewed several people with learning disabilities who lived in care accommodation who had similar experiences like Ian's:

> Anne: '. . . if you want anything, you have to ask for it . . .'
> Paul: '. . . The managers don't like you to speak your mind . . . you have to fight for what you believe . . . you're just a bad boy . . . because you're not being quiet . . . You're supposed to take what they give you, and not say no. We've got a voice, we should be able to use it.'
> SY: 'Do people listen to you?'
> Paul: 'No, they don't listen'.

> (Yates 2005: 72–3)

Yates analyses the interviewee's responses to his questions and points out that both Anne and Paul use the pronoun *you* when they talk about their experiences of living in the residential care and the rules that are imposed on them. They both seem to be very aware of the injustice that they experience daily, however they also seem to say that there seems nothing much they can do about it.

What we got out of being part of the drama group

Emma: I gained more confidence in myself and with others, and an ability to empathise with the others in the group. Everyone was treated like equals and it gave everyone a way of voicing their feelings without having to worry about rejection and having their opinion valued because everyone was important in the group regardless of what they did, like there was not really just one star role. In traditional plays they have a leading character and a definite hierarchy and in this one, to be honest, there were a fair few people that don't consider themselves that highly anyway, and the fact that there was no star meant it wasn't that one person was getting special treatment and the others were lower down, they weren't like the spare strings for a guitar.

Ian: It was really important for me to be involved in the project because it got me involved in things I wouldn't normally do. It makes me assert myself better and to speak up. We had to use our imaginations all the time which is a good thing.

Emma: I also learnt that people are more likely to listen to what you are saying and understand what you are saying if you perform it through drama, art, song or dance, than if you just say it. I think that humanity needs to grab onto as much as they can to enable their understanding.

Liselle: I became more aware of the multifaceted role of the facilitator and specifically the level of power instilled in this role. I still believe ethically the facilitator/director must de-mystify this role and indeed find accessible, creative and collaborative ways to hand-over this power to the participants; ways that are guided by a self-advocacy model. In order for this to happen, the facilitator needs to ensure that there are structures which are integral to the process that enable participants to have choice, and to gain the skills and insight needed to create performance. One of the key ways of achieving this is to rely on the participants' own judgements and choices.

The future

Emma: [If the project were to continue] I would like the project to use the same formulae; everyone having the opportunity to speak up and perform at the same time. I would like there to be places all around South East London where people came to do workshops as well. The aim of it would be an opportunity for people with learning disabilities to voice their opinions and thoughts on life through a creative medium. I also think dance and song are all expressive too, some messages might come across through dance, and through dance you wouldn't have to worry about dialogue, and those with communication difficulties would have a real voice through their bodies to give people a better understanding of themselves and what they go through.

Liselle: Following the success of these two performances, we had to move venue and change the day of the weekly sessions which meant that some of the original members could no longer attend. We were then told by the committee that we should make a musical play that would be performed at the next annual event for committee members and their families. I was aware that I felt uncomfortable with being told to do this, feeling as if we were perhaps owned by the committee. I started to become aware of a divide between the ethos of the drama group that we had developed over the past eight months, to that of the ethos of the committee, which seemed to see the group as more of a show-case opportunity for the organisation. I wanted to create more of a bridge between the participants in the group and the committee so that the actual members could vocalise how they wanted the group to develop. I tried to instigate a meeting to discuss the long-term aims however; unfortunately, a three-way conversation was never able to happen. I started to feel that my belief in a self-advocacy approach was being really challenged and unacknowledged. It was at this point that I made the decision to resign as I felt I could not and did not want to be accountable to the committee. I wanted, rather, to be accountable to the members of the drama group.

Aftermath

Following the interviews with both Ian and Emma they each commented that they had gained a great deal from revisiting, discussing and reflecting upon their own experiences as participants in the project. They felt that having this reflective time following the project was just as important as it was being part of the actual project itself. Ian and Emma were constantly making connections to their own lives and they said that they had gained a deeper understanding and awareness of the process that they had been part of. Both participants commented that reflecting on the process had enabled them to gain more of an insight into themselves and that they would use this as a way of challenging the constant prejudices and ignorance's experienced by people with learning disabilities that has been normalised within our society, that they both still experience in their everyday lives.

By revisiting the project as well, I have also been able to find clarity within my own practice (led by a self-advocacy approach) and place it within the wider political context of the discrimination still experienced by people with learning disabilities. On reflection, I believe that at the outset of the project I should have perhaps communicated more succinctly my intentions and indeed ideology to the committee/key worker. Prior to this project I had made the naive assumption that this organisation would have had self-advocacy embedded, so that the participants would be able to use the project as a way of gaining as much ownership as possible. Perhaps my own key learning curve is not to make these assumptions in the future, but to make the politics of this work explicit for all involved.

Bibliography

Buchanan, I. and Walmsley, J. (2006) 'Self-advocacy in Historical Perspective', in D. Atkinson and G. Grant (eds), *British Journal Learning Disabilities*, Oxford: Blackwell Publishing, pp. 133–38.

Yates, S. (2005) 'Truth, Power, and Ethics in Care Services for People with Learning Difficulties', in S. Tremain (ed.), *Foucault and the Government of Disability*, Ann Arbor, MI: University of Michigan Press, pp. 65–77.

Notes

1   Heart 'n' Soul is an arts organisation led by artists with learning disabilities http://www.heartnsoul.co.uk (accessed 8 January 2007).

2   http://www.peoplefirst.org.uk/aims.html (accessed 12 May 2007).

Chapter 49

L. Dale Byam

SANCTIONS AND SURVIVAL POLITICS

Zimbabwean community theater in a time of hardship[1]

COMMUNITY THEATER, AS A component of applied theater, is a relatively new endeavor in Zimbabwe. It came to prominence as a recognizable element of both art and education in the post emancipation era in Zimbabwe. Before then, Community Theater strived as a vestige of indigenous theater and could be found primarily in the rural areas serving an important social role as a mechanism for preserving the collective memory of the society primarily through ritualized events. Those efforts were occurring at a time when strict laws forbidding the growth and development of Black African theaters were encouraged by the then Rhodesian government. After years of armed struggle, which forced valuable human resources into exile, independence in 1980 unveiled the promise for free education, economic independence, and the growth of a national cultural identity. The Zimbabwean Community Theater movement was applied to community development as one aspect of this promise.

While the arts had always been considered an element of Zimbabwean identity, before independence no prominence had been given to its role as an instrument of human development. Inspired by earlier arts projects that had already been tried in the region such as the highly publicized Botswana project which had been informed by the educational strategies of Paulo Freire, Ngũgĩ wa Mĩrĩĩ and Ngũgĩ wa Thiong'o's Kamirithu experiment in Kenya, which broadened the community agenda to focus specifically on literacy, and efforts in Zambia that nurtured the infamous Chikwakwa Theater, Zimbabwe took the initiative of spearheading the country's government sponsored theater arts movement. The surrounding regional projects had reinforced the importance of connecting education to the performing arts while also developing close ties with the communities that it aimed to represent. This idea gained further momentum with the establishment of the parastatal ZIMFEP, the Zimbabwe Association for Education and Production and the subsequent formation of its subsidiary the Community Based Theater Program (CBTP). In time, Ngũgĩ wa Mĩriĩ, who had fled Kenya because of his community theater activities there, spearheaded and developed ZIMFEP's Community Based Theater Initiative.

The CBTP satisfied the country's need for a cultural movement that would create a consciousness of free utilization of indigenous arts, for a community oriented theater not directed towards foreign adjudication, and for a theater that was not tied to the existing theaters and playhouses built by the colonial regime. To that end, the project organizers' approach entailed conducting intermittent training workshops for community artists throughout the country. These workshops sometimes led to the creation of original scripts, but in other instances groups adapted the plays and or legends of their communities as a means of attracting popular interest. Later as the CBTP's influence broadened throughout Zimbabwe, the project was weaned into an independent umbrella agency through the Zimbabwe Association for Community Theater (ZACT) assumed primary responsibility for the training and development of community theater artists throughout the country.

Development agencies acknowledged ZACT's potential as an important training agent for the development of new types of community theaters by the continued financial support from major donors such as the Humanistic Institute for Cooperation with Developing Countries (HIVOS) and the Swedish International Development Agency (SIDA). One such community theater was Amakhosi, formerly a small karate club headed by Cont Mhalanga in the southern district of Bulawayo. Amakhosi's turnaround to theater was swift and markedly successful. In 1982, after a brief exposure to theater training, Mhalanga began developing techniques for incorporating the martial arts into his new-found interest. His determination coupled with access to training catapulted his organization into one of the more formidable theater companies in the southern region of Zimbabwe. Mhalanga immediately adapted a strategy of writing one play per year for the first ten years and managing and directing his organization by recruiting a core base of actors while also offering open training workshops in Bulawayo to interested school leavers. As for an audience, Mhalanga focused primarily on presenting Amakhoi's work to diverse communities, addressing the political and social concerns of the country while maintaining no formal ties to government institutions and deriving funding from various European development agencies.

Amakhosi's support base widened and it wasn't long before it began receiving international support. The group performed in local schools, when such performances were permitted, presenting plays in both the rural and metropolitan areas but also traveled extensively offering workshops in Europe and North America. Perhaps because of its relatively independent beginnings, Amakhosi didn't hesitate to identify government as one source of Zimbabwe's development problems. Consequently, its experience with the government censorship bureaus dated back to a much earlier time than other community arts agencies that were otherwise linked to government. In 1987, *Workshop Negative*, a play highlighting government corruption, was banned from touring the western region of Zimbabwe. For Mhalanga, his was not a voice against government, but rather one for the communities he served. Zimbabwean playwright and cultural analyst Stephen Chifunyise disagreed.

> In the final analysis, we use that argument that African artists must totally
> commit themselves to the development of Africa and freedom of Africa;

and if that freedom of Africa means advancing Africanism and even the positiveness of Africa for a change and minimizing the weaknesses of Africa, you can call it propaganda, but to us it's the responsibility of Africans.

(Chifunyise 1989)

Plays such as *Workshop Negative* and Amakhosi's affiliation with NTO, a theater organization that had catered to whites during the pre-independence era, kept it at odds length from ZACT. Though ZACT and NTO offered training and administrative support to theater companies, ZACT saw NTO as an organization at cross purposes with the development of community arts in Zimbabwe.[2] Others viewed NTO's turnaround policy of inclusion in the post independence era as a strategy 'to continue obtaining financial support from the new black government and private sector' (Chifunyise 1990). Still, Amakhosi persevered in the aftermath of NTO's demise in the late 1990s. And in spite of its occasional run-ins with local government officials, it continued to present plays both locally and internationally while deriving the bulk of its sponsorship from international development agencies (Mhalanga 2006). ZACT, considered to be in its prime in the 1980s (Byam 1999; Mahoso 2005; Chifunyise 2005; McClaren 1986) plummeted in popularity during the 1990s as it faced the economic hardships that confronted both the rural and urban poor.

Economists argued that it was the government's heavy investment in health and education that catapulted the country into the economic hardships of the 1990s (World Bank 1996). As public expenditures increased, private investment marginalized and inflation spiraled. In an effort to amend this imbalance, the government then introduced the Economic and Structural Adjustment Program (Gibbon 1996). The intention was to develop a more open market economy by encouraging private investment while cutting back on government expenditure. However, by 1991 the country was confronted with a major drought that lasted close to two years. The attendant social and economic stability informed by both the economic and environmental circumstances impacted the community arts movement along with other sectors of the economy. Close to 30,000 workers in the public service lost their jobs. (World Bank 1996). Sadly, the severance packages could not support the needs of the aforementioned. These problems coupled with increases in food prices adversely affected the living standards of lower income workers in Zimbabwean society. The implications were severe for various civic groups including community theater artists who held down informal or low level jobs in the informal and formal sector as few could depend solely on theater to sustain themselves. As government expenditure veered away from parastatals and the public sector, community artists could no longer rely on government for training programs or facilities for the presentation of theater works in their communities.

Foreign sanctions equally took its toll on Zimbabwe. Following the government's efforts to reclaim farm lands for redistribution, several countries withdrew aid and imposed sanctions against Zimbabwe. On December 21, 2001, United States' endorsed Zimbabwe Economic Recovery Act halted loans and the extension of debt to Zimbabwe (Whitehouse 2001, web reference). The sanctions led to critical shortages and forced the country into a rationing system for the distribution of food and gasoline. Workers waited in long queues to purchase gasoline. Decreased manpower in sectors relying on transportation impaired the mobility of community artists. Theater companies found it difficult to conduct regional workshops through which artists exchanged skills and experiences. For both Ngũgĩ and Mhalanga, the economic crisis sorely affected their community theater work in Zimbabwe.

> That [fuel shortage] has made sure that there's no audiences anymore . . . no audiences at all . . . if you look at our website very carefully you'll find that we stopped updating it because there isn't [sic] any plays anymore, there isn't anything worth talking about. And we said to ourselves, let's let the world see for itself that something has happened . . . something has stopped happening . . . and then we left it there to send a message to people that nothing is happening here . . . no audiences, you can't put up plays anymore . . . it's really pathetic . . . you can't budget, you can't do anything.
>
> (Mhalanga, 2006)

Spiraling unemployment figures, radical price increases in both the informal economy, and the attendant mass migrations towards urban areas typify contemporary Zimbabwe. Internecine conflicts among local political parties also threaten the country's stability. 'We are in a political environment that is very rigidly two sides who can't meet . . . very polarized . . . to such an extent that the members of Parliament don't even want to shake the hands of the President' (Chifunyise 2005). Such a precarious environment prompted donor agencies to take action. In 2001, SIDA granted ZACT close to $Z300 million, ZACT's largest grant to date, to develop a theater program addressing the subject of political tolerance in civic education (Ngũgĩ 2006). No sooner than the project had begun, ZACT members became embroiled in in-fighting with one faction hurling accusations of financial impropriety at the other. Donor agencies suspended the project to conduct a full audit. And though the audit allayed the funding agencies concerns, new conditions were added to the funding contract requiring the participation of political parties and other civic groups to ZACT training programs – a condition that Ngugi rejected.

> But artists are not members of those organizations. My idea was to have a neutral political theater program which would be able to benefit both parties. I didn't want a theater that showed that everything was coming from the government . . . so I couldn't take the route. So from that time I said I wouldn't take any donor funding from them. We managed our offices for a year, but then we had no more money to pay.
>
> (Ngũgĩ 2006)

In the absence of such funding, ZACT retreated to a voluntary hiatus by 2003. The very agencies that had helped nurture the arts movement into vibrancy had brought it to its slumber. With international sanctions creating uncomfortable restrictions for these donors, it seemed inevitable that the donor agencies would withdraw from Zimbabwe. 'If you focus on women's rights and AIDS, those can be funded anytime,' Ngũgĩ mused while questioning the motivation of the political tolerance program in Zimbabwe and recognizing that ZACT's history of reliable international funding had came to an abrupt halt. But AIDS education is standard fare in Zimbabwe and necessary in light of the epidemic status of AIDS and HIV in

Zimbabwe. Community Theater has been one vehicle for taking educational AIDS campaigns into both rural and urban areas. It can also be the starting point for the identification of other social concerns in the community as was the case of Amakhosi when its AIDS campaign in the largely Shona speaking district of Umguza in the northern province of Matabeleland[3] became the conduit for its newest community arts project in the district.

Throughout 2005, Amakhosi traversed the district presenting 30–35-minute plays supported by post-performance discussions as part of an AIDS campaign. During this time, the theater company used its standard criteria for gathering information about the community:

1   an identification of its local champions – community members who assist in organizing community workshops for the theater company by providing critical information about community practice;
2   a formation of focus groups – groups that the theater organizes according to specific principles or demographics such as age, gender, and head of household;
3   an exploration of subject/knowledge gaps – indicators of the community views on the subject;
4   the development of intervention strategies – the process that places Amakhosi in a specific village or community.

As was typically the case with Amakhosi's community-based work, the post-performances of the AIDS plays in Umguza comprised discussion and the organization of more specific categories to determine AIDS' affects on the family unity. Focus groups were subdivided into child-headed families, married women of specific age groups, adult-headed families and decision makers i.e., people running church projects or other community organizations. The discussions generated a wide variety of important community issues, but the subject of women's empowerment was identified as the significant knowledge gap as the Amakhosi artists observed an overall reticence from women during post-performance discussions. Knowledge gaps become the basis for the development and presentation of the community arts project. The process through which Amakhosi artists develop and train the rural artists to address the knowledge gap through performance is referred to as the intervention. As Mhalanga explained:

> One of the things that came out is that women do not communicate enough . . . and they communicate among themselves – internally, and therefore there is a need to turn out their communication into the community. There is a perception in this culture that men tend to grab things quicker. They tend to talk louder, and they hardly listen within the cultural context of these three districts. Women don't normally speak enough, they don't get up and they wait until men decide what needs to be done.
>
> (Mhalanga 2006)

As part of the intervention, Amakhosi sought out a social partner or development agency to assist in implementing the project. The Canadian International Development Agency (CIDA) as Social Partner invested in excess of 80,000 Canadian dollars in support of a twelve-month gender project through the arts for the year 2007. The program is on-going and funding supports the payment and transportation of Amakohsi artists into the Umguza district along with supplies necessary for training and the development of the performances. Three wards within Umguza were selected for the development of the project. Within these wards, six villages were identified for involvement. With the assistance of local champions two representatives (male and female) from each of these villages were invited to a central area to participate in skills-training workshops with the Amakhosi artitsts. The village artists were subsequently trained and charged with returning to their villages to recruit 24 artists and to create performances on the subject of gender equality for their communities. As this multi-tiered project develops, it is Mhalanga's hope that the Umguza district will present a series of productions by year's end surrounding the subject of gender equality.

Notwithstanding these developments, most community theater companies are not in a position to undertake such mammoth community arts programs at this time. For one, funding is scarce. The British Council, HIVOS, and SIDA have gradually withdrawn their support for social programming in Zimbabwe. The Swedish International Development (SIDA), the last to withdraw support, in its final phases of funding chose not to support individual agencies, but to channel its support through a central agency, the Zimbabwe Cultural Development Fund, in an effort to create a more 'systematic and consolidated funding system' (Maduna 2006). Though welcomed, the approach continues to stymie the development of the performing arts in Zimbabwe since, in face of adversity, more arts agencies have become reliant on donor funding for sustainability.

Artists have no alternative but to join other members of the unemployed labor force in their movement to the towns in search of jobs. The burgeoning migration exacerbates a critical problem. In 2005, the Zimbabwean government tried to counter urban crowding through the introduction of Operation Murabatsvina (operation restore order) – a clean up operation intended to remove squatters and illegal structures from urban communities. The clean up resulted in the removal of thousands back to the rural areas and raised the ire of humanitarian organizations to the point that a UN fact-finding mission was dispatched to Zimbabwe. The mission deemed the operation disastrous further pushing Zimbabwe into the international spotlight (Tibaijuka 2005). But also, it affected so many urban poor that even community artists, particularly those living in temporary housing, could feel the consequences of the operation.

Months later, Mhalanga was arrested under the suspicion of cavorting with human rights agencies to create Community Theater focused on critiquing Operation Murabatsvina. His detainment – though brief – points to the closer scrutiny and censorship that artists face in times of political hardship. Mhalanga sees this as an obvious progression for Community Theater in face of the dire circumstances.

> Community Theater is very developmental. You'll find that the political issues in the country are a very burning issue so Community Theater does not avoid that discussion. Every time you call for people to discuss, they start from the political situation in the country and those things will always come out in discussions and that irritates government.
>
> (Mhalanga 2006)

One learns quickly that everything is relative in Zimbabwe even the opinions on the role that art should take at each stage in the country's development.

> The process has had to change. You can't talk development issues without saying "what will this group of people say about this? Am I being a mouthpiece or a propagandist?" I am now self critical. We have to speak on things that we strongly feel about. And some of the things that we strongly feel about we can't articulate them because the time to articulate them in a more rational way is not now!
>
> (Chifunyise 2005)

Ngũgĩ counters:

> I don't see what censorship these guys talk about. You know proper censorship is when you can't do anything or where things are banned and you can't move. If these people experienced what people like us went through in Nairobi [Kenya] twenty five years ago! my view is that censorship is non existent in Zimbabwe . . . Even now there is a lot of critical work, almost bordering on inciting in Zimbabwe, but it is still going on.
>
> (Ngũgĩ 2006)

Whatever the challenges, few theaters have been able to survive into the millennium, and the major players in the theater movement are now Rooftop Productions led by Daves Guhza and dedicated to producing theater in the popular outdoor urban venue Theater in the Park; CHIPAW, the Children's Performing Arts Workshop, led by Robert McClaren and Stephen Chifunyise and Amakhosi. The proliferation of European plays has dwindled and Zimbabwean theater is being produced. But for now it is commercial theater. 'It does not go touring into rural communities. It will go to people who can afford to pay' (Chifunyise 2005).

Is this enough for a country that cut its teeth with a vibrant community arts movement? It is evident that theaters who wish to continue during Zimbabwe's hardships must rely on their banked talents. For Chifunyise, the hardships in Zimbabwe have closed the door on community arts. 'We have not sustained ourselves. The cultural sector has suffered so drastically in the last ten years. The whole community theater movement that was thriving is collapsing or almost completely gone' (Chifunyise 2005). But for Conte, hope centers in laying low in the rural areas of Zimbabwe and producing simple theater at very low cost.

As for those companies formerly attached to ZACT, without training who can predict what the future holds? Existing companies do the best that they can within their own communities. Many, however, have left the theater and have continued their work as community activists, or are pursuing careers as musicians where more opportunities seem to be available at the present time (Chifunyise 2005). Ngũgĩ remains optimistic and positive, 'All the people we trained are in to cultural work either as administrators or trainers. They are using the skills in community development' (Ngũgĩ 2006).

One hopes that there will always be a place for diverse viewpoints in Zimbabwe and that the community arts movements will one day return to its vibrancy. For now, Ngũgĩ works as an independent consultant to the Southern African region and will soon venture into Prison Theater using local community theater artists as part of his training team. Could this be the precursor to a new stage of ZACT? Cont Mhalanga vows to return to the rural areas while also presenting his work in national playhouses. And like Ngũgĩ, Mhalanga will continue to work independently – writing, producing, presenting plays, and encouraging young artists to present their works within their communities.

Perhaps that is the common denominator that unites Zimbabwean community artists. The Community Theater movement has been indelibly altered by heavy reliance on donor funding in the past and political and economic challenges in the present. But perhaps all is not lost if artists can continue to negotiate their hopes in the hardest of times – hopefully giving rise to a new form of community art in this stage called independence.

Bibliography

Amakhosi Actors (1993) Interview by author, New York, June.

Amakhosi Culture Center and Performing Arts Academy, available at www.amakhosi.org (accessed September 16, 2006).

Bush, G.W. (2001) 'President Signs Zimbabwe Democracy and Economic Recovery Act', available at www.whitehouse.gov/news/releases/2001/12/20011221-15.html (accessed March 3, 2006).

Byam, D. (1999) Community in Motion: Theater for Development in Africa, Connecticut: Greenwood Publishers.

Chifunyise, S. (1989) Interview by author, Harare, Zimbabwe, September 23.

Chifunyise, S. (1990) 'Trends in Zimbabwean Theater Since 1980', Journal of Southern African Studies 16 (2): 276–89.

Chifunyise, S. (2005) Interview by author, tape recording, Harare, Zimbabwe, July 26.

Gibbon, P. (1996) 'Structural Adjustment and the Working Poor in Zimbabwe: Studies on Labour, Women Informal Sector Workers and Health', Journal of Modern African Studies, 34 (3): 527–30.

Gokova, J. (2002) 'The Intensified Struggle for Democracy in Zimbabwe: What Options for NGOs/Civil Society?', available at www.kubatana.net/ (accessed July 10, 2006).

McLaren, R. (1986) 'Art and Revolution: Problems of Cultural Policy (Zimbabwe)', Faculty of Ars, Drama, University of Zimbabwe (Unpublished essay).

Maduna, T. (2006) 'Sweden Terminates Funding to Some Zimbabwean Arts and Culture Organizations', available at www.kubatana.net/ (accessed June 10, 2006).

Mahoso, T. (2005) Interview by author, tape recording, Harare, Zimbabwe, August 5.

Mhalanga, C. (1993) Interview by author, tape recording, New York, June 7.

Mhalanga, C. (2004) 'Workshop Negative', African Theater: Southern Africa, New Jersey: Africa World Press.

Mhalanga, C. (2006) Interview by author, tape recording, New York, October 10.

Ngũgĩ wa Mĩrĩĩ (2006) Interview by author, tape recording, New York, October 12.

Tibaijuka, A.K. (2005) Report of the Fact-Finding Mission to Zimbabwe to Assess the Scope and Impact of Operation Murambatsvina by the UN Special Envoy on Human Settlements Issues in Zimbabwe.

World Bank (1996) 'Structural Adjustment and Zimbabwe's Poor', Operations Evaluation Department No 105.

Zimbabwe's National Theatre Organization (1997) 'No. 3', available at www.infozine.com/ miror/theatre/nto/bira97b.html (accessed July 10, 2006).

Notes

1   The editors note with sadness the untimely death of Ngũgĩ wa Mĩrĩĩ, who died since the writing of this chapter.

2   At its first national convention in 1989, ZACT mandated an exclusion policy forbidding its members from dual membership (Byam 1999: 125).

3   Zimbabwe is divided into provinces and within these provinces are districts that are further subdivided into municipalities or wards. Several villages comprise each ward.

Chapter 50

Michael Etherton

CHILD RIGHTS THEATRE FOR DEVELOPMENT WITH DISADVANTAGED AND EXCLUDED CHILDREN IN SOUTH ASIA AND AFRICA

IN THE MID-1990S A NUMBER of development agencies, whose work was intended to benefit children and young people, started to promote Child Rights as the basis for their aid and assistance. These agencies included UNICEF at its headquarters in New York and the Save the Children organisations in the UK, Canada and the Scandinavian countries. This new approach followed the drafting and acceptance of the Convention on the Rights of the Child (CRC) by the United Nations General Assembly in 1989 and its ratification in 1991.[1] The CRC is part of the UN's international human rights order.

It is often claimed that this international legal code of human rights is a concept of Western democracy that has been imposed on the rest of the world, in the interests of the affluent Western economies. The CRC has had similar charges levelled against it. However, it is increasingly seen that the UN Rights system, despite flaws, protects individuals, including people in poor and failing states, against the harsh might of large corporations and powerful countries. This protection is generally at a macro level. At a micro level there are also many instances of the CRC protecting impoverished children from the institutions in their states, from their dictatorial and often violent governments, and, in particular, from the pervasive patriarchal beliefs and practices. Paradoxically, while these institutions have power over impoverished individuals, the states are themselves often powerless to do otherwise within an unfair global economic order that favours large corporations and their affluent host states. Civil rights needs to work at the local and the global levels simultaneously.

Rights-based initiatives are predicated on agencies such as the UN and non-governmental agencies [NGOs] ensuring genuine participation of local people in their projects. The basic principle is to do what unrepresented groups of people, including children, want. In order to achieve their aims — with the help and the 'clout' of international agencies — these disadvantaged groups also need to have control over their own local institutions and associations. Agencies often say that they want children's participation in 'their' projects when they actually mean, the 'agencies' projects. Young people want change for the better and they would like development agencies to help them achieve this. Ideally this should be a process in which young people mobilise adults, rather than vice versa.

Active participation in civil society needs to be responsible, enduring and measurable. Enabling active participation is sometimes hard to achieve and requires careful strategies, particularly in the case of children and young people.[2]

In 1998, when I was working for Save the Children UK in South Asia [SC UK], we used a Theatre for Development [TfD] process to see if it would achieve active participation by young people in civil society in the countries where SC UK had programmes and projects, which was what the agency wanted. The choice of TfD was ours, and sprang from the drama background of two of my Bangladeshi colleagues in Save the Children, Asif Munier and John Martin, and my own involvement in popular theatre in Africa in the 1970s and 1980s. TfD, emerging from the initiatives of the popular theatre of the poor and oppressed in Africa, Asia and Latin America, seemed to us to be largely free of agenda and ideology. The methodology was, in effect, a vacant platform on which young people could express the injustices in their lives and then propose their initiatives for change.

The first workshop took place in Bangladesh in 1998, and was followed by workshops in Pakistan, Nepal, India and Ladakh in South Asia. Many of the South Asian facilitators of this TfD process now run training programmes in and for some other organisations. I left SC UK in 2001. The organisation then used me to run TfD Training-of-Trainers [ToT] workshops within their programmes in a number of African countries, between 2001 and 2005. The TfD training was to be part of a wider SC UK initiative called 'Working better with children and young people' which aimed to increase the impact of projects on the lives of young people.

All these workshops showed that once young people had a platform, literally and figuratively, they unequivocally identified oppressive forces affecting their lives. These were invariably violent adults, dangerous places and hostile institutions. Participants also subtly challenged the direction of the NGO's projects and programmes. They wanted the cooperation of sympathetic adults to change things on their terms.

The aim of each of the TfD training workshops in South Asia and Africa, therefore, was to give adult field workers some specific skills in enabling young people to find a collective voice for their aspirations, with which to speak to adults. The methodology uses drama to help children acquire devising skills, public performance skills, skills in articulating cause and effect and, finally, an ability to negotiate directly with adults.

The format for the training was to set up two consecutive full-time ToT workshops. The first workshop took the adults who wanted to work on an equal basis with young people through a four-day process that functioned at their own experiential level. Through a structured series of drama games and exercises, the TfD process enabled them to articulate their problems and hopes.

The subsequent TfD workshop was also four full days and gave adults from the first workshop the immediate opportunity to practise, under guidance, facilitating the games and exercises with a group of young people, by taking them through that same process they had just experienced: status games, the so-called 'hot-seat' and 'mirror' exercise which are often extended into pairs improvisations and sometimes built up into wider improvisations showing contradictory behaviour. The problems of the young people, like early child-marriage, sexual abuse of children and hazardous near-slavery work by young people, are often stated simply. Hopes are often modest: girls want to continue with education after the early marriage; young people want to be able to negotiate better working conditions with their employers. Their over-riding concern is for justice and 'fairness'. The two workshops constituted learning through experience.

In both workshops the participants – the adults on the first and the young people on the second – use imaging to collectively realise their problems, first in drawings; and then through stories and devised dramas in small groups. The improvised scenes are always only part of the story; they are therefore deliberately uncompleted. These scenes are criticised by the whole workshop group. Are the characters interesting? Do we really want to know what happens to them as the story develops? The scenes are then revised in the small groups, extended, characters made more paradoxical, ironies introduced. These improvisations are further commented on and further revised, until everyone feels that all the plays devised are communicating precisely the contradictory complexity of the problems that we all know, in our hearts, echo the truth in our lives. All the plays, however, end with the issues still to be resolved. Early child marriage is not going to be solved through a short improvised drama, but the issue can be opened up for constructive discussion. This is the case with most of the 'big' issues which the plays raise: in Sri Lanka the young people successfully raised the issue of pervasive alcoholism and what first steps might be taken collectively to deal with it and protect children.

The plays are intended to capture the human condition, rather than simply raise issues. The complexity of the problems in the participants' lives underlies the narrative structure. The reason for the emphasis on an evolving narrative, full of irony and paradoxes, is to escape from the prevalent NGO view of drama which targets audiences with message-laden plays for pre-determined behavioural outcomes.

Within the four-day process of each of the workshops there is also an emphasis on negotiation. To start acquiring negotiation skills, participants are trained to conduct discussions effectively with groups of adults among the audience at performances of their plays. The substance of these discussions is left to the participant groups. The facilitators help each small group to structure an informed and responsible discussion with those officials whom the young participants want to meet in order to put their case. It is informed in so far as the young people have a grasp of the wider implications of what they are saying, of proximate and ultimate causes. For example, in Nepal the young people began their discussion with the District Governor and Head of Education with the question: 'Can you tell us what your budget is for education in this District?'. They explained that if they knew the financial constraints they could suggest what expenditure mattered more to them. The discussion is responsibly conducted in that the young people are consciously unconfrontational with officials: they remain polite, good listeners, reacting carefully to what adults tell them. The District Officials in this district of Nepal reacted positively in this workshop.

The training emphasises drama-devising and negotiation skills, a duality that defines this particular process of TfD with young people. It links the process to

Child Rights because it enables young people to speak out, in ways they want to, against the violations and injustices they experience.

The dual aim was not, however, present in the first Bangladesh workshop. When we started, we concentrated mainly on adults and young people making good plays that were performed for audiences within the communities of the participants. We facilitated non-theatre people to realise a piece of theatre of their own devising in powerful performances before ad hoc and unplanned audiences drawn from their impoverished communities.

By the time we did the TfD training programme in Ladakh, in the Himalayas, in 2000, the emphasis had shifted. The facilitators were now combining adults and young people in both workshops, and the focus was on developing negotiation skills alongside drama skills. Furthermore, the participants themselves determined precisely who that audience should be. We went through a traumatic experience in Ladakh in which it was made clear to us by the young participants that it was they, and not we the facilitators, who should determine an appropriate audience for the plays about education.

Adult staff and participants in the Ladakh workshop had intended from the start of the training that the process would culminate in the young participants performing their plays to the Ladakh Council, explaining to officials through discussions afterwards what the problems were in state education in Ladakh and how education could be improved. The young people devised some very good, but controversial, plays. They then discovered, within the workshop process, that some of the adult facilitators did not in fact support their analysis or their plays, even when they said publicly they did. Ideological differences surfaced among the adults in the workshop, particularly on the issues of the language of instruction in the schools, and the problem of teacher violence.

The young participants felt that they could not, in these circumstances, successfully lobby officials if they were unsupported by the agency that had set up the workshop for them. They recognised the views of the dissenting adults; but at the same time they stood by their plays, which most of us thought were honest and thoughtful theatre. They told us in a meeting that they would not take them – yet – to the Council; instead they wanted to take them into a couple of schools and see if the students there agreed with what their dramas were saying. They did this, with considerable success, performing to over 400 students in each of the two schools visited. I believe that Child Rights and TfD have expanded in Ladakh and negotiation skills among the students have evolved.

Two other TfD training workshops, in Angola in 2003 and most recently in Sri Lanka in 2005, further modified the methodology and the process. The Angola training had an initial adult workshop, followed by three simultaneous workshops in different parts of the country. The TfD methodology was integrated into the work of the organisation and there were considerable additional resources that enabled the views of the young Angolans, in their dramas and discussions, to be transcribed, checked by the young people, owned by them and published in Portuguese, for wider advocacy with government. Furthermore, the dramas of the young people, which in other TfD workshops existed only in oral performances, now existed in written scenarios. Each scenario was in a version accepted as the most appropriate by the group of young actors who had developed it.

In 2005 in Sri Lanka the training operated in the Tamil district of Jaffna in the North and the Singhalese district of Galle as the first stage of a comprehensive way for young people and adults to change society. The strategy specifically related the initial TfD methodology to the changes that young people in these districts wanted, enabling them to spell out ways in which they and the agency together might actually make this happen.

Each of the TfD training workshops succeeded in terms of its objectives. Good plays were performed and impressed the audiences. Young children as well as adolescents participated, and girls as well as boys. Some of the subsequent TfD workshops facilitated by newly trained South Asian TfD facilitators resulted in negotiations with officials, parents and adults in authority. In Nepal some young people developed TfD clubs which they set up and ran; and initiatives by a Nepali film-maker, Karna Maharjan, in the training programme there extended the methodology into enabling poor and excluded young people to use video for advocacy alongside TfD.

On the whole, however, these successes were not systematically developed within SC UK. The enthusiasm generated by the immediate success of most of the workshops has now been dissipated. It has left some good memories but an overriding disappointment in the absence of follow-up and further development of the methodology. We had personal experience of this when in 2005 Asif Munier and I visited the young people who had participated in a notably successful workshop in North-West Bangladesh in 2000. They were now young adults, some of them married. We visited them in a personal capacity.

Why wasn't this work sustainable within the international organisation that had initiated it? One outcome of a lot of these training initiatives was the articulated opposition of young people to current strategies and projects. Any agency would, therefore, in its country offices or its Head Office, find itself in a corporate dilemma over the future of TfD within its programmes. On the one hand the policy-makers in an organisation might clearly recognise both the validity and significance of what the young people were so clearly and so effectively telling senior staff through the training workshops, while on the other hand senior financial management in that organisation were aware that the way international NGOs are set up and the nature of their fund-raising would make it difficult to do what young people variously proposed as their alternatives. Put simply, donors would not, in the case of SC UK, continue to give the organisation the money for what, in shorthand, could be referred to as 'Rights-based drama by children'. It would seem too political.

The difficulty for an international development agency is that TfD can seem unable to compromise with institutional corporate requirements. Some international organisations are therefore hostile to drama and tend to buy in drama expertise on a commercial rather than a collaborative basis. Because they are paying, they dictate the product and ignore the process. The TfD process that SC UK pioneered in South Asia and in eight African countries between 2001 and 2005 was unique. It was a genuinely open-ended and empowering TfD process, initiated within the programmes of an international NGO, and given support and resources. It always represented a considerable risk to the agency. However, in practical terms, children could not dictate policies and practice.

I understand this dichotomy within development organisations, so I have been prepared to compromise on the TfD methodology. The overriding aim we share is to ensure that all young people achieve a recognised right to have a say in decisions that affect them. This commitment, when followed through in a TfD process, has almost always resulted in dramatic improvisation that is humanist, impressing audiences as being more truthful than they had ever imagined it could be.

Can the impact of this TfD process result, over time, in measurable social change in the tough lives of young people in poor communities? How can this impact be measured? Within development, *impact* differs from *monitoring and evaluation*.[3] All the Rights-based TfD workshops were evaluated and considered successful by all the participants. But SC UK did not follow up on this success; and so it missed achieving any longer term impact, either on those particular young people growing into adulthood or on their communities. Asif Munier and I found in our meetings with the young adults that it is difficult to separate measuring the impact from continuing to be involved in the facilitation of new drama skills within the process – that is, extending the process in new directions, which adolescents growing into adulthood say they want.

Save the Children's corporate mandate is to work for the mass of poor and abused children, and the agency cannot commit to extending drama skills with small groups of young people as they become young adults. Of course, five-day training programmes in drama improvisation are insufficient. Young participants need more drama facilitation, at intervals, as they grow up, by TfD-trained adults.

What the young people can go on doing by themselves is to develop their negotiations with those in authority. Ironically, improvisations give them the confidence to speak to officials and parents in constructive ways that often achieve results. Young people trained in the first workshops need to be able to train the next generation of young people in these same drama skills. The ability to organise powerful performances gives them the organisational skills necessary to initiate their lobbying campaigns. They also need to be able to pass on these organisational skills to the next generation of young people.

Sustaining the link between drama and social change needs a shared sense that the drama element in this strategy is what brings young and old in the communities together through creativity, organisation and representation. These skills provide the young people with the best kind of platform to address change.

Bibliography

Etherton, M. (2004) 'South Asia's Child Rights Theatre for Development: The Empowerment of Children who are Marginalised, Disadvantaged and Excluded', in R. Boon and J. Plastow (eds), *Theatre and Empowerment*, Cambridge: Cambridge University Press.

Etherton, M. and Prentki, T. (2006) 'Editorial: Drama for Change? Prove it! Impact Assessment in Applied Theatre', *Research in Drama Education*, 11 (2).

Munier, A. and Etherton, M. (2006) 'Child Rights Theatre for Development in Rural Bangladesh: A Case Study', *Research in Drama Education*, 11 (2): 175–83.

Notes

1   The text of the Convention on the Rights of the Child can be read in a published version in English, titled *A World Fit For Children*, UNICEF, New York, 2002.
2   For TfD initiatives in South Asia and Africa, I use the term 'young people' to include all children from about 9 to 20 years. The CRC uses to term 'children' to refer to those between the ages of 0 to 18 years.

PART 8

Applied theatre and globalisation

Chapter 51

Tim Prentki

APPLIED THEATRE IN A
GLOBAL VILLAGE

T HE CONTRIBUTORS TO THIS READER have ably demonstrated the
breadth and depth of the kinds of processes that operate under the term Applied
Theatre. Its reach is not limited by gender, race, age, disability, legal status or any
of the other means by which people are categorised in the interests of social cohesion
or political expediency. Each article bears witness to the attempts of facilitators
to support the self-empowerment of the groups with whom they have shared the
possibilities arising from the application of theatrical processes. Through all the
barriers, frustrations, resistances, twists and turns, the conviction that theatre can
play a role in improving the quality of life has sustained them in tasks for which
the monetary rewards are normally slight. The work has been about the restoration
of dignity, the reclaiming of rights and the rediscovery of the person beneath the
label; frequently one that attracts opprobrium and condemnation such as prisoner,
child-soldier, homeless, young offender. The underlying assumption that drives these
activities forward is that individuals and the societies in which they live are capable
of transformation:

> The applied theatre operates from a central transformative principle:
> to raise awareness on a particular issue (safe-sex practices), to teach a
> particular concept (literacy and numeracy), to interrogate human actions
> (hate crimes, race relations), to prevent life-threatening behaviors
> (domestic violence, youth suicide), to heal fractured identities (sexual
> abuse, body image), to change states of oppression (personal victimiza-
> tion, political disenfranchisement).
>
> (Taylor 2003: 1)

There are, however, dangers in the pursuit of this transformative mission. Besides
the tendency to suppose that theatre might be the answer whatever the problem –

the ever-ready bandage to apply to the wounds in the social fabric – who is determining who is in need of transformation? Are paedophiles more in need of the process than politicians? Criminals more than company executives? Drug addicts more than doctors? The tendency to work with those who are the victims of the way the world is run rather than with those who run the world can tempt applied theatre into the territory of the therapist, encouraging the participants to adapt more effectively to the world, rather than nailing its colours to the mast of social change by encouraging analyses and actions aimed at adapting the world to the needs and rights of the majority of the species. By going down the route of social inclusion, practitioners can easily find themselves operating as the 'soft' arm of government policy, representing civil society and voluntary sector partnerships. As several contributors have suggested, apparently democratic endeavours can quickly tip over into domestication in situations where the power to set the agenda and to act upon it has not been shared with the participants.

There is a double-edged quality to the practice of applied theatre, frequently expressed in the phrase 'a safe space' referring to the place where a workshop or project is happening. At worst it can be 'safe' in the same sense as a comfort zone is safe: a place where habit and identity are confirmed; familiar stories are retold; and ancient prejudices affirmed. At best it can be a place where it is 'safe' to speak the unspeakable and to imagine the unimaginable without fear of reprisal or ridicule; a laboratory from which new understandings emerge and new relationships are forged.

The context-specific nature of much applied theatre is at once its strength and its limitation. In keeping with its emergence in the postmodern period, it is a form or series of forms which encourages personal rather than master narratives; a plurality of voices rather than a spokesperson on behalf of the group. Whether these narratives ever coalesce into meaningful social action, may depend alike upon the interventionist strategies of the facilitator and the capacity of activist organisations to support the discourses developed by the theatre process. The plethora of possibilities may wrap the participants in a wet blanket of powerlessness; trapped, as it were, in the Internet, instead of being empowered to take control of communication channels for the community's own self-expression.

Yet evidence is all around us that applied theatre is needed more now than ever before. It is needed because it can enable hitherto passive members of groups to transform themselves into active citizens; needed because it is by definition a collective activity in a world where the mass of people lead lives of increasing isolation and fragmentation. The global imposition of the neoliberal economic agenda has resulted in more and more aspects of human life, such as health, education and even the function of parent, becoming reduced to business transactions. In the global 'free' market of buying and selling, people are defined by what they own, by the exercise of purchasing power. Those with nothing to sell and no means of buying are excluded not only from economic participation but, increasingly, from partici-pation in the spheres of culture, education and health. When economics and its accompanying business practices become the emblems of worth, those whose pockets are empty, be they individuals or nations, are excluded from the transactions that make life meaningful; so much rubbish blown across the wastelands of the neoliberal landscape.

Where Ulysses, in Shakespeare's *Troilus and Cressida*, outlines the consequences for human relations resulting from neglect of 'degree', we are tempted to transpose his vision to a world in which all other ways of relating have been subordinated to the economic:

> Then everything includes itself in power,
> Power into will, will into appetite;
> And appetite, an universal wolf,
> So doubly seconded with will and power,
> Must make perforce an universal prey,
> And last eat up himself.
> (Shakespeare 1951: 793)

Whatever the specific aims of an applied theatre project in relation to its particular context, it is almost certainly going to have to engage with a process that works towards the restoration of the participants' identities as citizens in the face of the neoliberal agenda which seeks to confine them to the role of consumer. These kinds of business relations have even encroached upon the art form of theatre through the concept of emotional labour and the progressive Disneyization of the environment. Disney employees are referred to as members of the cast and the customers as guests in an effort to recreate an entire world, its history and dominant myths, as a commercial enterprise dressed up as a fantasy of painless, effortless existence; not a theatre of cruelty, rather a theatre of comfort. Workers are trained, like actors, in responding to the public in a manner which will make them more susceptible to participating fully in a Disney experience that requires parting with money. When even the territory of the emotions has been consigned to 'labour', it is small wonder that the bulk of the populace exists in a state of self-alienation.

In this global context a version of Brecht's *Verfremdungseffekt* becomes a key prerequisite for applied theatre processes. Until participants are supported in efforts to make the familiar world of neoliberalism strange through finding different ways of looking at that world, it is unlikely that they can embark on a journey towards a new self-definition that is not bound by the dominant discourse. For example, it is customary to talk of international debt in terms of what 'poor' countries owe to the governments and financial institutions of the hitherto dominant Western nations but this notion of debt is predicated upon a particular reading of history that ignores those aspects of the story that constitute 'an inconvenient truth':

> This accumulation of debt has been accompanied by a massive transfer of natural resources from the poor world to the rich world. If these resources were valued according to their utility, the nations of the poor world would surely be the creditors, and the nations of the rich world the debtors. As the Native American leader Guaicaipuro Cuautemoc has pointed out, between 1503 and 1660, 185,000 kilogrammes of gold and 16 million kilogrammes of silver were shipped from Latin America to

Europe. Cuautemoc argues that his people should see this transfer not as a war crime, but as 'the first of several friendly loans, granted by America for Europe's development'. Were the indigenous people of Latin America to charge compound interest on this loan, at the modest rate of ten per cent, Europe would owe them a volume of gold and silver which exceeded the weight of the planet.

(Monbiot 2003: 157–8)

This turning on its head of conventional wisdom is part of the critical and curious attitude recommended by Brecht for those attending theatre performances. In attempting to employ applied theatre as a practical, critical tool of social analysis, it behoves the facilitator to offer alternatives, to ask questions and to provoke new ways of seeing. The great strength of the process is its ability to combine reality and fiction in previously unimagined ways but this strength can only be realised when the participants release themselves from the habitual thought patterns of this information-saturated age; when information is transmuted through experience into knowledge and thence into wisdom.

The other element of applied theatre that forms an antidote to the way in which most lives are experienced is that of collectivity. The process brings people together and requires them to listen to each other before engaging in a joint action. In other words it reaffirms humans as social beings whose creativity and imagination is stimulated by the experience of working together; achieving more than each alone and undergoing a qualitatively different recreation from that of the passive, isolated response to television or video-games. The process is frequently built up from the stories told by the participants, thereby ensuring that the ownership of the material rests with the subjects of the material; not only ownership but artistry as well. In telling a story, the teller is the artist, ordering the events of her life into a coherent form that can be made meaningful to the listeners. There is no mystery here; no separation of the artists from those who sit back and admire the art. All the participants are at once both artists and audience; critical and creative beings linked by a common intention.

Underlying the uses to which applied theatre is put lurks a contradiction that contains the source of its *raison d'être*. It is both a means by which people can try to make their worlds better places in which to live and a method of playing, of enjoying themselves in 'time off' from their 'real' worlds. Because applied theatre is associated with forms which were developed in the second half of the twentieth century, such as Theatre in Education and Theatre for Development within the broader community theatre movement, there is a tendency to focus upon its social functions and the efficacy of its interventions at the expense of the aesthetic pleasure to be derived from participation itself; from the exercise of the imagination in the context of collective play. There may be no clearly defined social purpose, no outcome expressed in terms amenable to a log-frame, and yet the action of engaging in these processes can make a profound impact upon all those who participate. Richard Andrews, writing about the annual process of staging the Monticchiello play in Tuscany, captures this sense of what the event came to mean in the lives of the inhabitants:

The message was that the generation of *ex-mezzadri* might soon be coming to an end, but that in Monticchiello at least they had used the theatre to come to terms with their lives, past and present, and were not going to abandon their identity or their self-knowledge. The other Tuscans who formed the majority of their audience had clearly seen their own history articulated by this one small village over the years, and had experienced indeed a level of empowerment. The danger of sterile nostalgia always threatens, perhaps; but communities like individuals, must ultimately be allowed to use their own past for whatever purpose they choose. It is, after all, the only one they have. To dramatise it, ruefully and ironically as well as nostalgically, is more productive than to forget it.

(Boon and Plastow 2004: 54)

The very act of engaging in this kind of theatre can, of itself, constitute a process of community building without regard for any specific social outcomes. The applied theatre has been applied to life with consequences, in terms of impact, that may be measurable but rarely, if ever, predictable. This kind of application links the process with origins in Carnival – time off for play – that can turn out to be subversive or domesticating in relation to the dominant social formation. These twin impulses for social change, whether reformist or revolutionary, and for the licence to play meet in the character of Azdak in Brecht's *The Caucasian Chalk Circle*. Today the most effective examples of applied theatre are those which manage to coordinate the post-Enlightenment notion of social improvement with the medieval one of community Carnival; a folly of social intervention. The social worker and fool who meet together in the person of the applied theatre practitioner offer participants an alternative to the ultimately doomed agendas of neoliberalism. Through the highlighting of contradiction, they show that another world is possible and that, as citizen artists and human becomings, we are always walking on the edge of possibility.

Bibliography

Andrews, R. (2004) 'The Poor Theatre of Monticchiello, Italy', in R. Boon and J. Plastow, *Theatre and Empowerment*, Cambridge: Cambridge University Press.

Monbiot, G. (2003) *The Age of Consent*, London: Harper Perennial.

Shakespeare, W. (1951) *The Complete Works* (ed. P. Alexander), London: Collins.

Taylor, P. (2003) *Applied Theatre: Creating Transformative Encounters in the Community*, Portsmouth, NH: Heinemann.

Index